FAITH IN THE FACE OF
MILITARIZATION

FAITH IN THE FACE OF MILITARIZATION

*Indigenous, Feminist,
and Interreligious Voices*

EDITED BY

Jude Lal Fernando

PICKWICK *Publications* · Eugene, Oregon

FAITH IN THE FACE OF MILITARIZATION
Indigenous, Feminist, and Interreligious Voices

Pickwick Publications
An Imprint of Wipf and Stock Publishers
199 W. 8th Ave., Suite 3
Eugene, OR 97401

www.wipfandstock.com

PAPERBACK ISBN: 978-1-7252-8399-2
HARDCOVER ISBN: 978-1-7252-8398-5
EBOOK ISBN: 978-1-7252-8400-5

Cataloguing-in-Publication data:

Names: Fernando, Jude Lal, editor. | Cowan, Colin, foreword. | Singh, Sudipta, preface.

Title: Faith in the face of militarization : indigenous, feminist, and interreligious voices / edited by Jude Lal Fernando; foreword by Colin Cowan; preface by Sudipta Singh.

Description: Eugene, OR: Pickwick Publications, 2021 | Includes bibliographical references and index.

Identifiers: ISBN 978-1-7252-8399-2 (paperback) | ISBN 978-1-7252-8398-5 (hardcover) | ISBN 978-1-7252-8400-5 (ebook)

Subjects: LCSH: Militarization—Religious aspects. | Indigenous peoples. | Imperialism—Religious aspects. | Women and war.

Classification: BT736.2 F35 2021 (print) | BT736.2 (ebook)

Contents

Foreword vii
  COLIN COWAN
Preface xi
  SUDIPTA SINGH

Introduction: Faith that Hopes for Liberation 1
  JUDE LAL FERNANDO

EMPIRE, MILITARIZATION, AND INDIGENOUS VOICES

1.Michael Lujan Bevacqua
    Guam: Chamorro People's Resistance at the Tip of America's Spear 27
2.Wati Longchar
    The Empire, Powerlessness, and the Power of the Oppressed:
      The Struggle of the Indigenous Peoples of North East India 45
3.Nidia Arrobo Rodas
    Indigenous Peoples and Liberation Theology: Resistance to
      Imperialism and Militarization in Latin America 65

WARS, WOMEN, AND FEMINIST VOICES

4.Rasika Sharmen Pieris
    Hope that Confronts Oppression and Suffering:
      Faith and War-affected Women in Sri Lanka 89
5.Lilian Cheelo Siwila
    Trampled Women, Forests, and Sacred Sites:
      An Ecofeminist Reading of Effects of Militarization in Africa 112

STRUGGLES FOR JUST PEACE
AND INTERFAITH DIALOGUE

6. Young-Bock Kim
Spirituality of Resistance to the Total Militarization of Global Society:
Perspectives from the Korean Peninsula 131
7. Dan Gonzáles-Ortega
Plurality of Faiths and Dialogue for Just Peace:
A Call to End Violence in Mexico and Beyond 155
8. Erin Shea Martin
"Walking in Evil": Liberation and Dialogue
through Afro-Brazilian Capoeira 175
9. Mark Braverman
Facing the Challenge of Zionism: Theological, Hermeneutic,
and Interfaith Issues for the Church Today 198

SOLIDARITY AS LIBERATION

10. Joshua Samuel
Crucified Bodies and Hope of Liberation: Re-viewing the Cross in the
Context of Black and Dalit Suffering 223
11. Phil Miller
Countering Counter-insurgency in Grenada, Belize, Bahrain, and
Sri Lanka: Investigative Journalism as Resistance to Imperial
Militarization 242

Contributors 265

Bibliography 269

Index 283

Foreword

MILITARIZATION WORKS ON THE premise that a country should maintain a strong military capability and be prepared to use it to defend or promote national interests and maintain peace. The reality is that this makes the world less, not more secure. Those who live in contexts of war and militarization constantly challenge such myths of security, protection of national interests, and peace as promised by the powers that be. Their existential reality of death, destruction, and displacement (hell on earth) tell a different story. Empire, by divinizing itself as all-powerful, promises peace while in a permanent state of war, bent on crushing and desecrating life. The agents of Empire, those keen on militarizing society with the myths of security and peace, want us to believe that they have our well-being and the common good at heart.

The Council for World Mission (CWM) stands in the Christian prophetic tradition that advocates and hopes for a different kind of peace and security: that which works for and embodies the sacredness of all life and God's promise, in and through Christ, of flourishing life for all. While the peace offered by the occupying Roman Imperium privileged the royals and was achieved through the socio-economic, political, and military oppression of the masses, God's desire as embodied by Jesus pointed to a radically different kind of peace. It is a counter-imperial one where the poor are fed, the lame walk, the deaf hear, debts cancelled, prisoners are freed and there is a re-ordering of relationships. The gospel accounts on the life and ministry of this Galilean Jew is a trenchant theological critique of the demonic reach of Roman military occupation, of a people with overwhelming military-style force, of co-opted collaboration, and of the disfiguring of people's humanity. That reach is there in the slaughter of babies and the crucifixion of an innocent Jesus. It could not, however, kill God's desire of flourishing life for all. In the spirit of the One who rises-up, CWM seeks to partner with all committed to 'chanting down' the military might of Babylon and 'chanting up' a radically different kind of peace.

This volume is a timely intervention and contribution. And, I am delighted that CWM could have facilitated both opportunity and space at two conferences (Mexico City and Seoul), in our commitment to continually discern together ways to decolonize mission and theology in response to the cries and hopes of the peoples who resist war and militarization.

The contributors of this volume come from some of the most highly militarized lands in the world. Their reflections witness to faith that hopes for liberation in the face of the harsh realities and consequences of war. Their essays have emerged out of their prophetic denunciation of imperial peace that results in death, destruction and displacement, while proclaiming just peace that guarantees fullness of life. The work offers a sharp critique of theologies of whatever brand that justifies imperial peace based on military power. The indigenous, feminist, interreligious, Black and Dalit voices of this book demand our discipline and dedication to an alternative consciousness and commitment to transformative praxis. Above all, they call us to overcome isolation from each other in our particular struggles; and to form horizontal and intersecting solidarity across the borders amongst diverse oppressed peoples ,believing that the arc of justice is on our side in history, however grim the reality seems to be.

For me, the contributors in this volume affirm the prophetic calling that Jesus places on our lives to be agitators of a new epistemology, rooted in an understanding of God's love for the world, a love that is relentless in making all things new. There is evil, despair and injustice in our world, but this work and CWM's witness is all about defying this reality with hope, hope which is audacious and daring like these texts. Through this publication we mark our solidarity with the diverse peoples — and their numerous social and political movements — who have been tormented by war and militarization, but continue to hope, believing that not only another world is possible: indeed, another world is also necessary.

Collin Isaiah Cowan
General Secretary, CWM
26 July, 2020

REV DR COLLIN ISAIAH COWAN *is the General Secretary of the Council for World Mission. He is originallly from Jamaica and was the General Secretary of the United Church in Jamaica and the Cayman Islands. Known for his courage, passion and commitment to justice, peace, integrity of creation, and building of life affirming communities, he has inspired many socially engaged groups and communities across the globe through his preaching and writing. He challenges the churches to move away from Christian triumphalism associated with empire and promotes a new understanding of Christian witness and praxis that speaks Truth to the power and empower the powerless. His contribution towards developing capacities of churches to resist all imperial forces is immense.*

Preface

THE EMPIRE'S MANIPULATION OF geographical borders belies the violence at the heart of its methods of conquest and control. In order for its neocolonialism to be sustained, the Empire uses its brutal military machine, both overtly and covertly. Meanwhile co-opted ethno-religious allies propagate exclusivist nationalist ideologies and foment persecution of those who resist. In neocolonial contexts, militarization by the Empire and the militarism of ethno-religious states have an umbilical relationship.

The Empire utilizes conventional weapons, ranging from precision-guided munitions to small arms and light weapons around the world to destroy, kill, and maim. High-tech weaponry such as nuclear weapons are used as a tool to manipulate international relations and geopolitical power structures. Many emerging weapon technologies such as drones, robots, and space weapons are meant to further maximize destruction of our planet and resisting peoples.

There are direct correlations between enormous resources spent on war and weapons on the one hand and global social and economic inequalities and poverty on the other. War destroys lives, livelihoods, infrastructure, and well-being creating a culture of fear and violence. This impedes development by upsetting social programs, education, transportation, business, and tourism, which in turn prevents economic stability, social and mental well-being, and sustainable livelihoods. The manufacture and use of weapons also undermine sustainable ecological development and preservation creating inequality in access to resources which further impedes poverty-reduction initiatives. In the search for alternatives to militarized security, it is necessary to problematize justification of war and military expenditure while fully recognizing the need to uphold human rights obligations, including socio-economic rights. These issues cannot be addressed in isolation from one another. The COVID-19 pandemic has exposed, more than ever before, the brutal interconnection between the war paradigm and social inequalities that had been concealed by imperial peace and security.

War and militarization are morally justified under certain political and ideological conditions which give rise to particular militarisms, both in the main domain of the Empire, and its vasal states where battle-lines are forged on the oppressive overlap of religion and race, ethnicity, gender, class and caste. Religiously forged militarisms are pitted against one another causing deep polarization between diverse faith communities. Ethno-religious or religio-nationalist conflicts continue to rise at the communal, national, and international levels. One-third of the world's population meets hostility because of their religious affiliation, be they Christians, Muslims, Jews or people of other faith traditions, including indigenous traditions. We discern the violence and dissension of the Babylonian Empire at work in the modern neocolonial Empire. These imperial designs and moves come as a coordinated, deliberate effort to undo the work and progress of decolonising undertaken by many resisting peoples and to prevent their civil and human rights movements that are geared towards reclaiming human dignity and the integrity of creation by posing alternative visions of the eco-human community. Some of these movements are inspired by the liberative thrust of faith that offers a permanent critique of the oppressive forms of religion that justify the existence of the Empire.

In problematizing the justification of war and militarization, it is necessary to integrate a gender perspective into our analyses and initiatives for just peace. We need to take a comprehensive view of all genders and gender identities in order to analyze and challenge conceptions of masculinity and femininity as they relate to war and militarization. Ideas about gender affect the way people and societies view war, militarization, and militarism. Inside and outside of war, the so-called gun culture is overwhelmingly associated with cultural norms of masculinity. Men are perceived to be protectors and warriors whereas women are seen as helpless victims who need men's protection. Men fight to protect the Mother-Nation! Inversely, rape of women who belong to the enemy nation becomes a tool of war as a form of subjugation. To disgrace a man, rape his woman! This is the most perverse logic of patriarchy that is associated with war and militarization. Highlighting the ways in which the possession and proliferation of weapons are underwritten and supported by a particular construction of masculinity enables us to see just how dehumanizing, dangerous and illusory is the image of militarised security promised by the war paradigm of the Empire. Extension of the same analysis can also help demonstrate that the enshrinement of nuclear weapons as an emblem of power is not a natural fact, but a social construction.

Militarization of the natural habitats of the indigenous peoples all over the world which are highly rich in biodiversity has an intergenerational impact that is difficult to reverse. Military power is used not only to violently suppress indigenous movements for self-determination and autonomy, but also to promote the enterprises of the states as well as transnational corporations that transmute natural resources into global capital while meshing these regions with urban centres of industrialization. Militarization deprives indigenous peoples of the freedom of movement, destroys their environment, and gives rise to sexual violence against women and girls.

The eschatological vision of the prophets looked forward to a liberated era where there will be no more war and weeping. The same vision is reflected in the expectation of the new heaven and new earth in the *Book of Revelation*. This vision cannot be separated from the creation of a new human being as someone who is compassionate, enlightened, and free. In traditional terminology, this is a person who is saved. In the Christian tradition, liberation theology and the Peace Churches have looked into this biblical vision by critically reflecting on war and militarization whereby war mongering images of the divine and valorisation of sacrifice and suffering that theologically legitimize the imperial ways are outrightly rejected. The language of 'just war' is challenged not only as a logic of justification, but also in terms of political and ideological conditions that justify war. Instead, Kin-dom values that counter different forms of neocolonial structures of violence are upheld as principles that provide us with an alternative model of peaceful co-existence.

Despite the fact that the world is continuously being threatened with death and destruction by the imperial war paradigm, we hear multiple counter-stories of resistance. People are dreaming dreams, imagining a different world, building alternative communities of hope, and restoring the earth. The Council of World Mission (CWM) as a community of churches stands for hope as it continues to bear witness against imperial systems of death and destruction. On every continent, the leaders who have embraced the imperial consciousness and its systems are having to face the strength, resilience, and resistance of the ordinary people who are relentlessly opposing oppression. They embody not only a cry and a lament, but also a liberated vision. CWM stands with them and celebrates their joys and sorrows. This publication serves as a means to provoke and inspire churches and communities to rise up in faith with the oppressed peoples who are on an ongoing struggle against war and militarization across the world, and in creating a new human being and declaring the integrity of creation. A critical reflection of faith on this historical praxis is not simply for the sake of reflection, but for a commitment to just peace. Critical confession of faith and radical discipleship cannot be separated in this new vision and theology.

This publication comprises of indigenous voices of those who are relentlessly resisting war-mongers in many ways, hopes of feminist theologians who have engaged with the collective experiences of women affected by war and militarization and categorically refuse to glorify suffering and victimhood, and the prophetic and dialogical visions of interreligious leaders for a just and peaceful future. We pray that these articles will inspire all of us and strengthen our common struggle against the Empire and militarization across the world. We urge that through this publication global solidarity against war and militarization will be strengthened.

I take this opportunity to thank all the contributors and reviewers of the articles as well as participants of the conferences on Resistance to Empire and Militarization that were organized by CWM in 2018 for their thought-provoking reflections. Our thanks go to Andrew Pierce, John Robinson, Caroline Clark, Ari Fogelson and Freya Dasgupta for helping us with proofreading and Jose Antonio Gutierrez for his translation work. We are indebted to the staff of Wipf and Stock for guiding us patiently and diligently through the process of publication. Finally, I must say that the whole project would not have been possible without the supervision, meticulous planning, and editing by my friend Jude Lal Fernando. Kudos to him.

Sudipta Singh
Singapore
2020

SUDIPTA SINGH *was the mission secretary for research and capacity development of the Council for World Mission. Originally from India he is a renowned social activist involved with a range of people's movements around the globe. One of his key activities is to explore how different faith traditions could come together to resist the empire and religious fundamentalisms. He has organized many international conferences and promoted a range of publications on this theme.*

Introduction

Faith that Hopes for Liberation

Jude Lal Fernando

"Shadrach, Meshach, and Abednego,
is it true
that states
that see National Security
as the supreme value
are like Nebuchadnezzar
with his golden statue
that the king commanded
to be adored?
Adoration today
consists in the idea that,
in defense of the supreme value,
everything is permissible:
kidnappings, tortures,
disappearances, murders.
Everything is permissible
to safeguard
National Security.
Is this
when one must be willing
to be cast
into the fiery furnace?
Clearly, the Spirit of God
inspires a new song
that will encourage

the victims
of the idolatries of every age."
—DOM HELDER CAMARA[1]

WHAT DOES BELIEVING MEAN in the face of both empire and militarization? Many of the essays in this collection were written before the worldwide outbreak of COVID-19 and the widespread protests against racism in the USA and beyond. Yet the themes they address—empire, poverty, oppression, racism, environmental destruction, militarization, and liberating faiths, have surfaced in an even more forceful way in the midst of the pandemic. These essays articulate the critical and liberating consciousness shared by oppressed peoples across the world, arising from a faith in the God of the oppressed, expressed in radically diverse ways, and resisting the imperialist deities of materialism (read economic growth), racism, and militarization that falsely appear as the saviors of humanity. These are the false gods—which form the modern empire— worshipped by the most dominant militarized states in the world and followed by their allied states even in the midst of a worldwide pandemic; and they are being resisted directly or indirectly by a vast majority of peoples on the globe in multiple ways. In the words of Samuel Ryan, these false gods are "anti-human gods."[2]

In these essays, most of the authors who undertake critical theological reflections situate their faith within the context of empire and the militarization of societies. Militarization is among the most brutal forms of repression unleashed by the imperialist powers and their allies on the resisting peoples who defy the falsely deified hierarchical order. War and militarization are analyzed here as an intrinsic part of the empire and its allied nation-building projects across the world.[3] Two essays that adopt a non-theological language and are written by critical political analysts—who yet recognize the significance of faith in resistance to militarization—throw light on the depth and breadth of militarization while identifying different ways of resistance. This collection is the result of an ongoing conversation between theologians and secular political analysts who are *engaged* as activist scholars in different conflict zones

1. Camara, *Hoping Against All Hope*, 12–13.

2. Ryan, "Outside the Gate, Sharing the Insult," 141.

3. For an insightful analysis of the principles and mechanisms of empire, imperialism and militarization see D'Souza, "Wars Beyond the Armed Forces," 25–44.

in the world, conflicts constituted by modern imperialist agendas.[4] They invite the reader to join them in *evoking* a critically reflective praxis amongst the oppressed in our societies for whom faith plays a crucial role in resisting the empire and militarization, and *envisioning* a liberated future.

The term "oppressed" should not be used in an abstract and romanticized way. The experiences of oppression are not the norm, but they provide the location and hermeneutical lens in critically reflecting on faith. It is the critical and liberating consciousness and praxis found amongst the oppressed that transforms them into subjects of history who do not aspire to be accommodated by the hierarchical order or replace it with another oppressive one; but, rather, engage in a struggle to respond to a divine and human command to transform totally the system for the sake of the whole of humanity and the cosmos.

Empire, COVID-19 and Liberating Faiths

Let me highlight a few examples of how the themes of this collection are manifested in the midst of the outbreak of COVID-19 so that the reader will be able to appreciate the timely significance of the authors' contributions in a more nuanced and perceptive way that can help us to think through and beyond the pandemic.

"Free Michigan" and "Free Virginia" were the tweets that the executive of the White House sent in support of the protesters in some states who were demanding that their governors lift the lockdowns meant to contain the spread of COVID-19. The protesters, who were led by well-funded and organized far right groups, held placards stating: "Be Open America," "Liberty is Rising," "We the People," "Land of the Free" and "Set us Free." Some were wielding guns. It is the belief in white supremacy, in the individual freedom to amass wealth for a few no matter what happens to the rest, and in the right to kill that has been proclaimed—belief in the false gods (anti-human gods) upon which the modern capitalist military empire is built. In many states, the African American community has been disproportionately and seriously affected by the virus due to systemic poverty and lack of healthcare.[5] In photos that went viral,

4. For an analysis of the importance of the interaction between critical secular political analysts, scholars of religions and theologians see my introduction to *Resistance to Empire and Militarization: Reclaiming the Sacred*. Fernando, "Introduction."

5. Brooks, "African Americans struggle."

two health workers in Denver appeared to block the way of the protesters in silent defiance. In Pennsylvania, some health workers held posters, which read "I do not want you in my ICU. Stay home," "I am on the frontline, Stay home." Their choice to stand with the weak, the sick, the dying and for the wellbeing of many as opposed to the ideology of the neo-fascists is commendable; but soon there arose a radically different resistance from the margins led by Black and Brown people, whose bodies have been mercilessly stricken by the "pandemic of racism" and the "pandemic of poverty" for centuries. As Erin Shea Martin, a young, white American graduate in intercultural theology and interreligious studies, and a practitioner of Afro-Brazilian capoeira, in solidarity with the oppressed peoples in her country writes in her contribution to this book (chapter 8, p.176):"[a] country founded on stolen land with stolen bodies is not the land of the free." People on the margins could not stay at home for different reasons.

With the killing of George Floyd by a white policeman who held his knee down on the man's neck as the Black American pleaded for breath, there was an eruption of widespread protests across the country and beyond. Armed only with the love for humanity, those on the margins came out to the streets, forming communities of solidarity across race, faith or no faith, sexual orientation, etc. They defied the lockdown restrictions (but wearing face masks unlike the neo-fascist groups), seeing the centuries old systemic and socially internalized pandemic of racism as more destructive than the pandemic of COVID-19. Joshua Samuel in his brilliant essay in this book (chapter 10), sees Black as well as Dalit bodies (in his native India) as the "crucified Christ." The white supremacist protesters who demanded an earlier ending of the lockdown were encouraged by the country's leadership, but widespread protests led by a large number of communities of solidarity against the killing of George Floyd were threatened with military action. The governor of New York who was hailed as someone who cared for the health and wellbeing of the citizens by taking prompt action—like a "wartime president"—to contain COVID-19, opposed the protests led by communities of solidarity against the killing of George Floyd, and justified police action against the protesters, nakedly exposing the hidden racism amongst liberals. In a prophetic statement released on June 4, 2020 that reflects their liberating faith, the board of directors of the American Academy of Religions, in unambiguous terms, showed the interrelationship between the health crisis and racism, and appealed to those who study religion and other humanities to engage in interrogating race relations:

> Black bodies have been under assault in this country since the very framing of the nation. The extrajudicial violence levied overwhelmingly against black people must stop. Over the past three months, a pandemic has exposed yet again how social and economic inequities that affect black and brown communities make them more vulnerable to illness and death. Police violence and mass incarceration are but two excruciatingly painful facets of those inequities.[6]

This statement made a daring appeal to the universities and to wider society to reflect seriously on the social dimension of religions and their commitment to justice and equality.

> As a society of scholars who study religion, who take religion in its social and sacred dimensions seriously, we are deeply grieved by the wrongful loss of life. Great religious leaders across traditions have called on their followers to live up to standards above themselves. As scholars of religion, we draw on the best of those traditions to insist on several responses...Recognize the classroom as a source of power in the fight against racism and white supremacy...

In Brazil, the president, who has been glorifying the era of military dictatorship, joined with protesters who were led by white middle class supporters of the government, demanding military rule to overrule the local governors' lockdown measures. Again, "freedom" was the slogan. It was a proclamation of worship of the freedom of a few, as opposed to the emancipation of the wretched of the earth. In several tearful interviews, the mayor of Manaus, the biggest city in the Amazon rainforest region, appealed to world leaders to help stop the virus spreading amongst the indigenous communities who are the most vulnerable population in the country.[7] Meanwhile, an indigenous poet who lives in the Ecuadorean side of the Amazonian forest, wrote a poem that embodied her deep interrelationship with the earth, believing that the power of the cosmic imaginary could end the pandemic.[8] Indigenous communities believe in a sense of this-worldly sacredness in which the interdependence of

6. AAR Board of Directors, "AAR Statement on Racism and George Floyd Murder."

7. AFP, "Brazilian Amazon Mayor Pleads for World Help."

8. Tomaselli, "Journey Towards Mother Earth."

eco-human reality is upheld, as opposed to the exploitation of human beings and the commodification of nature by the capitalist empire. Wati Longchar from North East India, and Nidia Arrobo Rodas from Ecuador, tell us in their essays in this book how indigenous peoples in their lands continue with their resistance in the midst of the "divide and rule" politics promoted by Indian governments and the heavy militarization of Latin America aided by the USA.

In India, millions of people who subsist on daily wages were brought to the point of starvation due to the government's unplanned and callous lockdown, and in some places the police and the military assaulted people who were seeking some means of income for mere survival. Much as a vast section of the population in the USA believed that the virus was spread by China (named as "Wuhan virus" by the top US leaders) to destroy the US economy, a vast segment of the Hindu population, led by the Hindu nationalist ruling party, accused India's Muslims of spreading the virus (some Hindi-language media outlets call it "Corona-Jihad."). Yet, in the state of Kerala, people of diverse faiths came together, coordinated by political leaders and civil servants, to contain the virus while attending to the needs of migrant workers, the poor, and the most physically and mentally vulnerable sections of the population.[9]

In Sri Lanka, the Sinhalese majority has glorified its president—a former military officer who, as defense secretary, led the brutal war against the Tamils in 2007–2009—and the security forces for coordinating plans to contain the virus while the government engaged in further militarizing every public sphere, particularly against Tamils and Muslims in the country.[10] With the massacre of thousands of Tamils in 2009 by the Sri Lankan state (which is perceived as a great military "victory"), undertaken with the full support of the UK/USA axis, and heightened by the Easter Sunday attack in 2019, the belief in militarized security and racism has engulfed the Sinhala majority to the extent of collectively blinding them to the immense poverty amongst them. Women, belonging to different faiths, are those most affected by war, militarization and poverty. As perceptively demonstrated by Rasika Sharmen Pieris (chapter 4) they are slowly beginning to speak out against these false deities and false doctrines of the state, which have been embraced by the religious hierarchies of the island who preach the virtue of bearing suffering and accepting

9. Biswas, "Coronavirus."
10. Adayaalam Centre for Policy Research, "COVID-19."

karma, while individualizing the experience of women and treating the militarized unitary state as a deity. Most remarkably, the Tamils in the North and East of the country, in the midst of the lockdown, showed utmost courage under the threat of arrest in commemorating those who were massacred in the last phase of the war on May 18 (Mullivaikkaal Remembrance Day). They gathered at several public memorial sites, strictly adopting social distancing measures and wearing face masks, and enduring constant intimidation on the part of the Sri Lankan security forces. Some were arrested. Every church rang its bells in memory of the thousands who were killed.

God of the Oppressed vs. The Imperialist War Paradigm

It is warlike language that has been used by the world's most powerful states and its allies in the midst of COVID-19. Language not only communicates reality, but also constructs or reinforces existing reality, presenting it as a given which is believed to be sublime and absolute. In this way, militarization has not only been legitimized, but has also been justified, morally and spiritually, for a "common good," which is defined in favor of the dominant class, gender, race, ethnic, and religious groups. War and militarization are an extension of politics (or, more accurately, of geopolitics), which is grounded on the above oppressive social relationships and upon which the capitalist military empire and its allied states have been built. In this book, Michael Lujan Bevacqua from Guam (chapter 1), writing from an anti-colonial position, shows how his native island has been converted into a military colony by the USA in its attempt to control the Pacific Region and Asia, thereby suppressing his own indigenous Chamorro people. Nidia Arrobo Rodas (chapter 3) laments and defies the ways in which her Latin American continent has been brutally militarized through the aiding and abetting of repressive regimes by the USA, which has led to mass atrocities against resisting peoples. Phil Miller, a British investigative journalist—following the methodology of Dharmeratnam Sivaram (a Tamil Eelam journalist murdered by the Sri Lankan state) and Ambalavaner Sivanandan (a Tamil Eelam writer) who held that the function of knowledge is liberation—exposes in detail how his government has been involved in counter-insurgency warfare in Asia, the Middle East and Latin America as part of its imperialist agenda in the world (chapter 11). Young-Bock Kim from South Korea (chapter 6) calls the USA a 'Planetary Empire' which aims to militarize space in a way that will leave a destructive impact across generations. This is the paradigm of war that over-determines and overpowers the resolution of many conflicts across the world through military means, thwarting peaceful political settlements and the liberative achievements of oppressed peoples (the Korean Peninsula, Palestine, Tamil Eelam, to name but a few).

The empire and its allies present themselves as idols and demand that the oppressed peoples offer themselves as sacrifices for economic success and above all for state security, as all the while sickness, starvation and death abound. The wretched of the earth are the collateral damage of the war-paradigm embraced by the allied international system of states. This is the logic behind the response to COVID-19 by many states who follow the imperial gods. Amongst many others, Black and Brown bodies in the USA; indigenous and the other most impoverished communities in Brazil; millions of migrant workers, Dalits, indigenous communities, and Muslims in India; the essential workers who are engaged in cleaning jobs who have no choice between life and livelihood; and the elderly population of the world have to be sacrificed for the health and wellbeing of the imperialized and militarized relationships. This is the result of the war-paradigm that is being constantly pushed forward by the US-led system in the world, as opposed to the peace-paradigm of the oppressed peoples agitating for a different world. Criminalizing the struggles of oppressed peoples is a way of justifying the elimination of any threat to the deified military order, which aims at keeping the world in a permanent state of war in the name of imperial peace and security.

Faith in a God of the oppressed does not rely on the war-paradigm, its language, rationale and structure, but rather demands a radically different outlook, language, and a sociopolitical and geopolitical formation that secures just peace. The peoples who are militarized and dehumanized embody a language of lament and liberation. Paradoxically, they are the crucified and risen Christ at the same time. They are not a bunch of helpless individual victims, as the imperial statistics on human rights violations depict them. They confront the deadly ungodly designs and proclaim their faith in a God of Life (zoegraphy) as opposed to the gods of death and destruction (thanatography) as prophetically stated by Young-Bock Kim (chapter 6). Their moves of resistance are imbued with love, following the example of Jesus Christ, not only for the oppressed themselves, but also for whole of humanity. As Cornel West tells us, this is "tragic comic" because those who resist out of love knowing that they will be crucified hold the highest spiritual and moral ground. They are "ready to get crucified with that kind of love...from generation to generation... lifting up that spiritual and moral banner...in the midst of wars..."[11]

God Who Does Not Liberate Is No God

The authors of these essays who are engaged in diverse struggles across the globe with deep love for the oppressed, have embraced not only their collective experience of oppression, but also their aspiration for liberation. They believe that there are no silent voices, but only silenced ones or those easily ignored by the dominant powers, both political and religious. These essays capture their critical voices in multiple locations, evoking the collective liberating consciousness amongst the oppressed, and rejecting the notions of silent voices, helpless victims, and individualized subjects. The authors' God-talk or theologizing is grounded in the believing voices of the subjugated ones who yearn for liberation in the midst of different forms of militarization that are aimed at silencing voices. This believing is totally different from blind obedience to religious teachings that justify the status quo and falsely deify it as an absolute.

In this book, interrogating the meaning of the official motto of the USA, "In God We Trust," Nidia Arrobo Rodas asks the question "Which god?"(chapter 3). Is it God of Life or a god of death? Young-Bock Kim (chapter 6) makes a prophetic declaration against the global militarization of the planet by the USA as the "Story of Death and Destruction" as opposed to the "Story of Life." No nation can claim to rule the whole planet. It is idolatry par excellence! A god who does not liberate is no god. Faith that does not instill hope of liberation from multiple forms of oppression is a blind faith that enslaves, maims, rapes, and destroys life. Therefore, the primary task of theologizing is not faith seeking understanding, but rather faith that hopes for liberation; liberation from constellations of oppressions that instrumentalize a majority of distinct peoples across the globe and the cosmos as mere tools for the aggrandizement of power, prestige and wealth (Mammon), aiming to turn human beings into dust and nature into a pile of toxic waste. Liberation means the recreation of a new people who continue incessantly resisting being turned into dust (non-persons, crowds of individuals, or atomized individuals), and the reclamation of the sacredness of the cosmos—which

11. West, "Cornel West Moves."

ensures the continuation of all forms of life—rejecting the technocratic and military barbarism that desecrates the integrity of creation.

God-talk and talk about the sacred, in this collection of essays, takes place in defiance of the most gruesome form of oppression, the militarization that is necessitated by modern imperialist structures. Militarization is the most coercive method of "resolving" political conflicts by which mass atrocities are committed against those who resist. The "new normal" of the lockdowns related to COVID-19 in many countries is the "continuous normal" lasting decades in the most militarized lands across the world which are doubly affected by the pandemic. The faith of the tormented people in these lands—who demand radical change and not reform, with great urgency—coming from whatever religious tradition they belong to, is seen as a transformative act of hope that envisions a liberated future not only for themselves, but also for the whole of humanity and creation. As Gustavo Gutiérrez reiterates,

> In the last instance, we will have an authentic theology of liberation only when the oppressed themselves freely raise their voice and express themselves directly and creatively in society and in the heart of the People of God, when they themselves 'account for hope' which they bear, when they are protagonists of their own liberatio.[12]

The Basis of Liberation Is Material Spirituality

The critical voices of the oppressed form "the third magisterium," a term coined by Aloysius Pieris. "Neither the academic nor pastoral magisterium is conversant with this evangelical idiom."[13] The faith-language of the oppressed has a distinct character with a particular spirituality. Pieris identifies several features of this spirituality: it is, first, a material spirituality or a "this-worldly spirituality" based on the need for liveable conditions.[14] Life does not exist as an abstract category for the oppressed. It requires conditions that make it liveable. Judith Butler notes:

> To say that a life is injurable, for instance, or that it can be lost, destroyed, or systematically neglected to the point of death, is to underscore not only the finitude of a life (that death is certain)

---

12. Gutiérrez, *Theology of Liberation*, 174.
13. Pieris, *Fire and Water*, 156.
14. Pieris, *Fire and Water*, 156.

but also its precariousness (that life requires various social and economic conditions to be met in order to be sustained as a life). Precariousness implies living socially, that is, the fact that one's life is always in some sense in the hands of the other.[15]

Second, as they do not have powers of the world (anti-human gods or false gods) at their service, the oppressed are utterly dependent on the God of life for their basic needs. This is "the only God of this life and, of course, the only God of their life."[16] Reflecting on the oppression of Dalit people in India, and referring to the "atheism of Jesus" on the cross, Samuel Ryan tells us that "the experience of godlessness" is "common to all the oppressed."[17]

> But within this barren godlessness, the lineaments of a new divine Face begin to show, the Face of the Crucified God, the oppressed God of the oppressed, whose very agony undermines and shatters the thrones of Powers and Domination.[18]

In the context of war and militarization—which have been waged in the name of the idols of national security—as they have been repressed, displaced from their beloved homelands, traumatized, wounded, maimed, raped, orphaned, widowed, massacred and reduced to non-persons by the powers of the world, the oppressed rely totally on this God who is the God of justice and peace. Justice that secures liveable conditions is the basis of peace. They demand their homeland and natural habitat, envision themselves not as a bunch of individuals as presented by the statistics of imperial human rights and development projects, but as a people, and desperately in need of knowing the truth about their loved ones who were tortured and made to disappear. This faith is at once a lament, a defiance, and a hope. They do not believe that what has come upon them is individual, but collective. It is not the will of God or karma, but the result of structures of power that have been deified. Their faith is neither materialistic nor utopian. It is not about a better life after death, but about a transformed world in which their tears will be wiped away, and justice and peace will dawn in their lands in their own lifetime, or at least in the next generation to come, and those who were killed will

---

15. Butler, *Frames of War*, 13–14.

16. Pieris, *Fire and Water*, 157.

17. Joshua Samuel in his essay (chapter 10) speaks of the experience of Black and Dalit peoples in the same way.

18. Ryan, "Outside the Gate, Sharing the Insult," 141–42.

gain a new life amongst the living. In short, faith in a God who walks with them, confronting the empire and ending wars, and who delivers ultimate justice, forms the root of their spirituality. The peace that they envisage is not metaphysical or merely personal and spiritual, but political. Inner peace and outer peace are not dichotomized. Piety and political justice are not set apart from one another.

Third, the deep sense of materiality amongst them is intrinsically interwoven with indigenous traditions which uphold the sacredness of the cosmos. Hence, their material spirituality is "not secular, but cosmic" and is therefore ecological.[19] In this sense, the land they yearn for is not a piece of private property that can be possessed by the state or sold to a multinational company, but a homeland which is sacred with all its forests, beaches, rivers, and creatures. The indigenous peoples in the Andes name it *pachamama*, the goddess-earth or earth-mother. The sense of the sacredness of land is found not only in age-old indigenous traditions, but also in modern national liberation struggles in Ireland, Kashmir, Kurdistan, Palestine, and Tamil Eelam, as well as in people's movements that oppose military bases and the privatization of land in places like Ryukyu and Jeju islands.[20] Furthermore, Mitri Raheb's magnificent work *Faith in the Face of Empire: The Bible Through Palestinian Eyes* separates the Zionist (both Jewish and Christian) understanding of "Holy Land" which has openly imprisoned millions of Palestinians—by forging one of the most militarized states on earth—from the biblical imagination of land which has to be realized only from the perspective of the people who are oppressed by the empire. The sense of sacredness that the oppressed give to the land, that they yearn for, emerges from their faith in God who is "above" the empire and who is the creator of the cosmos.

> Believing that there is something more powerful than the empire is an important and necessary step toward questioning the empire...Whereas armies might not dare to challenge the empire because of the power imbalance, faith in God can provide the necessary motivation to go against the empire even if doing so means sacrificing one's life.[21]

19. Pieris, *Fire and Water*, 157.

20. For a theology of land see Fernando, "People, Land, and Empire in Asia," 125–40.

21. Raheb, *Faith in the Face of Empire*, 85–86.

In this way, the indigenous and biblical sense of sacredness of land is dynamic, non-essentialist and inclusive, and is diametrically opposed to the static, triumphalist, and sectarian understanding of sacredness of land which one finds in religio-ethno-nationalist projects like Christian Fundamentalist Evangelicalism in the USA, Hindutva, the Islamic State, the Sinhala Buddhist state, and Israeli Zionism.

Fourth, in contrast to all the major religious traditions which are entrenched in patriarchy, in the cosmic spirituality of the oppressed "the women find some space to express at least symbolically their state of oppression."[22] Moreover, through their popular religious beliefs and practices, women have resisted the traditional patriarchal religious teachings that deify the existing oppressive order. They reject the glorification of suffering and sacrifice as the means to salvation. Reflecting on her own personal experience of WWII in Japan and challenging the Christian doctrines of atonement, Rita Nakashima Brock states.

> For too long, doctrines of atonement have also propped up indefensible ideas that divinized Jesus' maleness and vilified femaleness as fallen, lesser, and in need of male control. For centuries as well, he was white-washed and used to colonize, enslave, kill, and oppress dark-skinned people who were deemed lesser, fallen, subhuman, or evil…These consequences of atonement theologies are not secondary conceptual mistakes that can be elided with improved language and inclusiveness. They are designed to support white male Christian hegemony and violence, and they must be interrogated…If God is love, as Christians claim, why would that love lead to division, domination, and fear of punishment instead of human flourishing? Because love is defined as enduring trauma, as self-sacrifice. My dissertation addressed this question by redefining love as mutuality and interconnection.[23]

In the contexts of war and militarization, these women refuse to believe that widowhood and the experience of sexual violence are simply individual conditions rather than the result of oppressive structures of power. The God in whom they believe demands ultimate justice in and through their continuous resistance that is filled with creativity and hope.

---

22. Pieris, *Fire and Water*, 157.
23. Borck, "Anamnesis as a Source of Love," 38.

In that sense, the opposite of war is not militarized peace (imperial peace which is at permanent war), but creativity.[24]

The fifth feature, as Pieris points out, is the most powerful means of communication of the faith in the God of the oppressed, namely, the use of story. "Human liberation, which constitutes their only religion, is the story of a God among his/her people. The world is the sacred theatre."[25]

Finally, the aim of interreligious dialogue should not be to develop a common language of each other's understanding of ultimate reality, but to embrace the cosmic and material spiritualities of the oppressed as the starting point of dialogue.[26] In other words, the oppressed masses come to know each other's distinct faiths through their cries and hopes, which create space for the formation of "Basic Human Communities" or to say communities of solidarity, which must be the location of interreligious dialogue. The world religions have to be religions-in-the-world.[27]

The authors of these essays follow the above methodology in their theological articulations of the cries and hopes of various peoples in the face of militarization. They tell us that, without a grounding in the material spirituality of the oppressed, our theologizing is nothing but philosophical speculation that has no affective, transformative thrust. Without such an approach, as Gutiérrez describes, our theology turns "into a kind of religious metaphysics or a wheel that turns in the air without making the cart advance."[28] In fact, to recognize that every theology is contextual is intellectual honesty, but to say that a theology that does not liberate is no theology amounts to taking a position, a political/ideological position. It means a particular commitment to liberative practice. A theology that is not grounded in a liberative material spirituality separates faith from critical thinking and looses its currency, relevance, and significance for those who yearn for liberation from a constellation of oppressions.

In recognizing and embracing the material spirituality of the oppressed, it is essential that theologians ground their work in the critical analysis of the sociologists and political analysts who form part of the various peoples' struggles for justice and liberation. In fact, these analyses, undertaken and presented in non-theological language with a deep

---

24. For a feminist praxis that resists militarism see Kim and Wonhee, *Feminist Praxis against US Militarism.*

25. Pieris, *Fire and Water,* 157.

26. Pieris, *Fire and Water,* 157–58.

27. Pieris, *Fire and Water,* 157–58.

28. Gutiérrez, *Theology of Liberation,* 38.

sense of love for human dignity, stand out in their own terms as embodiments of the cries and hopes of the oppressed.[29] The theologians of this collection are closer in their hearts and minds to critical secular political analysts than to their official religious teaching authorities. Similarly, the secular political analysts are closer, in their spirit of scholarship,to the indigenous, feminist, and liberation theologians than to the academics who analyze sociopolitical reality, justifying the *realpolitik* without any reference to ethical politics. An alternative academic collegiality is needed at a time when knowledge is increasingly being commodified in the service of materialism, racism, and militarization. This collection has emerged out of critically reflective practices in Africa, Asia, Latin America, the Pacific and the USA. It starts and ends with essays that have been written by critical political analysts who recognize the significance of faith in human liberation. The rest of the articles are theological, combining faith and critical thinking grounded in a this-worldly spirituality. The papers were presented at two consultations convened by the Council of World Mission with the theme of promoting resistance to empire and militarization.The first set of papers of these consultations has been published under the title *Resistance to Empire and Militarization: Reclaiming the Sacred* (Sheffield: Equinox, 2020). We have divided this second collection into four sections in a way that recognizes the above-mentioned different features of the material spirituality of the oppressed; indigenous, feminist, interreligious, and basic human solidarity as liberation.

Indigenous Voices

The first section on indigenous voices is comprised of three articles from the Pacific, Asia and Latin America. The first article is written by Michael Lujan Bevacqua, a political analyst and an indigenous Chamorro language scholar in Guam. Taken over by the USA from Japanese occupation during WWII, Guam has been converted into a key strategic military site for controlling Asia,which has led to the dehumanization of the Chamorro people as colonized and racially inferior subjects, while their land is desecrated and contaminated with military arsenals. The writer guides our thoughts with an anti-colonial orientation, and lucidly

29. See Higginbottom, "Colonialism Still Matters," 251–69 and Galarza, "New Imperialisms and Struggles for Peace," 270–87.

points out the ways in which the USA's empire-building project in Guam and the other islands has been unfolding as part of its Pacific Pivot that has made Guam "the ideal portrait of a densely militarized space." Deeply committed to the revitalization of the Chamorro language as part of the anti-colonial struggle against the USA, Bevacqua states how Chamorro people who have made Guam their home for thousands of years have been restricted from visiting their ancient sacred sites with which they have a deep relationship. The community activists have revived the traditional practice of hiking to these sites to reclaim the sacredness of their land and sea. The essay invites us to challenge the very colonial status of the island under the USA, which is being used as a weapon against other nations, particularly China and North Korea, and reiterates the need to transform the island into a peacebuilder between East and West. In this account, the resistance of the oppressed Chamorro people embodies glimpses of a liberated future. The sense of sacredness they accord to the island constitutes their material spirituality. Without recognizing this, any analysis of Guam would not generate liberative knowledge.

In the second essay, Wati Longchar, who is from Nagaland in North East India, through his writings as a theologian and with his lifelong commitment to the liberation of his indigenous community and many other such communities in Asia, points out how modern empire is built on a range of layers of oppression. After capturing the land of the indigenous peoples, either by brute military force or agreement via treaties, the dominant power engages in social and cultural colonization to impose its own belief system on the oppressed. In this sense, militarization is not only a physical phenomenon. Christianity, as part of the project of empire building, has engaged in this cultural domination to the extent of destroying the indigenous cosmovisions and languages, and constructing a superior-inferior binary which also justifies development schemes that exploit the indigenous people and destroy nature. Longchar's location of theologizing is this critically reflective historical praxis, which makes him believe that the living core of the Biblical message is nothing but the collective struggle of the indigenous peoples for land and wellbeing. Faith in the face of continuous oppression is connected with the struggle for justice in which God takes the side of the oppressed indigenous peoples. Their historical experience of oppression embodies the paradox of powerlessness and liberation. They are despised by anti-human gods, as Samuel Ryan stated earlier on, and therefore they are dependent on the

God of liberation who journeys with them in their struggle, as Aloysius Pieris reminded us.

From Latin America, we have the contribution of Nidia Arrobo Rodas who, with great passion and conviction, highlights the indispensability of the indigenous peoples in resisting the empire and militarization. Rodas, who leads the Foundation for Indigenous Peoples in Quito, reminds us that the death and destruction of the indigenous peoples by the colonial powers is the biggest holocaust in history, and has yet to be recognized as such. It is this genocide, carried out through a combination of military, cultural, economic, political, and religious actions, that laid the foundations for the capitalist empire. Throwing light on the rich cultural heritage and biodiversity of the region, she awakens us to the cosmovisions and the liberative struggles of the indigenous communities which are diametrically opposed to the exploitative and destructive rationale of the capitalist military empire. The writer, who worked closely with the late Bishop Leonidas Proaño of Ecuador, shows how his pioneering work in the empowerment of indigenous peoples has become an inspiration for many churches and liberation theologians in Latin America in their pastoral commitment and theological reflections. Her account, written with a powerfully prophetic tone, tells us that pastoral intentionality and theology should be grounded in the cosmic spirituality of indigenous peoples who have been struggling for liberation from imperialism and militarization for centuries in Latin America. The history of her people is not only a history of genocide, but also a history of unceasing struggle for liberation.

Feminist Voices

The two essays in the second section are written by feminist theologians who have engaged with the collective experiences of women in the contexts of war and militarization in Asia and Africa. They focus sharply on the ways in which the bodies of women are objectified as weapons of war, as victims of sexual violence, as widows and as "mothers of war heroes," as well as on how the interrelationship between women, livelihood and natural resources is destroyed in war, making women and children the most vulnerable section of an affected people. Patriarchal views and practices of all the religious traditions have heavily conditioned the ways in which gender relations are imagined and structured in wars and post-war contexts. Wartime often reveals what goes unseen during peacetime.In the face of oppression, however, women have mounted a formidable resistance to their dehumanization, both by religious and secular powers. These essays highlight how women who are affected by war are engaged in transformative and liberative gender practices that subvert the traditional patriarchal religious practices. By doing so, they redefine what it is to be spiritual and religious, providing us with a new hermeneutic of radical equality and hope. Similarly, the women who face destruction of natural resources—upon which whole communities depend for their day to day sustenance through the work of women—awaken us to ecological and gender justice.

Rasika Sharmen Pieris, who, as a religious nun, has committed herself to the war-affected women in Sri Lanka, gathers the liberative voices of widows who resist the reduction of their suffering either to individual factors or to the religious reasons put forward by their respective religious authorities. Widows of war have become the most vulnerable segment of the population in conflict-ridden societies. Their widowhood is a result of racialised and masculinized power structures that lead to war. Challenging these powers (both religious and secular) through their alternative narratives, embodies the hope of liberation which gives rise to a new feminist theology in the context of war and militarization. The voices of widows challenge the traditional understanding of widowhood. After critiquing traditional Christian teaching that presents suffering as necessary for salvation, Pieris appreciates the contribution that liberation theologians make to our understanding of structural sin, but she problematizes their emphasis on sacrifice as a means to liberation by joining with a range of feminist theologians who vehemently oppose the glorification and romanticization of suffering. Through a range of interviews with war widows in Sri Lanka who are mostly Tamil (Hindus and Christians), as well as those widows who belong to Buddhist and Muslim faiths, Pieris testifies to the power of resistance and energizing hope within them in the midst of oppression and suffering. The writer situates their voices in defiance of the nationalist/political and military conditions that created widowhood. She tells us the stories of Annai Poopathi, a Tamil woman leader who fasted to death resisting the military occupation of her homeland, and many other women who continue resistance as an embodiment of both oppression and hope of freedom. Any theology that attempts to reflect on peace will be superfluous if these voices of real experiences of oppression and hopeful resistance are not taken seriously.

Adding an invaluable nuance, Lilian Cheelo Siwila, an eco-feminist theologian in South Africa whose work has focused on the relationship between women and nature, makes an earnest appeal not to separate the search for security by women during war from destruction of natural resources. Militarization of religious spaces, as well as natural habitats that are considered to be sacred, has increased in many countries in Africa, a factor which has had a destructive impact on women and children. Even though it is they who bear the heaviest burden of war and conflict they are totally excluded from the structures of power that determine the politics of conflict and peace. It is not possible to articulate a theology of just peace without realizing the interrelationship between women, children, and natural resources. The sense of sacredness given to natural locations in African indigenous traditions can act as a spiritual basis for resistance to the rape of women and destruction of natural resources in the contexts of war and militarization.

Interreligious Voices

The four articles in the next section take us on an interreligious path to justice and peace. They are written by a Korean minjung theologian, a Latin American liberation theologian, a Jewish liberation theologian and a capoeira practitioner who is an emerging interreligious scholar. These interreligious perspectives emerge not from a normative approach to justice and peace, but from a deep sensitivity to the collective experience of peoples who have gone through slavery, oppression, militarization, and war. Their theologies emerge out of the spirituality of these oppressed peoples whose encounter with God demands the transformation of structures of power and an end to war.

Young-Bock Kim, one amongst the few remaining *minjung* theologians of the first generation, invites the reader to tap the spiritual resources of his Korean religious heritage which has been formed out of the historical oppression and suffering that the people endured for centuries as a result of imperial invasions. *Chŏndogyo* (Korean: religion of the heavenly way), formerly *Donghak* (eastern learning), an indigenous Korean religion that combined the spiritualities of Confucianism, Buddhism, Taoism, Shamanism, and Roman Catholicism emerged as a collective response to this oppression. It is the Story of Life. It invokes the creative power in the universe for unity amongst people and for union with God, the two concepts being inseparable. He lays emphasis on the main feature of this creative response: the convergence of different spiritual, moral, and political forces in East Asia to resist the Story of Death and Destruction told by the empire and its militarization. With a prophetic tone he exposes the extent to which the USA has been militarizing the world and reminds us of the urgency of embracing the Story of Life that is emerging from the oppressed peoples on earth.

Dan Gonzales-Ortega, the Executive Secretary of the Latin American Ecumenical Theological Education Community, expressing a great sense of urgency to end rampant violence in Mexico and beyond, calls to all peoples of faith and of no faith to engage in self-criticism in the face of death and destruction and enter into mutual transformation that can enhance life, life in abundance. In the face of violence he reminds us that the opposite of faith is fear. Faith is strengthened when it is proclaimed in dialogue and solidarity with each other. Therefore any public action, he tells us, taken by faith communities, needs to have a spiritual reference point that takes ecumenical and interreligious perspectives seriously. The Mexican Movement for Peace with Justice and Dignity states that the need to end violence is a "national emergency." The author tells us that this is not simply a national imperative, but a global one. Mexico is not only on a challenging journey to end violence in its own land, but is also resisting the most militarized state on earth that borders it.

Our next essay is written by Erin Shea Martin by combining her practice of Afro-Brazilian art form of capoeira and emerging interreligious scholarship. Drawing insights from Enrique Dussel's philosophy of liberation and Raimon Panikkar's theology of religious pluralism in a mutually complementary way, she explores the creative possibilities in capoeira as a pedagogy for interreligious liberation. Capoeira, formed in the context of slavery, is the practice of a people at the periphery of social and economic systems, and can provide a way of resistance to oppression and militarization in religiously pluralist contexts. This art form embodies a spirituality of being together that facilitates the subversion of subjugation, and which radiates creativity, resilience, and the dignity of Black people telling us that Black lives matter. She concludes that it is only by recognizing the dignity of Black bodies that our collective liberation is possible.

The last author in this section, a Jewish liberation theologian, through his life-long unwavering commitment to the Palestinian liberation struggle and his utmost familiarity with the Christian and

Jewish prophetic sources, tells us how the modern state of Israel is fully an apartheid state and a manifestation of the global neoliberal order. He challenges the "church theology" that justifies the Zionist project as a deceptive means of overcoming Christian supercessionism over the Jewish people. This theology, directly or indirectly, has justified the decades-long brutality against the Palestinian people. Braverman invites the reader, following South Africa's Kairos Document, to embrace the age-old prophetic heritage in confronting the Israeli occupation of Palestine. This essay blends together in highly perceptive and astute ways theological, sociological and political analyses and thereby revitalises faith with a critical consciouness.

Solidarity as Liberation

The above voices of resistance are distinct from one another, something which is necessary to capture diverse contexts and layers of oppression. However, it is equally important to identify the spiritual and theological ways in which solidarity amongst oppressed peoples can be pursued, without which building a path to liberation is not possible. Solidarity energizes particular struggles, increases hope, and helps resist the temptation posed by a parochialism that can arise within a particular struggle. Above all, as the empire and its militarization has gone global, and even planetary, without solidarity amongst the oppressed peoples across borders, resistance will not be formidable. Therefore the material spirituality of the oppressed peoples should be necessarily accompanied by a spirituality of solidarity that forms Basic Human Communities or communities of solidarity. The two authors in this last section invite us to a spirituality of solidarity. One is an Indian Dalit theologian and the other is a British investigative journalist who recognizes the role of faith in resistance.

Joshua Samuel—following the historic liberative example set by B. R. Ambedkar and W. E. B. Du Bois in trying to understand each other's Dalit and Black liberation struggles respectively and to extend solidarity—employs the meaning of the cross for both peoples in seeking theological resources to articulate their experience of dehumanization and their hope of liberation. As a Dalit theologian, without conflating distinct ways of dehumanization through caste and race, Samuel goes back and forth from Dalit theology to Black theology, and sees the murder of Dalits and Blacks by caste and white supremacists, aided by social and cultural systems and their states respectively, as similar to the crucifixion of Jesus. The cross was as universal as the Roman empire itself. The crucifixion of Jesus was not simply a punishment of a criminal, but a crushing of the resistance to the deified hierarchical order. In that sense, the cross is a statement of maximum threat issued against those who challenge that absolute power. Black and Dalit bodies are perceived as transgressive. Blacks are killed because of their blackness, Dalits are killed because of their dalitness. These bodies are eliminated to restore the deified imperialist order of the world which is both epistemically and socio-politically structured. It is a *godlessorder* in the face of the wretched of the earth!

Nevertheless, Blacks and Dalits see the crucified Jesus as one of them, but also as one who rises up with them in and through their communities of resistance. As God did not tolerate the murder of her son, she would not let the cross be the destiny of her Black and Dalit children. Samuel tells us, in evocative language, that the defeat of the cross has been and is being turned upside down with the help of the Spirit by the various communities of solidarity who unceasingly resist the godless and deified order. The outcry is not simply against the individual killings of Floyd, Brown or Garner in the USA, and Ilavarasan or Gokulraj in India, but against the caste and white supremacist system that has deprived these human beings for centuries of their God-given dignity. The goal of resistance is the reconciliation of humanity, but it must start with the suffering and liberation of oppressed peoples from the foot of the cross.

We began with an anti-colonial political analysis with an indigenous spirituality, and our concluding chapter is also not a strictly theological reflection. It is written by one of the most prolific investigative journalists from Britain whose work has exposed the ways in which his country has been involved in some of the most brutal counterinsurgency wars across the globe that are aimed at repressing resisting peoples. Driven by a spirituality of countering counterinsurgency warfare, spending days and days in the UK National Archives at Kew in south-west London, and through close encounters with human rights activists from Bahrain and Sri Lanka, Phil Miller "mines the truths" of mass atrocities for which his government is responsible. His approach is twofold: the recovery of truth and doing so from an international perspective. Here, the truth about what happened to loved ones reinvigorates the memory of the past and helps liberative consciousness to continue to flourish. His exposure of what has happened is a call for solidarity. The international perspective that brings together Grenada, Belize, Bahrain, and Sri Lanka invites and challenges readers to see the interconnectedness of these locations in order to globalize the resistance to counterinsurgency warfare, dismantling the isolation of one group of victims from another, and helping to increase social and political consciousness, offering resilience and hope. It prevents the victims from falling into despair and embracing narrow nationalism. Counterinsurgency war is an onslaught on the basic humanity within all of us, a humanity that is imbued with the will to freedom. Miller provides the testimonies of some faith groups (both Christian and Muslim) who are engaged in protecting basic human freedoms that have been repressed by militaristic regimes with overt and covert support given by Britain. Through his writings, and by providing us with the testimonies of commitment to human rights by faith groups, the writer presents a spirituality of solidarity that has been formed as resistance to war and militarization. This spirituality is not an affirmation of individual human rights as presented in Western liberal human rights discourse, but a consciousness emerging from a collective struggle for human dignity. Each one who has lost life, been tortured, raped, made to disappear, or imprisoned, is part of a collective struggle from different locations. Could the Tamils in Sri Lanka, Muslims in Bahrain, and the Christians in Belize and Guatemala help form the "global human community" (as an extension of local "Basic Human Communities") and share their cries and hopes for liberation from empire and militarization? It is only through such a path that different forms of religious fundamentalisms – the products of neo-colonial empire that create deep polarization amongst diverse peoples – as well as capitalist technocratic secularist forces can be overcome.

Concluding Remarks

Building horizontal solidarity—triggered by the collective experience of godlessness and inspired by the God of liberation—amongst distinct, oppressed peoples across borders, as opposed to appealing to the imperialist gods for accommodation and reform, empowers the oppressed as subjects of history beyond racial, religious and national boundaries.

> For that to happen, that hope will have to transcend its particu-
> lar (Jewish, Christian, Islamic, or any other) denominational
> divide and speak a metaphysics of liberation beyond the theol-
> ogy of one or another divisive claim on God. The particularity of

that theology will have to speak a universal language, from the bosom of its particularity.[30]

Such moves strengthen the faith of all in a mutually enriching way, dispelling fear from one another. In its own way, the practical aim of this collection is to help the reader to journey towards that non-imperialist alternative world. The human spontaneity filled with empathy and creativity—extending solidarity to one another and resisting racism, materialism and militarization—that erupted amongst the peoples across the world in the face of COVID-19 and the killing of George Floyd cannot be sustained without a consistent and continuous critical praxis of liberation imbued with a spirituality of solidarity across borders.

30. Dabashi, *Islamic Liberation Theology*, 255.

Empire, Militarization, and
Indigenous Voices

Chapter 1

Guam: Chamorro People's Resistance at the Tip of America's Spear

Michael Lujan Bevacqua

"In many ways, I feel that being a poet is not about mastery and manipulation of language, but more about struggling with and failing at conveying meaning and emotions. Sadly, I've never felt fluent in English, and my Chamorro language skills are very fragmented and incomplete. Most of the time I don't even know what to say about how I feel or what I remember or what [we] have lost or how [we] can recover and heal. Yes, the scars will remain. But for me the goal is not to fully recover, the goal is to strive towards a life of dignity, self-respect, and empowerment. In terms of language, that means keeping it alive, vibrant, and an essential part of our existence. Yes, it is already happening."
— Craig Santos Perez[1]

Hacha (1)—Tinituhon[2]

The 2010 documentary *The Insular Empire: America in the Mariana Islands* begins with the following quote from U.S. Founding Father

1. Craig Santos Perez is a Chamorro poet. Briggs, *Craig Santos Perez*, 66.

2. "Tinituhon" is the Chamoru term for "the beginning." Each section of this chapter is designated with an Ancient Chamoru number. Hacha = 1, Hugua = 2, Tulu = 3 and so on. As part of Guam's colonization, these numbers were replaced with Spanish numbers and later English numbers. As part of my own personal decolonization I

Benjamin Franklin, "A great empire, like a great cake, is most easily diminished at the edges. Turn your attention, therefore, first to your remotest provinces."[3] This notion is apt in terms of understanding Guam's relationship to the United States, and also the U.S. role as a global military power.

Guam is the southernmost and largest of the Marianas Islands, a chain of fifteen islands in the western Pacific that is sometimes represented to tourists as the place "Where America's Day Begins." Despite this moniker, Guam remains largely unknown to the majority of the people in the United States. Guam and the Marianas have been the home of the Chamorus, the islands' indigenous people for thousands of years, but today exist in a colonial relationship to the United States. Guam is a strategically important asset to the United States. Some military commanders have even gone so far to refer to the island as "the tip of America's spear" leveled towards Asia.[4]

Within the United States, Guam is known as one of its unincorporated territories; meaning that the island belongs to the United States and those who reside there have limited rights determined by the U.S. Congress. Within the United Nations, Guam is referred to as a non-self-governing territory, meaning it is one of seventeen such places left in the world that has yet to undergo a genuine process of decolonization.[5]

Although Guam's political status has changed in various ways since 1898 when it was taken by the United States from Spain during the Spanish-American War, the island remains a colony of the United States. As of today, residents of Guam are considered to be U.S. citizens, but the island does not receive Electoral College votes and, therefore, does not get to cast votes for the President and Vice President of the United States. Furthermore, Guam has no voting representation in the U.S. Congress, but elects a single non-voting delegate who sits in the House of Representatives. Despite its lack of participation in the basics of U.S. democracy, Guam is nonetheless bound by U.S. federal mandates and laws.

Guam is in many ways an ideal portrait of a densely militarized space. U.S. military facilities currently occupy 29% of Guam's 212 square miles. Partially due to the island's World War II history, but also due to

---

structure my academic articles using the counting system of my ancestors.

3. Warheit, *Insular Empire*.

4. Evans, "Tip of the Spear."

5. United Nations Secretariat, "Working Papers on Non-Self-Governing Territories."

its general poverty, Guam boasts some of the highest per capita level of enlistment in the U.S. Armed Forces of anywhere in the U.S. and its territories. The largest celebration on the island annually is Liberation Day, a huge parade held on the island's largest central road, "Marine Corps Drive," meant to honor the U.S. military for its role in liberating the island from Japanese occupation during World War II.

As the U.S. continues to plan its "Pacific Pivot," preparing for future threats from Asia by militarizing its Pacific Island possessions, the fate of Guam is easily missed due to its lack of standing within the U.S. and in the international community. The location of Guam on the edge of Asia, as well as its liminal political status have led to recent attempts by the U.S. to dramatically increase its presence on the island. As will be discussed in this article, in 2005 the U.S. Department of Defense (USDOD) first announced plans to transfer thousands of U.S. Marines and their dependents from Okinawa to Guam. In late 2009, the U.S. Navy released their Draft Environmental Impact Statement (DEIS), which provided a broad outline of the massive multi-billion-dollar buildup the U.S. military planned for Guam.

In response to this, Guam has also been the site of sometimes unexpected outbursts of peaceful public mobilization against U.S. military plans. Plans by the U.S. military to build new training areas and transfer thousands of troops to Guam have been met with public outcry over the potential cultural, environmental, and social damage to the island. These protests make clear a desire among the island's residents, most importantly its indigenous people, the Chamorus, that they have a greater say over U.S. military increases and U.S. military use of the region. This account is about the continuous colonization of Guam, mainly as a U.S. military colony and Chamorro people' resistance to it.

Hugua (2)—War by Other Acronyms

Within the strategic U.S. military framework, Guam falls under the purview of PACOM, the acronym for the Pacific Command. PACOM does not necessarily envision the region with respect to its member nations' own boundaries or interests. Instead, what PACOM signifies is the designs of the U.S. to imagine this half of the world according to its own strategic desires. The military arms of the U.S. do not see this part of the world as individual bases or islands or countries, but as an entire region which belongs to them and is theirs to control, theirs to defend—even, sometimes, against the people of that region who do not want them there.[6] PACOM is identified on its website as follows:

> U.S. Pacific Command (USPACOM) is a Unified Combatant Command of the Armed Forces of the United States. It encompasses about half the earth's surface, stretching from the west coast of the U.S. to the western border of India, and from Antarctica to the North Pole. There are few regions as culturally, socially, economically, and geo-politically diverse as the Asia-Pacific. The 36 nations that comprise the Asia-Pacific region are home to more than fifty percent of the world's population, three thousand different languages, several of the world's largest militaries, and five nations allied with the U.S. through mutual defense treaties. Two of the four largest economies are located in the Asia-Pacific along with 10 of the 14 smallest. The AOR [Area of Responsibility] includes the most populous nation in the world, the largest democracy, and the largest Muslim-majority nation. More than one third of Asia-Pacific nations are smaller island nations that include the smallest republic in the world and the smallest nation in Asia.[7]

This strategic military behemoth is just one of many which the U.S. has, which carves the world up into 10 different unified commands. But these commands are neither abstract nor without form; they are instead communities imagined and forged together in the name of American interests.

We can see this imperial imagining at play in how the U.S. seeks to operate in and around Guam. In 2010, USDOD established the Marianas Island Range Complex, or MIRC. This innocuously named complex is a half-million square nautical live-fire training range area that surrounds Guam and its neighboring islands in the Marianas chain: Rota, Tinian and Saipan. It authorizes live-fire training activities in the air, on the land and at sea.[8]

At the time of its creation, a USDOD official referred to MIRC as the largest training area in the world. In 2015, the USDOD expanded MIRC by formalizing the Mariana Islands Training and Testing study area (MITT), which almost doubled the potential training area, to around one

---

6. Hossein-zadeh, "Globalization of Militarism."

7. United Pacific Command, "USPACOM Facts."

8. Commander, Joint Region Marianas, "Marianas Island Range Complex."

million square miles (U.S. Navy). The MITT allows for 12,580 detonations of various magnitudes per year for five years and 81,962 takings of twenty-six different marine mammal species per year for five years due to detonation, sonar, and other training and testing activity. Additionally, the MITT allows the damage or destruction of over six square miles of endangered coral reefs, plus an additional twenty square miles of coral reef around the island of Farallon de Medinilla, through the use of highly explosive bombs.[9]

As evidence of this military value the United States routinely holds large-scale multi-national training exercises in Guam and the surrounding Marianas. For example, in 2006, the U.S. coordinated the largest ever-peacetime naval exercises, "Valiant Shield." In all, these exercises included navies of a dozen different nations, which, from the U.S. military alone, consisted of 22,000 military personnel, two hundred and eighty aircraft, twenty-eight ships, and three aircraft carriers.[10] The exercise was so successful that the United States repeated the exercise in 2007 and 2010 and has since made it a bi-annual activity.[11]

The heavy militarization of Guam has led to a significant amount of contamination. After World War II, hazardous and toxic chemicals were dumped and buried around the island and are still being cleaned up until today. There are at least 80 contaminated military sites on the island today.[12] While the United States military was conducting nuclear testing in the Marshall Islands, their ships were regularly brought to Guam for cleaning and servicing. It is more than likely that fallout from the radiation tests and contamination from the cleaning has affected the health of people living in certain areas, resulting in dramatically high rates of certain types of cancers.[13] In addition, since the United States military regularly uses Guam and the waters around it for training purposes, there is always the possibility for accidents to take place. From 2007 to 2008, there were seven crashes of aircraft in and around Guam.[14] In 2008, a

9. Terlaje, "MITT SEIS."

10. Associated Press, "China Watches US Guam Maneuvers."

11. Williams, "15,000 Troops on Guam."

12. Borja, "25 Years Later."

13. Natividad and Kirk, "Fortress Guam," 10.

14. Bevacqua, "Adios Benit."

nuclear submarine also leaked trace amounts of radioactive waste into the waters around Guam.[15]

Tulu (3)—What a Difference Being a Colony Makes

The strategic value of Guam can be divided into two basic parts: its location and its ambiguous political status. In a 2006 interview, the head of PACOM, Admiral William Fallon, made this clear. According to him, one need only look at a map to recognize the value of Guam's location to the United States.[16] In terms of targets in Asia, where the Pentagon sees most of its future threats, Guam provides a secure base for land, naval, and air forces, and is much closer than the continental U.S. or Hawai'i.[17] As Guam lies within just a few hours of all the major nations in East Asia, it has played a key role in supporting every major U.S. conflict in the region since World War II.

The second aspect is the territorial or ambiguous political status of the Marianas.[18] In the same interview, Fallon also articulated this point, when he noted that the advantage of having bases in Guam is that it is an "American territory" and that "(t)he island does not have the political restrictions, such as those in South Korea, that could impede U.S. military moves in an emergency."[19]

Guam is a colonial possession of the United States, and, as such, is neither a full part of it, nor its own independent country. The United States military is given more freedom in Guam and in the Commonwealth of the Northern Mariana Islands (CNMI), than they are in other countries in the region. As such, the U.S. military does not need to ask permission for many of their activities, as they are required to do for their bases in foreign countries.

This point was well exemplified in the text *Pacific Passages, World Culture and Local Politics in Guam,* by Swedish anthropologist Roland Stade. He conducted an interview with a Captain Douglas from the U.S. Air Force, which articulated quite clearly this value of having an island like Guam as a colony:

15. McIntyre and Mount, "U.S. Sub Leaked Radioactive Water."
16. Halloran, "Guam Seen as Pivotal U.S. Base."
17. Lizama, "No Secrets."
18. Stade, *Pacific Passages,* 47.
19. Halloran, "Guam Seen as Pivotal U.S. Base."

People on Guam seem to forget that they are a possession, and
not an equal partner . . . If California says that they want to do
this, it is like my wife saying that she wants to move here or
there: I'll have to respect her wish and at least discuss it with her.
If Guam says they want to do this or that, it is as if this cup here
[he pointed at his coffee mug] expresses a wish: the answer will
be, you belong to me and I can do with you as best I please.[20]

Fatfat (4)—From Coaling Station to Wartime Occupation

Since it was first taken by the U.S. military in 1898 during the Spanish
American War, Guam has played a key role linking the United State to
Asia, especially in terms of its economic and military interests. Initially
used as a coaling station for U.S. ships crossing the Pacific, Guam was
run by the U.S. Navy prior to World War II, but was not seen as particularly valuable. From 1898 to 1941, the island would be a largely quiet U.S.
Navy base, where the base commander held autocratic control over the
civilian Chamoru population.[21]

Guam's value to the U.S. would change dramatically in World War
II and after. Just a few hours after Japanese forces attacked Pearl Harbor
in December 1941, Japanese bombs fell on Guam, with a full-blown invasion force arriving two days later. The subsequent 32-months of Japanese
occupation were traumatic for the Chamoru people, who were subjected
to forced labor, forced marches, sexual slavery and eventually massacres.[22] When the U.S. invaded and retook the island in July 1944, Chamorus called it a liberation, and celebrated the end of Japanese occupation.

Chamorus in Guam had exhibited significant political ambivalence
toward their U.S. colonizers prior to World War II.[23] The U.S. Navy had
controlled the island and Chamorus were not given U.S. citizenship or
allowed to participate in their own government. They lived at the legal
whims of a parade of Navy governors who could pass any law they saw fit.
This often racist and infantilizing treatment was not lost on Chamorus,
who recognized the hypocrisy of the U.S. in its autocratic, undemocratic
military regime. But, in the ashes of World War II, Chamorus in Guam

20. Stade, *Pacific Passages*, 192–94.
21. Rogers, *Destiny's Landfall*, 114.
22. Palomo, *Island in Agony*, 7.
23. Underwood, "Afterword," 7.

seemed eager and ready to pledge their allegiance to the United States, and, for the first time since 1898, saw themselves as a community that should be patriotically connected to the United States.

Chamorus who had once been skeptical of the ideals America preached but did not practice seemed to develop very personal and intimate understandings of those American ideals, when compared with the blood and mire of Japanese occupation. As a result, the end of World War II saw Chamorus joining the U.S. military in significant numbers, partially as a means for economic advancement, but also as a means of repaying perceived debts owed to the U.S. for its expulsion of the Japanese during the war. Chamorus had joined the U.S. Navy in small numbers prior to the war, but now appeared eager to sign up for Navy, Army, or Air Force service. Chamorus have become regular participants in U.S. conflicts since the end of World War II and enlist, along with others on Guam, at some of the highest per-capita rates of any community in the United States or its territories.[24] Chamoru men were drafted into the Korean and Vietnam wars in large numbers, which also helped to create a feeling of familiarity and tradition with the U.S. military in many Chamoru families.[25] The high levels of U.S. military service continue until today, and it remains one reason why community resistance to U.S. military plans in Guam, remains complicated.[26]

Lima (5)—Islands in an American Lake

Fighting formally ended in the Marianas in 1944, but the war itself was not declared over until the following year. Whereas U.S. interests in the Asia-Pacific region had waned significantly in the decade leading up to World War II, U.S. strategic interests shifted dramatically in the wake of that major conflict. As the world power that received the least direct damage from the fighting and did not exit the war with massive destruction or human casualties, the U.S. became the main architect in rebuilding the post-war world. Pre-war United States sentiment had a strong strain of isolationism, but the post-war United States had strong imperial aspirations. Across the map, in the lands of both enemies and allies, the

---

24. Cagurangan, "Guam Number 1."
25. Pena, "Afghan Deployment."
26. Santos, *Paradox of Guam.*

U.S. began to build a network of military bases aimed at protecting its interests; it played a role in the governance and rebuilding of key countries.

Guam, once a sleepy navy base on which Washington didn't want to spend a dime, soon became a key point in securing the new American strategy in Asia. Guam, along with the other newly secured islands in Micronesia, would become part of an "American Lake."[27] Guam would be akin to a frontier fortress that could be used to quickly project force into Asia, or strategically sacrificed as part of a buffer zone.[28] It is only after World War II that Guam eventually comes to be known as "the tip of America's spear."

Despite new feelings of patriotism, Chamorus in Guam chafed against the possibility of another era of military control. Chamoru discontent was spurred on by a number of factors, none more central than the taking of lands by the U.S. military in order to build up its presence on Guam. After the initial American retaking of Guam, Chamorus had been eager to give up their lands to the U.S., as it represented a means of supporting the war effort against the Japanese. There was an assumption amongst Chamorus that, when the war was over, their land would be returned to them and things would return to their nascent pre-war state.

With new strategic plans for Guam, the U.S. military's appetite for land only grew stronger in the immediate post-war years. Military land-taking continued for four years after the fighting in Guam had stopped. The taking of land was carried out in cruel and haphazard ways, sometimes not for critical military needs, but rather, as families displaced from Tumon witnessed, for recreational sites for military servicemen.[29] At one point, an estimated 66 percent of Guam's land had been "condemned" and taken for military purposes. While testifying in Congress about these land takings, a military official acknowledged that some of the land takings in Guam had not been legal, but argued that everything is legal in war.[30]

In 1949, Chamoru frustration with the U.S. Navy in Guam reached a pitch and a protest was staged: a walk-out by the Guam Congress. This Congress was elected by the people of Guam, but held no actual power,

27. Hara, "Micronesia and the Postwar Remaking."
28. Webb, *Micronesia and US Pacific Strategy*, 75.
29. Hattori, "Righting Civil Wrongs."
30. Phillips, "Land," 9.

acting only as an advisory body to the naval governor.[31] The walkout, and news of the Navy's treatment of Chamorus in Guam, reached the level of national news and also became a topic of international debate at the United Nations.[32] Partially to diffuse the controversy, but also to create a path for legitimizing the land takings, in 1950, the U.S. Congress passed an Organic Act for Guam. This act provided limited self-government and U.S. citizenship to residents of Guam. Soon after it went into effect, the U.S. Navy re-filed the condemnation orders for the lands taken from Chamorus, retroactively asserting their legality.[33] Despite the machinations of the U.S. government to legitimize their land-takings in Guam, the issue of land loss remains a bone of contention in the throat of Americanization in Guam. This issue has radicalized certain Chamoru families and turned them into intergenerational activists, who continue to protest U.S. militarization in the islands until the present day.[34]

Once Guam had been remade according to the new imperial aspirations of the U.S., with Air Forces bases in the north and Navy bases in the south, the island became the strategic asset it is today. As it sits on the edge of Asia in the Western Pacific, it becomes the tip of America's spear, ideal for the projection of force against friendly and hostile nations across East Asia. Guam lies within just a few hours of all the major nations in East Asia. As such, the island has played a key role in the transportation of troops and weapons to every major U.S. conflict in Asia since World War II. Guam has also acted as a link to the United States in terms of the migration of refugees from U.S.-involved conflicts. Guam was host to more than 100,000 Vietnamese refugees in 1975 as part of Operation New Life. In the years since, Guam has also hosted refugees from Burma and Kurds from Iraq, who were in transit to the United States.

Gunum (6)—The Guam Doctrine

The U.S. defeat in Vietnam led to a widespread rethinking of its military and imperial priorities. Even prior to the loss, however, a change in strategy had already been articulated, in what is sometimes known as the Guam Doctrine or the Nixon Doctrine. This foreign policy outline is

31. Rogers, *Destiny's Landfall*, 219.

32. Hattori, "Righting Civil Wrongs."

33. Rogers, *Destiny's Landfall*, 230.

34. Underwood, "Teaching Guam's History," 201.

drawn from a speech that President Nixon gave while visiting the island in 1969.[35] Whereas previously the U.S. military commitment to global policing had been open-ended, and was, after President Truman, shaped to follow and curb the spread of communism around the globe, Nixon called for a retraction or at least a change in focus. The U.S., rather than fight communism directly, was to act in a supporting role to countries, rather than fighting their wars for them.[36]

Part of this strategy called for a retreat or withdrawal of U.S. bases and assets away from contested to uncontested sites. As Pacific historian David Hanlon notes, this meant "the shifting of the American military perimeter from 'contested bases', or *contested sites*, in Asia to more secure locations throughout the Pacific," such as Guam, the Northern Marianas, and elsewhere in Micronesia.[37] Bases in Asia were subject to international agreements and subject to possible interference from local governments, especially those with populations that would protest or challenge U.S. interests. The islands in Micronesia, including Guam, were seen as secure sovereign U.S. territories, with populations too miniscule to matter and governments that were merely an extension of U.S. power in the region.

For Guam, this meant that it could be considered even more essential to U.S. interests, as it would be a fallback point should the U.S. be forced to leave its bases in Asia. With the perceived loss of U.S. power and stature in the world due to the Vietnam conflict, a base such as Guam, not subject to shifting geopolitical or diplomatic winds in the region, was even more important.

Fiti (7)—The Rumsfeld Doctrine

The end of the Cold War led to changes in the U.S. global military complex. Although the USDOD engaged in discussions over base reductions due to the loss of their primary enemy in the Soviet Union, the global footprint of U.S. bases did not change substantially. Instead the justification for the massive network of bases shifted from fighting communism to fighting terrorism. For a time, Guam distinguished itself as one of the few locations in the U.S. and its empire that was welcoming base closures, which would lead to the return of those lands that had been taken

35. Rogers, *Destiny's Landfall*, 243.
36. Gholz, "Nixon Doctrine."
37. Hanlon, *Remaking Micronesia*, 219.

illegally after World War II.[38] Guam in the 1990s was known to some U.S. military commanders as the "Sleepy Hollow" of the Pacific, a nod to its erstwhile military value, a relic of the pre-World War II era.[39]

The September 11, 2001, attacks in the United States led to a major shift in U.S. military and strategic priorities. In 2002, then-President George W. Bush dubbed the twenty-first century "the Pacific Century."[40] This was echoed by a number of other political leaders, including U.S. Secretary of State Hillary Clinton in 2011.[41] Such a description is tied to changes in U.S. interests and priorities in the world, due to the rise of several Asian nations, especially China. In U.S. strategic military terms, this has been referred to as a "Pacific Pivot," a realignment of U.S. military forces away from Europe and toward eastern Asia and the Pacific Rim.[42] This led to new military and strategic value being infused into Guam. With changes in technology and changes in potential threats, it wasn't simply a matter of strategic denial or buffer, but also of force-projection, or a large-scale, secure forward-operating base.

The sea of American bases that maintain its military power around the world are not at all uniform in their power, size, visibility, or history. At one point, the size of military bases was a primary concern, as their size correlated to the amount of force they could project and amount of might they could support. However, in a world connected by globalization and dramatic technological innovations, the size of a base is no longer its most important dimension. In global technocracy, the invisibility of a base, or its ability to avoid detection, is paramount.

In the post-9/11 world, this was initially articulated through the Rumsfeld Doctrine, from Secretary of Defense Donald Rumsfeld under U.S. President George W. Bush.[43] Rumsfeld's revolution in military affairs extended to many aspects, such as upgrading technology, privatizing the military, and developing the next generation of nuclear weapons. Regarding Guam specifically, he emphasized smaller, less visible bases overseas, a departure from the prior array of large existing sites. These bases, scattered around the globe, would be cheaper, easier to maintain, and better

---

38. Ifil, "Guam, Against the Tide."

39. Desirlais, "Andersen AFB."

40. Bumiller, "Bush Affirms U.S. Role."

41. Clinton, "America's Pacific Century."

42. Robson, "Pivot to Asia."

43. Business Week Online, "Digital War."

located in terms of strategically allowing the United States to strike more quickly and easily anywhere in the world.[44] In short, Rumsfeld's dream was that the United States could bomb and destroy any place in the world within two hours.[45]

A key illustration of the Rumsfeld Doctrine can be found in a 2006 *Foreign Affairs* article that listed the six most important United States military bases in the world: Camp Anaconda in Iraq, Bezmer Air Base in Bulgaria, Manas Air Base in Kyrgistan, Guantanamo Bay, the island of Diego Garcia in the Indian Ocean, and lastly, Guam.[46] Anaconda is most visibly associated with the doctrine, due to being born from the "shock and awe" invasion of Iraq in 2003. The need to establish new American bases in the Middle East was part of a shift in vision by the United States to anticipate potential threats from Asia, and so Iraq and Afghanistan were ripe for both "regime change" and "permanent bases."[47] In the case of Bezmer and Manas, the Rumsfeld doctrine was in full effect through the creation of a leaner, more high-tech, and, crucially, a less visible military. Bezmer and Manas were, first, "forward operating sites" with all the weaponry and technology of a base, including missiles, airstrips, telecommunications equipment, and support staff, but without any significant military presence. They were also "cooperative security locations," "bare bones" facilities which U.S. military personnel would only use in case of emergencies, which at all other times would be operated by local host-country contractors.[48] These sites were designed to elide the older rules of military engagement by, instead, projecting a force that metaphorically duplicated the thrust of a missile: quick, surgical, and loaded with "shock and awe." Rumsfeld's vision was never fully implemented, but there are ways in which we can see the U.S. military incorporated the proposed ideas of a leaner, meaner and less visible fighting force.

Gualo (8)—The Behemoth Buildup

Guam, as a politically ambiguous and largely unknown piece of sovereign American real-estate on the edge of Asia, fit well within the parameters

44. Phar, "Pentagon's Paradigm Shift in Asia."
45. Klare, "Imperial Reach."
46. Widome, "List."
47. Engelhardt, "Can You Say Permanent Bases?"
48. Klare, "Imperial Reach."

of the Rumsfeld Doctrine. It is for that reason that in 2005, USDOD announced their intention to move thousands of Marines and their dependents from Okinawa to Guam. The U.S. bases in Okinawa have long been a subject of community protest and have at times strained relations between the U.S. and Japan. In an effort to close Futenma, one of the most controversial bases in Okinawa which is located in the middle of crowded Ginowan City, the U.S. planned to move some of its forces into expanded bases in northern Okinawa and the rest to Guam. This move was speculated to cost several billions of dollars, as it would require the construction of new housing and training facilities for troops and their dependents.

In 2009, the USDOD released a Draft Environmental Impact Statement (DEIS) outlining its intentions for increasing its military presence in Guam. A number of concerns were immediately apparent. The DEIS stated that Guam's population, then at 160,000, could increase by 60,000 in just a few years with the so-called buildup.[49] Plans to build a berth for nuclear aircraft carriers would require the destruction of seventy acres of beautiful coral reef. In order to create a firing range complex for the Marines, places such as Pågat, which are culturally significant to the Chamorus, were to be closed off to the public. The U.S. military would require one thousand to twenty-four hundred acres of land for the buildup, possibly increasing its percentage of land ownership on Guam from 29 to 30 percent.[50] In addition, the population increases were thought to represent a danger to the integrity of the existing infrastructure of the island, especially around social services and utilities. A Government of Guam estimate claimed that it could cost at least $1 billion in improvements in order to prepare for the population growth alone.[51]

Sigua (9)—Protect and Defend Pågat

Pågat became a central point for those critiquing and resisting this U.S. military increase. Pagat is in the northeastern side of Guam and features freshwater caves, limestone cliffs and was the site of an Ancient Chamoru village. It is a favorite hiking spot and a place where traditional healers gather rare plants. It has also been a place where Chamorus today seeking

49. Dumat-ol Daleno, "20 Years of Growth in 5."
50. We Are Guåhan Coalition, "Buildup Basics."
51. Harden, "On Guam."

to reconnect to their ancient ancestors hike in order to pay respect amongst the artifacts and stone ruins of the ancient homes there.[52]

At present, the U.S. military controls close to 1/3 of Guam's land mass and restricts access to several sacred spaces where numerous artifacts can be found. Frustration over the loss of the proposed site first appeared in social media, primarily through the sharing of Facebook posts and images that contrasted images of soldiers firing and training with cultural symbols important to Chamorus. The images were accompanied by questions asking "Do We Want This for Our Island?"[53] A coalition of environmental, cultural and political organizations banded together to begin taking people on regular tours of the Pågat area, so that Guam residents could experience its historical qualities themselves. Thousands of people were taken to Pågat on what became known as "Heritage Hikes" meant to illustrate for people what the cost of the proposed military increase might be.[54]

From this initial activism, a collection of demilitarization groups stepped forward to protest the military build-up, all of which rallied under the banner of *"Prutehi yan Difendi"* which is Chamoru for "Protect and Defend." This coalition consisted of older groups that had long sought the return of Chamoru lands that had been taken following World War II by the U.S. military to build their bases, as well as groups made up of younger professionals who felt that Guam's culture and environment were not being treated fairly in this process. The phrase *Prutehi yan Difende* is drawn from the Chamoru pledge or Inifresi, which is taught to all public-school children on island.[55] Through this idea of protecting and defending Pågat, a wider critical conversation about the U.S. military presence on Guam began to develop.[56]

In talk radio, social media and public meetings, people began to express more and more discontent over the U.S. military plans. People were unhappy that one of the few places where the public could travel freely to enjoy Guam's natural beauty or to pay respect to their ancestral spirits might soon be blocked off. The idea of a firing range built in the area was also considered offensive. If the U.S. military carried through with

---

52. Hattori, Palomo, and Bevacqua, *Unified Chamorro Response.*

53. Naputi, *Charting Contemporary Chamoru Activism*, 188.

54. Naputi, *Charting Contemporary Chamoru Activism*, 178.

55. Bevacqua, "Adios Benit."

56. Naputi and Bevacqua, "Militarization and Resistance."

their plans, tens of millions of bullets would be fired from a hill above that area, frightening hikers and desecrating the remains of Chamorus that are resting in Pågat. More people were frustrated with the idea that even though the military already controls so much of the island it was nonetheless seeking to acquire new lands.

Community activists, worrying about the great potential for environmental and social harm to the island should the buildup be completed, mobilized during the ninety-day public comment period to build awareness and outrage.[57] The potential catastrophe of this military buildup was clear from the size of the document itself, as the potential environmental impacts to Guam required an unprecedented eleven thousand pages to disclose. Resistance continued to grow, as protests, teach-ins, petitions, and lawsuits were carried out.[58] At the end of the comment period, more than ten thousand comments, most of which were critical of the proposal, had been submitted.[59]

Despite the enormous number of comments and the critical protests of the people of Guam, the U.S. military's plans were delayed chiefly by outside forces, primarily economic downturns in the U.S. and Japan, rather than any concern for the indigenous people or civilian populace. With a price tag in excess of seven billion dollars, both governments agreed a scaling down of this transfer was necessary. In 2011, in response to a local lawsuit saying that the USDOD had violated federal environmental protection law in the selection of Pågat for a firing range, the DOD agreed to temporarily delay that selection and conduct further study, an SEIS (supplementary environmental impact statement).[60] In 2014, when discussions over the military buildup started again, USDOD had selected a new site for their firing range: Litekyan, a culturally significant site in northwestern Guam. Resistance continues, as once again the island community was shut out of the decision-making process.

Måno' (10)—From Spear Tip to Bridge

In August 2017, Guam garnered international attention for a few weeks, as it was at "the tip of the spear" in a hyperbolically violent war of words

57. Aguon, "Guam Gets 90 Days to Review EIS."
58. Natividad and Guerrero, "Explosive Growth of U.S. Military Power."
59. Flores and Camacho, "We Are Guåhan."
60. Camacho, "Resisting the Proposed Military Buildup."

between the North Korean and United States governments. Threats to Guam from North Korea have been common for many years, as Guam is one of the closest and most aggressive U.S. military bases to North Korea, and so there was not more than usual local attention when the island was once again targeted through rhetoric that month. However, when the infamously volatile President Trump offered his own aggressive, exaggerated barbs in response, the world turned to Guam to cover the ensuing Twitter war.

Much media coverage at the time only focused on the military logistics of missile launches and missile defenses. Some discussed Trump's tone and the probability of this new American president launching a nuclear war. Other media coverage extended space to the voices of people on Guam, asking them to express their concerns or fears. Among the people of Guam, some expressed faith in the U.S. to defend the island. Others expressed long-felt worries that the U.S. might not be seeking to defend the island, but rather use the island as a buffer zone to defend itself in the event of conflict, just as it had strategically done in World War II. As hundreds of news agencies made their way to Guam or sent emails or text messages to people with even the most minute connection to Guam, the island's colonial status clearly played a role in the conflict.

While the media could portray voices that expressed deep fear, that expressed faith in the U.S. military, or that expressed anger or sadness, all of these were simply ethereal comments on the situation; none of them played a material role in determining Guam's place in the potential conflict. While no country can control its fate in a conflict, the U.S., North Korea, South Korea, Japan and others were engaged in the potential conflict as actors, as entities that played substantive and acknowledged roles in the process. They chose sides, they outlined strategies, they spoke aggressively or encouraged peace. This was not the case for Guam. Facing a life-and-death situation for their island, their participation was limited to media soundbites. The fate of the island and its people belonged to the U.S., to determine what its plan or what its purpose was. The Chamoru people and other inhabitants of Guam could only comment, as if they were mere spectators, on the dire and absurd sequence of events unfolding.

The historic nature of the widespread, indigenous-led public resistance to the U.S. military's plans to build up its presence in Guam is inspiring, yet it can also be distracting. It distracts our attention from the fact that, whether through historical colonization or more recent negotiation, Guam remains stuck in a subjugated political status. Its indigenous people, as well as other residents, do not have a substantive role in decision-making over what military activities take place in their lands and waters. The people and land are simply fodder to be are used by the U.S. to achieve its strategic purposes. As Guam lacks any formal role in U.S. power and governance, there isn't even the pretense that its peoples' interests be taken seriously in the implementation of foreign or military policy by the U.S. As such, their ability to provide comments is one of the few ways they are allowed to participate in decisions over militarization. But considering the far-ranging decisions being made with Guam in mind, such participation is negligible and, indeed, merely a humiliating reminder of the people's actual colonial subjugation.

So long as Guam remains a colony of the United States, its existence will continue to be inundated by U.S. militarization and dictated by U.S. military interests. Looking to the future and wanting to ensure the safety of our island and children, it is imperative that Guam not be victims of regional conflicts or a chain of weapons to be used by one against another. Those of us in Guam should be active participants, sitting at the table with others, negotiating defense or peace agreements. We must strive to be a bridge between East and West, not a spear leveled from one end of the Pacific to the other.

Chapter 2

The Empire, Powerlessness, and the Power of the Oppressed

The Struggle of the Indigenous Peoples of North East India

WATI LONGCHAR

Introduction

GOD TOLD PROPHET EZEKIEL:

> Tell my people, "God says: I'll bring your hope back to life—O my people! I have given that responsibility to the people who still have love and compassion in their hearts. When they bring your hopes for justice back to life, you'll realize that I am God. I'll breathe life into you, and you'll live. Then I'll lead you straight back to a time of justice, and you'll realize that I am God. I've said it, and I'll do it—God's Decree."
> God grabbed me. God's Spirit took me up and set me down in the middle of an open plain strewn with bones. He led me around and among them—a lot of bones! There were bones all over the plain—dry bones, bleached by the sun.
> God said to me, "Can these bones live?"
> I said, "God, only you know that."
> God said to me, "Prophesy over these bones: "Dry bones, listen to the message of God!"(Ezek 37:1–5)

The passage reflects situations of hopelessness and despair of the oppressed peoples. People in exile were living like dry bones under the bondage of Empire without hope. Seeing people without land, political rights, and identity, Ezekiel despaired. "Can these bones really be brought back to life?" God, only you know that. Dry bones represent powerlessness. Restoring justice to the powerless people is a divine imperative. This chapter examines how the Empire makes indigenous people powerless, with a particular focus on the people in North East India. Oppression and exclusion is justified by manipulating religion by the Empire. Without listening to the collective experiences of those in the margins we would run the risk of serving the interests of the Empire. A transformative theology must be located in the context of the margins.

Oppression under the Imperial Structure

Empire refers to an unjust structure/institution and mindset. This includes ideologies, cultural practices, economic, social, political, and military structures of power. The Empire defines the value system and imposes it upon the others. Though it has many different layers, we can broadly categorize them into two. The first is the domineering structure where a group of people exert maximum power to dominate the other. They set the norms for the other based on the structures they created for their exclusive interest. The other group is the dominated ones who are forced into servitude and suffer exclusion. This imperial power structure excludes the other to marginality. Oppression is justified by manipulating religion and God. The personhood of the other is controlled or denied by the Empire or annihilated by military means in the most brutal way. Here are some of the power structures of the Empire:

- *Anthropocentrism* excludes other segments of God's creation. Affirming its human might as the point of reference, the Empire denies the integrity of God's creation. The nature is a mere object for gaze, enjoyment and above all to be used as a commodity. In the imperial value judgment, the world and its resources are mere objects to be exploited, abused and discarded.

- *Androcentrism* defines women as meek, inferior, and weak. Women are subordinate to men. Affirming male superiority women are excluded from leadership roles in church and society. Women are objectified as mere property and forced into cheap labor and flesh markets.

- *Racism* defines black people. People of color are inferior and less valuable. They are seen as cursed by God without morality and born to be slaves.

- *Indigenous People* are seen as primitive, backward, and illiterate people without religious values and ethics. The most disrespectful and dehumanizing one is commercialization of their culture whereby musicians, dancers and other artists are forced to compete with one another to earn a living which destroys their communal relationships.

- *Casteism* defines and excludes dalit, adivasi, and other "backward" classes from the power structures of society and religious life by imposing false doctrines of pollution. Affirming the superiority of Brahmin and the other high castes, the dalit and Other Backward Communities (OBC) are denied of right to life.

- *Ableism* excludes persons with disabilities from the mainstream society. Affirming a perfectionist prosperity theology Persons with Disabilities (PwD) are seen as dependent, inferior, sinners, and cursed by God.

- *Heterosexism* excludes LGBTIQ peoples from the mainstream society and the right to family life. Affirming heterosexuality as the sole norm of divine creation people with other sexual orientations are considered abnormal, deemed psychologically sick, and denied justice and right to life.

- *Militarism and Militarization* are associated with the above layers of oppression depending on the context. Militarism is the justification of violence by racial, religious or caste-based enslaving ideologies embraced by the dominant group and militarization refers to a range of repressive measures adopted to silence the voices of the dominated ones as they resist the Empire.

These imperial structures are built on a false ideology. Religion and culture are manipulated. These structures are sustained by manipulative legal systems and intentional misrepresentations of reality. Social power structures are organized in which the others are defined as inferior, not intelligent, weak, incapable, unclean, impure, uncivilized, backward, and primitive. Thus, subjugation of the other is framed as divine will or the dominant class is portrayed as the savior of the dominated. Resistance is seen a sin. Obedience is a virtue. Laws are introduced to justify repression of those who resist. These false presuppositions, beliefs, practices, and institutions are created by the Empire to protect its accumulated power, prestige and wealth. It is within this framework of the Empire that the indigenous peoples' struggle for justice needs to be located.

Colonization of Indigenous Territory, Culture, and Language

Affirming imperial value system colonization was/is justified. Colonization refers to the exercise of power and control over one people by another. Both formal and informal methods (behaviors, ideologies, institutions, policies, and economics) maintain the subjugation or exploitation of indigenous peoples, lands, and resources.[1] The first phase of the colonizing process involves land or territory confiscation of the others militarily or sometimes through diplomatic dialogue or agreement through treaties. In many cases, the colonized people are forcefully evicted; sometimes by creating fear and tension to drive them away—often in the name of religion, national integration, security and development. In extreme cases, the whole community is subject to genocide to facilitate the capture of land and resources. With the loss of land which is the main source of their livelihood, indigenous peoples are forced to live in abject poverty.[2] Along with the loss of land, their cultural patterns are disrupted leading to an identity crisis. However, for the Empire colonization is divine providence to spread the Gospel of Jesus to the "heathen" and the "dark world." In the name of civilizing them killing, domination, and confiscation of land are justified. In this colonizing process, the oppressed peoples are denied access to their own resources as well as their economic, political, cultural, religious and social activities. This denial affects the quality of life of both individuals and society. They are always at the receiving end, treated as objects that bear the brunt of the Empire's oppressive structures and social systems.

After disarming and controlling the territory the second phase of the colonization process is imposed which is called cultural and social

1. Waziyatawin and Bird, "Beginning Decolonization," 2.
2. Longchar, *Transforming Cultures and Praxis*, 95.

colonization. Robert Odawi Porter expounds the process of cultural colonization as follows:

> Cultural change at this level could be called "acculturation" or "assimilation" but the more accurate term is "social engineering." At first, the colonizer uses violence to force the colonized people to change who they are as people. This occurs through the application of new laws and punishments that outlaw traditional behaviors, such as religious practices, dancing, and certain family and marital relations. The next phase is equally as violent, but takes the less overtly threatening form of taking children away from their home and raising them in the colonizer's educational institutions. This "educational" process, often referred to as "promoting civilization," involves beating, hard labor, and psychological abuse. The "benefit" associated with this is that the seeds of the colonizer's culture are planted deeply in Indigenous Peoples at a very early age.[3]

Social and cultural colonization is done in several ways. First, the Empire changes the name of the native villages, towns, and even mountains and rivers. The people are not allowed to identify places by their indigenous names; the Empire gives them new names. Naming is controlling. This process was strategically done in countries like Taiwan, Australia and Argentina, among many others. Second, indigenous names, icons, symbols, and cultural practices are replaced or used by the Empire in an undignified and demeaning manner to inculcate feelings of lower self-esteem and to generate negative images and feelings of indigenous cultures and wisdoms.[4] In some cases, people would be forced to change their religious beliefs, educational practices, and economic and political systems.

Language is power. Language is one of the greatest gifts of God. It gives an identity to a particular community and it is through the language we analyze, express, and relate to the world around us and understand it. A major function of language is to act as a reservoir of people's identity and self-expression. It helps people to dream their future and assists them to articulate their hopes and visions of a new society. Language is also one of the most important social agencies that create feelings of community by providing distinct cultural identity.[5] Recognizing the power of language, the Empire, in the name of national integration, forbids people

---

3. Porter, "Decolonization of Indigenous Governance," 89.

4. Harjo, "Just Good Sports," 31.

5. Joseph, "Introduction," 6.

from speaking their own language. In the cases of Taiwan and Australia, indigenous people were punished for speaking native languages.

The Empire value system denies the right to life to many indigenous peoples all over the world. We may cite some examples:

1. As the British Empire carved its imperial borders in South Asia the Kingdom of Nepal claims that it is the only "Hindu Kingdom" in the world. This claim denies the existence of about 30 tribal communities. The government of Nepal denied not only the existence of the indigenous peoples, but they also try to wipe out the tribal culture and traditions by declaring their slash and burn cultivation as illegal. The tribal culture and traditions are deeply rooted in the rotation of agriculture and the cycles of nature. Their culture and spirituality cannot be separated from their livelihood. They have been dependent on the forest for centuries. Conditions have been created for them to wander in despair like dry bones searching for life and livelihood. They have become landless, foodless, waterless, and homeless. They have been reduced to a cheap labor community who sell their entire lives for mere survival. Life is not mere survival, but they barely survive.

2. In the name of national integration, peace, and security the governments have forbidden the teaching of ethnic languages in Myanmar. Children are denied the right to learn, write and, speak in their own mother tongues.

3. The indigenous people in Thailand like Laos and Karen region in Myanmar have been living for centuries in their homeland. But today, in their ancestral home, many are struggling to obtain Thai citizenship. As they are being denied citizenship their forests have been taken over by the government. They cannot hunt, fish, and cultivate in their ancestral land.

4. The Japanese government has declared that there is only one homogeneous community in Japan denying the existence of indigenous people like Ainus.

5. In Medan city in Indonesia, the indigenous people are still denied the ability to construct their places of worship because the government of Indonesia does not recognize indigenous religion as a distinct spirituality.

6. Thousands of indigenous communities have been evacuated from their ancestral lands by the government of Taiwan to develop a park and wildlife sanctuary.

7. The indigenous people in Sri Lanka and North East India and many parts of the world kill each other because of divide and rule policies of the Empire.

Christianity and Colonization

The expansion of Christianity towards Asia took place during the modern era with the might of the Empire. Some missionaries embraced the Empire's ideology. Upholding that imperial culture as "superior" in terms of religion, race, political structure, economic system, education and culture, missionaries went across the world.[6] They saw the "others" as primitive, uncultured, and uncivilized people and thus in need of "civilizing." Indigenous people were seen as people without culture or inferior culture, savage life-styles, and ways of life. Indigenous people's religion and spirituality was thus derided as demonic, superstitious, and evil. They perceived and portrayed them as part of the world/nature to be conquered by the Christian faith. Separating humans from nature was seen as development. Some missionaries even went to the extent of banning indigenous peoples' songs, dances, and even musical instruments like drums and flutes, making them rootless and nameless. Seeing colonial power and Christianity working hand and hand, Waziyatawin exposes the motivations behind the biblical translation.

> While most invading Europeans never attempted to learn or understand Indigenous languages, when they did they often did so only to facilitate the conversion of Indigenous Peoples to Christianity. If missionaries could deliver sermons in an Indigenous language, more potential converts could be reached. Among such missionaries, indigenous orthographies were often

6. The Western missionaries introduced Christian faith to the indigenous people. They set up ecclesial structures, education institutes, and medical services. I am not questioning their personal good intensions, but the imperial structure within which they operated and the way in which Christian faith was interpreted in a triumphalist manner. In the people's struggle for freedom, the ecclesial and educational structures they introduced have become major tools that help organize the indigenous people's resistance to oppression. Christian faith is being reinterpreted as a faith of the oppressed people rather than of Empire.

quickly created so that the Bible could be translated and printed in the Indigenous language. This practice was not developed out of love or respect for indigenous language; it was developed to more rapidly acquire souls for Christianity's kingdom. When indigenous people converted to Christianity, they were expected to learn the colonizer's language, whether it was Spanish, English, or French.[7]

This shows a superiority–inferiority value system. The Empire value systems imposed on indigenous people have made tremendous negative impacts on their lives and cultures. Indigenous people also internalized inferiority complexes with regard to their culture. The idealization of the imperial culture and religion have brought the greatest damage to God's rich blessing of cultures. Even today many indigenous people think that their religion, spirituality, economy, and culture are inferior and backward, and aspire to adopt an imperial lifestyle. Even though colonialism has come to an end, neo-colonial violence continues in this manner. Violence is not only the physical destruction of someone. It also included colonization of hearts and minds that destroys critical thinking and devalues one's dignity.

Internalization of indigenous culture as inferior and imperial culture as superior is one of the greatest threats for the existence of indigenous community today which is a clear indication of neo-colonial violence. I had the privilege of facilitating a training session for the Council for World Mission (CWM), in India, Taiwan, and Fiji. Students mostly came from Asia, Africa, the Pacific, and Caribbean countries. Once I asked them to define "beauty" and their answers were—fair, slim, long hair, long leg, good breast, pointed nose, etc. All these answers depict Western-influenced beauty norms. I told them that they are excluding majority of humanity—the black, brown, and yellow—because their definition reflects a "white is superior" mindset. Once I also posed a question; "Slaves were taken out from Africa, true or false?" All ten students including those from Africa said, true. Then, I reversed the quote; "Good and innocent people were kidnapped from Africa and made them into slaves by the colonizer." They said the reversed sentence is true. If children were asked to color the pictures of an angel and a devil, they will color the angel white and the devil black. We have several books entitled *From Darkness to Light* depicting superiority of white. We often affirm saying "He/she is the black sheep in the family." When I asked students at Yushan seminary

7. Waziyatawin, "Relieving Our Suffering," 190.

in Taiwan to put down words associated with "religion," they would normally write God, scriptures, temples, prayers, singing, ethical life, Lord's supper, chapel, preaching, etc. Although most of them are indigenous students they would not mention land, water, ocean, mountain, myths, stories, oral tradition, dance, drum, animals, trees, rock, community life, sharing, etc. This shows how deeply the imperial mindset has taken root in our ways of thinking, words and deeds. Accordingly theology is articulated from imperial lenses.

Development, Denial, and Subjugation

The imperial development ideology is rooted in the conquest of nature and the demonization of indigenous people's spirituality which is rooted in the sense of sacredness given to land. The Empire visualizes a highly mechanized and industrialized relationship with nature. The booming of economies with high-tech and throw-away life-style is perceived as attainment of a higher quality of life. Material growth is seen as the only principle of human progress. This paradigm of development is a serious threat to the indigenous people's existence. Crying out that business must benefit all in society, not the multi-nationals, a tribal farmer in Thailand narrated as he talked with me:

> The government asked the people to plant only one kind of plant and allowed them to borrow money for this endeavor. They planted trees according to government advice using chemicals. They borrowed money and used it for business. But after they planted and got the fruit, they could not sell it because the companies refused to buy from them. People have a lot of debt . . . The people from the villages go to the cities to work, especially the young people. But they get a very low salary. Many women are sold into commercial sex.

Crying out that decision making should consciously include the excluded and vulnerable, an indigenous leader in Philippines lamented in one of my visits:

> Just like King Ahab and his wife Jezebel grabbed the vineyard of Naboth after killing him the government of Philippine continues to take away the land from the indigenous people. For instance, the indigenous peoples of Binga and Ambuclao were forced to resettle in Palawan to make way for hydroelectric plants. The

Ibaloys of Benguet were displaced. A massive Marcos Sports Complex with a huge bust of President Marcos was built. Almost all the mountains of Abra that belonged to the Tinguians of Abra were given to the Cellophil Corporation as a logging concession. The government built several dams along the Chico and Abulog rivers that would submerge at least sixteen municipalities of the Kalingas.

Crying out that people and nature are not mere instruments of production an indigenous activist in India deplored at a meeting which I attended:

Many unfortunate tribes have already bid farewell to the world they loved most. Modern civilization has squeezed them out of this world. The rest are facing a serious threat of extinction or a life of slavery. Our big brothers want us to be their coolies (bonded laborers); when we refused, they plan to finish us. Ruthless exploitation, deprivation of human rights, alienation from land, suppression of our ethnic identity, and derogation of our culture and traditions have been paralyzing us.

Crying out for social equity, identity and respect for diversity, an indigenous brother from Cambodia spoke with me about the discrimination of their tribe:

In Cambodia, some ethnic groups (for example, the Cham) are not given equal opportunities for jobs and education. If they want a job they have to change their name to a Khmer name. They hide their own identities in order to survive. Even though some indigenous communities are given official recognition, there is still discrimination in employment, political and economic opportunities.

Crying out that economic growth alone will not ensure inclusive and sustainable development, an indigenous person from Vietnam said to me:

In Vietnam, rivers have dried up because the trees are uprooted indiscriminately. But it is not the indigenous people who do this. Others come from afar to seize our land and forest. Our identity as indigenous people is rooted in our land and its trees. The land, as we have said is the Mother; the giver of life, she gives everything that we need for life to go on.

We can cite many indigenous peoples' cries for justice in Asia. Their testimonies speak of fear, threat, pain and despair as well as resistance, hope and life. With the slogan "minority should sacrifice for the sake of majority," many indigenous people in Asia have been forced to sacrifice their land, forest and water. The imperial extractive growth model has become a threat to survival.

- It threatens the waters that are sacred to people and means of life for all human beings and all of creation.

- It removes people from their traditional lands, and threatens the food web that human beings and all creation are dependent upon.

- It enables genocidal effects on human beings, where indigenous peoples, vulnerable peoples, and the poor are displaced, poisoned, and killed so that multi-national economic systems can reap the benefits for the sake of a few beneficiaries.

In summary, the sole objective of economic growth and expansion is mere profit making. It does not respect life, culture and spirituality. It denies the right to live in dignity especially to the poor and marginalized people. According to the imperial ideology there is nothing amazing about the cosmos. God is separated from the natural world. Nature has only an instrumental and surplus value determined by the extent to which humans can utilize it and profit from it. The imperial market operates to affirm this destructive ideology.

We can notice that the root causes of wars, ethnic conflict and tension between different religious communities are all directly related to control of land and its resources. Indigenous people's spiritual heritage, traditions, and culture are slowly disappearing in the name of peace, development, national integration, tourism and preservation of the environment. The inalienable rights of indigenous peoples over land and resources have been forcibly taken away. Repressive laws have resulted in massive displacement. People have been uprooted, dislocated, and evicted from their ancestral homes. Land, mountains, and rivers are polluted and forests laid to waste.[8] People's sacred areas have been destroyed and have resulted in a disconnection with their culture and spirituality. Deprivation produces poverty, which contributes to child labor, forced labor, human trafficking (including children and women), drugs and substance abuse, armed conflict, and violence. These are all justice issues that demands life to dry bones. Indigenous communities continue their

---

8. It has to be recognized that there is no social justice without ecological justice. They are inseparably interrelated. Indigenous people heavily depend upon the labor and sustenance provided by the eco-system for their survival.

quest for a community where justice is expressed in equality and sharing, and affirms a community economic system with reciprocal sharing and hospitality. It involves a personal, communal, social and ecological commitment.

Indigenous People's Struggle in North East India

The independence movement of North East India (NEI) needs to be located within the larger context of indigenous peoples' struggle for justice around the world. There are about 30 insurgent groups active in the region. Some movements started alongside India's independence movement in the 1930s and 40s. The recent ones are born out of unjust policies, market capitalism and heavy militarization by the Indian government. Some conflicts are created deliberately by the Empire to divide and rule. The strategy is to suppress the justice movement in the name of security and national integration. All forms of violence like killing, kidnapping, torturing, raping, extortion and ransacking are the daily experiences of the people in NEI. Everyday many live in uncertainty and insecurity. They feel insecure even in their own homes. People have to pay multiple taxes to the underworld outfits. At any time, the underworld outfits or army personnel can torture or ransack homes, shops, and other local government establishments. Yet their suffering and misery are not well known to the outside world due to isolation. The region is strategically kept isolated from the rest of the world so that the world will not know the truth; the cries and hopes of the indigenous peoples. Some factors that contribute to the present crisis in NEI are as follows:

(a) Historical negligence of government on basic services, resulting in worsening marginalization, poverty and food insecurity among tribal peoples. Contributing factors include geographical distance and racial and religious differences.

(b) Poverty is massive due to lack of development. After more than sixty years of India's independence, the government has not undertaken any tangible development program in the region. The dominant society treats them as second-class citizens because of racial and cultural differences. More importantly, most of the tribals/indigenous people are Christians, who are portrayed as betrayers of the nation. They are seen as anti-national.

(c) The local government is unstable. Economic dependency is the key for political instability. Most of the local governments are proxy governments of the ruling Indian party at the center.

(d) Many parents cannot pay school fees for their children, leading to increased school dropouts. This is one of the reasons for all kinds of social problems flourishing in the region. The region ranks highest for crime cases in India.

(e) There is unequal treatment of citizens on the basis of tribe, ethnicity, and religion.

(f) Racism is rampant and there are many cases in which top positions in government service and the army have been denied to minorities.

(g) Tribal culture is treated as inferior and Hindutva ideology is imposed. Institutionalized discrimination and cultural chauvinism are experienced in the education system and even in the media establishment.

(h) Taking advantage of the unstable situation, the officials and the contractors often misused or manipulated people's funds. This corruption not only hinders the development work but also create gap between the haves and have-nots.

(i) There is constant fear among the people due to increasing militarization of the region. There are many who have been killed and made to disappear. The Indian government which is a main conduit of the imperial system in the present day world strongly believes that repression is the only way to counter the indigenous people's resistance, not peaceful negotiation. As human progress is measured by economic growth, international commerce, and stability of the Indian state the imperial system of states, as a god who has no ears and eyes, does not hear the cries and hopes of the indigenous people.

The tribal communities in NEI are highly militarized by the Empire. The communal riots are engineered to weaken the people's movements. In recent years, we have experienced riots related to Meiteis-Naga, Naga-Kuki, Karbi-Kuki, Karbi-Assamese, Assamese-Bodo, Chakmas-Mizo, Arunachali-Chakma, Bengali-Tripuri, Garos-Khasi, Khasi-Nepali, etc. In all these communal riots and unrests, one will notice the hand of the Empire. These conflicts weaken the unity of the oppressed peoples across the NEI and strengthen the imperial agendas. Yet the struggle against the organized greed of the Empire that exploits the people and plunders their land is unstoppable. Critical consciousness against the manipulative divisive politics is at work helping build solidarity that can overcome conflicts. Amid many temptations they are on a journey:

(a) demanding their ancestral domains and territorial integrity against systematic and massive land grabbing,

(b) resisting anti-people and anti-ecological development aggression

(c) resisting militarization of their sacred habitats and communities, and violation of human rights,

(d) fighting against institutionalized discrimination and cultural chauvinism, and demanding celebration of diversity,

(e) resisting commercialization of their culture,

(f) demanding rectification of the long historical government neglect of basic services that has resulted in marginalization, poverty, and food insecurity,

(g) demanding the right to own, manage, and develop their territory and resources therein,

(h) demanding to recognize the right to practice and develop their socio-political systems including customary laws, justice systems, rituals and beliefs, and other cultural practices, and to maintain their cultural integrity and ethnicity.

God with the Powerless

God's voice can be heard through the words of the wise, especially the poor, the oppressed, and the rejected ones. The God of the Bible is the one who journeys with and ahead of the people who are outside of the deified imperial power structures (idols). To hear God's voice we need to listen not only to the testimonies, pains and sufferings of the people who are outside of the power structures, but also to their hopes, dreams and collective aspirations. It is the marginalized people's cries for justice that become God's cry. Their faith in God who promises liberation gives them hope. A theology that does not articulate this faith and hope has no relevance, currency and significance for the oppressed peoples on earth.

The incarnation of God in Christ Jesus took place among the people at the margins in Palestine, a Roman colony. Jesus was not born in a palace, but in a manger, a ragged cowshed, an open and unprotected place. At the time of the birth of Jesus, people who gathered around him were people outside of the religious and political power structure of Palestine. They were people without any political power, nor religious authority, women, children and the poor people like the shepherds who were landless and did not have legal protection and from whom the rich people even refused to buy milk and vegetables. The wise men, strangers in Jerusalem who brought precious gifts to Jesus, refused to be subjected to the imperial laws and obligations. They were asked by the Empire to report about the birth of Jesus. Instead they left by another route to Galilee to protect the life of Jesus. People who welcomed Jesus were those outside of the hierarchy of power. These people were not allowed to enter the temple and did not have any political influence. People who were missing during the birth of Jesus were the rich men, rich women, the king, queen, princes and princesses, high priests, nobles, and other high officials. The birth of Jesus was astonishing and threatening news for those holders of power. Threatened by the news, Herod, the king, ordered to kill all children two-years-old and younger in Bethlehem (Matt 2:16). They never wanted God to take liberative action among the lowly people. Revelation is a liberative proclamation; "God is with us." The angel announced the message, "Peace be with you" among the marginal people. God chose the margin—the people on the underside of history—to inaugurate Her Reign, bringing justice and peace. God was and is encountered among the powerless and in unexpected locations like manger, but not in the palace. If the God of the Bible took the side of marginalized people, then it is clear that God continues to take the side of marginalized people even today, identifying with the dry bones and challenging their oppressors in NEI sharing their cries and hopes for justice and freedom. The Bible testifies that the Divine participates in history to defend those who are victims of power. James Cone has rightly said:

> Yahweh is known and worshipped as the One who brought Israel out of Egypt, and who raised Jesus from the dead. God is the political God, the Protector of the poor and the Establisher of the right for those who are oppressed. To know God is to experience the acts of God in the concrete affairs and relationships of people, liberating the weak and the helpless from pain and humiliation. For theologians to speak of this God, they too must

become interested in politics and economics, recognizing that there is no truth about Yahweh unless it is the truth of freedom as that event is revealed in the oppressed people's struggle for justice in this world.[9]

God's Healing Power dawns through the Struggle of the Oppressed People, not from Empire

The gospel writer tells us the story of two persons—one at the "Centre" (the rich man) and the other on the "Margin" (Lazarus; Luke 16:19). Lazarus, being subjected to miserable inhuman conditions knew what it meant to be thirsty, hungry, in pain and to beg in front of someone's gate without dignity. The rich man who was partying with sumptuous meals every day could not understand the pain of Lazarus. Similarly, the rich who are protected by unjust power structures cannot understand the pain of the marginalized people. People who cannot understand the suffering of the oppressed people cannot bring solution and transformation. Tribals, dalits, women, persons with disabilities and other marginalized groups who have been marginalized for centuries know what affirms life and what denies it, what helps communities and what hurts them, what contributes to their well-being, and what denies their rights. From the margins they bring first-hand liberative knowledge of the suffering to unmask the forces that work against God's will in the world.[10] Through their lives and struggles for life, they hold forth what God wants in the world that is needed to remain faithful to the promised Reign of God. The change can take place only when marginalized people raise their voices believing that God is on their side. In fact, it is this faith that prompts them to speak out, organize themselves for collective action and journey together. In this sense, believing is not accepting the inhuman conditions as God's will as traditional Christianity taught us. It is just the contrary.

There are many testimonies both in the First and Second Testaments that show how people in the margins were used by God as instruments for transformation and change. For example, 2 Kgs 5:1–19 presents a story of how people in the margins became the agents of healing. Naaman suffered from leprosy, though he was also a successful commander of the army of the king of Syria and had won favor from the king and the people

9. Cone, *Black Theology of Liberation*, 57.

10. World Council of Churches, "Just and Inclusive Community," 1.

because of his skillful and dedicated work. And the nameless little girl—the prisoner and victim of war, displaced from her family, her people and land—was put to force labor, working for Naaman's wife, but she became an agent of healing. We see the following contrasting positions of the two—Naaman and the Nameless little girl:

> Naaman is powerful. The Nameless girl is powerless and
>   helpless.
> Naaman is a ruler. The Nameless girl is ruled.
> Naaman is a conqueror. The Nameless girl is conquered, abused
>   & misused.
> Naaman is an army commander. The Nameless girl is a victim
>   of the army.
> Naaman is a slave owner. The Nameless girl is a slave.
> Naaman is a predator. The Nameless girl is a victim.
> Naaman needed healing. The Nameless girl offered help/
>   healing.
> Naaman has a name. The girl does not have a name.[11]

In her pitiable and pathetic experience of war and dislocation, the Nameless girl knew what Naaman was going through in his life. She knew the pain and sorrow of Naaman. Instead of rejoicing and revenging over his misfortune and pain, the Nameless girl offered words of healing. It was indeed difficult for the ruler to listen to the words of the ruled. The ruler wanted to get healed by maintaining the royal power and offering wealth. The exercise of power and money is paramount for the people who never experience pain and suffering. First, he obtained an official letter from the king of Aram thinking that the royal authority and power would be respected and obeyed by the subjects. Second, he took ten talents of silver, six thousand shekels of gold, and ten sets of clothing to impress and to appease prophet Elisha. As was common protocol at that time, Naaman expected that the prophet would come out, bow down before him, perform rituals like calling on the name of God, touched over his body, and cure his leprosy miraculously. The ruler thought that he would be healed. But it happened in quite a different way. Instead of going and meeting Naaman, Elisha sent a message through a messenger, "Go and wash in the Jordan seven times, and you shall be clean" (II Kings 9). People in power, like Naaman, always want protocol. He felt insulted and took this as disrespectful not only to him but also to the king. He became angry and decided to go away without obeying what Elisha asked him to do. But

11. Rao, "Centred on the Margin," 8–10.

then another Word of healing came from his servant; another person in the margins. He said "My father, if the prophet had told you to do some great thing, would you not have done it? How much more, then, when he tells you, 'Wash and be cleaned'" (II Kings 13). Only when he listened to the voice of his servant did he finally get healed.

What is the meaning of washing in the Jordan River? The river did not have, of course, substances within it that could cure leprosy. There is a deeper meaning in the act of washing in the dirty river seven times. It was the river where the poorest people lived, where they drank, and where they bathed. To be healed from leprosy, Naaman needed to wash himself in the river where the poor washed their bodies too. By washing his body seven times in the river Jordan, Naaman expressed solidarity with the people at the margins. To wash himself seven times in the river would compel Naaman, a military general and a fighter, to be humble in front of the prophet, in front of the Nameless girl and his servant, and become a servant of the people he had conquered. In this dirty river that Naaman despised, he could get his holistic healing. It was in solidarity with the people in the margins that he could find the power of healing. Listening to the least ones with obedience, humility, and solidarity is the basis of transformation.

The Power of the Powerless

To live a life of dignity, respect, and freedom is the intrinsic right of all human beings. It is a divine gift to all. Victims can celebrate God given life in abundance only when justice is restored to them. Forces that threaten celebration of life must be resisted. It is not an option, but a divine imperative and a mandate. Therefore, the words of Jesus—"The Son of Man did not come to be served, but to serve" (Mark 10:45)—should not be understood in *submissive and idealistic terms*. It is a *radical and costly leadership*. It involves *liberating marginalized people from the yoke of religious formalism, legalism, misuse of power, and unjust economic structures that oppress and marginalize them.* Jesus' uncompromising defense of life led him to a life of conflict with the Empire of his time. This conflict resulted in Jesus' death on the cross. Similarly, the disciples and followers of Jesus of Nazareth confronted the principalities and powers of structural/institutional/systemic Empire that exploit the poor of their times. They risked their life for Christ's sake and became martyrs for justice.

Women were the most powerless people at the time of Jesus, but God prepared ordinary womenfolk to be the agent of the transforming power of God. We see this testimony in the Gospels—who will roll the stone away? (Mark 16:1–4; Luke 2:1–5; Matt 28:1–10). The tomb was sealed in three ways: First, a large stone was rolled against the tomb. The stone was not only large, but it was also sealed by the Empire. Palestine was ruled by the Romans, the most powerful empire at that time. Nobody could challenge the Romans. Disobeying them and removing the stone was punishable by death. Second, it was guarded by the most powerful Roman soldiers. They were armed. The Roman guards were strict and disciplined fighters who knew that failure on duty was punishable by torture and death. The soldiers were there by order of the Emperor. Third, the Roman seal was affixed on the stone by the order of the king. The seal symbolized the power and authority of the Empire. Moving the stone from the tomb entrance would break the seal, thereby deserving execution by crucifixion upside down. The mighty Roman Empire trampled down. Womenfolk in the Roman colony had no weapon. They had no money, no political connection, and influence. They were mere ordinary rural women. Their only weapon against the mighty Romans was courage, solidarity, commitment, and love. With this weapon they went to the tomb to fight the Empire. The Romans could not suppress the truth of the resurrection of Jesus Christ.

The feeding of 5000 speaks of solidarity, care, and love for one another, which Jesus embodied. The Reign of God is always a shared meal, which challenges the imperial greed. The Risen One transformed the hearts and minds of the oppressed from fear to fearlessness, from despair to hope and from sadness to joy which constantly energized them to walk on the journey steadfastly. Repression caused by brute military force could not stop their journey. The early Christian community, motivated by the spirit of Pentecost, resisted the Empire in all its forms; cultural, social, political, and militaristic. Instead of turning to the Empire that presents itself as a god, they turned to the power of the Spirit of Jesus Christ and became new human beings who radiate the liberating hope wherever they went. They collected what they have and shared among them forming an alternative community. They gathered the victims of the Empire and embodied the dawned of a new world through their selfless solidarity with one another. This is how the dry bones gained a new life, the deadly imperial power structures were overcome and life in abundance was guaranteed. It is this faith that needs to be recaptured in the day to day struggle of the indigenous peoples in NEI.

Conclusion

To fight against the Empire we have to awaken ourselves to the faith in the liberating God revealed in Jesus Christ who prompts us to build solidarity among the peoples. Faith without solidarity is dead. Solidarity without faith would not last long, particularly in times of extreme hardships. Without faith and solidarity it is not possible to face the unjust imperial system that cause dehumanization and desecration of the earth. The journey of the indigenous peoples in NEI is a long and arduous one like in the biblical wilderness. Liberation is not an idealistic utopia or something of the past that is not possible in our times, but a continuous struggle and a commitment to *transformation of the sinful social structures*. It involves constant *raising consciousness* by critically reflecting on the historical praxis of the oppressed people. In that, it is necessary that the Christian communities among the indigenous peoples engage in a critical reflection of their faith in Risen Christ and realize the promptings of the Spirit here and now in NEI in contributing to the emancipation of the tormented indigenous peoples across the region, no matter what their religious affiliation be. The critical biblical reflections of this essay were done as part of my journey with my people in NEI with the intention of revitalizing faith in God who raised Jesus from the dead and assured life in abundance for all the struggling oppressed peoples on earth against the imperial masters who falsely claim to be all powerful.

Chapter 3

Indigenous Peoples and Liberation Theology

Resistance to Imperialism
and Militarization in Latin America[1]

Nidia Arrobo Rodas

"We need to take action before it's too late, before the ambition
and madness of a few men turn our planet into a dead moon, in
a space graveyard."—Msgr. Leonidas Proaño

Introduction

From times immemorial, in Abya-Yala, our continent, until the arrival
of the Europeans, native peoples have lived peacefully, enjoying their
own culture, worldview, science, knowledge, and technologies which
were exceptional and admirable in every sense. They had their own as-
trology and cosmology, social and political organizations, medicine and
odontology, agriculture and architecture/civil engineering, and different
forms of arts and spirituality. Genuine civilizations were formed such as
the Maya, Aztecs, Incas, and so on, just to name a few.

That scientific, cultural, spiritual, technological, and social development was interrupted violently by the European invasions, which led
to the biggest holocaust in history—which has not been recognized nor

1. Translated from Spanish by Jose Antonio Gutiérrez.

compensated for until the present—which exterminated at least 70 million human beings and turned others into the most highly oppressed peoples on our planet to this day. Many cultures were destroyed and the never-ending plunder of abundant natural resources was set in motion. From the beginning the stated aim of the invader was creating a "New World." It was solely driven by the lust for gold, silver, and precious metals. A totally alien culture, economy, and religious and political system was imposed as part of the genocidal process which established exploitative social and ecological relationships as the norm of "the newly created world." This grotesque violence and accompanying exclusion and marginalization were practiced with a cross and a sword. The Chilean sociologist Hervi Lara Bravo states,

> between 1503 and 1660, hundred and eighty five thousand kilos of gold and sixteen million kilos of silver arrived to the port of Seville in Spain. All that wealth plundered from the New World stimulated economic development in Europe, and in many ways, made it possible. This was the dawn of the age of capitalist production, after the discovery, conquest, and colonisation of America, which was one of the biggest genocides in history. This was like the iron age which laid the foundations of what we are experiencing today.[2]

The history of my continent is not only a history of genocide, but also of continuous struggle for liberation. This account is a small attempt to capture some glimpses of that struggle. The spirituality inspired by the indigenous cosmovisions sees land as sacred and liberative reflection of Christian faith has not only contributed to the struggle immensely, but also shaped its character in Latin America. As a result there emerged a fundamental reorientation of understanding faith and doing theology in our modern times. I have chosen the life and work of one pioneer of this spirituality as the main focus of this essay, which will follow after a very brief analysis of the unfathomable richness of eco-systems that support life in its entirety and the brutal imperialist onslaught against it.

Eco-Systems and Flourishing of Life

In the vast territory of Abya Yala, which comprises a little more than two billion hectares, representing 15 percent of the world's surface, there

2. Lara Bravo, "Ethical Crisis."

is great wealth and cultural diversity thanks to the ancestral peoples whose existence is continuously being threatened today. There are over sixty million indigenous peoples who have co-existed during millennia in a symbiotic relationship with nature. The Amerindians account for 13 percent of the world's linguistic diversity. Alas, 60 percent of those languages are endangered or on their way to extinction. Our continent is also the source of 30 percent of fresh water in the world; a third of the total amount of renewable hydric resources in the world. South America has 30 percent of the world's overflow water circulating freely on a drainage basin's surface. Moreover, it houses various ecosystems such as mangroves, glaciers, and moorlands (páramos). These ecosystems are insufficiently known despite being paramount for the environment and humanity.

A lot of research indicates that in these territories there exists the highest biodiversity on the planet in terms of species and eco-regions as well as several precious resources such as oil, minerals, and fresh water. In this continent, there are 35 percent of the mammals, 35 percent of the reptiles, 41 percent of the birds and 51 percent of the amphibians in the world. The indigenous peoples managed to domesticate several plants such as potatoes, quinoa, maize, avocados, cocoa, and chilies, many of which have contributed to feeding the world and overcoming famine elsewhere. Stephen Leahy claims that Costa Rica alone has some 800 endemic species which are not found anywhere else in the world. Canada, with a surface almost 200 times bigger than the small Central American nation has merely 70 unique species, scattered in an area of nine million square kilometers of land.[3] According to the Argentinian co-president of the Intergovernmental Science-Policy Platform on Biodiversity and Ecosystem Services (IPBES) for the Americas, María Elena Zaccagnini, in the American continent there is 40 percent of the ecosystemic capacity of the planet to produce the biological resources required by humanity. "In other words, we have thrice as much biocapacity per capita than the average global citizen."[4]

It is these rich eco-systems that nourished life from generation to generation. The very foundations of indigenous peoples were built on this diverse bio-sphere which is revered as sacred. Nonetheless, the vast majority of the population of Abya Yala live in poverty and the majority

---

3. Leahy, "La protección de la biodiversidad en América Latina."
4. DW, "Latin America."

of the indigenous peoples survive in a truly stoic fashion. This is truly the genocidal process that continues by the alienation of the majority of peoples and destruction/desecration of nature. The so-called modern lifestyles of the New World are often disconnected from the local natural environment or there is no natural environment that nourishes communities. As nature is plundered her children are made orphans crying out in desolation. It is not simply a physical destruction, but also an epistemological and spiritual one. The social-cultural values such as the sense of place, linguistic diversity, and ecological knowledge are being erased.

Alberto Acosta, the Ecuadorian social scientist, states that there is an "apparently perverse relationship between natural resources and underdevelopment, causing abundance to be a curse."[5] As defined by Joseph Stiglitz that is the "paradox of plenty" or "the resource curse of plenty" which is derived from the biocidal model ruling those countries which are totally dependent on nature's rents.[6] This curse of plenty is threatening the lives of the indigenous peoples, of all of us who live in these territories, and of mother earth. Moreover it violates human rights and doesn't take into account the rights of indigenous peoples and of nature. It is even threatening democracy and most of all it has reduced the Amazon—the lungs of humanity—to being the periphery of the periphery.

When Alexander Von Humboldt arrived, over two hundred years ago on his historical tour of the Americas, in what we know today as Ecuador, he marveled at the geography, the flora, and fauna of this region. It is said that he regarded its inhabitants as beggars sitting on sacks full of gold because of its enormous natural wealth which was not being "taken advantage of." Since then, adhering to this view, which is no different to that of the Spaniards when they conquered these lands, the various Ecuadorian governments, time and again, have aspired to extract the treasures from those sacks, writes Alberto Acosta.[7] Eduardo Gudynas articulates this gruesome reality in the following way:

> According to the classical ideas on development abundance of natural resources was key to reach a better standard of living. In Latin America, it was often insisted upon that the abundance in minerals, fertile soil, fresh water and other resources was

5. Acosta, *La maldición de la abundancia*, 16.

6. Humphreys et al., *Escaping the Resource Curse*.

7. Acosta, *La maldición de la abundancia*, 10.

enough to guarantee the road towards prosperity and welfare. However, the countries of this continent, among them Ecuador, still suffer from serious social ills; poverty persists and inequality is evident. It is as if wealth slipped away from our hands and got lost beyond our borders, to the rivers of the international trade, without causing the qualitative leap forward on the national level . . . it is a history replete of contrasts, such as the opulence of the oil companies and the poverty of local communities, or the records of crude oil exports while this country suffers from serious energy problems.[8]

This paradoxical context of abundance and dispossession and of extraordinary cultural-biological-natural wealth and plunder is the hallmark of modern imperialism and its accompanying militarization. From the outset, the Western empires on their expansionist drive in our continent aimed at appropriating—in an uncontrolled fashion—the abundant natural resources of the region which they considered as their "backyard," exploiting them as if the resources and mother earth were inexhaustible. This has been an oppressive situation for our peoples, a situation even more violent for the indigenous nations which, for centuries, have been subjected by colonial and neo-colonial nation-states that never valued, let alone respected and protected, these native peoples. Neo-colonial states of the continent are hardwired into the Empire. These states have become conduits of extractivism for the Empire. At the same time new social classes have been formed locally in the image and likeness of the New World that believes brutal exploitation of masses and attacks on mother earth are "natural" for economic wellbeing. Accordingly racism and military repression against the indigenous peoples have not only been legitimized, but also morally justified. The sons and daughters of *pachamama* (mother earth) are the biggest barrier for the creation of the New World.

Throughout modern history imperialism has exerted its power through military, cultural, economic, political, and religious means and waged multiple wars that have resulted in thousands of deaths and deep scars. The impact of imperialism is deeply felt in the sorry state of the economy of our dependent countries, in the generalized impoverishment of the population and in the dispossession of the indigenous nations severed from their territory. This is the "accumulation by dispossession" of the capitalist imperial market that "determines the wounded and

8. Gudynas, "Prologue," 16.

the dead."[9] The ever-expanding environmental destruction, the carbon footprint, climate change, and the escalating environmental disasters with unforeseeable consequences are treated as "externalities" that are not part of the economic growth which are never taken into account by the accumulated and organized lust of the Empire which has no eyes and ears. The main victims are the impoverished people and our raped mother nature. Yes, it is a history of genocide, but this is not the end of our story.

Msgr. Leonidas Proaño, Indigenous Peoples and Liberation Theology

Pastoral Work as Liberation

The history of my continent is a history of continuous struggles of liberation which cannot be stopped. There have been many anti-imperialist and anti-militaristic struggles that have been fought by the indigenous nations and by social organizations in Ecuador and the rest of the continent who have stood against dispossession and plunder of nature. Without doubt a pioneering role in these struggles, particularly of the indigenous peoples, was played by Msgr. Leonidas Proaño from Ecuador who is popularly known as the prophet of the poor, bishop of the indigenous, and father of the Church.

> There is no doubt that the Ecuadorian Liberation Theology recognises Leonidas Proaño as its most inspirational and significant figure. His, is an emancipating, lived, spoken and written theology, with a pastoral intention rather than a speculating one, a theology which inspires the historical trajectory of the social and ecclesiastical actors towards and from the hope of the people of God in Ecuador.[10]

Early in his career he started a process of raising awareness of the dire conditions of the poor as an intrinsic part of evangelization and unheard of politicization of the indigenous peoples. This was done through a range of liberating pastoral activities that were designed jointly between the indigenous communities and the people's movements of the other impoverished social classes of society. As someone who journeyed with

9. Arizmendi, "Necropolitical Capitalism," 289.
10. Solano, "La Teología de la Liberación," 390.

him as a co-worker I have always been inspired by his pastoral action which was defined by an inseparable intersection of faith and politics. He taught us that in order to build the Utopia, which in political terms is a new society and in spiritual terms is the Reign of God, you have to walk on two feet. One foot needs to step firmly with the Gospel and the other with the people's organizations. The faith in the Gospel gives the spirit, and the organizations give the mode of resistance that are necessary to achieve structural changes to exercise, respect, and guarantee human rights and the rights of the people.

Juan José Tamayo, a Spanish theologian, points out four reasons behind the origins of liberation theology:

> To sum up, they were the irruption of the poor in history, the liberation movements, dependency theory, and the entry of Christians as important conscious actors and not as mere mass, in the political process of liberation. These are the conditions which allowed the liberation theology to come into being in Latin America, with its distinctive originality vis-à-vis the theological reflections after the Council.[11]

To talk about liberation theology is to look for an answer to the following question: What's the relationship between salvation and the historical process of humanity's liberation? The bottom line of liberation theology—according to Gustavo Gutiérrez—is not political, social or economic arguments, but theological arguments which are essentially biblical:

> Theology as critical reflection on historical praxis is a liberation theology, a theology of the liberating transformation of the history of humankind and also therefore that part of humankind—gathered into ecclesia—which openly confesses Christ. It is a theology that does not stop with reflecting on the world, but rather tries to be part of the process through which the world is transformed.[12]

God, according to the Bible, stands side by side with the poor who are in a struggle for liberation. She loves them and announces good tidings, God's Reign, to them through Jesus Christ. Msgr. Proaño's liberation action and liberation theology were rooted in the Word of God and in the burning reality of oppression and exclusion of our peoples. He critically reflected on the meaning of the following text within his people's historical praxis:

11. Tamayo, *Para comprender la Teología de la Liberación*, 35.

12. Gutiérrez, *Theology of Liberation*, 15.

"The Lord said, 'I have indeed seen the misery of my people in Egypt. I have heard them crying out because of their slave drivers, and I am concerned about their suffering. So I have come down to rescue them from the hand of the Egyptians'" (Exod 3:7). Jesus Christ embodied this Word as testified by the Gospels. "The Spirit of the Lord is on me, because he has anointed me to proclaim good news to the poor. He has sent me to proclaim freedom for the prisoners and recovery of sight for the blind, to set the oppressed free, to proclaim the year of the Lord's favor" (Luke 4:18). In the historical context of Latin America, the God of Jesus Christ journeys with the poor and the oppressed and leads them in their struggle. She is with them and ahead of them. This is how Msgr. Proaño radicalized Christian faith in our continent. In this sense, proclaiming the Gospel is an emancipatory political project as opposed to the oppressive Western proselytization which aided and blessed imperialism. During the thirty years of his episcopate and three years of presiding over the indigenous pastoral office of the Bishops' Conference of Ecuador he personified the liberative Gospel message not simply in words, but in deeds by leading many revolutionary campaigns that empowered the oppressed masses, particularly the indigenous communities.

His pastoral work made the indigenous masses wake up from centuries of slumber. They stood up on their feet and asserted their dignity. In the religious and spiritual sense, he made them realize that the Gospel and the church were on their side and their aspiration for liberation is the will of God, not the existing inhuman condition. They revived their spiritual bond with mother earth as part of the liberative praxis. In the social and political sense, he gave leadership to them as a true pastor to challenge the feudal relationships of centuries-old oppression in the Ecuadorian rural regions. Gradually they started forming their organizations, particularly during the last two decades developing and promoting their own liberative cultural, economic, political, and theological proposals. As a result they have achieved an active presence in public life as an undeniable political, social, and spiritual force.

Taita Proaño during all of his life was a faithful disciple of both Jesus Christ and the indigenous peoples.[13] He was proud to proclaim within his country and abroad, in universities, conferences, and meetings: "The indigenous people have taught me." "My university was the people and they were my best teachers." He trembled with emotion when he repeated

---

13. Taita is a Kichwa expression, meaning father, daddy.

Jesus' prayer: "I praise you, Father, Lord of heaven and earth, because you have hidden these things from the wise and learned, and revealed them to little children" (Luke 10, 21). With his actions, Msgr. Proaño embraced the principles of liberation theology:

1. preferential option for the indigenous people which he considered to be the poorest among the poor;

2. critical response to reality and to challenge people's oppression;

3. recognition of the poor as an active subject in their own liberation process;

4. the notion that there can be no Christian salvation without economic, social, political, spiritual, and ideological liberation, all visible signs of human dignity; and

5. the notion that sin is not only individual but is above all collective and structural, for our burning reality is based on social sinfulness which denies the historical design of God for the oppressed peoples: life and life in abundance.

François Houtrart comments,

> Liberation Theology makes explicit its analysis of society in terms of structures, antagonistic social relations which derive mainly from the appropriation of economic power. Its role is to discredit the economic system as such (the market's idolatry) and to give ethical support to the social movements in resistance, while looking for alternatives and keeping a critical distance from the means to achieve this.[14]

On the basis of the above principles, but most of all, by the living experience of the liberating Gospel, all of the actions of Msgr. Proaño in Ecuador constitute a historical praxis and the beginning of a process in which the revolutionary potential of the indigenous nations was made visible. This process had a national and a continental impact among the indigenous masses. Totally in keeping with his option for the poor and the indigenous people Msgr. Proaño in his relentless struggle to transform social structures and to achieve justice made a revolutionary move based on the method of See, Judge and Act.[15] This was something extraordi-

14. Houtart, *Deslegitimar el Capitalismo*, 216.

15. A well-known revolutionary method of the Young Christian Workers, which was created by the Belgian priest Cardijn, influenced the Medellín Conference and the

nary in Ecuador, that is, the restitution of lands to the indigenous people which up until then belonged to the Church of Riobamba, as an act of justice and reparation. In fact, the church possessed land as a result of its colonial heritage in Latin America. The return of land to the dispossessed on earth is an act of conversion to the covenantal relationship between God and people. Here faith and political action for justice become one.

The God of Liberation and enslaving gods

He found imperialism and capitalism to be the root cause of oppression.

> God created the world for all men, not for a few privileged men. God created men to love one another, so in their love, they helped each other to progress in life. God condemns with terrible words, threats and punishments everything that has to do with injustice, and the oppression of the poor, the widows, the orphans, the workers, and the labourers, and everything that has to do with slavery. God is not happy when some men are enslaved. God repudiates, therefore, everything that means domination of some men over others. God repudiates everything about imperialism because that is domination of some men over a multitude of peoples.[16]

He denounced capitalism in unambiguous terms and called it cold and heartless:

> Capitalism is cold, cold as anything made of metal. It does not care about men or peoples. It only cares about profits. And it only cares about men and peoples to the extent that they can generate profits. To devour profits, it devours men and peoples. It is cold and heartless . . . Our country, like other countries in Latin America, has fallen victim to the claws of this monster long ago. We are dependent of it in many ways. We are its toy. It makes us think as it does. It makes us act the way it wants us to act.[17]

Church of the Poor in Latin America.

16. Proaño, *Fe y Política*, 4–5.

17. Proaño, "El Profeta Del Pueblo," 118. "El Profeta del Pueblo"was published in Riobamba in 1983, and it expresses a position developed after a long process of reflecting and being side by side with the indigenous and peasants harassed by the U.S. policies and religious authorities. Second edition was published in Quito in 1992.

He clearly identified neo-colonial violence in Latin American countries speaking truth to the oppressed in the following manner:

> In this game a prominent role is played by the INTERNATIONAL MONETARY FUND. They have repeatedly come to give advice. In our situation of dependency, this advice is tantamount to PRESSURE. But the capitalist monster does not only live abroad in the so-called developed countries, in the United States and Europe. It also lives in the Latin American countries and in our very country too. Its thick and deep root has ramifications. That monster has tentacles here too, among us.[18]

He explicitly named the main driver of the empire and exposed and denounced its interventionism, particularly, its brute military onslaught on Latin American countries:

> The United States have interests of their own. President Reagan, the General Secretary Alexander Haig, they both have expressed on multiple occasions that their intervention in El Salvador, Guatemala, Honduras, Nicaragua, and all over Central America is because their interests are at stake . . .[19]

> Bringing together political interventionism with a military interventionism they have invaded countries such as Dominican Republic. They have taken over territory of other countries, such as Guantanamo in Cuba. The U.S. marines have invaded Nicaragua back in history. And they have found other means to change governments in Chile, through the CIA, through the ITT, through other agencies working inside the country. And there is political interventionism each time that organisations such as the Peace Corps or others, which have CIA members, start destabilising from within those governments which are at odds with the U.S. interests.[20]

The USA, thus, not only make "their interests" the central argument, but they translate them into programmatic actions to defend them with fire and blood. The core of the Monroe Doctrine, "America for Americans" has been and is still in place, a doctrine of thought that originated in the context of the imperial-colonial project of the European powers. He lamented over the plight of the whole of nature and people in Latin

18. Proaño, "El Profeta," 119.

19. Proaño, "El intervenxionismo norteamricano en Américan Latina," 10.

20. Proaño, "El intervenxionismo norteamricano en Américan Latina," 10.

America. Those who claim to be all-powerful and act like gods have enslaved them. This lament emerges out of his deep faith in the God of
creation and the oppressed peoples who wills their liberation.

> The great wealth of the soil, the subsoil, and the sea belongs to
> the Latin American countries only nominally . . . Latin America
> is not free: it is terribly manacled by the whims of powerful
> countries . . . Why men put so much effort in subjecting other
> men to slavery? How deeply entrenched is in men the tempta-
> tion to be like a god, to be a god![21]

The Church with the Crucified People

The imperial plot in the murder of Msgr. Óscar Arnulfo Romero on
March 24, 1980 is *vox populi*. He was the archbishop of San Salvador and
he centered his pastoral work in the liberation of the poor and oppressed.
He denounced the systematic violations of human rights in El Salvador
and demanded an end to repression believing that the tormented people
of his country are the Crucified Christ here and now. In order to murder
him, Marino Samayor Acosta, a military sniper, had received US$114
under the instructions of Colonel Arturo Armando Molina and Major
Roberto d'Aubuisson. The latter was the founder of the right wing political party Nationalist Republican Alliance, (ARENA) a man who was
trained in the School of Americas (which is called the School of Assassins
by thousands of victims of military dictatorships in Latin America who
were aided by the USA). Romero's prophetic voice continues to challenge
the imperialist establishment and its neocolonial governments in Latin
America. His canonization as a saint by Pope Francis is a powerful statement that the church has made against the USA's imperial designs and
their local actors in Latin America.

We should also remember here, how on November 16, 1989, in El
Salvador, members of the Atlacatl battalion, trained in the School of the
Americas entered the Central American University (UCA) and mur-
dered the liberation theologians Ignacio Ellacuría, Ignacio Martín-Baró,
Segundo Montes, Juan Ramón Moreno, Amando López, and Joaquín
López y López together with their co-worker Elba Ramos and her daugh-
ter Celina. Of the twenty five soldiers who participated in this massacre,
nineteen were trained and graduated in the School of Americas. Because

---

21. Proaño, "El Profeta," 120.

of the massive number of cases of torture and the murder of priests, nuns, and Christian activists in the 1980s, the Latin American church during this period was called "Church of the Martyrs." In Central America alone there were 1800 priests and nuns who were tortured and had to flee into exile and sixty-nine were murdered. In the age of the gods of imperialism, capitalism, militarization and neo-colonial violence—who plunder the earth and deprive millions of masses of their life and livelihood and brutalize them when they resist—the theme of Christian martyrdom gains a new theological meaning. The call is not to give up one's life for the sake of religion in the traditional sense of martyrdom, but for the oppressed peoples. Liberation theology, in this sense, is not only a critical reflection of the historical praxis, but also of one's commitment to justice and liberation.[22]

All of these struggles of the Christian communities reflect the historical journey of the Latin American peoples against the ongoing genocidal process unleashed by imperial powers and their local allies. After the historic conference of Medellín (1968)—in which prophetic bishops of the stature of Dom Helder and Proaño actively participated—the Latin American Conference of Bishops redefined the pastoral work of the church in accordance with the historical struggle of the oppressed peoples. The preferential option for the poor, and the struggle for justice and the transformation of those structures based on social and political sinfulness that ruins the lives of the marginalized were seen as essential to the practice of Christian faith and mission. The USA was terribly upset with this new move in the Roman Catholic Church. It could not accept this and had to do something about it. And they did. The empire struck back with its might as Msgr. Proaño explained:

> The U.S. State Secretary asked a U.S. entity, Rand Corporation, to do an exhaustive research into the positions of the Catholic Church in the Latin American continent. They carried out the research for over two and a half years. The result of this study was the profiling of bishops, priests, religious communities, and groups of lay Christians. Those of us who desired the renewal of the Church, its commitment to the poor, and its commitment to

22. However, Rasika Sharmen Pieris's chapter in this collection has clearly shown suffering and martyrdom should not be glorified. The feminist theologians have warned us against such mythologization and absolutization of suffering which justifies suffering of women as the norm in a patriarchal system. Suffering is an outcome of the commitment one makes to justice, not the end. It is not suffering that saves us, but resistance—moved by faith, hope and love—to all forms of oppression.

> justice, we were PROFILED in order to be DENIGRATED, in
> order to be DISCREDITED, in order to be EXPELLED, in order
> to be DISAPPEARED![23]

And I would add murdered too. He went on, pointing out how the church continues to pay a heavy price due to its commitment to the peoples' struggle:

> The Catholic Church has paid and is still paying a dear price for
> its "sin," having opted for the poor, for justice, for the liberation
> of the oppressed. The so-called and well-known Plan Banzer,
> was conceived by all the profiling done by the Rand Corpora-
> tion, and it was not only applied in Bolivia, but in other Latin
> American countries, against priests, nuns, and bishops consid-
> ered to be dangerous.[24]

Msgr. Leonidas Proaño himself was persecuted and harassed by the political and religious authorities. A Vatican diplomat was sent to Ecuador to evaluate his pastoral work in his dioceses in 1973. He was arrested by the military dictatorship, together with seventeen other Latin American bishops, priests, religious and lay people in 1976. He received multiple death threats and in order to counter his liberative pastoral action the Empire sent hundreds of fundamentalist Christian sects to Chimborazo. Later, in May 1980, during the presidential campaign of Ronald Reagan in the USA, the document *Santa Fe I* was written. In it, for the first time, liberation theology was officially included as a target to be fought as part of the National Security Doctrine. Within this oppressive imperial setting the faith in a God who journeys with the oppressed peoples in and through Jesus Christ towards their liberation—the key theme in liberation theology—defies U.S. imperialism and militarization in Latin America. In this context, the struggle of faith is not with secularization as in Europe, but with the imperialism that deprives people of their human dignity and desecrates the earth. With this liberative faith many communities joined the historical struggle against the genocidal onslaught of the Empire, in seeking the liberation of all.

---

23. Proaño, "El intervenxionismo norteamricano en Américan Latina," 11.
24. Proaño, "El profeta," 73.

Struggles against Militarization

"The School of Assassins"

The imperial National Security Doctrine emerged in the context of the USA-USSR rivalry during the Cold War and was used by the USA in order to make sure that the Latin American armies served to contain or totally repress revolutionary processes in their own countries resorting to systematic means of violence, which in essence is state terrorism. This goal was achieved through putting governments in power in various countries who were completely submissive to the U.S. imperial agenda in the continent. Based on this doctrine, in July 1963, the United States Army Caribbean School, which was created in 1950, became the military training school we today refer to as the "School of the Americas," a veritable training center for Latin American criminals. Here, the highest military ranks of most of the Latin American countries have received "mis-training": Rafael Videla (Argentina), Hugo Banzer (Bolivia), Manuel Contreras (Chile), Efraín Ríos Montt (Guatemala), Romeo Vásquez (Honduras), Jaime Lasprilla (Colombia), Manuel Noriega (Panama), Roberto d'Aubuisson (El Salvador), and a long list of army men such as Ollanta Humala, Vladimiro Montesinos, Luis Posada Carriles (a former CIA agent), and General Roberto Eduardo Viola (the man behind the Argentinian coup in 1976). In this century, those who graduated from this school were involved in the attempted coups in Venezuela in 2002 and 2014, and in Honduras in 2009 when President Manuel Zelaya was toppled. The vast majority of the intelligence departments and death squads involved in the systematic violation of human rights in our continent were indoctrinated and trained in counter-insurgency warfare by the U.S. Army. By July 1, 1999, 61,034 students had graduated from this school. It is estimated that in 2015 an average of 1500 Latin American and Caribbean soldiers and policemen were still being trained under the ideology of the USA army, which promotes all forms of attacks against our people, in the name of their National Security. On the subject of this military training school, Msgr. Proaño spoke with a prophetic zeal:

> There, police have been refined in the art of unspeakable tor-
> tures, revealing their lack of respect or notions of what is hu-
> man dignity. They have received this training there, there
> they have absorbed the National Security Doctrine, that kind
> of hatred, that kind of cruelty we see in practice across Latin

America, in some countries in a more callous and frequent way, but ultimately we can see it everywhere. All of that is military interventionism.[25]

The Summer Institute of Linguistics was also created on the basis of the National Security Doctrine. This is a wolf in sheep's clothing, which suddenly arrived in the very heart of the Amazon with the alleged objective of translating the Bible into the languages of the indigenous nations, which was obviously a fraud. In Ecuador, they even received government funding to achieve their real goal, which was to pave the way, in every sense, for the "Pacific" arrival of the big multinational corporations. In Venezuela, during the 1970s, that institute penetrated the country hand in hand with the New Tribes Mission, having an infrastructure and logistics capacity as powerful as that of the state. Through institutions like the SIL in the Amazon, not only was our national sovereignty violated, but a fresh wave of genocide, ethnocide and dispossession unfolded.

In a geopolitical context, Latin America has a strategic importance and therefore is under the watchful eye of the Pentagon. U.S. imperialism has a global stake in our region, for we provide it with at least 25 percent of the commodities it requires. As a continuation of the Cold War the USA is carrying out irregular warfare in Latin America. For this reason the 2010 budget of the Pentagon had resources destined to support counter-terrorism, non-conventional warfare tactics, the internal defense of foreign countries, counter-insurgency and stabilization operations. Another avenue for the strategy of plunder and interventionism is the presence of U.S. military bases all over the world. In our Abya Yala, there are dozens of these bases. In Colombia alone, in 2009, there were seven of these bases in operation. We cannot forget the Southern Command; the military organization in charge of Latin American operations, from Mexico all the way down to Patagonia, including the Caribbean, with headquarters in Miami.[26] The strategic objective is to "secure" the defense of the USA, promote its "prosperity," and guarantee continental "stability." These militaristic moves are intrinsically interwoven with the Free Trade

25. Proaño, "El profeta," 74.

26. The Southern Command has a staff of some 1200 military officers and civilians. It is present in the majority of Latin American countries through a number of military bases and through bilateral agreements with governments for joint military exercises and patrols as well as training of naval, aerial, and land military exercises with those armies in agreements with the U.S. empire.

Area of the Americas (FTAA), the FTAs, the IMF, the World Bank, and the IDB which maintains the hegemony of the U.S. empire.

Liberative Praxis that Confronts Militarization

We have always been active as social movements in the defense of our right to exist as a people and our sovereignty in the continent. We know that only organization and mobilization can guarantee social change and the defense of our human rights. Our way of defining human rights is radically different from the individualization of human rights by the Europe–USA axis. Our understanding of human rights is inseparably linked to socio-economic and political justice and care for mother earth. We have developed creative actions in the streets and roads to confront U.S. interventionism.

In the 1990s, Ecuador was the scene of systematic protests against the IMF "recipes," the FTAA project, and the pressures to impose Free Trade Agreements (FTA). Jointly with the indigenous movement in the overcrowded streets of Quito we brought big puppets of Uncle Sam, we shouted slogans, and we organized sit-ins. We gathered frequently in front of the U.S. embassy. Eventually to avoid all the protests they had to take the embassy to the outskirts of the capital. In 1998, the former president Jamil Mahuad (El Comercio) leased the Ecuadorian air force installations of Manta to the U.S. government for ten years. For ten years the U.S. soldiers were stationed in the Manta base turning it into a U.S. enclave supposedly to fight drug trafficking and to detect pirate ships with illegal migrants. Since that moment we organized multiple and systematic protests together with the indigenous movement for the defense of our sovereignty. "Llukshi kaimanta gringos de Manta . . ." was the unanimous cry in the various demonstrations and protests.[27] I remember in one of the events organized in memory of Msgr. Proaño we called upon people to "bombard" the U.S. embassy with thousands of paper planes carrying protest messages against U.S. interventionism and against the Manta military base. At an agreed time we gathered and swiftly threw those papers into the garden of the embassy. Unsurprisingly, soon we had to leave the protest strip as the "forces of law and order" rushed into the scene to charge against us. Finally, after ten years of struggle, we succeeded. In 2008, the National Constituent Assembly

27. This means in kichwa "Out of Manta gringos."

recognized the people's mandate in article 5: "Ecuador is a territory of peace. We will not accept the establishment of foreign military bases or any other foreign installations for military purposes . . . it is forbidden to lease national military bases to foreign armed or security forces."

Liberation theology has also stimulated throughout the continent, especially at the U.S. border with Mexico, various actions against the School of the Americas (SOA) since 1990. On November 16, 2018 we celebrated twenty-eight years of these protests with vigils, advocacy, demonstrations, and non-violent direct action to demand the end of repressive U.S. policies in Latin America. These protest actions were led by Fr. Roy Bourgeois, the founder of SOA Watch, who has been arrested on many occasions. These actions started on the first anniversary of the blatant assassinations of the six Jesuit priests and their co-worker, Elba with her sixteen-year-old daughter Celina Ramos, in the UCA in El Salvador by the graduates of the School of the Americas. In the Third Border Conference of SOA Watch, in November 2017, the U.S. interventionist politics that has had a devastating impact on our continent and the strategies of the U.S. border control imperialism were denounced. The hideous border policies have destroyed lives of refugees, young people, indigenous communities, and black communities at the border. Once again, in the strongest possible terms the conference demanded the following:

- The shutting down of the School of the Americas (SOA/WHINSEC) and an end to the economic, military, and political intervention of the USA in Latin America.

- An end to the Merida Plan and of the Alliance for Prosperity.

- Demilitarization and de-investment in the borders.

- An end to the racial system of oppression which criminalizes and murders migrants, refugees and people of color.

- Respect, dignity, justice and the right to self-determination of communities.

For their part the native peoples have resisted throughout 528 years of dispossession. They have opposed the oppressive structures that were systematically imposed upon them first by the colonial and imperial foreign powers, and later, by U.S. imperialism and the local powers. The so-called national leaderships which were forged after the war of independence operated according to the same colonial logic and therefore were neo-colonial in their essence. There have been many indigenous uprisings in Ecuadorian soil. *Under the green fields there's much blood on our land*, cried a poet. Even though the imposition of so-called Western civilization on the great Amazon civilizations did not take place at the time of the Conquest, it is this region that suffers the most from extractive, imperial and militaristic policies. We are heirs to the liberating and mobilizing praxis of Msgr. Proaño who in the 1980s, following a request made by the church grassroots communities, formed the Solidarity Front of Chimborazo in Riobamba. This Front was not only local. It had a continental outlook. It organized many actions in solidarity with the other people's struggles. Some of these were: Mothers of the Plaza de Mayo in Argentina, Farabundo Martí Front of National Liberation in El Salvador, the Sandinistas, the government of Fidel Castro, and the campaigns against the tyranny of the military dictatorships in the Southern Cone. Through collective action Msgr. Proaño promoted the struggle for the expulsion of the SIL, which was decreed by president Roldós, an action that cost his life. A day after the expulsion he died in a mysterious "plane accident." Msgr. Proaño stated: "If we have managed to fight for the expulsion of the SIL from our country we have also to fight to expel all other U.S. agencies from our country, because their mission is to serve U.S. interests." He said that his dream is an Organization of American States without the USA.

The heroic and exemplary resistance of the Amazonian Kichwa people in Sarayaku against the oil multinational companies is well known. Their struggle managed to get these companies out of their territories. They also won a court case in the International Criminal Court in spite of the militarization of their territory and the continous bomb attacks they had to face. In their freed land (*pacha*) they are developing *kawsak sacha* (living forest) as part of their collective life plan: *Our living territoriality is, and will be, free from any type of extractivist activities such as oil, mining, logging, biopiracy, and others. Kawsak sacha is for everyone.* This program of the living forest is a powerful testimony to the possibility of gaining juridical recognition of the territorial and natural rights of the native peoples all over the world. Likewise, in the other regions of the Amazon, there are exemplary struggles of the indigenous nations like Cofán, Siona, Secoya, etc. who together with peasant communities created the Union of Peoples affected by Texaco, an association which brought a litigation of international reach. This was known as the "trial of the century" and it was against Chevron-Texaco, which was started in

Ecuador in 1993. Their arguments were clear. The company was directly responsible for the environmental impact of oil exploitation which not only affected nature, but also had an impact on human health.[28]

I can also think of a group of partners in our struggle who have become aware of our role in the defense of life and who are indignant about the protection given to the multinational oil companies by the Ecuadorian army. We have formed a collective called "Birds against Shotguns." The objective was to create awareness among the people and the Ecuadorian army so that they would stop protecting the companies. Thus, on the anniversary of our independence, August 10, 2006, we made a protest action and planned to present to the president our White Book with details of a new set of national policies. Forty "birds" dressed in white showed up at the event to present our manifesto to make visible our disagreement with the protection given by the armed forces to the foreign oil companies in the Amazon, and to protest against the killing and disappearances in the Amazon because of the military actions. We were surrounded by two hundred men in uniform who were trying to silence our voices that were raised in defense of the natural resources, our freedom and sovereignty, and disarmament. We were held by them for some time. Later we were released after pressure mounted by the media and human rights organizations.

On the one hand the above and many other ongoing liberative struggles define the way in which we relate to God and do theology. On the other hand this new way of being Christian has strengthened the struggle of the indigenous peoples and many other oppressed social classes to continue with the journey towards liberation. In concrete terms there are many unaccomplished tasks, some of which have been identified by the Christian Secretariat of Solidarity with Latin America (SICSAL) in keeping with the spirit of Saint Óscar Romero. They are summarized below.

First, the shutting down of:

- School of the Americas, and therefore of all military and police training which promote violence and war as a means to solve conflicts in Latin America and beyond.

- Research centers developing biological weapons, among them, the Centre for the Research of Tropical Diseases of the U.S. Marines (NAMRU-6) in Peru.

---

28. Acosto, *La maldición de la abundancia*, 73.

Second, the end of:

- The arms and nuclear race which is endangering the very existence of humanity.

- Persecution of refugees and migrants—which took place even against the well-known Honduras' caravan. All of them are compatriots running away from violence and poverty which originated as result of the economic and security policies promoted by the USA in Latin America.

- The border wall. The world doesn't need any more walls, but solidarity bridges.

- The interventionist policies of the USA and the closure of all the U.S. military bases in the world, especially in Latin America, including Guantanamo Bay.

Third, respect for the self-determination of the peoples worldwide (Palestine, Tamil Eelam, Kashmir, Kurdistan, indigenous communities, etc.).

Conclusion

The people's struggle in Latin America is an anti-capitalist, anti-imperialist and anti-militaristic one that is aimed at stopping neo-colonial violence, which is a genocidal process that deprives a majority of masses of their life and livelihood while desecrating the earth. To achieve its goals imperialism resorts to militarization that demands blood sacrifice and the rape of mother earth for the glory of the Empire. Liberation theology expounds faith in a God of compassion and justice who unconditionally sides with the oppressed in and through the Crucified and Risen Jesus Christ—a radically different "defense pact"—against the mighty empire which only believes in its brute force (idolatry) while proclaiming "In God we trust." Which god? In our continent, the pastoral action of the Church of the Poor has always been committed to the anti-imperialist and anti-militaristic struggle signifying the true faith in the God of liberation, for a God who does not liberate is no god or a false god. Msgr. Proaño is a faithful disciple of the Gospel and of the oppressed peoples, particularly the indigenous ones, who exemplified and embodied this struggle which is highly relevant and significant for today.

The liberation struggle is not only an opposition to the Empire, but also a recreation of a new community of peoples; a covenantal community. The capitalism and imperialism that necessitate militarization need to be replaced with an alternative system of socioeconomic and political relationships based on peace, justice, solidarity, integrity of creation, and life in abundance for all. In that, as François Houtart asserts, the search for new paradigms for a "social economy" as opposed to production for private capitalist accumulation is necessary. This is an economy which will be built from a very different logic to capitalism.[29] In this regard, the cosmovisions of the indigenous peoples who uphold an interdependent relationship with the mother earth and the covenantal relationship between God and the oppressed peoples that enshrines the politics of compassion and justice, can certainly provide us with a spiritual and theological basis for the struggle of reconstruction. Houtart reminds us: "Capitalism is not going to come to an end by itself, it is imperative that all of the social and political struggles converge towards this, both in the Global North and South."[30] The best form of solidarity is anti-imperialist struggle until we achieve the utopia prophesized by Isaiah: "They will beat their swords into plowshares, and their spears into pruning hooks. Nation will not take up sword against nation, nor will they train for war anymore" (Isa 2:4).

29. Houtart, *Deslegitimar el Capitalismo*, 57.
30. Houtart, *Deslegitimar el Capitalismo*, 58.

Wars, Women, and Feminist Voices

Chapter 4

Hope that Confronts Oppression and Suffering

Faith and War-affected Women in Sri Lanka

RASIKA SHARMEN PIERIS

"Poopathy amma transformed depressing, individual emotions into positive social action. Poopathy knew that her experiences were the experiences of countless numbers of women. She came into contact with the Mother's Front in Navatkerni and through this organisation was able to support, help and inspire other women who were going through the same traumas as she herself had been."—ADELE ANN BALASINGHAM.[1]

Introduction

My Personal Encounter 1

TWO YEARS AGO, I stayed in Kepappilavu, a village in the war-affected northeastern district of Mullaitivu, Sri Lanka, with a few nuns from my religious congregation who lived there for they had realized that our

1. Kanpathipillai Poopathy, affectionately known as Annai Poopathy (Mother Poopathy) fasted unto death in 1988 for 30 days demanding demilitarization of her homeland. She is from Batticaloa district, a mother of 10 children, whose two sons were killed by the Sri Lankan security forces. Adele Ann Balasingham was a Tamil political activist who is the author of *The Will to Freedom: An Inside View of Tamil Resistance*. London: Fairmax, 2001. Balasingham, "Annai Poopathy's Fast for Freedom."

religious commitment has no meaning if we do not identify ourselves with the oppressed in their struggle for liberation in the midst of state repression. During this stay, I was really awe-struck by the sharing we had every evening as a group. We reflected on the life struggles of the people, the root causes of their unjust suffering, their hope and courage in hopelessness, and their dream to live as dignified human beings in their homeland. I met many who showed me how their land has been occupied by the military. Their lament and dream was to get back to the soil where they grew up and belong to as it is this land that makes their lives livable.

My Personal Encounter 2

During the stay in Kepappilavu with the other nuns, we were invited by the women related to the persons of enforced disappearances to attend the memorial ceremony of Annai Poopathy, a woman leader, who fasted to death through hunger strike in demanding the withdrawal of Indian troops from her homeland in the late 1980s. These mothers whose husbands or children were forcibly made to disappear during the last phase of war in 2007–9 have continuously engaged in public demonstrations seeking the truth about their loved ones amidst frequent military intimidation. I was determined to stand with them to commemorate the selfless Poopathy *amma* (mother) despite threats and military surveillance. Confronting grief and sadness with unbeatable courage, resilience and selflessness rather than allowing herself to be drowned in perpetual morbidity, Poopathy *amma* transformed depressing, individual emotions into positive social action. Poopathy *amma* knew that her experiences were the experiences of countless numbers of women.

Faced with "everyday ordinariness"—militarization, state brutality, Sinhalaization and Buddhisization, land grabbing, and oppression of women—the war-affected Tamils whom I met in Kepappilavu and beyond are not prepared to accept the status quo and be silenced. In my observation, the majority of the war survivors in the North and East who are engaged in the struggle that seeks truth and justice are women. Being a woman myself, I was struck by the vulnerability of the women struggling for the dignity and liberation of their people in the midst of military occupation. Surviving/living through the everyday ordinariness that causes immense suffering they refuse to accept the state of oppression and accompanying militarization as normal. They embody the power of resistance to decades-long oppression of their people and radiate the hope of liberation that makes it possible for them to live in their homeland as a free people.

In my other visits to meet the war widows in the Sinhala (Buddhist and Christian) and Tamil (Hindu and Christian) communities, and Muslim women, partly for my doctoral work, I felt their longing for dignity and freedom. Some of them, even though small in numbers felt that they no longer wanted to be mere victims within the oppressive frameworks defined by the social, cultural and religious power structures. In their search for "life" in an alternative society, some war-affected women had moved away from dehumanizing conventional patterns of living and had deconstructed the oppressive socio-cultural and socio-political norms and practices, so that they could live in freedom as dignified human beings.

All these women I met in Kepappilavu as well as in my other visits, carry an enormous potential and the capacity to struggle for their full humanity by confronting oppression and suffering. They have challenged me spiritually and intellectually to touch and embrace this potential that they embody as vulnerable women who have the power to transform society in seeking full humanity. As they come from one faith tradition or another they have provided me with a radically new perspective of looking at faith as opposed to the traditional understanding of what it is to believe. Their struggle to find new ways of dealing with their suffering is the location that has to define the meaning of faith. This essay adopts primarily a Christian theological language and has chosen the experience of war-affected women in Sri Lanka as the hermeneutical key in redefining faith; faith that hopes for liberation by confronting oppression and suffering.

My encounters with the war widows revealed the influence of their religions on their daily experiences. They prompted me to examine how religion can be misused to marginalize widows through oppressive teachings, customs and rules and at the same time can be a supportive element to overcome their marginalization. I will explore how the teachings on suffering in Christian theological thinking affect the lives of widows in Sri Lanka. Therefore at the outset, I will briefly focus on the notion of suffering in Christian theological thinking on three levels with the intention of engaging in a theological and contextual exploration of Christian war widows' resistance to their marginalization on three main levels. The three levels are the perspective of institutional classical Christian theological teaching on suffering, how this teaching is challenged by liberation theologians who speak of suffering from the perspective of the poor and analyze it as a result of unjust social structures, and how feminist theologians interrogate suffering from the perspective of women, based on critical analysis of their daily experience/everyday ordinariness. Finally, I will situate the struggle of war-affected women in Sri Lanka for dignity and freedom at the heart of theological reflections by inviting the reader to be attentive to their voices of resistance and hope.

Suffering in Multiple Theological Contexts

Glorification of Suffering

The official teachings of the church on suffering can be identified under three main points. Firstly, in the view of the official church, the origin of suffering has its roots in the fall of the first parents. This implies, in particular, the fall of the woman, as a result of which women are condemned as the cause of evil. Secondly, suffering is understood in relation to the suffering and the death of Jesus, the savior who redeemed the world through his blood, as was the plan of God. Thirdly, following the example of Jesus, who "sacrificed" his life to save humanity, the followers of Christ are encouraged to embrace suffering as a meaningful way of participating in the suffering of Jesus as the means to salvation.

Many Christians who believe in the "Almighty" and "All powerful" God ask the question: Why is suffering there in the world if God is good and powerful? This questions the very existence of God. Those who believe in the existence of God question the nature of God—If God exists, is God powerful or powerless? Is God merciful or cruel? Does God cause human suffering as a punishment for sins? Where is God in our suffering? Why is God silent in our suffering? Does God participate actively or passively in our suffering? According to the *Catechism of the Catholic Church* (CCC): "God is infinitely good and all his works are good. Yet no one can escape the experience of suffering or the evils in nature, which seem to be linked to the limitations proper to creatures."[2]

On the question of why evil does exist in this world created by God, the CCC claims that there is no quick answer, yet "[O]nly Christian faith

2. *Catechism of the Catholic Church*, part 1, section 2, chapter 1, article 1, no. 385.

as a whole constitutes the answer to this question."[3] However, "[O]ur experiences of evil and suffering, injustice, and death, seem to contradict the Good News: they can shake our faith and become a temptation against it."[4] John Paul II claims, "[At] different moments in life, it [suffering] takes place in different ways, it assumes different dimensions; nevertheless, in whatever form, suffering seems to be, and is, almost inseparable from man's [sic] earthly existence."[5] The lack of a sufficient human answer to the question of evil and suffering is reflected in the book of Augustine, Confessions: "I sought whence evil comes, and there was no solution."[6] John Paul II in his apostolic letter, Salvifici doloris, defines suffering as the experience of evil. The understanding of evil as the cause of suffering suggests that suffering and evil should be defined alongside each other. John Paul II identifies suffering as having either a passive or active relationship to evil.[7]

The traditional teachings of the church connect suffering with evil through women. The church Fathers, for example Augustine, Tertullian and Thomas Aquinas in their interpretation of the "Fall" in the Genesis story, had the notion that sin entered human history through the weakness of the woman: Eve. Therefore, they condemn women as the cause of evil and death, leading to "women" being considered subordinate or secondary to men. They also considered women to be the temptresses of men. The profound impact of this teaching is reflected in the negative attitudes Christians have had towards women, and this perception of women negatively affects the lives of women in their family, faith community and society.

Pope John Paul II expands his understanding of the meaning of suffering as follows:

> This is the meaning of suffering, which is truly supernatural and at the same time human. It is *supernatural* because it is rooted in the divine mystery of the Redemption of the world, and it is likewise deeply *human,* because in it the person discovers

3. *Catechism of the Catholic Church*, part 1, section 2, chapter 1, article1, no. 309.

4. *Catechism of the Catholic Church*, part 1, section 1, chapter 3, article1, no. 164.

5. John Paul II, Introduction to *Salvifici doloris*, no.3, February 11, 1984.

6. Augustine, *Confessions*, 7, 7, 11.

7. Cf. John Paul II, *Salvifici doloris*, chapter 2: "The World of Human Suffering," no. 7.

himself (*sic*), his (*sic*) own humanity, his [*sic*] own dignity, his [*sic*] own mission.[8]

He also claims that as the meaning of life is found in giving and receiving love, the same love gives meaning to suffering and death. Justifying the existence of suffering, John Paul II instructs: "[L]ove is also the richest source of the meaning of suffering, which always remains a mystery: we are conscious of the insufficiency and inadequacy of our explanations. In the view of John Paul II, suffering is a punishment for sin when it is connected to one's fault." In his words: "Punishment has a meaning not only because it serves to repay the objective evil of the transgression with another evil, but first and foremost because it creates the possibility of rebuilding goodness in the subject who suffers."[9] He affirms that "While it is true that suffering has a meaning as punishment, when it is connected with a fault, *it is not true* that *all suffering is a consequence of a fault and has the nature of a punishment. Suffering has the nature of a test.*"[10] Pope John Paul II claims that in love, the Christians who suffer, find salvific meaning of their sorrow as Jesus has taken upon himself all the suffering of the people of all times. Love is a main source of the answer to the question of the meaning of suffering as per the official teachings of the church.[11]

The official teaching of the church is, that with the fall of man and woman, the bond between God and human beings was destroyed, but Jesus restored this relationship through his death on the cross. The church receives Jesus Christ as the savior, and this doctrine considers (a) Jesus to be truly God and truly man; (b) The two natures of Jesus as united in the one person of the Son of God; (c) Jesus to bring the fullness of God's revelation; (d) Jesus to have saved everyone through the sacrifice of his cross; and (e) The paschal mystery of Jesus as the supreme revelation of God's love.[12] The CCC claims that Jesus has fulfilled what God asked him to do from the moment of his incarnation, and the church understands

---

8. John Paul II, Conclusion to *Salvifici doloris*, no. 31.

9. John Paul II, *Salvifici doloris*, part III: The Quest for an answer to the Question of the Meaning of Suffering, no. 12.

10. John Paul II, *Salvifici doloris*, part III: The Quest for an answer to the Question of the Meaning of Suffering, no. 11.

11. John Paul II, *Salvifici doloris*, part III: The Quest for an answer to the Question of the Meaning of Suffering, no. 31.

12. Dupuis and Neuner, *The Christian Faith in the Doctrinal Documents of the Catholic Church.*

the suffering and death of Jesus in relation to the will of God. Hence, the church teaches that "Jesus' violent death was not the result of chance in an unfortunate coincidence of circumstances or a result of a religio-political conflict, but is part of the mystery of God's plan . . ."[13] The church also claims that Jesus died for the sins of all people in accordance with the Scriptures, and that his life was an offering to God.

The notion that suffering is redemptive—as is understood and taught by the church—has been criticized, and suffering that is perpetrated unjustly by oppressors is problematized. If God is loving, then why does God allow suffering in the world? Is it correct to justify the suffering that exists in society? Is it morally right to console a sufferer saying it will bring heavenly rewards? Can we equate people's suffering with the virtues of sacrificial love and obedience? Is it correct to say that there is no salvation without suffering? Was it the only way or was there a way for Jesus to save people other than "sacrificing himself on the cross?" Did God want Jesus to suffer a violent death in order to save humanity? Keeping these critical questions in mind, the next effort is to critically analyze the official teachings of the church on suffering from the perspective of liberation theologians.

Suffering is Structural

The relation between theory and praxis is a crucial point in the method of liberation theology. In the view of liberation theologians, praxis is not only the starting point—the locus of theology—but it is also the aim of liberation theology. Liberation theology can be considered to be a fundamental shift in the history and methodology of theology. The praxis that many liberation theologians speak about, is the suffering of the poor who struggle for their liberation on a structural level.

In general, many liberation theologians are careful not to fall into theological abstractionism. Their understanding and theologies of suffering are rooted in praxis, and accordingly, they are critical about the existing traditional interpretations of suffering in the church. For example, Gustavo Gutiérrez and Jon Sobrino being rooted in a praxis where many people are suffering in poverty, view suffering from the eyes of the

---

13. *Catechism of the Catholic Church*, part I, section 2, chapter 2, article 4, no. 599.

poor—"crucified people"[14] or "non-persons."[15] For them, suffering is the result of social sinfulness and without removing this social sinfulness, the salvation the church speaks of in relation to the next life will not be complete. They challenge the prevailing doctrines of God, sin, salvation and the theology of the cross. Paying attention to the liberating aspect of Jesus' mission on earth, they highlight the importance of commitment to the mission of the liberation of the poor as God too takes the side of the poor. They also appreciate the martyrs who have offered their lives for the "poor" in their struggle for true liberation.[16]

In the view of many liberation theologians, God is on the side of the poor/non-persons therefore they recognize God as the "God of the poor." For Sobrino, the poor or the crucified people in the unjust social and political system of his continent reflect the suffering and death of Jesus who offered himself for his people. In his understanding of Jesus as a martyr, Sobrino recognises the crucified people as martyrs who participate in the suffering and the death of Jesus.[17] Hence, the crucified people are the bearers of salvation who bring light to the world through their martyrdom. Many liberation theologians would take the side of the oppressed, especially the poor, and they do not consider the suffering of the poor as a punishment from God or as their fate. Their main effort is to highlight the need to release the poor from their suffering.

Many feminist theologians appreciate the liberation theologians because they do their theology from the perspective of the oppressed and assert the need to overcome suffering without glorifying suffering in oppressive social structures. However, many feminist theologians are critical of some of the notions of the liberation theologians whose efforts encourage the value of voluntary suffering or self-sacrificial love. According to the majority of feminist theologians, women are the ones who are called to sacrifice themselves in their role as women in general and in particular as wives and mothers, and also in their belonging to the poor. Many liberation theologians do not recognize male domination and the oppression of women as major issues in relation to the unjust social structures that they highlight repeatedly. The experiences of the women who are oppressed in society due to their race, sex, class, and caste challenge

14. Sobrino, *Jesus the Liberator*, 195.

15. Gutiérrez, "Task and Content of Liberation Theology," 28.

16. Sobrino, *Witnesses to the Kingdom*.

17. Sobrino, *Witnesses to the Kingdom*.

both traditional and liberation theology's view of suffering. Hence, many feminist theologians search for a theological understanding that reflects the experience of oppressed women.

The Feminist Critique of Suffering and Self-Sacrifice

According to many feminist theologians, even though suffering is a common aspect of human life, it is a particular reality in the lives of women in many societies. Both men and women are oppressed in existing social structures that marginalize them due to their ethnicity, social status, class, and caste. Despite oppression being common to both men and women, in many societies women are marginalized within the patriarchal structures in society just because they are born a woman. Women are not a homogenous group, therefore "the" woman does not exist. Women of colour, lower social status, caste, and class are the ones who suffer most in society. As a result, many feminist theologians understand suffering from the perspective of the lived experience of women who are suffering in their societies under concrete cultural, religious, and socio-political conditions.

Feminist theologians are very critical of the understanding of suffering in the traditional teachings of Christianity which uphold the views of male theologians. The significance of feminist theology lies in the emphasis on women as the most vulnerable, and on their oppression and suffering as a starting point or the primary locus of their practical theological reflections. They argue that women who are oppressed and suffer as a result of patriarchal structures, are not simply victims, but agents of societal transformation by providing vision and hope through their resistance to unjust social structures as well as oppressive traditions.[18]

Many feminist theologians, coming from different social backgrounds, not only explore the complexity of the suffering of women in today's world, but they also note that suffering was and is not a simple reality, as it is interwoven into the broader spectrum of the social, religious and political spheres. They insist on the importance of reading and understanding suffering from a broader perspective. Their reflections on suffering reveal on the one hand, the inhumanity of women's oppression; on the other hand, how religion encourages suffering by making it imperative as a means of expiation. From their Christian background,

18. Brock, "Ending Innocence and Nurturing Willfulness."

many feminist theologians contend that personal sin is the main Christian doctrine highlighted in traditional Christian theology, while the social dimension of sin is neglected. For them suffering afflicts not only an individual, but an entire community. Therefore, the suffering of an individual woman cannot be treated in isolation, but needs to be considered in relation to the wider social reality of evil in society, especially within the patriarchal and hierarchical social structures. For them, suffering is both personal and communal. It has a social dimension. Since sin is both personal and social, they see the need to speak of Christian soteriology on both a personal and a social sphere. They also uphold the idea that salvation is not something to be experienced after death, but they speak about the importance of experiencing liberation even on earth: in everyday life as well as in life after death.[19]

In their discussion of the ideology of suffering and salvation, feminist theologians reject the prevailing traditional Christian theology of satisfaction/atonement because it encourages women to embrace suffering passively on the basis that Jesus was obedient to his "Father" (sic). They claim that such a theological vision never helped women to experience true salvation or to experience the reign of God. Observations by many feminist theologians, are that the death of Jesus on the cross was wrongly and brutally used to give value to the suffering of the oppressed, in this case, women. Hence, they reject the notion that the death of Jesus was the plan of God. Instead, they see the death of Jesus as a consequence of his mission of justice for the oppressed and as a result of challenging the political and religious leaders of his time. Feminist theologians feel that women in today's context undergo the same suffering as the marginalized and oppressed in Jesus' time due to violence in society.

The most important fact is that many feminist theologians reject *any kind of suffering*, as suffering should not be considered as the fate of life and therefore should be overcome through resistance. They also connect suffering with hope: hope to overcome suffering through the struggles of women. It became clear that "Christian teachings" did not necessarily mean the traditional teachings of the church, but included the different views and experiences of all Christians. The latter might differ from (or be deeper than) the teaching authority of the church. Similarly, Christians are not a homogenous group of people: they differ due to their race, religious denominations, class, gender, caste, and many other categories.

19. Williams, *Sisters in the Wilderness*.

The diversity of the people cannot be the reason for separating one from the other or the reason for dehumanizing, marginalizing or oppressing the "other." So far I have discussed analyses of suffering in Christianity from different perspectives so that we can situate it within a broad Christian theological spectrum not limiting ourselves to the official teachings of the church.

A Re-evaluation of Suffering: War Widows at the Center

Liberative Struggle as the Norm

Exploring the experience of war widows who were/are placed on the "margin" by oppressive social, cultural, religious and political systems in Sri Lanka, the effort of the present section is to theologically analyze the theme of suffering, placing the experience of war widows at the "center": war widows as subjects rather than objects. Elizabeth Schüssler Fiorenza's four crucial points of the feminist category of experience provides perspectives that are imperative for awareness of the importance of the "experience" of war widows as a source for theological thinking. She says:

- Experience is mediated linguistically and culturally. There is no "pure experience" that can be distilled from its *kyriocentric* contexts and texts.

- The personal is political. Personal experience is not private but public: it is socially constructed in and through race, gender, class, caste, heterosexuality, ethnicity, age, and religion.

- Since personal experience is determined socially and religiously, it demands critical analysis and reflection that can explore the social location of experience.

- Experience is a hermeneutical starting point, not a norm. Only certain experiences, namely the experiences of struggle and liberation for justice and radical equality, can be articulated as feminist norms.[20]

Similarly, Christ and Plaskow, while highlighting women's experience as a critical principle that can disrupt traditional theological discourse, state, (1) "All theology begins in experience"; and (2) "Experience

---

20. Schüssler Fiorenza, *Wisdom Ways*, 171.

is embodied. It is through the body that people experience and respond to the world."[21] Some war widows, moving away from the understanding of their present suffering as the result of *karma* or the will of God, embody a unique experience that leads to articulating new ways of reflecting on their experience and new social, cultural, religious, and political constructions. The experience of war made some widows aware of their social and political condition, which made them move beyond passive victimization. They are undeniably the ones who carry the greatest potential for change and are in a better position to articulate their resistance than others.

Rethinking the Root Cause of Suffering: Structural Sinfulness

"Suffering is part of Christian life," "suffering is redemptive," "there is no joy without suffering," these are the recurring themes known to many Christians in Sri Lanka. Understanding any suffering as the will of God, was a recurring theme which some of the women interviewed challenged, as in how could a person say, "If God wants me to suffer, I cannot avoid it," or "This is my cross, I have to bear in my life." The reason for the existing dominant assumption among many Christians that suffering is part of Christian life can be understood through the explanation of suffering in the institutional Christian thinking discussed in the previous section.

Due to the fact that the interpretation of the "violent death" of Jesus is not perceived as the result of circumstances within an unjust social, political and religious context of his time, the emphasis of the institutional Christian doctrine of sin has been on sin as a personal and singularly individualized reality. In church teachings, especially in liturgy, it is portrayed that Jesus died on the cross or that he sacrificed his life, but not that Jesus was killed. Unlike institutional and traditional Christian thought, some war widows, similar to many Catholic liberation theologians and feminist theologians challenge the rather abstract and individualized notion of sin in institutional Christian thinking. Pointing to the social aspect of suffering, the war widows consider people's suffering today to be the result of the existing unjust social structures. Many Tamils along with a few Sinhalese and Muslims named the cause of their suffering as follows.

Discrimination against the Tamils:

21. Christ and Plaskow, *Goddess and God in the World*, 290.

My husband was in the (Liberation Tigers of Tamil Eelam) LTTE movement and I am proud of him as he fought for the rights of our people until the last moment. Anyway, we the Tamils still as a nation have no freedom to live in our homeland as "human persons." All the Sinhala-centric governments continue to oppress as they think that the country belongs only to the Sinhala-Buddhists. They brutally killed our people who were longing to live with respect and freedom in our own homeland. It was a massacre. Even after the end of war the state still discriminates against the Tamils without listening to the demands of our people. Where is justice in this country? (Tamil Christian war widow).

Brutal war between the Sri Lankan state and the LTTE:

I happened to become a widow due to the brutal war of the country. Even though many people blame me for the death of my husband, nothing wrong with me or I am not an unfortunate woman. Our political leaders promoted war and it was a business for them; finally, people like me lost their husbands and children lost their fathers. This is the result of thirty-year-long war. (Sinhala Buddhist war widow)

Militarization:

How many soldiers and check points did you pass on your way to meet me? I still cannot overcome the pain and anger when I remember what happened to my own sister. While we were crossing to the side of the army we had to forget that we were women. We know what really happened to us, especially to the women. It was terrible. I do not like to see the uniform of your soldiers (Sinhalese). My sister was in the LTTE and the soldiers knew about her, so they did everything to destroy her mentally, physically and sexually. The pain is still within me. We do not want to live with them, but now we have to live in the presence of the military. That is our fate. We also have to take permission for everything [Her face was aggressive]. This is our village, not their [Sinhala soldiers] village, but we are like their slaves. Does the country not belong to us? The situation is very pathetic. (Tamil-Hindu war widow)

Sinhalaization/Buddhisization of the Tamil traditional homeland: With her experience of journeying to the North after the war and witnessing how the state has tried to create a Sinhala-Buddhist atmosphere within the area, Kumari Kumaragamage states in her book *Ureippu Sappada, Noasu Kan Walata* (To Unheard Ears):

> Why do we make such an effort [erecting the statues of the Buddha] to prove to ourselves that we are Buddhists, and to show it to others? Is it because we ourselves feel that we do not own the real Buddhist qualities within ourselves? Or is it because we doubt our own Buddhistness? Perhaps are we trying to forget something by hiding behind these exhibitions or do we have a need to cover up the whole thing from the others? If we live according to the teachings of the Buddha, and our friendly ways are a sign of that kindness preached by him, it is not necessary to make it known to others by making a big noise. If so, why so much trouble to express that we are Buddhists?[22]

Enforced disappearances:

> Life has not been a bed of roses since the end of war in 2009 as we handed over our children to the armed forces like many did towards the end of war. We have been on streets for more than one year and feel that our pleas have fell on deaf ears. Some of us fell sick being exposed to dust and lack of basic needs, and being on the streets we become vulnerable. We are not demanding comforts, knowing well the difficulties we had to face we took to streets looking for our loved ones who were forcibly made to disappear. We will continue our struggle until we find our loved ones. We have lost our confidence in the governments which are responsible for the unimaginable human massacre that took place while the whole world was awake. Seeking for justice is not a single day journey, we are aware. I am determined that I would look for my lost children and the children of others while seeking for justice though many have given up believing that the Sinhala state would not deliver justice for Tamils. But we are a people who fought for our political goal for decades. (Tamil-Christian war widow in Mullivaikkaal, which is known among Tamils as the final "killing field" of the war is an area on the North-eastern coast of the island where thousands of Tamils were massacred during the last phase of the war between the Sri Lankan state and the LTTE)

State brutality:

> After the end of war between the Sri Lankan state and the LTTE in 2009, we the Muslims have been targeted by many

22. Kumaragamage, *Ureippu Sappada*, ix.

Sinhala-Buddhist groups with the support of the government due to which we suffer different types of discrimination. My personal feeling is that apart from a few people, no one speaks for us as most prefer to remain silent or add to the tensions. (Muslim war widow)

Land grabbing:

The land that belonged to us for generations is not accessible anymore. My desire is to breathe my last breath in the land where I was born. I also admit the fact unfolding that the military would not evacuate from our land soon. We took to streets demanding the armed forces to release the land especially the private lands. It is really painful to see the military dwelling in the lands with newly built posh buildings while we are on streets. (Tamil-Hindu war widow in Kepappilavu)

These reflections of war widows reveal the importance of naming the social sinfulness (unjust social structures) as the cause of their suffering rather than the individual sinfulness of people: the fate of an ethnic group or widows, suffering as the will of God and all kinds of suffering due to one's *karma*.

Rejecting Justification of Suffering

As discussed earlier, feminist theologians reject the glorification of any kind of suffering. According to them, it is problematic to consider suffering as redemptive because it threatens the humanity of women in society, and they disapprove of redemptive violence as irrational. For instance, Delores Williams challenges the pioneers of black theology, such as Martin Luther King, Jr. as their vision was to lead black women "passively to accept their oppression and suffering."[23] Rita Nakashima Brock underlines that innocence is not a survival skill, it does not nurture and empower anyone, rather it makes passive scapegoats.[24]

Kwok Pui-Lan raises the point that alongside the familial and social pressures, religions play a major role in the oppression of women. She contends that women, although being the majority in the Asian churches, are marginalized through the power structures, and are neither recognized nor respected by the male hierarchy of the church due to misogyny

23. Williams, *Sisters in the Wilderness*, 200.
24. Brock, "Ending Innocence and Nurturing Willfulness," 77.

within the Christian tradition and notions of purity and taboos in Asian religious traditions.[25] For a woman to reject what the dominating structures dictate is a taboo in the Asian context. In the view of Song, "what we have in many countries in Asia is a culture of suffering within a culture of domination."[26]

Given the context in which their existence was threatened, their bodies abused and their womanhood denigrated, the Christian widows asked, how can war widows think suffering is good or accept suffering as part of womanhood or Christian life? From the perspective of the war widows, the endurance of unjust suffering did not give them happiness in life; in such instances the norm was reversed, making suffering neither a Christian nor humane virtue. The voices of the "silenced war widows" in Sri Lanka, their verbal, physical, individual and collective reactions to their suffering provide us with a way of rethinking and deconstructing the established norms that oppressed them for centuries, as well as a way of reconstructing a theology that supports them in their resistance to suffering.

Women do not deserve suffering:

> Suffering is a common aspect in all beings, yet it cannot justify the unjust suffering of women. We women were not born to suffer in this life. If we cannot change the mentality of women, we women should become conscious of the value of ourselves. Then no one could misuse us or control us. (Muslim war widow)

Challenging male-domination:

> Men are not aware that we suffer mainly because of their oppression, instead they simply say that to be born a woman is to suffer. How unfair for them to look at women with this perspective? Many are afraid to challenge the views of men. In many societies, men decide everything for women: how to dress, behave, speak and every aspect of life. I think many women are scared of challenging men thinking that it is not womanly, but challenging male-domination is not unwomanly. (Sinhala Christian war widow)

"Why only women have to sacrifice for others?":

> After the death of my husband, our village monk said to me as a woman coming from a very good family, I must keep the name

25. Kwok, *Introducing Asian Feminist Theology*, 98–99.
26. Song, *Theology from the Womb of Asia*, 71.

of my father and husband. For this, he asked me not to think of another marriage since I am a mother of a daughter. Do they say the same for men? I do not think . . . They expect all sacrifices only from women. (Sinhala Buddhist war widow)

Women are not the sexual property of men:

Once when I went to an officer to get a document, he asked me to come after five days without any reason. When I asked him why he was asking me to come again and again, he said that until he gets a positive reaction from me to his "proposal." I got angry and immediately made a complaint to the head office against the officer. I am not scared of anyone. (Sinhala Buddhist war widow)

Breaking silence:

Being a Tamil, if I keep silence in the midst of unjust suffering, the people who oppress us will continue to use violence against us. The present experience of our suffering teaches us that we have to stand against the unjust suffering that we undergo due to ethnic domination. Having faced challenges in the past, now I have become a strong woman. I have nothing to lose other than freedom to live in our land. I lost all my family members during the war. When injustice happens to our people in the village I am the first one to speak against the oppressor. The army soldiers also know about me well, but I am not scared of them. The worst thing that they could do is to kill me as they killed brutally my other family members. It is better to die standing for truth and justice. (Tamil Hindu war widow)

Saying no to oppressive elements of culture:

To speak honestly, I was in the LTTE for some time and we were totally against the traditional view of women in our culture. We fought for our rights; we were against the dowry system. We had the freedom in the movement and we were not considered as secondary to men. We were equally treated as men in the society. But now our people have forgotten everything and they try to impose all the harmful cultural norms on us. (Tamil Christian war widow)

Opposing social discrimination:

Our Sinhala people consider me as a bad omen. They don't like to see widows when they are about to go out for an auspicious event. I myself have lots of experience. But I never take those cultural ideas seriously. If you get hurt by what others say, you cannot survive. Some people say, directly to me you are a *Kanawandum* (widow), an unfortunate woman. (Sinhala Buddhist war widow)

Being critical on religion:

Even though many of us can use religion as a weapon to change this society, we don't take that responsibility, instead being followers of our religions, we just keep silent. I do not think that my religion should help people only to be pious, but it should be a guide to promote peace, unity and respect for each and everyone in the society. Whatever the teachings in my religion be, I did not want to have a child from a man who killed thousands of our people. I would rather go for abortion, than having the child. (Tamil Christian war widow who became pregnant after rape)

A new image of God: Despite their rejection of unjust suffering, some of the Christian war widows, in the midst of their daily suffering and oppression, shared a new image of God, an image different from the image of God that exists, in the heights of heaven or as a co-sufferer prevalent among Christians in Sri Lanka. Moving away from these images of God, the war widows recognized God as being with them to resist their oppression. For example, a widow said, "God does not want me to suffer. My suffering is not the will of God. God is with me in my struggle of overcoming my suffering" (Tamil Christian war widow).

As with many feminist theologians who reject the glorification of suffering, the war widows resist the suffering that threatens their very existence. Their day-to-day experience of new ways of dealing with their own suffering is a powerful starting point for hermeneutics and theologizing, their experience being essential to the process of theologizing. Their voices call for a theology that resists valorization of suffering and a theology that helps resist the oppressive structures in society, culture and religion. They search for a theology that is grounded on a faith that hopes for their full humanity, rather than a theology that keeps on justifying their oppression and suffering as the will of God. For war widows, suffering is not the norm and end in life, but life and the struggle for life. Their struggle embodies the hope of liberation.

Seeking Pathways to Overcome Suffering

Being in a context, where on the one hand women are oppressed based on their gender, ethnicity, religion, class, and caste, and on the other women's struggle for freedom is systematically restrained and their voices are deliberately silenced, a few war widows are creatively and critically searching for pathways to dismantle their chains of oppression in their journey towards liberation. Since the unjust social violence is not accidental, the war widows highlighted the principal need for liberation within their context. For them, the suffering caused by the brutal social violence cannot be hidden with the promise of liberation after life. They challenge the traditional redemptive language, which emphasizes salvation after life—"eschaton." Christ and Plaskow assert, "if the meaning and purpose of human life is to be found in embodied life on this earth, then many of the ways we have been taught to think about theological questions no longer make sense or provide the orientation we need." [27]

The understanding of a few war widows who are critical of the official teachings of Christianity is that traditional Christian language at present does not in any way resonate with the present experience of struggling communities. The believers are forced to view liberation as coming totally from outside: from God's action in Christ. In their search for liberation, the war widows like the feminist theologians, turn towards their own contexts and utilize their own experience as well as the experience of their oppressed people to break the imposed silence.

Remembering "stories":

> For Tamils, story-telling is a means of resistance to the deliberate silencing of their voices by the oppressive powers. Therefore, they keep [her] story alive through the revelation of their stories of the past in order to prevent a repetition of the massacre. A widow said: "no one can erase our past memories by destroying our cemeteries. We daily remember our people who died in war and who fought for our rights. The daughters and sons who died in the war are heroes for us" (Tamil Christian war widow). In the process of story-telling, the war widows conveyed their inner feelings, aspirations and meanings. As Chung asserts, "the power of story-telling lies in its embodied truth. Women talk about their concrete, historical life experience and not about abstract, metaphysical concepts."[28]

27. Christ and Plaskow, *Goddess and God in the World*, 289.
28. Chung, *Struggle to Be the Sun Again*, 104.

Life giving power of war widows:

> Whatever happens, I used to share it with my friends. Since they too are widows, it is easy for them to understand my life. (Muslim war widow)

> After becoming conscious to the pain of my people, I decided to take an initiative to go to the concentration camp as a group of women whose husbands and children are missing to look for our loved ones. (Tamil Christian war widow)

Speaking through silence:

> Our women's movement in the village as a group decided to boycott the last election as we were aware that no Sinhala regime would listen to our demands" (a Tamil Hindu war widow)."We publicly demonstrated against the government for the continuous injustice done to us. It was a silent protest as we all strapped our mouths, holding banners we expressed our demands. (Tamil Hindu war widow)

Collective struggle for freedom:

> I express my ideas, feelings, grievances, for I am assured that I would be accepted and listened to, thus being part of my suffering as we do go through the moments of suffering in life. We all have lost our husbands due the brutal war that took place over past three decades. Not all the questions have answers, yet the freedom of expressing my view is important. (Muslim war widow)

The war widows, while breaking the social myth, "woman's place is in the home, whereas man's place is in the society," have crossed from the "private" to the "public" sphere through their various involvements in women's associations. As Virginia Fabella suggests, "women from the base are the best equipped to speak on Third World reality."[29]Being in a society where leadership, decision-making and the public domain are the privilege of men, coming together as a group without male leadership is itself a message that widows are not mere victims: they are the agents of social transformation. The women's movements are a safety net for war widows to accomplish their task and the place where hope is assured. My numerous encounters and meetings with them made me realize that these movements are the places where women came together and discussed

29. Fabella, *Beyond Bonding*, 111.

both their agonies and hopes, took decisions to resist oppression, and stood together for each other, their wellbeing and the wellbeing of their oppressed people, while challenging the structures of power that dehumanize them.

Connecting Suffering with Hope

There were some women who have undergone continuous atrocities throughout their lives, yet had the courage to face life and find hope to rebuild their lives, rising out of the ashes. These widows connect suffering with hope, not with individual sin and evil. This is the hope of overcoming suffering by joining the struggles of each other as women. As with many feminist thinkers, the hope of war widows is that, harmful social and political structures and systems, traditional practices, and views on marginalized people, especially women, can be changed through new pathways. The following responses of some war widows represent the hope shared by many:

> Earlier I thought that changing our Buddhist culture was un-imaginable as it constituted an integral part of social life. My experience of suffering within the oppressive aspects of culture changed my thinking pattern: we can change our culture. We construct cultures and we have the power to change the cultures if it does not humanize us. (Sinhala Buddhist war widow)

> We are marginalized and oppressed by the society and dominat-ed by different groups of people due to our womanhood, wid-owhood, ethnicity and socio-political status. Yet, do not forget that we are women. We are women who have faced the utmost challenges in the past and even now we suffer in our struggle for our liberation. We have power to assert ourselves and stand for our dignity, overcoming barriers which make us unjustly suffer in society. Our power is our hope. (Tamil Christian war widow)

> My daughter was raped while we were in the refugee camp, my two sons were abducted by unknown people because they were in the LTTE and I still do not know what happened to them. See, I even do not have a proper place to live. We are suffering because of your people, yet we are not defeated. We still have hope. (Tamil Hindu war widow)

Another Sinhala Buddhist war widow, who lived in the eastern part of the country where both Sinhalese and Tamils live, testified that she was involved in politics and also in an inter-religious and inter-ethnic group. She said:

> I believe that when we come together, there is strength among us. That is why I try to unite women together. In this village each and every woman is involved in at least one association. We can energize one another. That is our hope. We belong to different religions, ethnicities, and castes, yet we feel that we all are in the same boat on our life journey. Here, we learn how to respect other religions, how to listen to the different views of women and how to work together as one family. If not, we know that we cannot reach our goal, because we all have a dream to live as free people.

Hope lies in the fact that the war widows have begun organizing themselves autonomously to make their voices heard: emergence of hope in the midst of suffering. For them, liberation begins the very moment they reject and resist their oppression as widows. From a Christian perspective the salvation war widows speak about is a total and concrete reality. It is the salvation of the whole person in the present context. Alleviating suffering here and now is the priority, and understanding the challenges posed by these women to the existing oppressive Christian theologies in particular, and religions in general in Sri Lanka is a precondition for all those who intend to find true meaning of their faith; faith as liberative knowledge.

Conclusion

Breaking the cultural, religious and political silence, war widows have rediscovered their hidden power to express themselves in their own "languages"—language is a powerful tool for the defining and redefining of one's own image and the image of one's surroundings—as resistance. They reclaim their "silenced" voices and experiences, which had been subjugated for ages. They are coming forward in their self-representation opposing any representation of themselves by the oppressive power structures. Even though the war widows are the poorest of the poor in the existing social, cultural and religious structures in Sri Lanka, as discussed throughout this essay, they have become a powerful theological subject as well as a catalyst for a new religious thinking through their challenging and creative ways of resisting oppression and suffering.

Schüssler Fiorenza insists, "simply belonging to an oppressed group does not necessarily guarantee the production of emancipatory knowledge."[30] The war widows who resist their oppression and suffering are a "democratic congress" (in the words of Schüssler Fiorenza) of full decision-making citizens who struggle for the liberation of the whole society, while transforming oppressive structures in daily life. The war widows in Sri Lanka who belong to four major religions—Hinduism, Christianity, Islam and Buddhism—are the icon of the poorest of the poor, struggling for liberation and full humanity. From a Christian point of view they have become the locus from where the contextualized theology originates in this country, via praxis, thus holding authority to speak about the divine. As Kwok asserts:

> For many Asian feminist theologians, theology is not simply an intellectual discipline or a rational reflection of Christian faith. Theologians cannot afford to engage in the academic exercise of mental gymnastics, when so many people are daily dehumanized … Theology must be embodied; and reflection and action must be integrally linked together.[31]

Critical reflection based on experience makes a strong claim that truth cannot be monopolized homogeneously, particularly in the case of theology. Evolution of theology based on the historical praxis "lived" through by a group or a community—a historical struggle—asserts the power of "naming," thus affecting both the method and the content of current theology, opening a window for transformation of patriarchal and other oppressive structures in society. Apolitically construed theology, given the context of war widows after the war and their power of resistance in Sri Lanka, would not contribute to a contextualized theology as war widows form a society that deconstructs the traditional patriarchally constituted societal structures. Theologizing in light of the war widows' "poorest of the poor" experience demands political inclusivity, because as stated at the beginning, socially constructed "personal" experience is political.

---

30. Schüssler Fiorenza, *Sharing Her Word*, 36.
31. Kwok, *Introducing Asian Feminist Theology*, 32.

Chapter 5

Trampled Women, Forests, and Sacred Sites

An Ecofeminist Reading of Effects
of Militarization in Africa

LILIAN CHEELO SIWILA

"We are either going to have a future where women lead the way to make peace with the Earth or we are not going to have a human future at all."—VANDANA SHIVA[1]

Introduction

When in the images of war, destruction of natural resources, loss of lives, and property is displayed on the screens of our televisions, it is very difficult to assess the human and ecological costs. The only way we are able to assess the hopelessness of nature and humanity, especially women and children, is by being on the actual scene. Africa's experience of neocolonial violence unfolds through wars and conflicts besides pandemics such as HIV and AIDS, Ebola and COVID-19. When wars hit a nation, the sense of humanity and sacredness disappears. Sacred sites become locations of human abuse spilled with blood. As the forests are trampled on by heavy war machinery the rivers swallow the dead bodies. Mother Nature weeps inconsolably with women and children whose vulnerability is inexplicable.

1. Goodreads, "Vandana Shiva Quotes."

Yet, not only the media outlets, but also most of the literature focusing on militarization tends to ignore the relationship between the groaning mother earth and the cry of women and children.[2] Most of what is said and written is about the power dynamics of the warring parties. Without essentializing and romanticizing the relationship between nature and women it is necessary to recognize the ways in which women and nature are affected in an interrelated manner in the context of war and militarization. The inhuman ways in which women and children are treated during wars also pose some serious feminist inquiries into the role that patriarchy plays in our societies. The aim of this chapter is to critically reflect on the effects of militarization on women and the sacred natural resources and on their interrelatedness.

This chapter adopts a post-colonial ecofeminist perspective. This is because within the African context discussions on militarization and the empire cannot be done outside the historical colonial influence on Africa, both on its people and their natural habitat. Therefore the recognition of the role that colonialism has played in forming militarized neo-colonial states in most African countries is of great importance in this study. The gendered nature of militarization and its multifaceted effects on humanity and nature requires an ecofeminist standpoint. Using ecofeminist theory, the chapter argues that, the destruction of natural resources and sacred sites as well as the rape of women which occurs during militarization and war requires a feminist curiosity that poses critical theological questions. In other words, the reality that women and nature undergo in the face of militarization needs to be taken into account for theological reflections to be liberative.

Neocolonial Violence and Militarization in Africa

Colonial masters who came to Africa introduced an economic, political, and military system that brutalizes its people, and loots and desecrates the natural resources. This helped most of the western countries to emerge as empires within the African continent even after the formal end of colonialism. Measures such as the slave trade, and the scramble for Africa were some of the practices that necessitated militarization of the continent. The impact of these colonial practices can deeply be felt in poverty, ethnic conflicts, epidemics and destruction of natural resources

2. Chirongoma, "Motherhood," 1–11.

in different countries in Africa. For example, the effect of slavery and the gold trade can still be felt in countries such as Ghana which were the trading centers en route to Europe. The stolen land in South Africa during the apartheid era still has serious effects on South African people, especially the black people, most of whom continue to live in townships with limited resources such as land and water supply. The loot of oil fields in Nigeria and other West African countries continues to cause ethnic conflicts among the indigenous peoples. The mines in DRC, and the privatized waters of the Kariba dam in Zimbabwe and Zambia in the name of development are just some examples of the extent of destruction of natural resources. The missionaries accompanied the colonialists. A wide range of scholarly texts written on the effects of missionaries on Africa demonstrates that missionaries were not very different from the colonial masters in their motives for Africa. Although their stated aim was to convert the "uncivilized Africans" to Christianity, their approach carried on an imperial capitalist spirit which made their work militaristic.

From a political perspective, in an attempt to liberate themselves from these empires, most African countries had to undergo political turmoil in order to gain their national independence. However at the dawn of independence from the colonial rule, African countries felt the sigh of relief and the new dawn was perceived as the end of all forms of oppression from the colonial masters. Zdenek Cervenka argues that:

> On reflection it is remarkable that the massive involvement of the military in the political life of Africa, at the time of the post-war wave of independence, was both unforeseen and unthinkable. The euphoria of freedom, optimistic concepts of nation-building and economic development, and the revival of traditional culture and values—symbolized by "the African personality," were all generated by Africans rejoicing over the collapse of the colonial empires. Arms were regarded as a legacy belonging to the colonial past. In December 1961, the eve of Tanzanian independence (then Tanganyika), Julius Nyerere told an audience at the London Africa Bureau that his country would not need an army after independence. His view was shared at the time by many analysts of African affairs, who were all impressed by the charisma of the new African leaders and their vision of a new era of peace, prosperity and the unity of Africa.[3]

3. Cervenka, "Effects of Militarization of Africa," 3.

This honeymoon however did not last long because, within a short period of time, African countries began to experience both internal and external conflicts most of which were consequences of colonial practice as well as neocolonial imperial designs. Due to the historical colonial experiences of African people, most of the wars in African countries are a result of the African people's dependence on neocolonial empire and of reaction to historical colonial trends that manifest themselves in different forms. For example, the continued migration and border conflicts in some parts of Africa are part of the colonial history. Colonizers formed these geographical borders which sometimes separated ethnic groups and clans creating conflicts among people of the same ethnicity. Amina Mama and Margo Okazawa-Rey state that Africa's modern history is deeply marked by the history of colonization, a project that relied directly and indirectly on the military superiority of the colonizers.[4] The current scenario is not different from the former. African countries are divided among themselves fighting for natural resources which were divided by colonial borders. Neocolonial violence is at its peak.

Today we not only speak of wars or conflicts in relation to governments fighting rebel groups, but also to situations where international and regional interventions have been militarized to the extent of committing war crimes. We also speak of new wars that involve exploitation of resources by legitimate global industries that have seized the opportunity to exploit as many resources as possible before the civil strife ceases. Turshen Meredeth speaks of these new wars:

> New wars—a contested concept—are those funded by sales of local assets like gold, diamonds and coltan to transnational corporations often through international criminal networks. New wars take advantage of financial deregulation to create new economic relations in the era of neoliberal capitalism. When protracted, new wars exacerbate the inability of states already weakened by austerity programmes to ensure human security and protect human rights.[5]

In all these wars, women and children are the main victims of lack of natural resources, and victims of sexual abuse and killings. The empire asserts its supremacy in new ways.

---

4. Mama and Okazawa-Rey, "Militarism, Conflict and Women's Activism," 99.
5. Turshen, "Women, War and Peace."

In this chapter, I argue that the power of militarization and empire is that it can operate remotely and cause conflict in between countries without being visible. This is what we mean by neo-colonial violence. History also shows that the colonial armies established in most of the colonies were not so much for the protection of the nation from invasion but for the suppression of these nations. A study by Mama and Okazawa-Rey reviews that the creation of colonial armies based on western military forms was only one aspect of the militarization of the continent.[6] Other forms of militarization that have emerged in the continent include economic and political militarization which have to a large extent contributed to the destruction of the continent's natural resources. Cervenka argues that:

> The plethora of conflicts that have taken place in postcolonial Africa and the high political, economic and cultural costs of military rule provide good grounds for arguing that African militarism has generated more insecurity than security, often terrorizing rather than protecting local populations, dominating the political sphere, blurring the boundaries between civilian and military, and thereby undermining all non-military forms of political and institutional authority and accountability. More broadly, militarism is conceptualized as an extreme variant of patriarchy, a gendered regime characterised by discourses and practices that subordinate and oppress women.[7]

Cry of the Earth, Cry of the Women

This chapter employs an African ecofeminist framework in critiquing militarization and empire that have a deadly impact on women and nature, especially sacred natural sites. Ecofeminism or ecological feminism defined by Rosemary Radford Ruether examines the interconnections between the domination of women and the domination of nature. Ecofeminism aims at strategies and worldviews to liberate or heal these interconnected dominations by understanding deeply their etiology and enforcement.[8] This chapter uses an African lens to assess how these structures of domination can be addressed. This is because, from

---

6. Mama and Okazawa-Rey, "Militarism, Conflict and Women's Activism," 99.

7. Cervenka, "Effects of Militarization of Africa," 4.

8. Ruether, "Ecofeminism," 22.

an African feminist perspective, we cannot separate women's struggles for security during war and conflict from the destruction of natural resources that take place during these wars. Besides sexual abuse which is rampant amidst war and conflict, one of the destructive effects of war on women and children is environmental degradation. Women who are at the center of food autonomy are also at the center of food insecurity and victimization during military invasions, making it difficult or impossible for them to protect the lands and rivers which are the sources of the daily survival of their families. The loss of the forests and streams to state-run military bases and rebel groups deny them the right to access basic resources for their own food, sovereignty, and shelter. The destruction of natural resources also means women who are the key figures in providing food to the family are affected with food insecurity for their households. It is within this collective experience of deprivation that an ecofeminist perspective becomes imperative as a lens to address the interconnected struggles of both women and nature against militarization. The struggle of women for life and livelihood is inseparably connected with the struggle to protect nature. Therefore they seek redemptive ways of emancipating both themselves and nature. It is only with such a struggle that the life of all can be sustained.

Another factor for proposing an ecofeminist approach to militarization and empire is that as long as literature on women focuses on the sexual abuse of women, girls, and child soldiers, the problem of environmental degradation, the loss of sacred natural sites and its effects on African heritage and worldview is sidelined. We hear little or almost nothing about these valuable sites that are destroyed or used as war zones at the expense of indigenous people's spirituality and heritage. Hence the call for an ecofeminist approach to confronting militarization is calling for a perspective that will respond to both the loss of women's dignity through abuse and loss of sacred natural sites from a feminist perspective.

> Ecofeminism can be described as a multi-faceted and multi-located challenging structure. It confronts systems of patriarchy, race and class. Ecofeminism broadens the scope of the cultural critique and incorporates disparate yet radically connected elements. Ecofeminists' standpoint reflects various positions that can be transformed through time and place.[9]

9. Siwila, "Tracing the Ecological Footprints of our Foremothers," 133.

Furthermore during these wars it is women who are left in the homes with the children to fend for food as household providers while men are either captured or killed by the enemy forces or have joined the armed forces and groups. Hence in our discussions on militarization, it is important to recognize the link between women and stewardship, and the relationship between food security (which is provided by women) and political instabilities, and its effect on women and children. Karen J. Warren, who authored *Ecofeminist Philosophy* (2000) and edited *Ecofeminism: Women, Culture, and Nature* (1997), has convincingly demonstrated that the ecofeminist lens is not only concerned with the connection between women and nature, but also with the ways in which the interconnectedness among environmental degradation (as a result of militarization), food insecurity and political unrest affects humanity's wellbeing.

The ecofeminist perspective also challenges the status quo which does not take into consideration the effect of war on human spirituality. Ruether contends:

> When I speak about the challenge of ecofeminism to theology, it is in the context of radicalization that takes place as ecological consciousness is incorporated into feminist theology and the struggles of women. One then realizes the need to question and reconstruct the cosmological framework out of which the Christian worldview grew from its ancient roots in the Hebrew and Greek worlds. A full treatment of the implications of these deeper questions is still very much in process. One awaits a full presentation of what an ecofeminist theology would look like.[10]

An analysis of ecofeminism from a religious perspective by Hyun Kyung Chung states that ecofeminism draws its resources for struggle from more egalitarian body-affirming, nature respecting religions, cultures, and ideologies. It searches for a spirituality which promotes the immanence of God, the sacredness of this world, and the wholeness of body. It aims at rediscovering the holiness of matter which is promoted in many ethnic indigenous religions.[11] An ecofeminist perspective helps us to realize the need for a theology of stewardship that was accorded to humanity by God which has lost its grip. As nature is groaning, sacred sites are being trampled on, families are being broken, women are wailing, and men are being beheaded or abducted for military defense.

---

10. Ruether, "Ecofeminism" 26.

11. Chung, "Ecology, Feminism and African and Asian Spirituality," 176.

Rape and Militarization

Most of the ecofeminist scholars have used the metaphor of the rape of mother earth when talking about the destruction of nature by patriarchal systems. In critically reflecting on the effects of militarization of natural resources, I use this metaphor to demonstrate the relationship between the rape of women in the forests by the soldiers and the destruction of the forests in the form of rape. Evidence on sexual abuse of women during wars has shown that some women raped during wars have faced the ordeal while they were searching for water, food or shelter. An ecofeminist perspective on these rape cases would argue that the earth is also raped by these military soldiers through the destruction of forests and pollution of rivers and seas. In the African context, sexuality and nature, especially sacred natural sites, cannot be separated. This is because both sex and nature are associated with life. In some indigenous cultural settings, having sex in the forest is a forbidden act because these places are seen as indwelling sacred abodes of the ancestors and the sex act would pollute the place and trigger the anger of the ancestors.

A study by Tina Sideris on the war in Mozambique reviewed how the indigenous people lamented over the loss of their land and how the spirits of their ancestors who were killed during the war are said to be still wandering in the forests. In this study Sideris provides empirical evidence of women's experience in war:

> Rape and other forms of sexual violence became weapons of terror and intimidation. Women were raped in front of their husbands, children, and compatriots. There are widespread reports from women and men testifying about husbands being used as mattresses—they were forced to lie on the ground, while their wives were raped on top of them. Children were raped in the presence of their parents.[12]

Sideris further quotes women's testimonies which capture their experiences of war in Mozambique. One of the women whom the author called Lucia had this to say:

> On the spot where the man raped me I was terribly shocked about seeing a man sleeping with a five year old—a very small child. That child couldn't even manage to walk. He took a panga and killed the child. Instead of caring about my own rape and

12. Sideris, "War, Gender and Culture," 715.

feeling for what happened to me, even today I still see that man sleeping with a small child and after that the child being killed. Most of the people who were taken by Renamo were teenagers and school children. I have seen many young people being raped by these Renamo.[13]

Looking at these gruesome realities one understands that sex is used as a weapon of war in the militarization of Africa. Continuity of life is related to sexual intercourse in the African context. Human beings are conceived through the sexual act and so, as plants and animals, are multiplied through the same process. This kind of belief also brings home the fact that the sexual act needs to be respected as an act for continuity of life. Molyneaux argues that the sexual union for male and female is a metaphor of creation in many mythologies. Commonly the earth is female reflecting the consonance between nature, fecundity and fertility of women.[14] In most of the African cultures, sexual acts during war were prohibited as it was considered a bad omen. Men going to war were not allowed to sleep with their wives as anything that is militant was not to be associated with sexual intercourse. A study by Kapya J. Kaoma, *God's Family, God's Earth: Christian Ecological Ethics of Ubuntu* (2013), found out that in the past one of the preparatory rules before going to war was for the whole community to abstain from sex over a number of days. The notion attached to this restriction is that of impurity. In most ethnic groups of Africa, sex is associated with many religious rituals and at the same time it is also seen as a threat to crop production and as polluting of the land. Death too is associated with some rituals that may be associated with impurity. Funerals and any rituals in some settings are deemed to be disturbing the ancestral spiritual order.

Despite indigenous beliefs that guard women and land, what is happening in reality is different. The forests are now used as space for raping women and children. Sacred sites have been demonized and polluted with semen and blood. Hence the connection between abuse of women, nature and militarization cannot be overlooked. Mama and Okazawa-Rey argue that feminist conceptualizations of militarization are broader than those prevailing within the field of conflict and security studies. In seeking to address militarization as a gendered and gendering phenomenon, feminist scholars have critically engaged with its more enduring

13. Sideris, "War, Gender and Culture," 715.
14. Molyneaux, *Sacred Earth*, 10.

cultural, ideological, political and economic aspects, as well as the gendered nature of military institutions.[15] Sigridur Gudmarsdottir states:

> When the earth is declared a body, violated by human consumption and greed, powerful transformations of language take place. On the one hand symbolic connections between nature and women are affirmed; on the other the experience of sexual violence that women especially suffer are addressed and intensified to a cosmic scale. For many ecothinkers, the body of the earth came to be seen as a sacred body, identified with a motherly or a goddess deity. Consequently, if nature was identified as a female body; the ecological crisis which the contemporary world faces was depicted as the abuse, rape or slaughter of the sacred mother. If thinking about the earth as a body is common in diverse ecotheological circles, the main contribution of ecofeminists to this kind of thinking was to apply feminist analyses of patriarchal oppression and ravishment of female bodies to the environmental debate.[16]

Amid all these setbacks and the subjugation of women during wars through the lack of natural resources, sexual abuse etc, research has also shown how women have stood up to protect mother earth against its exploitation by military troops. Women have groaned in labor pains together with mother earth seeking to birth a new world without bloodshed where sacred sites will be respected as the indwelling abodes of the spiritual beings; a world where rivers will cease to be polluted with dead bodies, where the land will be free of blood stains, and forests will retain their vegetation and cease to be sites for the sexual abuse of women and girls.

Sacred Natural Spaces as Sites of Resistance

The general African worldview is that the forests and rivers are sacred spaces because that is where the ancestors live. Therefore going to these forests and rivers means going to meet the Supreme Being and unite with the spirits of the living dead. The scenario of war has changed this paradigm. Most of these sacred sites have been invaded by war. People are now scared to visit these sacred sites for their own spiritual encounters as they have now become death traps. Hence deploying an African

15. Mama and Okazawa-Rey, "Militarism, Conflict and Women's Activism," 100.

16. Gudmarsdottir, "Rapes of Earth and Grapes of Wrath," 207.

ecofeminist perspective that fights for liberation of humanity and nature from all forms of oppression becomes inevitable. Such an approach requires a quest for a need to reclaim these sacred sites as useful resources for the survival of humanity and protection of nature.

Under normal circumstances sacred sites are well established and respected places in all parts of the world. Sacred sites can be natural sites with ecological, spiritual, and cultural values, or artificial sites such as temples, mosques, churches, synagogues or museums. These spaces are considered as sources of life and have a special relationship with nature and humanity. Natural sacred sites such as rivers and mountains are seen as embodiment of mother earth. They also act as the indwelling abodes of both the living and the living dead (the ancestors) as well as the natural world. They are the connecting point between the physical and spiritual world. Adam Hussein Adam argues that:

> Sacred Natural Sites are spiritually important as places created by God, or the Creator, and as resting places for the spirits of ancestors. They are places of potent energy, understood by many to be like acupuncture points in the body of Earth, forming energetic networks. The sacredness of the Sacred Natural Site reaches deep into the Earth and up into the sky. They are places of worship, like temples.[17]

Yaw Adu-Gyamfi demonstrates how among the Akan people land and other natural resources are respected and protected. The author argues that the sacredness of natural resources entail that land among the Akan people is not easily sold, but it is leased and when that happens the ancestors are informed about it:

> For the Akan people conservation of Land is sacred and a gift from God through the ancestors to be preserved and used on a sustainable basis for the good of the community—past, present and future. In addition, the Akans perceive land as Mother Earth, a living goddess, who needs a day of rest. So, in various communities weekly "Sabbaths" are observed for the land. Sacred groves in many communities demonstrate the sense of ecology of our ancestors. Sacred groves include patches of forest lands, on water catchment areas in hilly slopes, river beds and river edges. They are areas set aside as sacred sites and strictly protected by customary laws, beliefs and enforced taboos. Chiefs, communities or individuals for religious and cultural

---

17. Adam, *Recognising Sacred Natural Sites and Territories in Kenya*, 13.

purposes have reserved these areas for purposes such as royal
burial grounds, preservation of watercourses and sacred plants
and the abodes for traditional deities.[18]

These sites remain sacred because they are the indwelling places for the
mizimo ancestors. They symbolize the importance of the earth and the
powers inherent in nature. However these sacred sites are also threatened
and in some cases totally destroyed by increasing post-war development
schemes, which reconfigure the relationship between African countries
and the neo-colonial empire. J. Hubert argues that there is no doubt that
many sacred sites throughout the world are under threat. One major
threat is commercial development such as construction of roads, bridges,
shopping centers and dams.[19]

Sacred sites in the African context are imbued with communal
spiritualties. The community is also part of these sites. They are a meeting
place for the community to offer their prayers and supplications to the
ancestors. Each member of the community has a responsibility towards
these sites. Therefore if one member of the community trespasses these
sites the whole community is affected. African cosmology shows that all
things are arranged and human beings are like priests of the earth linking
the universe to God. From an ecofeminist perspective women should not
be seen as mere victims, but as preservers of nature and communities.
There is a need to shift from a model that sees women and nature as
victims of patriarchal oppression to seeing them as custodians of nature
as in the case of *mulela*.

Gendering Religious Spaces and Militarization

Religious spaces have always masked themselves as places where the
troubled, the discriminated, the abused, the hungry, the murderer and
the attempted-murder survivor all congregate in search for peace and for
answers to their everyday challenges. It seems to matter less whether it is
a church, a mosque or a shrine. These spaces have always attracted people
from different walks of life for a plethora of intents. Religious spaces are
regarded as particular places where human persons meet their deity in
the most intimate way and at the same time they are the spaces where

18. Adu-Gyamfi, "Indigenous Beliefs and Practices," 147.
19. Hubert, "Sacred Beliefs and Beliefs of Sacredness," 9.

communities perpetuate their identities and cultural heritages. This story is not foreign to Africa.

From an African indigenous perspective religion animates and permeates human activities and aspirations. Scholars like John Mbiti long held a presupposition that Africans are notoriously religious.[20] Although Mbiti restricts this observation to African traditional religions, I would extend it to incorporate what I describe as modern religions that have attracted a huge number of followers, most specifically since the beginning of the twentieth century. Today the continent boasts of an increased number of religious followers in both Christianity and Islamic religions as compared to how it was at the beginning of the twentieth century. In sub-Saharan Africa for instance statistics show:

> The number of Muslims living between the Sahara Desert and the Cape of Good Hope has increased more than 20-fold, rising from an estimated 11 million in 1900 to approximately 234 million in 2010. The number of Christians has grown even faster, soaring almost 70-fold from about 7 million to 470 million. Sub-Saharan Africa now is home to about one-in-five of all the Christians in the world (21%) and more than one-in-seven of the world's Muslims (15%).[21]

Despite this increase in numbers, religious spaces have not survived the wave of militarization currently shaping the social, political, and the religio-cultural landscape of Africans. These spaces have been seen as soft targets by combatant groups. Such groups perceive these spaces to be a means of expressing their dissonances with and retaliations against their opponents. Either the worshipers, the majority of whom are women and children, are taken as hostages, shot on the spot, and displaced or they are killed through suicide bombing. In most cases, when such events strike it is the women and children that face the worst of the consequences. In many worship spaces in Africa, women make up the largest proportion compared with men. Various studies have shown that "women generally tend to be more involved in religious practices than men. Women are more likely to attend religious services, pray privately, say religion is important in their lives, and depend on religion as a coping behavior."[22]

---

20. Mbiti, *Introduction to African Religion*, 30.

21. Stencel et al., "Tolerance and Tension."

22. Koenig et al., *Handbook of Religion and Health*, 329.

Militarization of religious spaces appears to be often justified especially where certain religious denominations see other religious groups as a religious threat. Like rigid ethnic identities "group perceptions of religious separateness may lead to conflict."[23] One of the countries that has experienced an increased number of religious-related military conflicts is Nigeria where confrontations between Christians and Muslims has led to a series of massacres of the most defenseless in the society. These have included the *Kaduna* riots between Christians and Muslims over the introduction of Sharia law in Kaduna in 2000. It is argued that while more than twenty churches and eight mosques were burnt down and between 2000 and 5000 people lost their lives in a span of just two months.[24] The country has experienced other riots with similar consequences such as the Jos riots that occurred between September 7 and 17, 2001, the *Yelwa* massacre which happened between February and May in 2004 and the Jos riots which happened on November 28 and 29 in 2008 where Christians and Muslims turned against each other over the results of a local election. With the rise of *Boko Haram* in 2009 there have been a series of killings. Some have happened in religious sites. For example on December 25, 2005 the Islamic militants are said to have bombed a Catholic church during mass. The Nigerian military was involved in the Zaria massacre that happened between December 12 and 13, 2015. The soldiers opened fire on a Shiite community as they prepared their worship space for prayer sessions. Apart from Nigeria similar incidents have happened in Egypt. The attack on the Coptic church on November 3, 2018 as pilgrims headed to their monastery is one of a series of attacks that the Coptic Christians have endured in Egypt. From 2013 to 2018 Egypt has experienced various attacks all targeting Coptic religious spaces.[25]

These experiences suggest that worship spaces are no longer places of peace and comfort where the most vulnerable of society, the abused, and the discriminated against are likely to find consolation. On the contrary there seems to be no difference between war zone areas and places of worship. In conflict-ridden Africa, religious spaces seem to fall into the most dangerous zones that continually perpetuate victimizations of females and children in our contemporary society. These zones intersect with hunger and drought zones, low level literacy zones, climate change

---

23. MacFarlane, "Taking Stock," 15–33, 26; Haynes, "Religion, Ethnicity," 305–17.

24. Human Rights Watch, "*Miss World Riots.*"

25. BBC News, "Coptic Christian Attack."

zones, domestic violence zones, sexual and reproductive health zones, patriarchal zones and many other zones that put women in the most vulnerable group of humanity.

As in other zones of female victimization, when religious spaces become militarized women and children command little authority in avoiding danger. In many cases, women are not part of the negotiating table for conflict resolution. Many of these committees, whether religious or otherwise, are headed by men who in most cases have the ability to flee when militias strike. Gender stereotypes are often at play during peace times which become prominent in times of conflict and war. In "mainstream thinking on war and violent conflict, women and men are still often positioned at opposite ends of a moral continuum, where women are considered peaceful and men aggressive, women passive and men active."[26] This can also explain why not as many women compared to men are seen on military parades of countries' defense forces. Furthermore it can also explain why even among those women who happened to be recruited into the security forces a very few are elevated to higher ranks. In situations where that happens the so-called elevated woman become celebrities of the army. This is also true when women are highly involved in conflict resolution in many of the African countries.

Women are not involved in decision making in militarization of religious spaces, but this does not protect them from being the prime victims. Although men too are victims of conflict situations they tend to be favored by socio-cultural privileges as compared to women. In conflict situations, the mobility of women is limited given their location as mothers who also carry their children on their backs. Not only do they have to carry their children but also to provide basic necessities such as food and water. Given this limited mobility, women are more likely to either be killed or maimed in conflicts. Where this is not the case they become the agents of the internationalization of conflict when they must cross international borders as refugees to escape from war situations at home. In other cases, where they avoid crossing international borders they are still "nevertheless internally displaced... Both these situations give rise to environmental conflicts, which further affect women and children adversely."[27] Environmental crisis arising from war and militarization cannot be separated from the struggles of women who continue to resist

26. Coulter et al., *Young Female Fighters*, 7.
27. Mwagiru, "Women and Children," 1–24, 5.

the status quo. Therefore the call for justice (gender, economic and political) and peace cannot be separated from ecojustice. An ecofeminist approach is necessary in making this connectedness.

Conclusion

In most African countries, militarization as part of the neo-colonial empire has turned women's quest for safe water, shelter, and safe forests to collect firewood into one of the most pressing and difficult challenges. As a result of this most women and children experience negative health effects, especially in the war zone areas. According to Peter J. Atkins (2018), in regions such as Nigeria's north eastern part, South Sudan, and Somalia where political strife is a daily experience, about twenty million people were estimated to be at immediate risk of dying of hunger in 2017.[28] Most cases are due to displacement from their villages where they were able to access food through farming.

It is also important to note that despite the fact that women have been victims of all these wars, women too have emerged as victors through resistance to abuse and oppression. This has been done through forming organizations aimed at protecting women and children or women joining the war to fight for themselves.[29] Nicole Itano argues:

> In other African conflicts, like Uganda and Congo, women have participated in rebel movements, but usually in supporting roles. They cook, clean, and often sleep with soldiers—not always by choice. But here in Liberia, often out of revenge for husbands slain at the hands of the enemy, women have fought on the front line as part of an elite and feared unit unique on the continent.[30]

These are some of the examples of resistance by women during wars that are often undermined. From a theological perspective, war, militarization and empire form the political context within which the liberation struggles of the slaves of Egypt and their subsequent generations unfolded based on the faith in a God who is both the creator and liberator. In that, the humanity and nature were inseparable. Journeying to Egypt with the good intention to look for refuge from a hunger stricken homeland,

---

28. Atkins, "Geography of Hunger and Famine."

29. Utas, "West-African Warscapes," 403–30.

30. Itano, "Sisters-in-Arms in Liberia's War."

the children of Israel found themselves in slavery in Egypt where they were forced to work for the empire. Their exodus journey back to a land of freedom turned out to be not only an experience of destruction of natural resources and loss of lives, but also a journey filled with hope and sustenance (water from the rock and manna). The ecofeminist lens and the African indigenous belief that sees nature as sacred, help capture the struggle for liberation of the present day people amidst war and militarization. Faith in a God who liberates needs to be seen within this ecofeminist African spiritual context, as opposed to both colonial missionary portrayals of God as well as Christian and Muslim fundamentalist caricatures of God. In fact, the latter are neocolonial representations of God.

In envisaging a liberated future Africa should get rid of its dependence on neocolonial structures that perpetuate war and militarization. Faith in a liberating God demands a radical conversion of hearts and minds concerning the ways in which our social, political and ecological relationships are organized. Throughout human history empire justifies militarization to maintain brutal exploitation of men and women and plunder natural resources be it land or minerals. At the end of wars the defeated party finds themselves in a state where they have to surrender their natural resources. Cervenka argues that the process of demilitarization of Africa will be a long and complex one, for it does not just mean a simple transfer of power from a military to a civilian government. It means, above all, a demilitarization of minds. The disillusionment and cynicism which has been bred by the succession of armed redeemers, promising things they never delivered during the past thirty years, may take another thirty years to heal.[31] It is in this context, an ecofeminist understanding of the liberating presence of God that can be found in the sense of sacredness given to the earth by African indigenous traditions can support the decolonizing of Africa where the people begin to believe that God is not out there, but amongst us, particularly amongst struggling women who see the interrelationship between humanity and nature.

31. Cervenka, "Effects of Militarization."

Struggles for Just Peace
and Interfaith Dialogue

Chapter 6

Spirituality of Resistance to the Total Militarization of Global Society

Perspectives from the Korean Peninsula

Young-Bock Kim

"In the Confucian tradition, changing one's last name is considered the greatest betrayal one can commit against his or her ancestors. To express one's dedication to something, a Japanese individual will say he would 'sacrifice his life' for it; however, a Korean will say he would 'change his last name.' Therefore the edict requiring Koreans to adopt Japanese names was truly an act of brutal violence. This order was related to the Japanese Imperialization Policy, under which they also introduced their conscription system…Throughout the entire country, Koreans lamented the loss of their name. It is very difficult for me even to remember my adopted Japanese name. Occasionally, the Japanese ask me what my Japanese name was out of curiosity, but I can never answer that question. It was one of the most humiliating experiences I have ever had."
— Dae-jung Kim[1]

1. Kim, *Conscience in Action*, 14.

Introduction

THE SETTING FOR OUR spiritual (Biblical and theological) reflections and practices related to "empire and peace" should be the actual situation of life. And spirituality itself should be understood in relationship with spiritualities at all levels of community among living beings. The history of empires from ancient to modern times has been shrouded in profound spiritual ambiguities. The ancient empires of West Asia and East Asia had their own peculiar religious foundations; and their modern counterparts have established their own religious and spiritual foundations up to this day. The story of the global empire and its militarization cannot be told in simple factual terms. Therefore, I want to propose as the primary context of our discourse the story of life of all living beings, which I will call Zoegraphy (Story of Life) vs. Thanatography (Story of Destruction of Life). The story of life of all living beings is a comprehensive sphere, with war and peace as juxtaposed realities. If the destruction of life by wars and militarization is the central issue, then Thanatography (the story of death and killing of life) is taken as the central concern. Any story of life (Zoegraphy) converges with the story of death of life (Thanatography). I will navigate my reflections in mapping the spiritual and political dynamics of these stories in exploring the role of spiritualties in revisiting empire and militarization in the Korean peninsula and beyond.

The Matrix of Zoegraphy and Thanatography

The Korean people have experienced hundreds of wars and violent conflicts. Let us adopt a Korean perspective to look at the suffering of diverse living beings during the history of human wars. This perspective starts from a local point, moves to a national and then a geopolitical paradigm, and reaches further to a cosmic framework. Several points must be considered in the Korean Thanatography. The Korean peninsula was invaded numerous times during its ancient history. Major conflicts and wars took place during the period of the Three Kingdoms, at the end of which unification was imposed through war and conquest by the Silla Kingdom in alliance with the foreign Tang military power in China. This was the first major military involvement and conquest within Korea. During this period of internal military struggle, the Korean people generated a Thanatography with the popular story of 3,000 royal women who, according to legend, jumped from a mountain cliff into the river, choosing death over the brutal violation of their dignity by the military forces of other Korean kingdoms and of Tang China. Though this saga is difficult to confirm historically, it is just as "real" as more recent stories of Korean women, such as the comfort women story under the Japanese Empire during the WWII.[2] In this context, the people deepened their resistance to violence and war within the "spiritual" wellspring of the Maitreya, the Messianic Buddhism that prevailed in the Baekje region. Here a Zoegraphy of the Korean people was formed, with spirituality as the foundation of life, and all living beings recognized as the subjects of life within the "messianic reign of Maitreya." This spirituality has been a major stream of the Zoegraphy of the Korean people throughout their entire history in resisting empire, colonialism and militarization.

At the same time, there arose an ironic and questionable legacy: the glorification of military culture through the Hwarangdo (Flower Youth), elite youth military corps of Silla Kingdom, which played a decisive role in the war of unification of the Three Kingdoms in alliance with the Tang military. This legacy has been reinforced through images of glorious nationalist heroism in various battles against foreign military invasions. Militarism in the form of war heroes has been deeply entrenched in nationalist ideologies during the history of Korea. Such military glorification can be found in almost every nationalist situation and military institution in the world, and it is an integral part of the Korean military today.

Another story appeared in the history of Korea through the codification of the Saga of Tangun, the founder of Korea, during the period of the Mongol invasion of the Koryo Kingdom. The Mongol invasion took the form of a 40-year-long, incredibly brutal siege against the people and their villages. The entire Korean peninsula was subjugated under the Mongol military forces, which used horses for rapid attacks. It is truly ironic that the Tangun Saga of the Korean people, the story of Korea's foundation, which shares spiritual roots with central Asia, provided the vision of resistance against the Mongolian Empire. It is a saga of cosmic benevolence embracing all humanity, true conviviality, and prosperity in Grand Peace which is the foundation saga of the Korean people that leads to a Fiesta of Life. This saga is a sort of Zoegraphy that constitutes the spiritual origin of living beings in the community of the

2. Between 100,000 to 200,000 women were used as sex slaves by the imperial Japanese military between 1935 to 1945. See Howard, *True Stories of the Korean Comfort Women*.

Tangun people and community. This is the vision of the Korean people that was consolidated in resistance to the brutality of the Mongolian Empire. The same vision empowered resistance movements against invasions by the Japanese Empire. During the Chosun Kingdom there were major military invasions by the neighboring powers of China, Mongolia (Mongol Invasion), and Japan (Hideyoshi Invasion). These tragic experiences deepened the matrix of Zoegraphy and Thantography in the history of the Korean people.

Korean Peninsula and Modern Imperial Geopolitics

Imperial Rivalries and the Spirituality of Korean Resistance

Let us turn to the modern history of wars affecting the Korean people in the East Asian region. During the last part of the nineteenth century, the first modern war took place, suppressing a peasant revolutionary movement that was seeking to transform the Chosun Dynasty. The ruling power of the Chosun Kingdom, unable to deal with this Donghak Peasant Revolutionary Movement, elicited the help of overseas military forces, first from China and then from Japan, who intervened to suppress the movement. This was the cause and context of the First Sino-Japanese War (July 25, 1894 to April 1895). In the first part of the twentieth century, Russian power was allowed to intervene in Korean royal politics and this led to the Russo-Japanese military conflict (1905). In these wars, it was the Japanese military that prevailed and consequently came to control Korea, establishing the Japan-Korea Protectorate (1905).

International activity prior to the Sino-Japanese war was a process of opening the Korean nation to the Western nations that were competing for geopolitical hegemony over the Korean peninsula. In the 1880s, Korea's King Gojong decided to establish diplomatic ties with the United States. After negotiations through Chinese mediation in Tianjin, the Treaty of Peace that ensured amity, commerce and navigation was formally signed between the United States and Korea on May 22, 1882. This first treaty between the Korean government and the U.S. became the model for all Korean treaties with Western countries. Korea signed trade and commerce treaties with Great Britain and Germany in 1883, with Italy and Russia in 1884, and with France in 1886. Commercial treaties were signed with other European countries as well.

In this geopolitical historical context, the Korean people cultivated an indigenous spirituality for radical transformation in resistance to many forms of violence—social, political, cultural, geopolitical, and military—being inflicted by the powers of China, Japan, and later Russia. Those countries carried out a politics of hegemony over the Korean peninsula and waged a series of military interventions, which led to the subjugation of the Korean Kingdom under the same hegemony-seeking international powers that had suppressed the revolutionary spiritual movement. The Japanese military was particularly aggressive in suppressing Korean resistance to unjust Korean rulers and their "allies." The First Sino-Japanese War (1894–95) was against the Korean people and against China. Defeating Imperial Russia in the Russo-Japanese War (1904–05), Japan made Korea its protectorate via the Eulsa Treaty in 1905, then annexed it by way of the Japan–Korea Annexation Treaty in 1910, thus starting its long military-enforced colonial occupation of the peninsula. Many Korean nationalists fled the country, and the Provisional Government of the Republic of Korea was established in 1919 in Nationalist China.

The Donghak Peasant Revolutionary Movement, which had a counterpart in the T'aiping Peasant Revolutionary Movement in China, was a crucial focal point of resistance in Korean history. It is estimated that the peasant force comprised more than 250,000 people, spread all over the peninsula. They were brutally suppressed. However, the Donghak Peasant Revolutionary Movement had presented a spiritual response to the wars and violence in the Korean peninsula. It was a major spiritual convergence of resistance against the imperial military powers in East Asia, with a core of spirituality centered around Chŏndogyo (Korean: "Religion of the Heavenly Way"), formerly Donghak ("Eastern Learning"), an indigenous Korean religion that combined the spiritualities of Confucianism, Buddhism, Taoism, Shamanism and Roman Catholicism. There is no concept of eternal reward in Chŏndogyo because its vision is limited to bringing righteousness and peace to the world. Toward this end, converts to Chŏndogyo dedicate themselves to God by placing clean water on an altar in a ritual called chŏngsu. They are instructed to meditate on God, offer prayers (kido) upon leaving and entering their homes, dispel harmful thoughts (e.g., of greed and lust), and worship God in church on Sundays.

The essence of Chŏndogyo is said to be contained in a 21-word formula in Chinese characters (chumun), a prayer that is recited as the way to enlightenment. It is translated: "May the creative power of the universe be within me in abundance. May heaven be with me and every creation will be done. Never forgetting this truth, everything will be known." This formula contains the basic principle of Chŏndogyo: "Human and God are one" (In-Nae-Chŏn); this oneness is realized by individuals through sincere faith in the unity of their own body and spirit and through faith in the universality of God. This religion was a response to the corrupt authoritarian regime of the Chosun Kingdom along with the Chinese and Japanese foreign military powers that were suppressing the Korean people in the most brutal fashion, with Japan utilizing a modernized military.

The Torment of the Korean People

The casualties of the Sino-Japanese war, the Russo-Japanese war, and the suppression of the volunteer resistance (the "Righteous Army" of the people) reached several hundred thousand. This Thantography was not merely the physical destruction of the people's lives; it was a deep historical wound that became the foundation of resistance against the violence of colonization and war that began in the last part of the nineteenth century and reached its peak during Imperial Japanese Wars and Total Militarization Against the Korean People (1905–45). After 1919, there was a Second Sino-Japanese War (1937–45) between the Republic of China and the Japanese Empire, from 1941 on, as part of World War II. Imperial Japan's military occupation of Korea, which lasted from 1905 to 1945, exerted great influence over geopolitical hegemonic politics. In this historical process, a pivotal resistance movement arose among the tormented Korean people. In 1919, they rose up in a major historical resistance, embracing and reconstituting the nineteenth century spiritual convergence of the Donghak Movement. This was the March First Independence Movement. In 1917, the Bolshevik Revolution had taken place in Russia. In 1918, the League of Nations met in Paris, declaring the "doctrine of self-determination of colonized people," and the Korean people sensed the signs of the times for radical transformation.

The 1905 Japanese Protectorate, imposed upon the Korean people by military force, kindled the vehement resistance of the Korean people in the form of the "Righteous Army." The spiritual foundation of this movement was Confucian "spirituality"—particularly the realist and reformist Confucianism that evolved in the later part of Chosun Dynasty.

This movement converged into the March First Independence Movement. Another stream that joined the resistance process of the March First Movement came from the Western liberal and Christian movement (mission). The Independence Club and the New People's Association also joined the movement of resistance to the Japanese military occupation of Korea. From 1919 to 1925 and even later, Korean communists led internal and external warfare against the Japanese. In China, the nationalist National Revolutionary Army and the communist People's Liberation Army helped organize Korean refugees against the Japanese military, which had also occupied parts of China. The nationalist-backed Koreans in the Burma Campaign (December 1941 to August 1945) and the communists fought the Japanese in Korea and Manchuria.

The Division of a Tormented People

The division of the Korean peninsula was the product of international power politics during the last part of the Pacific War, when the Soviet Union had just declared war against the Japanese Empire (1945). At the Tehran Conference in November 1943 and the Yalta Conference in February 1945, the Soviet Union promised to join its allies in the Pacific War within three months of the victory in Europe. Accordingly, it declared war on Japan on August 9, 1945, three days after the USA had dropped the atomic bomb on Hiroshima, and the same day that it bombed Nagasaki. By August 10, the Soviet Army had begun to occupy the northern part of the Korean peninsula. On the night of August 10, U.S. colonels Dean Rusk and Charles H. Bonesteel III, tasked with dividing the Korean peninsula into Soviet and U.S. occupation zones, proposed creating a border at the 38th parallel. This was incorporated into U.S. General Order No. 1, which responded to the Japanese surrender on August 15. The Korean division was solidified (1945–1949), thus sowing the fatal seeds of the Korean War and the Cold War.[3] The Korean War was the real beginning of global Cold War geopolitics.

3. At this point of history in imperial politics there arose two axial points on the global ellipse of geopolitics, one in West Asia and the other in East Asia. In West Asia, the pivotal point is Palestine, which was dismantled in forging the modern state of Israel; in East Asia it is the Korean peninsula that was divided. These moves made the two regions "permanent" theatres of war for the imperial powers. Since then the struggle for geopolitical hegemony in East Asia has not changed fundamentally, among the four big powers: United States, China, Russia, and Japan. Meanwhile,

According to data from the U.S. Department of Defense, the United States suffered 33,686 battle deaths, along with 2,830 non-battle deaths, during the Korean War. U.S. battle deaths were 8,516 up to their first engagement with the Chinese on November 1, 1950. South Korea reported some 373,599 civilian and 137,899 military deaths.[4] Western sources estimate the Chinese People's Volunteer Army suffered about 400,000 deaths and 486,000 wounded, while the Korean People's Army (North) suffered 215,000 deaths and 303,000 wounded.[5] Data from official Chinese sources, on the other hand, indicate that the Chinese PVA suffered 114,000 battle deaths, 34,000 non-battle deaths, 340,000 wounded, and 7,600 missing during the war. 7,110 Chinese prisoners of war were repatriated to China. Chinese sources also report that North Korea suffered 290,000 casualties, 90,000 captured, and a large number of civilian deaths.[6] *Encyclopædia Britannica* notes that North Korean civilian casualties were 600,000, while South Korean civilian casualties reached one million. The Chinese and North Koreans estimate that about 390,000 soldiers from the United States, 660,000 soldiers from South Korea, and 29,000 other UN soldiers were "eliminated" from the battlefield.[7]

As explained by a South Korean account focusing on the victims, the Korean War did not last for just three years; North and South have remained in a state of division and military confrontation for the past 70 years. In the war, the South Korean military suffered 138,000 deaths and 450,000 wounded, totaling 609,000; and the North Korean military suffered deaths and injuries of 520,000, rising to 800,000 when the figure includes the missing. The UN military forces suffered 58,000 deaths, and a total 546,000 casualties including wounded and missing. The Chinese military suffered 136,000 deaths, 208,000 injuries, and total casualties

---

in West Asia, a competition for hegemony has emerged between the United States, Europe, and Russia. Militarily, West Asia is in a very unstable situation due to the Zionist politics of Israel. Mark Braverman's perceptive article in this volume astutely analyzes how Christian theology that developed in the West after the Holocaust replaced one supersessionism with another whereby Israel is freely allowed to oppress the Palestinians. One can easily discern the Zoegraphy of the Palestinian people in the context of the Thanatography of Palestine perpetuated by an oppressive Christian–Jewish lobby in the West. See The Amman Declaration of Peace in Palestine (2006) and Kairos Palestine (2009).

4. Rhem, "Korean War Death Stats Highlight."

5. Hikey, "Korean War."

6. Lumen, "Korean War."

7. Millette, "Korean War."

of 973,000 including the missing. 245,000 South Korean civilians were killed, 130,000 were massacred, 230,000 were wounded, 85,000 were kidnapped, and 303,000 went missing, for a total of one million.[8] According to U.S. statistics, there were 600,000 deaths in the war with a total 2 million causalities, 85 percent of which were civilians. 10 million people suffered separation from their families and became refugees.[9] The imperial structures of division claimed scores of lives leaving deep scars in the collective memory of the Korean people. How to heal the wounds of the Korean War victims is a major question for the Korean people.

Global Militarization and the Korean Peninsula

Globalization and militarization are two phenomena which have attracted special attention not only from public opinion but from science and academia as well. For a long time, globalization was understood as military expansion, as practiced for example by Alexander the Great, the Roman and Ottoman Empires, the British, and Nazis. However, as a concept globalization has many meanings. In modern times, it is understood as spreading new scientific and technological discoveries, and expanding economic, trade, and transportation advances all around the world, which are seen as the ways in which the globe is interconnected. However, it is critiqued as a way of creating dependence of some countries on a powerful few that has engendered massive inequalities across the world. Its most destructive feature is militarization as a global process, which unfolds through the arms race and military trade generating invasions and armed conflicts. In response to it we can also find a global movement for disarmament as people's awareness about the wars and violent conflicts increases through new modes of communication and travels. In short, we could say that globalization has a military paradigm as well as a peace paradigm.

Militarization is the process by which a society or global/local community organizes itself for military conflict and violence at the global/local level. It is related to militarism, meaning predominance of the military in the administration or policy of a state. Militarism is an ideology that reflects the level of militarization of a state, and which is associated with the glorification of the military, armed forces, weapons

8. Millete, "Korean War."

9. CNN Editorial Research, "Korean War Fast Facts."

and military power, including through symbolic displays, religious underpinnings and actual use of force including warfare. The process of militarization involves many interrelated aspects, encompassing local, regional and global society in a cosmic dimension. The post WWII dynamics in our world history of wars and militarization settled into the starkly divided Korean society and were projected into the global network of Cold War politics up until the later part of the twentieth-century. Militarization for global geopolitical hegemony has produced the divided matrix of the Korean peninsula, which is interconnected with China, Russia, Japan and the USA. The divided Korean people are enveloped in the vortex of militarization amongst the four big powers. Militarization by empire in East Asia has to be understood as U.S. power with the strategy of militarization. The global power projection of the USA has been expressed by former President Barack Obama as "the leadership role of the USA." The subsequent emergence of "America First" politics is a crude variation of this same assumed global role of the USA. Due to this imperial global power projection we have the War on Terror as a total, permanent war doctrine, without geographical or time limits, and without limits on weaponry. This totalistic war has evolved through the forms of imperial war, modern colonial wars, world wars (WWI and WWII), and the Cold War. The War on Terror in the twenty-first-century has become a pervasive war throughout the globe. Traditional imperial wars have evolved into modern global warfare: technocratic war that is unrestricted in its weapon systems and configurations of violence and destruction, which has an unimaginable intergenerational impact on planetary scale.

New Global Technological Warfare

Warfare and Technology

New military technologies played a crucial role in determining the out-come of the WWII. Most of them were developed in the war period, some were developed in response to perceived lacks during the war, and in the post-war period. During the war there were tremendous improvements in the quality and efficiency of so-called standard weapons: artillery pieces, rockets, armored vehicles, airplanes, ships, and submarines. The new technological age came into being through the development of mis-siles, rocket technology, nuclear weapons, and electronic devices: radar, sonar, systems of weapons guidance, and nuclear technology. As the hot war transformed into the cold war, some hot-war allies gradually became cold-war enemies. Relying on the technological advances achieved in the WWII, scientists continued and intensified their research, development, and production of new, more efficient, and more deadly weapons. The arms race, especially in its technological aspect, assumed a planetary dimension.

The USA–Soviet ideological confrontation was a competition not only to produce more sophisticated weapons, but above all to gain control over space. To that end they made tremendous efforts in research on new materials and guiding systems needed to produce and utilize launching orbital vehicles. The results spilled over into the civilian sector, especially in the fields of electronics, optoelectronics, computerizing and internet. Products made on the basis of high technologies (transistors, TV sets, mobile telephones, etc.) entered homes and offices around the world. New communications and other such technological products marked the transfer of the spirit of Industrial Revolution into the spirit of Technological Revolution. Research on new materials, guidance and communication systems for military purposes contributed significantly to speeding up globalization in all its dimensions.

Main Engines of Globalization: Science and Technology

Globalization is not a wave carried across meadows and over horizons by some virtual force. Rather, it is a gradual process stemming from human activities in certain fields, such as science and technology, production and trade, communication and transportation, militarization, and pacification, etc. We can identify four basic aspects/fields of globalization: trade and transactions, capital and investment movements, migration and movement of people, and the dissemination of knowledge. Among scientists there are disputes regarding the effects military expenditures on development. Some think they contribute to employment and economic growth, while others think that military expenditures and military production stifle economic development. There is a symbiotic relationship between the capitalist economy and military regime, but the use of capital for military purposes associated with imperialism produces parasitic economic growth.

Environmental challenges such as global warming are linked with globalization. All of them, and others in interaction, embrace the globe and modify its very nature. They are directly related to the scientific discoveries and technological advances that are considered major engines of globalization. New scientific discoveries are promptly applied throughout the world, serving as the major driving force for accelerating globalization in economy and trade, communication and transportation, and other aspects. During the Industrial Age, production of technical goods was concentrated within developed countries, while the underdeveloped world, the South-East area, was "market taker" and "raw materials giver." In the new Technological Age, sophisticated goods are being produced in most of the major developing states that used to be "market taker" countries. The dimensions of modern militarization have diverse structural implications for the divided Korean peninsula and the four big powers around the peninsula.

Future Planetary Scale Changes

The Pursuit of Global Hegemony, War, Economy and Society

Geopolitical hegemony is being pursued by a global military regime with a network of military bases and camps transcending all geographical limits. The military presence, ubiquitous on earth, is now extending into cosmic space. The U.S. alone has a global network of 900 military bases around the globe, and the possibility of military bases in space appears increasingly likely. South Korea is essentially a big de facto U.S. military base, as the U.S. holds strategic control over South Korea and Japan through its so-called defense treaties. From the Cold War and Korean War situations, its designated adversaries have shifted to China and the Soviet Union, and then to Russia.

Contemporary militarization looks toward a future military technocracy characterized by the convergence of transhuman technologies. The number one goal in advancing militarization is to "build a more lethal force." Deterrence is to be enhanced by modernizing the nuclear triad. There is more emphasis on technological innovation for increased lethality. Military technocracy is penetrating East Asian societies, the East Asian ecosphere, and East Asian space. The recent U.S. Defense Department Report specifically details the following purchasing priorities for 2019: increase the strength of the Army, Navy, and Air Force; buy ten combat ships ($18.4 billion); and increase production of F-35 aircraft and F/A-18 aircraft ($12.7 billion).[10] The 2019 defense budget supports 883 overseas bases and is lethal to humanity.[11]

The political power structure of the modern nation-state is the primary agent of military action in the name of national security. It is the power of the modern capitalist state that leads modern wars. The primary notion used to justify war is "national security." In the name of national security, the democratic rights of citizens and the rights of all living beings in the cosmos (ecosphere) are violated and destroyed. In the case of South Korea, the U.S. chose the military as the agent to modernize the economy—a policy that was implemented in Brazil, Indonesia and Nigeria. The South Korean case was a sort of militarization of the economy, and South Korea's military coup d'etats and military regimes were emulated as a model in other regions.

The economic war is integrally related to the political and geopolitical wars. The current economic war under way in the national and global context is just as brutal as the earlier colonial domination carried out by kingdoms and nation-states. Economic globalization is closely intertwined with the global military regime bent on total hegemony. Global financial transactions and global trade are part of an economic war that engages in economic violence against a majority of world's population.

The military-industrial complex has been used strategically to boost the state economy by creating jobs and increasing industrial production. Now the war economy constitutes a major component of the globalized political economy, through arms production, production of strategic items related to war and militarization, and the arms trade. This is clear in the East Asian region as well as in the global context. The arms race among the four big powers is the apex of the hegemonic struggle.

Arms production and trade is an integral part of the global economy. In fact, the war economy itself is the actualization of military operations within the economy. Thereby the economy and sociology of militarization has subsumed the total political economy of the nation-states and the world as a whole. Militarization is now an integral dimension of almost everything. And the inner texture of this global power complex is the technocratic symbiosis that binds together global militarization, global economy, and global geopolitics.

10. Lopez, "DOD Finalizes Purchase."
11. Petrovich, "2019 Defense Budget."

The global military regime has created a matrix of social violence within the relationships of gender, race, class, culture and nationhood. Global militarization aggravates the conflicts and violence that characterize class wars throughout the earth. Only a fragile legal framework differentiates civic from military relations, due to the symbiotic relationship between the social nexus of global society and the global matrix of violent militarization.

Civil–Military Relations

The role and image of the military within society is another aspect of militarization. At different times and places in history, soldiers have been viewed as respectable, honored individuals (such as Allied soldiers who liberated Nazi-occupied Netherlands in WWII) or even as heroes (the Finnish sniper who killed many Russian invaders); as "baby killers" by U.S. anti-war activists during the Vietnam war; or as war criminals (Nazi leaders responsible for the Holocaust).

Structural organization is another process of militarization. Before WWII, the United States experienced a post-war reduction of forces after major conflicts, reflecting American suspicion of large standing armies. After World War II, not only was the army maintained, but the National Security Act of 1947 restructured both civilian and military leadership structures, establishing the Department of Defense and the National Security Council. The Act also created permanent intelligence structures (the CIA, etc.) within the U.S. government for the first time, reflecting the civilian government's perception of a need for previously military based intelligence to be incorporated into the structure of the civilian state.

How citizenship is tied to military service plays an important role in establishing civil-military relations. Countries with volunteer-based military service have a different mindset than those with universal conscription. In some countries, men must have served with the military to be considered a citizen. Historical Prussia, where every male was required to serve, and service was a requirement of citizenship, contrasts with post-Vietnam America's all-volunteer army. In Israel, military service is mandatory, creating a society where almost all people have served in the armed forces.

Race Relations, the Society, and Military

In imperial Germany, military service was a requirement of citizenship, but Jews and other foreigners were excluded. During the Holocaust, Nazi Secret Service units engaged in massive scale execution of millions of Jews and other civilians. In the United States following the Civil War, military service was a way for blacks to serve the country and later to appeal for equal citizenship during WWII. The military was one of the first national institutions to be integrated. In 1948, President Harry S. Truman issued Executive Order 9981 establishing equality within the armed services. The military was also a tool of integration. In 1957, President Dwight Eisenhower sent troops to Little Rock, Arkansas to desegregate a school after the Brown v. Board Supreme Court decision in 1954. Improved race relations was seen as a national security issue during the Cold War. Communist world cited American racism as a major flaw in the capitalist system, and America wanted to improve its image in third-world countries that might be susceptible to Communism. This sort of false dichotomy was continued further throughout the McCarthy era and the Cold War in general. Ethnic and racial relations played out in the society.

Class Wars

The military also serves as a means of social restructuring. In the Korean situation, the class question is not merely relevant in terms of social relations, but is the ideological reality in the divided society. In France after the Revolution, the lower classes could gain status and mobility within the military. Also, the officer corps became open to the middle class, although it was once reserved only for the nobility. In Britain, becoming a military officer was an expectation for "second sons" who were to gain no inheritance; the role of officer was assumed to maintain their noble class. In the United States, military service has long been advertised as a means for lower-class people to receive training and experience that they would not normally receive, propelling them to higher incomes and higher positions in society. Joining the military has enabled many people from lower socio-economic demographics to receive college education and training. As well, a number of positions in the military involve transferable skills that can be used in the regular labor market after an individual is discharged (e.g., pilot, air traffic controller, mechanic). In most of the countries in the Global South, military service has become one of the main opportunities among the impoverished social classes. Members of the upper middle class occupy high-ranking offices while the rank and file is constituted of the lower social classes.

Militarization of Police

The police system is intertwined with military regimentation in Korea and other societies in East Asia with military regimes. Police militarization involves the use of military equipment and tactics by law enforcement officers, which may include armored personnel carriers, assault rifles, submachine guns, flashbang grenades, grenade launchers, sniper rifles, and Special Weapons and Tactics (SWAT) teams. The militarization of law enforcement is also associated with intelligence agency-style information gathering aimed at the public and political activists and a more aggressive style of law enforcement.

Gender Relations, Global Culture and Military

The military also has a role in defining gender identities. War movies (e.g. Rambo) reflect the cultural identity of masculinity in the form of the U.S. warrior, displaying the male body as a weapon of war. Military prowess has been crucial to understandings of contemporary masculinity in American culture. During WWI soldiers who experienced shell-shock were seen as failures of masculinity, unable to withstand war as the ultimate task of manliness. The maintenance of military life relies on such ideas about men and manliness as well as ideas about women and femininity, including notions of the fallen woman and patriotic motherhood.

Women have been mobilized during times of war to perform tasks seen as incompatible with men's roles in combat, including cooking, laundry, and nursing. Women have also been seen as necessary for servicing male soldiers' sexual needs through (forced sexual service by the Japanese colonialists). For example, during the Vietnam War, Vietnamese women who worked as sex workers were allowed on U.S. bases as local national guests.

USA as Planetary Empire

The U.S. is now called a "unipolar superpower," the only superpower left on earth; and the goal of its "power structure" is to attain supremacy over the world—politically, economically, and militarily. But this is a costly enterprise. As of 2017, U.S. annual defense expenditure had reached $1.68 trillion. The sum of taxpayer dollars spent by the Pentagon from 2000 to 2017 was $9.87 trillion. With the ending of the Cold War, the threat of all-out nuclear war between the two superpowers receded. There was an opportunity to ban nuclear weapons. But the beginning of the twenty-first-century saw increased militarization, marked by the weaponization of outer space. George Friedman, a defense expert and co-author, with Meredith Friedman, of the 1997 book *The Future of War: Power, Technology & American World Dominance in the 21st Century*, said in an interview, "The age of the gun is over . . . He who controls space controls the battlefield." Friedman argues that other nations "lack the money and/or technology to compete with us in the development of space-age weapons." His book concludes:

> Just as by the year 1500 it was apparent that the European experience of power would be its domination of the global seas, it does not take much to see that the American experience of power will rest on the domination of space . . . Just as Europe expanded war and its power to the global oceans, the United States is expanding war and its power into space . . . Just as Europe shaped the world for half a millennium, so too the United States will shape the world for at least that length of time. For better or worse, America has seized hold of the future of war . . .[12]

As *New World Vistas: Air and Space Power for the 21st Century*, a 1996 U.S. Air Force Board report, states:

> In the next two decades, new technologies will allow the fielding of space-based weapons of devastating effectiveness to be used to deliver energy and mass as force projection in tactical and strategic conflict . . . These advances will enable lasers with reasonable mass and cost to effect very many kills. This can be done rapidly, continuously, and with surgical precision, minimizing exposure of friendly forces. The technologies exist or can be developed in this time period.[13]

12. Grossman, "Weapons in Space."
13. Grossman and Long, "Waging War in Space."

Who makes money on the use of nuclear devices in space? General Electric, which manufactured the plutonium systems, and, in recent years, Lockheed Martin, which took over that division of GE. Both GE and Lockheed Martin have long lobbied the government to use their plutonium systems in space. The U.S. military wants nuclear-powered weapons in space and that's been a key reason why NASA has been insisting on using nuclear power in space even when solar power would suffice. NASA coordinates its activities with the military. A book commissioned by the U.S. Congress, *Military Space Forces: The Next 50 Years*, urges the use of nuclear power in space, both plutonium-fueled radioisotope thermoelectric generators and nuclear reactors which are

> the only known long-lived, compact source able to supply military space forces with electric power about 10 kilowatts and multimegawatts . . . Cores no bigger than basketballs are able to produce about 100 kw, enough for "housekeeping" aboard space stations and at lunar outposts. Larger versions could meet multimegawatt needs of space-based lasers, neutral particle beams, mass drivers, and railguns.[14]

Time Magazine reported in a July 2000 article on missile defense:

> The heart of Ronald Reagan's 1983 Star Wars program lives on, kept beating by a mix of election-year politicking, behind-the-scenes defense-industry puppeteering and a fiercely committed group of conservative think tanks and antimissile-system advocates.[15]

Public awareness of the situation is low. Vaguely hearing of arms control talks at the United Nations, many people assume that the great powers are finally dismantling their weapons. Nothing could be farther from the truth. The U.S. is continuing to pursue its goal of military superiority, though there is no real enemy in sight. The weaponization of space represents a real threat to the security of all life on earth. Not only will it waste hundreds of billions of dollars that should be spent on education, health, housing, and decrepit infrastructure, it will accelerate a new arms race in space. Other countries may develop U.S.-style "Star Wars" programs. Ironically, it is the U.S. that stands to lose the most in a race to militarize outer space. In case of war, the U.S. would suffer greatly, its satellites blinded by anti-satellite weapons, its communications centers

14. Grossman, "Democrats and Star Wars."
15. Grossman, "Weapons in Space."

neutralized. The time to stop this madness, therefore, is now. The story of U.S. Empire is the Story of Death and Destruction not of one race, class and country, but of the whole planet. "In God We Trust." As Nidia Arrobo Rodas from Ecuador questions in her magnificent contribution to this collection (chapter 3), "Which God?" Where is the Story of Life? Where is God of Life?

The Return to Zoegraphy from Thanatography

A Spiritual Discernment

During the Cold War, U.S. military strategy divided the Korean people ideologically, and later went so far as to declare North Korea a part of "the Axis of Evil." Conservative religious belief in the U.S. led to the imposition of anti-communism as a religious-political ideology on the Korean people and other peoples around the world. This religious ideology was internalized by the Korean people during the Korean War and beyond, as the Cold War regime dominated the world.

Then there was the experience of the Korean people in the atomic bombings of 1945 in Hiroshima and Nagasaki, afflicting one hundred thousand Korean people. The second and third generations of those Korean victims are continuing their struggle to deal with this experience through the restoration of justice, healing, reconciliation and peace. A movement for this, the Hapcheon Process, is under way in South Korea.

In 2016 when President Obama visited Japan, Prof. Richard Falk urged him to make an apology to the victims of the U.S. bombing of Hiroshima and Nagasaki, calling this "one of the worst acts of state terror against a defenseless population in all of human history." Obama called for a "moral awakening," but did not apologize. Apology must also be made to the Native American people for the genocide committed against them during the European invasion and conquest five centuries ago. What is the nature of the foundation of U.S. Empire, in spiritual terms? Martin Luther King Jr. prophetically stated: "Nation that continues year after year to spend more money on military defense than on programs of social uplift is approaching spiritual death."

Korean Christians were indoctrinated with the belief that all the spiritualities of the Korean people were "pagan," and that communism was an atheistic, evil, anti-God political ideology. These beliefs became deeply ingrained in the hearts of the Korean Christian community.

Yet, the Story of Life that had formed the anti-imperial historical consciousness of the Korean people could not be fully subdued. Part of the Christian community has made a spiritual and political discernment in resisting empire and militarization joining other Christian and diverse faith communities in the world. As Christians around the world pray and organize for justice, peace, and integrity of creation joining hands with diverse faith communities across the world Global Empire has sought to justify its deadly ways by cloaking its operations in fundamentalist religiosities of all types.

Korean Spiritual Responses to U.S. Empire

The following are some of the episodes of the Story of Life:

1. 2019 is the centennial anniversary of the Korean people's resistance against Japanese imperial domination. Masses of Korean people, including some Korean Christians in a leading role, waged a spiritual struggle of resistance against Imperial Japanese colonization, including its forced emperor worship.

2. 1973 Theological Declaration of Korean Christians supported the Korean people's active resistance to the military dictatorship of Park Chung Hee, which was the product of the Korean division and of the Cold War regime dominated by the U.S. military. Their resistance was a demand for democracy and at the same time a rejection of the national division.

3. 1988 Declaration of the Churches of Korea for National Reunification and Peace expressed the spiritual commitment of the Korean Christian community to the struggle for democracy, peace, and national reunification and thereby reaffirming the spirit of the March 1, 1919 Independence Movement.

4. Statement Towards a Nuclear-free World (WCC Busan Assembly, 2012) unconditionally upheld a nuclear-free world.

The following are some of the main features of spirituality that have been manifested in the history of the Korean people as they resist the militarized might of empire. These features can create space for spiritual convergence for radical transformation toward peace for life together.

1. Spirituality as the Subjecthood of All Living Beings: All living beings are blessed as the inheritors of great peace. Biblical faith in the Creation, New Creation, and Omega Point of Creation converge with Korean spiritual traditions for the coming together of all living beings in a Fiesta Convivencia.

2. Resistance as a Spiritual Act of Affirmation for All Living Beings: Affirmation of the selfhood and subjecthood of all living beings for a cosmic convergence of peace is in effect a resistance against the reality of Thanatography.

3. Convergence of Spiritualities for Creative Transformation in Korea: The Donghak tradition of convergence for creative transformation was the historical paradigm of the nineteenth century Korean people. A new call has come to us today.

The March First Independence Movement was a paradigm of envisioning and resistance, with a creative vision of peace through the convergence of the following eight streams of Korean spirituality:

1. Original Vision (Tangun Saga) of Universal Benevolence, True Conviviality, and Great Peace in Fullness of Life.

2. Ecospirituality of Seon (Cosmic Peace).

3. Buddhist Maitreya (Messianic Nirvana).

4. Confucian Vision of Peace (The Heart of the People is the Heart of Heaven).

5. Donghak Vision of Cosmic Transformation for Unity of Life.

6. Christian Vision of Heavenly Lord and Messianic Peace.

7. Radical Vision of Freedom inspired by League of Nations, incubated by Western Liberal and Christian Movement.

8. Social Spirituality of Justice influenced by Socialist Revolutions.

Spiritual convergence can lead to radical creativity for transformation. Now we need a historic moment of Kairos (Breaking-in New Historical Era) with the creation of a convergent spirituality for peace on the Korean peninsula—opening a new horizon not only for the Korean people but for the people of East Asia and throughout the world, where all are invited to a grand Madang (a central gathering space for communicating, sharing and celebrating) for a "fiesta of conviviality." What is needed is a cosmic convergence of spiritualities for peace and life together in our universe, through the creative work of a global circle of prophetic witness in ecumenical communion, among African and Black spiritualities of peace, American Native spiritualities, Asian spiritualities, Pacific spiritualities, and West Asian spiritualities. I see the collection of essays in this book as an attempt to respond to that need. In the present global geopolitical context, a particularly urgent focus for convergence is the Palestinian people's ongoing spiritual resistance for peace.

When we gather in the Cosmic Madang for a fiesta of life together in our peacemaking processes, we will experience (1) restoration of right relationships (justice), (2) healing and restoration of conviviality, (3) reconciliation through spiritual action, and (4) peace and life together.

Conclusion: A Planetary Convergence for the Fiesta of Life Together

Vision of New Cosmos Overcoming Pax Romana

Then I saw a new heaven and a new earth; for the first heaven and the first earth had passed away,... And I saw the holy city, new City of Salem, coming down out of heaven from God, prepared as a bride adorned for her husband; and I heard a loud voice from the throne saying, "Behold, the dwelling of God is with People. He will dwell with them, and they shall be his people, and God himself will be with them; he will wipe away every tear from their eyes, and death shall be no more, neither shall there be mourning nor crying nor pain any more, for the former things have passed away." (Rev 21:1–4)

And he who sat upon the throne said, "Behold, I make all things new." Also he said, "Write this, for these words are trustworthy and true." And he said to me, "It is done! I am the Alpha and the Omega, the beginning and the end. To the thirsty I will give from the fountain of the water of life without payment. He who conquers shall have this heritage, and I will be his God and he shall be my people. But as for the cowardly, the faithless, the polluted, as for murderers, fornicators, sorcerers, idolaters, and all liars, their lot shall be in the lake that burns with fire and sulphur, which is the second death." (Rev 21:5–8)

Biblical Vision of the New City

And I saw no temple in the city, for its temple is the Lord God the Almighty and the Lamb. And the city has no need of sun or moon to shine upon it, for the glory of God is its light, and its lamp is the Lamb. By its light shall the nations walk; and the kings of the earth shall bring their glory into it, and its gates shall never be shut by day—and there shall be no night there; they shall bring into it the glory and the honor of the nations. But nothing unclean shall enter it, nor anyone who practices abomination or falsehood, but only those who are written in the Lamb's book of life. (Rev 21:23–27)

Covenant with All Living Beings, Overcoming Pax Babylon

Then God said to Noah and to his sons with him, "Behold, I establish my covenant with you and your descendants after you, and with every living creature that is with you, the birds, the cattle, and every beast of the earth with you, as many as came out of the ark. I establish my covenant with you, that never again shall all flesh be cut off by the waters of a flood, and never again shall there be a flood to destroy the earth." And God said, "This is the sign of the covenant which I make between me and you and every living creature that is with you, for all future generations: I set my bow in the cloud, and it shall be a sign of the covenant between me and the earth. When I bring clouds over the earth and the bow is seen in the clouds, I will remember my covenant which is between me and you and every living creature of all flesh; and the waters shall never again become a flood to destroy all flesh. When the bow is in the clouds, I will look upon it and remember the everlasting covenant between God and every living creature of all flesh that is upon the earth." God said to Noah, "This is the sign of the covenant which I have established between me and all flesh that is upon the earth." (Gen 9:8–17)

Covenant of Peace, Overcoming Pax Babylon

I will make with them a covenant of peace and banish wild beasts from the land, so that they may dwell securely in the wilderness and sleep in the woods. And I will make them and the places round about my hill a blessing; and I will send down the showers in their season; they shall be showers of blessing. And the trees of the field shall yield their fruit, and the earth shall yield its increase, and they shall be secure in their land; and they shall know that I am the LORD, when I break the bars of their yoke, and deliver them from the hand of those who enslaved them. They shall no more be a prey to the nations, nor shall the beasts of the land devour them; they shall dwell securely, and none shall make them afraid. And I will provide for them prosperous plantations so that they shall no more be consumed with hunger in the land, and no longer suffer the reproach of the nations. And they shall know that I, the LORD their God, am with them, and that they, the house of Israel, are my people, says the Lord GOD. And you are my sheep, the sheep of my pasture, and I am your God, says the Lord GOD. (Ezek 34:25–31)

These spiritual visions of cosmic peace against imperial peace emerge out of the bosom of Christian particularity and have a universal appeal. Similarly plurality of spiritualities among diverse faith communities across the globe does have such visions of peace that have a universal appeal. Convergence of these spiritualities gives us imagination and power to overcome Pax Americana to proclaim and live our Story of Life, Life in Abundance, through continuous resistance to the imperial peace, which is at permanent war not only with human beings, but also with the whole planet.

Chapter 8

Plurality of Faiths
and Dialogue for Just Peace

A Call to End Violence in Mexico and Beyond[1]

DAN GONZÁLEZ ORTEGA

Then the LORD *said to Cain, "Where is your brother Abel?"*
He said, "I do not know; am I my brother's keeper?"
(Gen 4:9)

They answered him, "Abraham is our father."
Jesus said to them, "If you were Abraham's children, you would
be doing what Abraham did, but now you are trying to kill me."
(John 8:39–40[a])

Introduction

DURING 2003 I WROTE an essay titled: "Globalization of Violence:
Rereading of Judges 19 from Eyes of the Murdered Women in Ciudad
Juarez." It was published in 2004 after some modifications that took into
account the developments during that year and I used the neologism
"femicide." One of the key arguments of the text in 2003 was a hypothesis,
but as time went on looking at the developing circumstances in Mexico

---

1. This paper was originally written in Spanish and was translated by Samuel E.
Murillo Torres.

155

I was able to convincingly state the following: killing women without apparent reason was part of a perverse strategy where criminals were engaged under the immutable gaze of authorities at all levels of the state. I suspected that this way of spreading violence seemed like a laboratory where people experimented with death and fear to achieve a macabre type of governability in a small town in northern Mexico, Ciudad Juarez. I was very surprised when, starting in 2006, the Mexican far-right government called for a "war against drug cartels," opening the "Pandora´s box" that plunged the country into an endless violence. The army on our streets has brought death after death through an uninterrupted wave of violence. Common sense tells us that you cannot put out fire with fire. However, the excess of power that was experimented in Ciudad Juarez was spread out to the entire national territory consolidating a form of government through death and fear. The results were instantaneous. Scores of civilians were killed everywhere. Thousands were made to disappear. All of these were considered just "collateral damage" necessary to kill delinquents and put an end to organized crime.

Remembering Jesus' words to those who wanted to assassinate him, according to the narrative of the Gospel of John 8:31, I call this form of government "apoctocrático," a government built on murder and fear. Perhaps that is why in the language of Jesus "fear" is the fundamental opposite to "faith." Jesus' constant invitation is "do not be afraid," but "have faith" in the face of an empire, that is, "son of his father the devil because he is a murderer from the beginning." Jesus calls us to be "keeper of our brother" and of our sister, strengthening us in faith. Faith dispels fear and confronts violence with the view of achieving peace, which is the focus of my contribution to this collection of essays.

Churches' Journey towards Peacebuilding

The visit of Pope Francis to Israel in May 2014 has left evidence of the importance of the role of religions in building peace. The call he made to the political leaders of Israel and Palestine is more than just a diplomatic gesture by the Vatican state to the two states who are in permanent conflict. It also means a deep public and political witnessing to faith, not only in God, but also in humanity. This action of the Bishop of Rome confirms the veracity of the words of the Swiss Catholic theologian Hans Küng who in his proposal to go towards a world ethic that builds peace affirms: "There will be no peace among nations as long as there is no peace between religions." In the twenty-first century, speaking of peace is to appeal to a deep ecumenical commitment and a strong interreligious cooperation. This ecumenism is built on the exchange of Christian perspectives that have in common the values of the ethics of Jesus and the awakening of the common human values of peace through interreligious cooperation.

The modern ecumenical movement was built thanks to the great spiritual and theological stimulation of Protestantism in the twenty-first century. Meetings of leaders from Baptist, Methodist, Presbyterian, and Anglican churches in Sweden and the United States resulted in very dynamic movements such as the Young Men's Christian Association (YMCA), the Young Women's Christian Association (YWCA) or the World Student Christian Federation (WSCF). These are spaces that exist today as a testimony to the great commitment of people like the Methodist layperson John R. Mott, Nobel Peace Prize winner in 1946, who upheld that the goal of Christian unity is the service to humanity. The "centrifugal" force of this movement had its fruition in the so-called World Mission Conference of Edinburgh 1910, which laid the foundations of the Christian ecumenical movement that led to the organization of the World Council of Churches (WCC) in 1948 as an effort to collaborate in building peace in the aftermath of WWI and WWII.[2]

In the scope of the Roman Catholic Church, we also find a strong ecumenical opening from the pontificate of John XXIII, the "Good Pope," with his proposal to walk towards the "aggionamento," through Vatican II, to open the windows of his church to get fresh air through the recognition of the contribution of the rest of the churches and Christian traditions. At the council the active presence of the Protestant voice through theologians such as the Latin American Methodist José Míguez Bonino was highly significant for peace among the churches. From a Protestant perspective, the result of Vatican II, with regard to the ecumenical dialogue is still ambiguous because of the Roman Church's "centripetal" impulse to invite "the separate brothers" to return to the bosom of its church. However, it was a promising starting point in envisioning a broad horizon of relationships and dialogue that has been strengthened and expanded subsequently over the years.

2. The history of the global ecumenical movement can be consulted at https://www.oikoumene.org/en.

Definitely peace has been the bulwark through which religions have managed to agree, evidenced by the formation of the first World Assembly of Religions for Peace (WARP) in Kyoto in 1970.[3] This is the broadest and most representative organization with efforts to influence the peacebuilding processes through interreligious cooperation:

> From the point of view of Religions for Peace, nothing is as important as working together to face the most critical problems of our times. It is an urgent need to build cooperation mechanisms and platforms at all levels because coordinated efforts enable the strengthening and expansion of our actions in favor of peace, justice and sustainable development. Interreligious cooperation shows a powerful force through which religions can contribute more significantly in the construction of peace, prevention or transformation of conflicts and be an active voice for a world without discrimination, injustice or destruction of the planet.[4]

With the above historical steps that motivate us we can start a new journey to engage in further ecumenical dialogue and interreligious cooperation that confronts violence fearlessly and build peace in the world through a "shared security" against politics of "national security" that tends to become "apoctocráticas." This is of paramount importance at a time of the rise of both religious fundamentalisms within all religions and far-right nationalist forces in many countries across the world that divides and destroys humanity. These forces instill fear within us and amongst us as opposed to faith in the divine and human. They represent just the opposite of faith, that is, fear.

For this reason, my contribution will be based on a moderately maieutic methodology where I do not intend anything else, but to invite the reader for a reflection on three questions discussed below. I do not intend to reach conclusions on these quasi-existential questions, but simply to ask them aloud in case it helps someone else in the world to reflect on these issues deeply and proactively.

---

3. The history of this movement can be consulted in https://rfp.org/wp-content/uploads/2017/09/Kyoto-Declaration-Final-Draft.pdf.

4. Conrado, "Manual de Capacitación," 7.

The Three Questions: Peace in Christianity Enriched by the Encounter with Buddhism

In what way can religions recognize their internal contradictions and admit that their original ideals and struggles of peace have been contradicted by a history of violence?

The Buddhist option for nonviolence is known in two key words: "To be pacified and to pacify (to be peacemakers)." Other religions would tune in to it too. But let's face it. One thing is the ideal to which religions aspire, but the historical reality is another thing. Each one has betrayed that ideal throughout its history. The Eighth World Assembly of WARP held in Kyoto from August 25 to 29, 2009 denounced the ways in which religions are manipulated and kidnapped by fanaticisms, extremist believers, unscrupulous politicians, and sensationalists. The theme of this conference was "Confront all Kinds of Violence: Advancing Shared Peace/Security." Its central concern was the ambiguous relationship between religions and violence. This conference made a commitment to peace four decades ago, but since then violence has increased. In many cases, it was provoked and nourished by fanatical ideologies in the very bosom of religions. With the theme "Confronting Violence" those of us who were called to this new assembly in 2006 were faced with three urgent challenges:

a. How do we to bridge the gap between the religious and the economic–political worlds so that we could cooperate with one another in building peace?

b. How do we mediate concretely to accompany the peace processes?

c. What are the ways in which we can self-criticize violence within religions to purge them of exclusivism outwards and inwards, "inquisitorialisms?"

The role of interreligious cooperation in the processes of pacification within the contexts of transitional justice was a key theme in this assembly. After the social trauma caused by human rights violations, both by brutal state repression and counter-violence of the militant groups, the paths to peace are often long, vulnerable and painful, and require a determined will of reconciliation in all parties involved. The punitive approach to compensatory justice is not enough. The final statement of the assembly emphasized a perspective of restorative, reconciling, and rehabilitating justice. The past has to be remembered in order to avoid a repetition. Taking responsibility for the past actions is necessary to build a new future. It is only through such actions fear of each other can be dispelled. To this end the initiatives taken up in recent years in various parts of the world (Sierra Leone, Rwanda, Bosnia, South Africa, etc.) should encourage us to capitalize on the resources of interreligious mediations in peace processes. The actions for peace should not be reduced to a mere prayer for peace. In fact, for religions to cooperate for building peace, an exodus is necessary. Each religion should give up itself. There are two common features in every religion. They all inherit traditions of peace, but they all betray these traditions with violence. In what way can we understand and overcome this contradiction?

Are self-criticism and reform within each religion doomed to failure?

The Catholic Church took a radical turn towards reforming itself in the days of Vatican II. However, half a century later a new counter-reform has caused a painful situation and unearthed the schisms that were buried. Will self-criticism and the urgent reform of the church be renounced or will uniformity and homogenization triumph under the pretext of unity?

A Buddhist spoke to me in the assembly in Kyoto about a spirituality of mysticism that is common to all religions. He said that "just as in a very different time and culture, when it comes to quenching our thirst and cultivating plants we need water either from rain, wells or rivers." Water is a metaphor for a spirituality of fearlessness based on faith that hopes for peace which needs to be accentuated in uniting us and fostering cooperation. Who does not want it? Soon after the initial optimism of discovering through dialogue what unites us we run into a contradictory reality. Within every religion there is fear of the other and arrogance that blinds them to reform and self-criticism. Isn't self-reflection the most fundamental human activity in every religion that combines faith with reason and gives some sense to faith?

In addition, with the good intentions of fostering unity there is a tendency to promote uniformity. Nowadays, everyone is invited by the White House to drink the same Coca Cola and from the Vatican to sing the same Gregorian Latin. The metaphor of water, used by my Buddhist friend is appropriate to talk about life and spirituality. It is one thing to be fed by water that is absorbed by similar roots or for the leaves and petals to be blessed with rain, but it is totally a very different thing to insist that all trees, flowers, and fruits are the same. In fact, such claims forcibly impose one's specific religion or tradition on the other. These aquatic metaphors also suggest "vitivinicultural" (wine production) allusions, for example, about the quality of "fancy wines." In Japanese, "ji-zake" means "wine of the country." When some Japanese visited Mendoza in Argentina they learned the secrets of wine making, but they could not take to Japan the sun, water, and air of that land in the luggage. The same applies to Japanese rice wine from Osaka. Water, chemically speaking, is always H_2O. But the local flavor of the respective wines depending on water, sun, and air of the land is non-transferable. Similarity and sameness have two different meanings. It is diversity that makes mutual growth and enrichment possible. Fear of the other can be overcome with this realization.

In religions, local plurality is their richness. Spirituality is not watered with distilled water. In each place, over time as the water flows downward from the spring—depending in what kind of regions it flows—it gets contaminated and loses the original flavor. Sometimes it can be poisonous to drink. There are places where water could be of good quality. These places may be foreign to us, but the contact with what is foreign makes us realize our own deviations and instills in us the urgency of self-criticism and reform. We have to go through an exodus of self-criticism to reach the "Pentecost" of our mutual transformation.

For Judeo-Christian and Islamic traditions will the encounter with non-theistic religions like Buddhism help reform or cause lockdowns within each one's walls?

I hesitated in formulating this third question. It seemed more appropriate or politically correct to refer either to Judaism or Islam. Certainly. However, in paraphrasing Paul Ricoeur, although we can have friendly relations with many people we cannot have an unlimited number of intimate friends.[5] This happens with religions as it happens with languages. If I know only my own language I do not even know mine well. Knowing at least one or two different languages I open myself to the transformation of mine, but to do so with three or four other religions—with the same familiarity that I have with Christianity at least for thirty-eight years—I would need to prolong my life beyond one hundred and fifty years! Evidently this is not possible. That is why I take one example, that

---

5. This is a phrase written originally in French on a wall under the title "Fonds Ricoeur" in the library of the Institute Protestante de Théologie of the University of Paris, France.

is, Buddhism, but without claiming to know it thoroughly or overvalue it or give preference to it over the other religions.

Buddhism like all others has its brightness and darkness and we have to acknowledge both these sides. On the one hand we observe that even a religion so well known for its emphasis on nonviolence has also fallen into violence (e.g. Sri Lanka, Burma, Japan). Will the encounter with Buddhism be fruitful in the next decades in contributing to Christian self-criticism? In the first place, Buddhism can correlate inner calm with social harmony; to be pacified and to pacify (to be peacemakers) and, thus, get out of the anomalous atmosphere of tension in which we live in our society and in our Christian Churches. Secondly it can help rediscover silence in the face of an excess of words and explanations. In Sanskrit, "Upaya" means something like "salvific resources" in different languages with which the "dhamma" is preached according to the capacity of each listener. There are not three or four different vehicles, but varied ways of leading each person to the discovery of the unique secret of life. To save all of humanity a unique truth is announced with different languages. Buddhism can teach us to relativize all languages and the value of silence. I do not share the concern of those who are afraid of relativism.[6] I am more afraid of dogmatism than relativism, especially in countries like ours in Latin America, which are prone to impositions of quasi-dictatorial religious systems.

Third, Buddhism gives us the capacity for tolerance, which is necessary to rid ourselves of the excesses of dogmatism, fanaticism, and fundamentalism that some western traditions have propagated for centuries. Finally, Buddhism can help rediscover something as evangelical as the practice of compassion, tenderness, and *agape* that free us from resentment, exclusivism and discrimination. The main question is whether we are prepared for such a dialogue. *Will we go through a Paschal exodus of self-criticism that leads us towards a communicative Pentecost in which we let ourselves be nourished and enriched mutually by our encounter with other sister religions?*

Prayer as Critical Self-Reflection of Praxis

A Buddhist friend once told me something that has been spinning in my head for at least eight years. "If we just taught our children to meditate

6. See Jediminas, *Dictatorship of Relativism*.

properly we would be able to eradicate violence in only one generation." I still have these words in my mind because they challenge my commitment as a Christian. How do I intend to build peace if I do not pray? How could I pretend that violence can be stopped if I do not motivate my children to pray and pacify their own life and their spirit? Prayer here means self-reflection that deepens faith and dispels fear. There is no doubt that the violence that we experience in our lives obscures our faith, but it is prayerful self-reflection and meditation that brings clarity of mind and heart and fathoms solidarity with others who seek ways to overcome violence and build peace.

There is a symbolic expression with which we Christians often clothe ourselves since it is an imperative for the identity given directly by Jesus as an inheritance to his believers; "Being Light" (Matt 5:14–16). Jesus as a true human being demands from his followers what he himself claims to be; "I am the light of the World" (John 8:12). This religious stamp can get us into some complications if we do not understand it in its rightful context. Although it is true the light "is not to be put under a box," but on the candle stand, for very obvious reasons, the purpose of the light is to give brightness to see clearly the place where it is illuminated. However the temptation is to hope that the light becomes an end itself. The light does not serve its purpose, but rather it becomes the main element of contemplation or bluntly speaking the light expects others to look at it rather than at the space it illuminates. If this is so light loses its function and can be destructive as it causes people to be dazzled and blinded.

Considering the violence with which we live in Mexico and the violence that shakes the whole world it is indispensable that those of us who consider ourselves believers in Jesus follow his example as a light in the midst of darkness. The church's intention cannot be to become just the point of attraction and glorification, but to turn into a small tool at the service of the innumerable victims of violence who struggle with life hoping for a different future that overcomes death and destruction. In fact, light means nothing less than fearless faith that confronts the cult of violence. One can be a light through prayerful self-reflection of the relationship between one's self and one's society and instill faith in each other to overcome violence. Prayer always has to have a praxis; a struggle for peace. In that sense prayer becomes a means and/or testimony of solidarity with those who are afflicted by violence.

In general, people associate Buddhism with silence and reflective meditation. However, the recitation and intonation of the teachings have been particularly important in the history of Buddhist practices. The voiced articulation, which manifests the faith and the religious oath in the form of a prayer, is a visible act or a witness for others. Nichiren Daishonin Buddhism emphasizes the intonation of prayer as an essential posture rather than silent meditation. To put it differently the outer expression invokes the inner reflexivity. Unlike a mere intimate spiritual abstraction the religious practice expounded by Buddhism focuses on raising the highest inherent potential that human beings have, within a given society, for the benefit of humanity and all other living beings. Nichiren used to quote the maxim of an ancient Buddhist philosopher who says: "The voice carries out the task of the Buddha." This interrelationship between inner and outer reality of our existence can awaken Christians to engage in socially engaged reflective prayer in the face of violence. Christianity often has a tendency to proclaim itself with numerous words as the light of the world without critically reflecting what it means to be that light in a given context. There are too many words without depth. In fact, what Buddhists remind Christians of is not totally new. Christianity has a tradition of mysticism of service, which needs to be retrieved, and Buddhism helps us to do so. By coming to know the other deeply I come to know myself better. This is the spirituality of contemplation and struggle that Dom Helder Camara upheld in his life during the brutal dictatorship in Brazil.

Prayer frequently leads the believer to experiences of "ecstasy" which is called "heaven" (in Japanese "ten"). This word defines the plane where the celestial beings live and also is translated as "deity." Originally it meant "brightness" in the sense of radiating light. In Buddhism, this "sky" is not conceived as a place where one's life ends after death, but as a state experienced in life at every moment. The world of celestial beings means the state of satisfaction that people experience when they realize their desires. This is what I want to connect to prayer. Prayers are shouts of light where good wishes turn into flashes of hope for the people who suffer continuous violence of all types. Prayers have to be embedded in the struggle of all those who aspire for peace that makes life livable. Brightness is not meant to dazzle us, but to illuminate and allow us glimpses of hope that provide us with alternative exits from the existing impasse of the cycle of violence. Reflective prayer constitutes celestial spaces in what sometimes perishes like a "hell" in our midst. As this brightness dispels darkness fear is overcome. Faith is strengthened and the hope flourishes.

May our collective voice, the multicolored clamor from all corners of the world, be the one that makes again the miracle of resurrecting the hope of peace through reflective prayer. Religions, but even more, religious expressions such as prayer should be opportunities to build solidarity that bring peace and eradicate violence. It is this spiritual dimension of faith based on reflective prayer that must be the one that supports the public action of those who profess the Christian faith. Without cultivating a spirituality based on contemplation and struggle which is nothing but the experience of faith on a daily basis it will be difficult to create ecumenical ties with other Christian traditions as well as build cooperation with other religious traditions. I return to my introductory point that was inspired by Hans Küng. "There will be no peace among nations if there is no peace between religions."[7] However, I want to go further. I believe that there will be no peace between the religions if we do not engage in religious practices that invite us to prayerfully reflect on the interrelationship between the inner and outer world of our life in society that has been conditioned by the politics and culture of violence. Without realizing this interconnectivity there cannot be peace in the world. I exist, not because I think. I exist because we exist! This is the light of faith that prompts us to see clearly and act justly to build peace.

Overcoming Barriers for Enhancement

If we analyze the Mexican context, except for some very modest local initiatives,[8] the Christian Churches and religions in general do not have organized ways to cooperate collectively in supporting, monitoring, or accompanying peace processes. We prefer to work alone and to accentuate differences. Therefore what we do is so little that it looks like we do nothing. It is like hiding a lamp that shines! The obstinate religiosity and the mutual ministerial jealousy that make us believe that we are the only bulwarks of truth and benevolence have prevented us from developing ecumenical unity between the Christian Churches and cooperation for peace between religions. I insist as in the previous section that this is the result of a lack of systematic cultivation of spiritualities that could

---

7. Interfaith Peacemakers, "Roman Catholic Theologian."

8. There are some notable small initiatives such as the Center for Ecumenical Studies, Churches for Peace, and Youth Network of Religions for Peace with Justice and Dignity.

promote solidarity in diversity. If we speak about Mexican Christianity the churches do not have a joint way of being attentive to the current issues and situations that allows us to be prophetic in responding to the cries and hopes of millions of afflicted people in this land. As long as we do not have a united voice we cannot be prophetic in giving hope to our tormented people.

The lack of unity among Christian Churches prevents developing broad articulations and alliances with the sectors of other religions and civil society to work together to eradicate violence and build peace processes. This happens frequently because of the difficulty we have in interpreting policies and the way of understanding the dynamics of civil society organizations (NGOs). Rather than singing as a symphony moved by the cries and hopes of our people we produce a cacophony that confuses them. In Mexico, it seems that the Christian Churches have not managed to build strategies of public and political advocacy that allow consistent engagement in the sociopolitical life of the communities and in society as a whole. Without joint efforts, sustainability of individual church activities is not possible. The crisis is collective and the responses have to emerge through togetherness.

When some ecumenical organizations, churches or religions carry out programs or activities for peace there is no significant diffusion. There is no presence of these initiatives in the media and this is because there is no efficiency in the plans of advocacy, publicity, and social communication. One of the main weaknesses in this sense is the lack of capacity among the churches, religions and their institutions of theological or religious education to organize systematic, continuous, and articulated programs for peace that could efficiently develop a civic awareness of social responsibility. Building capacity is always a collective effort, which needs to emerge out of a rethinking of what it means by faith in the face of violence that presents itself as inevitable, absolute, and therefore inescapable. Moving beyond strictly theological, spiritual, political knowledge as well as rigid institutional allegiances the churches and religions should engage in a serious conversation on how faith, in whatever way it is expressed matters, in the conjuncture of society, politics, economics, ecology, etc. in humanizing the society. It is through such a deep and decisive reflection that the organizational limitations can be overcome.

A Possible Roadmap towards New Horizons

The crisis of our society is a clear reflection of the crisis of our various religious affiliations. In response to this worrying situation, let me introduce some ideas that adopt a Christian perspective arising from my particular Christian tradition linked to the Mexican Protestant tradition, not as a triumphalist exaltation, but as an exercise in self-criticism and a possible roadmap that can be considered for a conversation. Each one has to start from where one is situated and enter into a broad conversation with each other to broaden our horizons for a joint struggle for peace.

The gospel of peace which is the life of Jesus and his emphasis on love and justice challenge the Christian Churches to awaken themselves to the ethical and social potential in their faith that gives them credibility in standing for peace and nonviolence. When the churches participate in peace initiatives it is this potential that gives consistence and coherence to their testimonies of faith through their speeches, actions and programs. The churches, according to the biblical tradition and theology, are communities of human beings and one of their strengths is to be generators of peace which implies giving an evangelizing witness that transmits and spreads the values of Jesus so that his faithful participate in social processes and actions for peace in all places where they are present. In other words, proclamation of Jesus Christ is standing for peace in the Mexican context that confronts the cycle of violence. Churches generate a sense of belonging to a group, which gives a sense of security against the powers that perpetuate violence. This sense has to be activated by the leadership of each "*Comunidad de Base*" (Base Ecclesial Community), parish, and neighborhood church in calling the people to participate in actions, movements, and networks of solidarity through prayerful reflection that strengthen the testimony of faith by demanding justice and equality that can lead to peace. It is only by doing so that the church communities can become places of sanctuary for the afflicted ones who find strength and hope in the midst of grief and despair.

As the churches gather people together in groups or communities it makes it possible to raise awareness and generate processes of participation in social and political actions for justice and peace, and thereby build bridges between different sectors or social networks who are engaged in the struggle for peace. Churches should use written and audiovisual media as well as electronic media in a coordinated manner to disseminate and encourage initiatives that promote a culture of peace. There is a lot of human talent within the church, which should be harnessed together in transmitting hope in the society. Often many Christian Churches do maintain international networks of relationships with many ecclesial and ecumenical communities which can be mobilized in building solidarity across the borders that strengthen local and global initiatives for peace.

Many churches, especially of the Protestant style, have deep pacifist roots. A good example of this is the churches that come from what is called the radical reformation of the sixteenth century. Churches like the Anabaptists have inherited deep convictions because of their origins. They have given testimony to a radical understanding of faith:

a. Solidarity with the suffering of Christ.

b. The total renunciation of the "I" (individualism).

c. To be strong until martyrdom.[9]

d. Practice of clandestine baptism of adults.

e. The simplicity of liturgy prioritizing companionship and community.

f. The life of faithful lay people dedicated to prayer.

g. High emphasis on fasting, faith and prayer.

Particularly the "Mennonites" were firmly opposed to violence, use of weapons for any purpose, military service, and even to civil service. They separated themselves from the coercive structures of society by refusing to carry arms, serve in the army, pay taxes for war, and swear or accept the office of magistrates. They defended religious tolerance including towards Jews and "Turks"[10] and upheld economic justice as acts of faith for which they developed a deep solidarity with the poorest. They promoted strict equality among their members and were extremely anti-clerical and anti-aristocratic. The emphasis of this spirituality was on the notion of the "inner light" in the form of an intuition or special spiritual sensitivity that guided the life of the believers. In this sense, they realized prayer as a "seeing" the inner light, which is a critical self-reflection of the praxis which is geared towards peace. These churches have a great openness, but above all wide and deep experience, in generating, promoting, convening and mobilizing dialogues for peace. In some instances, they have given

---

9. These Christians were brutally repressed and persecuted by both Roman Catholic and other Protestant Churches (Lutherans and Calvinists).

10. A common way to refer to "Muslims" during the sixteenth century.

leadership to promote peace processes in conflict-ridden countries. They consider giving such leadership as a God-given ministry.

An openness to developing common objectives ecumenically as well as interreligiously cannot be created without understanding the spirituality of people who are victims of violence. It is they who provide us with the motivation towards peace and reconciliation. It is in them that the churches can meet Christ who is journeying with them in building peace. It is this journey that unites the churches that are called to the same task of peacebuilding in diverse ways. Churches have an active role in being agents of hope in the midst of despair and in the recovery of the self-esteem and dignity of people as well as in building capacity to develop community bonds and encourage the formation of networks of cooperation for peace. This is what is meant by the proclamation of the Risen Christ. This is how one loses one's religion and becomes a light. When one drinks from the deep down wellsprings of faith one is nourished to be free to act fearlessly, ecumenically, interreligiously and universally. The testimony of faith is strengthened when we come together in fostering healthy ecumenical relationships that are respectful of differences, but animated by faith, dialogue, hope and love. Defending the dignity of every human being and the integrity of life makes us one with those who are in pain and strengthens our bonds of sisterhood/brotherhood and solidarity with them and with diverse churches and faith groups.

Being builders of peace is a demand of the gospel for the Christian people. This is achieved through the daily practice of just relationships based on the God-given dignity of every human being. Believers should not resign themselves and wait for God to "judge" evildoers in an apocalyptic future while injustices increase uninterruptedly day by day. Actions and programs to counteract the systems of oppression, repression and cycles of violence and reclaim dignity, justice and equality must be here and now. The Reign of God is here and now and at the same time it is a journey guided by the Word and the Spirit of God. The Spirit blows wherever she wills. The Word is proclaimed in a loud prophetic tone as well as in a mystic's silence. Consistency in action accompanied by patience leads us to breakthroughs. Overcoming violence is not a single act, but a life journey; a journey of a people.

Confronting violence demands creating social alternatives where the afflicted people get involved with the handling of conflicts, changing attitudes, and generating dialogues not only in the political and social sphere, but also in the ecumenical and religious context. There have to be short, medium and long range plans and goals of this journey. The total eradication of violence will be the result of the sum of processes planned and enacted over time, but each step taken every day makes up the journey towards that end. We bear witness to a widespread cycle of violence both by the state security agencies and non-state actors. It has conditioned our lives to the extent of violence becoming the norm in our day to day relationships making us as a society increasingly fragmented and lacking in the collective strength to confront the powers within us and around us. Truth, justice and memory constitute the cry of the victims. Yet, every little action we take can be gratifying and reveal the infinite presence of life-mystery. The vulnerability we experience can be the trigger of collective strength that pushes us towards a unified action towards shared security.

Conclusion

In Mexico, the Movement for Peace with Justice and Dignity has called on the people to respond to the prevailing violent situation as a "national emergency." However, without diluting the strength of this statement I would say that the "emergency" is not only national, but also global.

Beside the violence that we live with in Mexico we find outbreaks of violence on the continent, in Venezuela and Brazil in recent days and in the entire Mesoamerican region. We hear on a daily basis reports of war and violence in India, Syria and Yemen to name a few. Violence against African American people in the USA has triggered large-scale protests, which are being repressed with scores of arrests and threats of military measures by the country's leadership. From a Christian perspective the metaphor that can be given to this situation is "darkness." "The world is in darkness" and we need the light of hope to move on with life. A biblical principle that has become a Protestant (Calvinist) slogan reads as follows: "*Lux Lucet in Tenbris,*" that is, "The light shines in the darkness." "The world is the scene of the Glory of God." From the faith perspective of the most classical Protestantism it is impossible to believe or be satisfied that darkness can prevail over light in the world. Those who believe in Jesus Christ, in fact, have to affirm the commandment to bring light to where someone dwells in darkness.

On November 13, 2012, on the day of my birthday, it was a great honor for me to celebrate the Hindu festival of "Deepawali," Festival of Lights, that commemorates the death of Narakasura at the hands of Krishna and the release of sixteen thousand maidens that the former had imprisoned. From there began the tradition of lighting a multitude of lights during the night. The symbolism of the festival consists of the need of the human being to move towards the light of "The Truth" from ignorance and unhappiness, that is, to obtain the victory of "dharma" (virtue) over "adharma" (loss of virtue). In a true sense, light here means liberation, liberation from captivity. In 2012, as an act of interreligious gesture, the Roman Catholic Cardinal, Jean-Louis Tauran, President of the Pontifical Council for Interreligious Dialogue made an appealing invitation to the youth:

> At this point in time in human history when various negative forces threaten the legitimate aspirations in many religions of the world for peaceful coexistence we would like to use this cherished tradition of sharing with you a reflection to explore the responsibility that Hindus, Christians and others have in doing everything possible to form all people, especially the young generation, into peacemakers.[11]

These words resound again and again in my ears every time I hear of a husband who is violent to his wife, or of an adult who abuses a child, or of a military attack on any population or when I read about organization of "self-defenses" in the towns of Michoacán and Guerrero as the last resort to resist crimes and the inefficiency of the state.

The right to live in peace based on justice is the very essence of every religion in the world. Therefore it is our right as citizens of the world and as spiritual people from any religion to oppose any type of violence that denies justice and jeopardizes harmony and peace that every person deserves. We cannot allow femicide in Ciudad Juarez, violent racism against the African Americans, killing and rape of Rohingya people, attacks on Dalits, Adivasi people, Kashmiris, and Muslims in India, black and indigenous people in Brazil, and war against women and children in Syria and Yemen. In all these places religions play a crucial role.

Now, what is the greatest challenge of Christianity and religions in the face of violence? It is building peace between religions through a prayerful critical self-reflective praxis where faith is strengthened ecumenically and interreligiously that dispels the fear of the other. Neither the so-called "Christian West" nor the "Islamism of the Middle East"

---

11. Tauran, "Vaticano."

represents a faith that dispels darkness and unites people in solidarity with the most afflicted ones. Instead, these exclusivist religious entities propagate fear, death and destruction. Amartya Sen notes:

> Even the frantic Western search for "the moderate Muslim" confounds moderation in political beliefs with moderateness of religious faith. A person can have strong religious faith—Islamic or any other—along with tolerant politics. Emperor Saladin, who fought valiantly for Islam in the Crusades in the twelfth century, could offer, without any contradiction, an honored place in his Egyptian royal court to Maimonides as that distinguished Jewish philosopher fled an intolerant Europe. When, at the turn of the sixteenth century, the heretic Giordano Bruno was burned at the stake in Campo dei Fiori in Rome, the Great Mughal emperor Akbar (who was born a Muslim and died a Muslim) had just finished, in Agra, his large project on legally codifying minority rights, including religious freedom for all.[12]

Islam (total surrender to God) and salaam (peace) are inseparably interconnected. Shalom in Hebrew and Jesus' first greetings after his Resurrection "Peace be with you" resonate with the same meaning. When you surrender to God and to no other power you are at peace with yourself and with the other and you do not trample anyone. Instead you stand with the one whose humanity is oppressed. From the perspective of women, the Network of Muslims for Peace states as follows:

> Jihad means "fight or strive on the path to God." We are dedicated to fight any form of violence—especially that carried out in the name of Islam—in all its scales: from violent extremism to gender violence, we, as female Muslims, must reclaim the mantle of cultural, intellectual and religious authority, declaring our opposition to violence with an energy and unified voice.[13]

There is a dangerous trap here. There is a tendency to vilify only Islam as a tradition that violates the dignity of women without a self-criticism of all religions and societies, which do so. Such prejudices against one tradition can justify wars and further divide the world. War in Afghanistan was justified partly on the claim to "liberate" women. No one can bomb a people towards liberation! All the religious traditions are highly patriarchal. In fact, in them we find seeds of femicide. We do not

12. Sen, *Identity and Violence*, 15–16.
13. Muslim Network for Peace, *Jihad against Violence*, 9.

worship man, but God. Faith can brighten our lives as long as we realize this truth. As long as violence against women in whatever form continues there will be no peace on earth. In other words, worship of One God means an end to violence against women by all religions. Religions have to liberate themselves through the light of faith by identifying fully with the victims of violence, both within and outside religions.

All churches and all religions have, in themselves, difficult battles to fight "ad intra" and "ad extra" to recognize the fundamental human dignity of all and affirm peace. We will have to get rid of the negative dogmatisms that threaten our faith and darken its light. We have to protect the waters of faith that nourish our relationships with one another. It is only then shared security becomes a reality. A shared security articulates security needs, the way in which they are met, and the agents, instruments and relationships necessary to achieve it. To a large extent, shared security would emphasize the collective responsibility of all people to meet our common security needs. Shared security requires that all sectors of society recognize our common vulnerabilities and our shared responsibility to address them. It is undertaken collectively by multiple actors who recognize that each sector of society must confront violence if we hope to do so effectively.

On the political level shared security cannot be achieved without participatory and collective forms of government. Governments, international organizations, civil society and religious communities themselves can promote shared security equally. Effective shared security extends beyond the boundaries of geography, nationalities, ethnicities and religion. Shared security is radically different from state-driven security. The latter protects a few at the expense of the multitude of peoples. As Jesus said fearlessly before Pilate that his kingdom is not of this earth, the peace that all faith traditions enshrine emerges from a prayerful critical reflective praxis of a people's struggle where Jesus Christ lives. States and political movements that do not respond positively to such people's struggles will not last long as all the mighty empires collapsed like the Roman Empire. Building peace is not an easy task, but it is a task that we must prioritize if we consider ourselves as a people linked to some spirituality or proclaim to be part of a faith group. Christianity (Roman Catholic, Orthodox, Protestant or Pentecostal) as well as other religions of the world (Judaism, Christianity, Islamism, Hinduism, Buddhism and so on) have a great historical task which cannot be put to one side, that is, to join the people's struggle for human dignity and peace. This necessitates ecumenical dialogue and interreligious cooperation, which nourishes and strengthens each other's faith and generates fearlessness in the face of oppression and violence.

With such a standpoint I would like to call on the new Mexican government. "Mr. President Andrés Manuel López Obrador, 'The military to their barracks!' was your campaign promise. No to the law of internal security! No to the National Guard! Stop the war! No more arms! Enough of disappearances! Stop femicide! No more fear! No more blood! Not in our name!"[14]

---

14. Spanish statement: "Así que, desde acá, un llamado apremiante al nuevo gobierno mexicano . . . Señor presidente Andrés Manuel López Obrador: 'Los militares a sus cuarteles', fue su promesa de campaña. ¡No a la ley de seguridad interior! ¡No a la guardia nacional! ¡Alto a la guerra! ¡No más armas! ¡Basta de desapariciones! ¡No más miedo! ¡No más sangre! ¡No en nuestro nombre!'"

Chapter 9

"Walking in Evil"

*Liberation and Dialogue
through Afro-Brazilian Capoeira*

Erin Shea Martin

"Capoeira is our fight from the colonial era . It was born in Bahia Angola and Regional. It's a game practiced in the land of São Salvador."

"My father came from Angola, eh eh My mother came from Angola, Angola Angola eh eh, Angola is Angola Oh, I came from Angola Angola eh eh Angola is Angola."[1]

"Forward"

I FIRST WROTE THE majority of this article as my dissertation for a Masters of Philosophy in Intercultural Theology and Interreligious Studies at the Irish School of Ecumenics in 2017. At that time, I viewed my academic work through the lens of my previous professional experience working with refugees in the United States, Turkey, and Jordan. Because I was studying interreligious dialogue, the theme of the paper focused on

---

1. These two capoeira songs show the different understandings of its development (Brazilian vs. African).

interreligious liberation. Now, as I am writing and thinking through the major themes of the paper—violence, oppression, dehumanization, resistance, and humanity—people all over the United States are protesting the brutal State-sponsored murders of Black men and women. For the last two and a half months, the novel coronavirus has sent us to our homes because many of us recognized its danger, taking shelter and extra precautions against it. We have failed, however, to see the dangerous and lethal illness of white supremacy that has ravaged this land and people for centuries.

I do not know what will have happened between the time I write this paper and the time that you read it, but as a white person from the United States, I cannot begin without urging readers to become involved and support Black lives in this country. I may be preaching to the choir or more accurately to the minister, but I urge you to become engaged in local initiatives to defund police and fund community safety.[2] Many people have been working for a long time to rechannel funding from our police forces to projects that would much better serve and protect by funding our basic human needs—shelter, food, clean water, health care, education. We cannot move forward without humanizing Black and Brown lives in our legal system, our criminal "justice" system, our military policy, our foreign policy, our education, our housing, our taxation system, and so many other aspects of our shared civic life. Most urgently, we cannot continue to fund the police apparatus that continues to take Black lives.

This country began for some people as a cry for "liberty," but liberation is impossible as a selective act. A country founded on stolen land with stolen bodies is not the land of the free. There is no liberty while Black men and women are killed with impunity by our police; there is no liberty while Black and Brown people are rounded up and jailed or deported; there is no liberty while Black and Brown women's disappearances go uninvestigated; there is no liberty while Black and Brown people are enslaved by a violent economic system. Enough is enough. Black lives matter. Our white supremacy is fatal. Our world can be better; let us build it together.

---

2. There are many organizations all over the United States that are working to defund police and fund Black and Brown life. Some include Black Lives Matter, Black Visions, Reclaim the Block, Al Otro Lado, and local bail funds. This is specific to the United States, but given the context during which I revised this research, I chose to include a call specific to the context.

Introduction

Human life begins in relationship with other human life, but a social, political, economic, and cultural system establishes a narrative of human existence that begins and ends with alienation.[3] Within this context, "either we discover again and anew the neighbor in flesh and blood or we are heading toward a disaster of cosmic proportions."[4] When alienation replaces proximity as the norm of human life, the human encounter in plural societies becomes treacherous, reflected in systems of social domination, militarization, and racialized oppression. At the crossroads of alienation, oppression, and plurality, people require a different way of being in the world that liberates from oppression and dialogues across cultures, religions, ethnicities, and races. This paper examines the twin objectives of liberation and dialogue through the work of Enrique Dussel and Raimon Panikkar and explores the Afro-Brazilian art of capoeira as a way of being together in plurality that resists alienation and oppression. Capoeira was formed as a mode of resistance to the dehumanizing institution of slavery. It reflects the creativity, genius, and resilience of the African diaspora at the periphery of a system of domination, a liberative imagination continued today in many communities seeking to dismantle the current dehumanizing realities of militarization and racialized oppression.

Enrique Dussel and Raimon Panikkar: Becoming Human

Definitions of the human person—who is included and from whose perspective we understand what it means to be human—often reflect the dominance and violence of oppressive systems. Criticizing common definitions of the human person, Enrique Dussel and Raimon Pannikar attempt to reconstruct and redefine our humanity. Enrique Dussel, drawing from political philosophy, examines the history of the philosophical tradition from Pre-Socratic times to the current postmodern period to expose the ways in which philosophy of the human person is the product of unjust social orders. Given the contextual nature of all philosophical discourses, he calls for a critique of the philosophical tradition and for the establishment of philosophical discourse at the margins of society

3. Dussel, *Philosophy of Liberation*, 49–58.
4. Panikkar, *Intrareligious Dialogue*, xv.

that can contemplate the reality of life beyond the rim of social power. In a different way and drawing from the Buddhist, Hindu, and Christian mystical traditions, Raimon Panikkar considers the current definition of the human person: the person as either object or subject. Panikkar understands the human person as neither, but rather as being-in-relation. Panikkar calls for a more holistic understanding of the human person that does not deny the rational part of her character but rather transcends this emphasis on a mere part to regard the person as a whole. Dussel concentrates on social relationship whereas Panikkar devotes his efforts to interpersonal/intrapersonal relationship; I posit that understanding both contribute to liberation.

Enrique Dussel: Becoming Human through Liberation

Enrique Dussel asserts that the philosophical tradition examines the human condition and defines the human being from a place of social privilege[5]: the *ego cogito* ontology "did not come from nowhere. It arose from a previous experience of domination over other persons, of cultural oppression over other worlds. Before the *ego cogito* there is an *ego conquiro*; 'I conquer' is the practical foundation of 'I think.'"[6] Using the language of "center" and "periphery" to speak about people afforded or denied social freedom, Dussel contextualizes the philosophical tradition in social entitlement, developed as a justification of ruling classes and social privileges. The philosophies of the center produced ontologies of the human person that were a reflection and justification of their social standing.[7] Being human then becomes commensurate with being in power.[8]

Taking the reality of the center as the only reality, the philosophical tradition defines personhood accordingly:

> For Aristotle . . . the Greek was human. The European barbarians were not human, because they were unskilled; nor were

---

5. Dussel confronts the geo-political, economic an political context of the history of philosophy, but in order to avoid cumbersome adjectives, I will refer to the complex social, cultural, geo-political, economic, and political context with the term "social" throughout this paper. For Dussel's critique, see Dussel, *Philosophy of Liberation*, 3–4.

6. Dussel, *Philosophy of Liberation*, 3.

7. Dussel, *Philosophy of Liberation*, 4.

8. Dussel, *Philosophy of Liberation*, 4–5; Freire, *Pedagogy of the Oppressed*, 47–48.

the Asians human, because they lacked strength and character; slaves were not human either; women were halfway human and children were only potentially human. The human being par excellence is the free man of the *polis* of Hellas. For Thomas Aquinas, the feudal lord exercised his *jus dominativum* over the servant of his fiefdom, and the man did the same over the woman . . . For Hegel, the state that bears the Spirit is the "dominator of the world," before which all other states are "devoid of rights."[9]

The people of the center are; the people beyond their frontiers are not.[10] It is only natural that the periphery be at the disposal of the center. If Being is, then beings only "are" in relation to those who "Are." The development of this ontology depended on the subjugation of people at the margins of a social system.

Dussel sets out to "take space, geopolitical space, seriously"[11] and demonstrates that the philosophy of the human person is never without social context. When the context for the development of philosophy of the human person is dominating and oppressive, ontology often supports the system out of which it was produced. A philosophy that identifies "Being with the ruling system"[12] consecrates social order as natural. When Aristotle claimed, "the slave is a slave by nature,"[13] he identified the social with the natural order and social dominance became the nature of the enslaved person. If in order to be fully human, a person must embody the characteristics of the elite of a social system, the problem is not restricted to reforming a broken social system but is also a problem of false consciousness. The "classic ontology of the center" instilled in the people of the center and the periphery a definition of the human person that perpetuated social domination and oppression.[14] In light of the

9. Dussel, *Philosophy of Liberation*, 4–5.

10. Dussel, *Philosophy of Liberation*, 5–6: When "Being, the divine, the political, and the eternal are 'one and the same thing,'" those who exist beyond the margins of social power become "things, tools, instruments."

11. Dussel, *Philosophy of Liberation*, 2.

12. Dussel, *Philosophy of Liberation*, 7.

13. Dussel, *Philosophy of Liberation*, 6.

14. Dussel acknowledges that throughout the history of the philosophical tradition, voices from the periphery arose: "Pre-Socratic thought appeared not in Greece but in Turkey and southern Italy, from a political periphery (they were dominated), from an economic periphery (they were colonies), and from a geopolitical periphery (they were threatened by the armies of the center). Medieval thought emerged from

contextual nature of philosophy, Dussel demonstrates that an adequate philosophy of the human person contemplates the reality of oppression "not from the perspective of the center of political, economic, or military power but from beyond the frontiers of that world, from the periphery."[15]

Dussel's analysis of the human predicament focuses on social exclusion in the form of economic exploitation, political domination, and military intimidation to expose philosophy for what it is: a human endeavor. Nothing human escapes its context and its desire to justify any power it possesses. However, Dussel also sees that "a philosophy of liberation is rising from the periphery, from the oppressed, from the shadow that the light of Being has not been able to illumine."[16] This philosophy sets out from oppression and carries the possibility of liberation. If, as Dussel claims, the "classic ontologies of the center" continue to hold sway in the minds of the marginalized and oppressed as well as the oppressors, philosophy of liberation must also change mindsets and expose philosophies of the human person as justifications of exploitation. In this case, it is a matter of conscientization and necessitates a pedagogy that can overcome the pervading false consciousness about the nature of the human person.

Raimon Panikkar: Becoming Human through Dialogue

Whereas Enrique Dussel understands exploitative social systems as the central hurdle to a fuller humanity, Raimon Panikkar sees the false sense of separation from one another as the central issue. For Panikkar, the blend of extreme individualism and cultural and religious plurality leads him to advocate for neighbors and strangers to find their way back to one another, across borders of nationality, ethnicity, race, religion, or

---

the frontiers of the empire; the Greek fathers were peripheral, as were the Latin fathers. Even in the Carolingian renaissance, renewal came from the peripheral Ireland. From peripheral France arose Descartes, and Kant burst in from distant Königsberg" (Dussel, *Philosophy of Liberation*, 3–4). However, "those who had to define themselves in the presence of an already established image of the human person and in the presence of uncivilized fellow humans" consistently turned their philosophical eye from the periphery towards the center rather than considering the reality at the margin itself (Dussel, *Philosophy of Liberation*, 4). Therefore, while peripheral, these philosophies cannot provide a philosophy of the person for those who suffer social marginalization because it does not consider their reality. Instead, it continues to place importance on the reality of the center. The problem is still a false consciousness of the human person.

15. Dussel, *Philosophy of Liberation*, 9–10.

16. Dussel, *Philosophy of Liberation*, 14.

ideology.[17] He contends that misunderstanding the basic reality of the human person has led humans away from one another. When human relationships are reduced to the *Ich/nich-Ich* (I/non-I) relationship, humans inevitably see in one another a total Other. Reducing the human to the I/non-I dichotomy in a world of individualism and plurality engenders a definition of the human person where to be human is "to be like me."

Key to dismantling the I/non-I consciousness is understanding that "our relationship with the other is not an external link but belongs to our innermost constitution."[18] The other person is neither an external "object" of knowledge nor an external "subject" of sentiment, but is rather already a part of the Self and a Self in their own right. The awareness that the other is "not my ego and yet . . . belongs to my Self" makes dialogue and communion among people possible.[19] The false consciousness of the I/non-I gives way and "the thou emerges as different from the non-I."[20] However, the development of the awareness of I/Thou relationship must "overcome both the Cartesian dualism of the *res cogitans* and the *res extensa*, and the idealistic dichotomy of the *Ich* and the *Nicht-Ich*."[21] In other words, the I/Thou relationship depends on the ability to transcend the perceived opposition of rationality and corporeal being as well as the opposition of Self and Other.

In order to develop an understanding of the Thou, Panikkar outlines the ontonomous relationship of Self and Other. The Thou is "neither autonomous vis-à-vis the I nor dependent heteronomically on it. It presents a proper ontonomical relation, that is, an internal relation constitutive of its own being."[22] The human only is insofar as it is *with* other human beings. Therefore, to be aware of Self is also to be aware of the Thou that resides within; it is to be aware that I cannot exist without Thou. False consciousness places the Other as completely external to the Self and Panikkar calls for a "consciousness [that] is not only I consciousness, but it entails also a thou-consciousness, that is, not my consciousness of you but 'your' consciousness, you as knower, irreducible to what you (and I)

---

17. Panikkar, *Intrareligious Dialogue*, xv.

18. Panikkar, *Intrareligious Dialogue*, xvi.

19. Panikkar, *Intrareligious Dialogue*, xvi.

20. Panikkar, *Intrareligious Dialogue*, xvi. Panikkar is also drawing on the work of Martin Buber and his development of the I/Thou relationship. See Buber, *I And Thou*.

21. Panikkar, *Intrareligious Dialogue*, 25.

22. Panikkar, *Intrareligious Dialogue*, 25.

know."[23] Becoming aware of the Thou within the Self entails changing a mindset that Self and Other are ontologically separate.

Developing this thou-consciousness furthermore depends on "piercing, going through the logical and overcoming—not denying— it."[24] The dialogical reality that Panikkar proposes transcends the objective world of rational knowledge and the subjective world of sentimental experience in order to arrive at a human consciousness that can speak to the reality of the whole person. The "whole person" cannot be reduced to any one faculty of humanity nor can it be simply the sum of its parts. The Cartesian dualism that understood thinking as coextensive with Being therefore took one human faculty and transformed it into a totality. If "to think" is identical with *to be*, then the only people *who are* are those who *think*. Within plural world, it is a short step then to *the only people who are are those who think like me*.[25] The problem of Cartesian dualism therefore must be overcome by seeing the whole person as beyond "the objective world of the *it* [and] the subjective world of the ego."[26]

Panikkar fundamentally aims to dispel a false consciousness based in tearing asunder what belongs together; the whole human person is beyond objectivity and subjectivity and the Other lies within the Self. To heal the divided world then is to overcome the false consciousness of I/non-I and *res cogitans/res extensa*. Acknowledging this consciousness as false and developing an I-Thou consciousness that sets out from the whole person is a question of pedagogy. If Panikkar calls for a change of this magnitude, an accompanying method for transforming consciousness is necessary. The way forward, for Panikkar, is to practice the I/Thou relationship through dialogue.[27]

---

23. Panikkar, *Intrareligious Dialogue*, 25.

24. Panikkar, *Intrareligious Dialogue*, 28.

25. In addition, when the philosophy of the human person erases bodily experience in favor of the intellect, systems that subjugate bodies become more tolerable. If a person's personhood is located in her mind, what happens with her body is less significant than the capacity of her mind. This is a topic for another paper, particularly as it applies to racialized oppression, but worth mentioning as a part of the *res cogitans/ res extensa* paradigm.

26. Panikkar, *Intrareligious Dialogue*, 25.

27. Panikkar, *Intrareligious Dialogue*, 39.

Dussel and Panikkar: Becoming Human under Militarization

While Panikkar and Dussel write from different perspectives, method-ologically and contextually, both indicate alienation as a key problem: Dussel understands alienation as the domination of peripheral peoples whereas Panikkar takes alienation to be the I/non-I relationship. Both authors expose a false consciousness about the nature of the human person and urge that human peoples become aware of the false sense of humanity and the way in which it perpetuates alienation. Together, Dus-sel and Panikkar present a philosophy of the human person that speaks to the context of militarization.

Panikkar urges people to develop an I/Thou consciousness, wherein the Self and the Other are not wholly without one another, but are co-constitutive. However, when the Thou and the Self are related within an oppressive context, the I/Thou relationship can be repressive. If the Thou of the relationship benefits from a social structure and ontology that af-fords it Being while the Self is oppressed by the same social structure and ontology as non-being, then the I/Thou relationship is not as simple as finding the Thou within. For the non-being, the Being already resides within, dominating through an unjust social structure and ideology of personhood.

Paulo Freire describes the consciousness of the oppressed as dual because "they are at one and the same time themselves and the oppres-sor whose consciousness they have internalized."[28] Dussel describes how philosophy of the human person "was the theoretical consummation of the practical oppression of the peripheries" and was later instilled as the way of being human in the minds and lives of those at the center and the periphery.[29] Likewise, Freire posits that the oppressed "live in the dual-ity in which *to be* is *to be like* and *to be like* is *to be like the oppressor*."[30] Therefore, if within the consciousness of the oppressed, the oppressor lurks, regularly defining them as non-being, the I/Thou relationship can reinforce this false consciousness. Encouraging people to find the Other within their Self without also critiquing the domination of some as Being over others as non-being reasserts an oppressive consciousness.[31]

28. Freire, *Pedagogy of the Oppressed*, 48.

29. Dussel, *Philosophy of Liberation*, 3.

30. Freire, *Pedagogy of the Oppressed*, 48.

31. Dussel aptly describes the difference between people from the center and those from the periphery by relating it to a game of cat and mouse: "The cat can make a

Within the context of militarization, communities need a way to counteract and abolish the false consciousness instilled by systematic violence and oppression. Development of a new consciousness is a pedagogical task that calls for praxis. Capoeira, formed at the periphery of a time of extreme militarization and domination, is a pedagogy of resistance to social domination, militarization, and oppression.

Capoeira: A Brief Introduction

In order to understand how capoeira is a pedagogy of resistance, it is essential to have a basic understanding of what capoeira is. Practitioners and academics alike acknowledge the development of capoeira within the milieu of slavery. However, historical accounts of capoeira are written from the perspectives of European slave owners, colonizers and tourists who misunderstood and belittled the lives of African capoeira players (or *capoeiristas*). Labeling the art form as a "dance," "martial art," or "game" was the only way in which people foreign to the ritual of capoeira knew how to define it.[32]

Most scholars and *Mestres*[33] place the origins of capoeira in the Kongolese and Yoruban cultures of Western Africa while maintaining that as it is practiced today, capoeira was shaped by the experience of slavery.[34] Some theorize that enslaved African people planning rebellions had to disguise their training with music and dance to go undiscovered by European slave owners while others assert that capoeira was a ritual that was already a part of the enslaved peoples' Yoruban and Kongolese cultures.[35] It is very difficult to pinpoint with academic certainty the precise origins of capoeira, but capoeira was unequivocally formed within

---

mistake; it is only toying with its prey. But the mouse cannot make a mistake; it will be its death" (Dussel, *Philosophy of Liberation*, 14). I do not suggest that a conversation between two people of different social standings is a game of cat and mouse, but the dynamic is present in the interaction.

32. Talmon-Chvaicer, *Hidden History of Capoeira*, 3.

33. A *Mestre* is a capoeira master and generally the head of a capoeira school or academy. The process of a capoeirista becoming a Mestre differs widely among the different schools, but generally only Mestres can declare a capoeirista a Mestre. Typically, a person practices capoeira for 20 years or more before becoming a Mestre (Lewis, *Ring of Liberation*, 63; Capoeira, *Little Capoeira Book*, 146).

34. Talmon-Chvaicer, *Hidden History of Capoeira*, 3–4; Almeida, *Capoeira*, 3–5.

35. Talmon-Chvaicer, *Hidden History of Capoeira*, 3–4; Rörhig-Assunção, *Capoeira*, 5–6.

the context of the massive forced enslavement of people from Western Africa whose experience of slavery and cultural heritage mark capoeira today.[36]

Most capoeiristas and Mestres recognize that capoeira was a resistance to the completely dehumanizing institution of slavery. Capoeira was a way for enslaved African people in the territory of Brazil to assert, remember, and teach the inhumanity of the system of slavery. Today, Mestres frequently refer to capoeira as "a way of being" and emphasize that "capoeira training transforms practitioners' comportment in everyday life so that the cunning they learn in the game orients them outside it as well."[37] As examined below, capoeira is therefore a pedagogy of resistance to the inhumanity of extreme domination—slavery, militarization, and police states.

The *roda* is the central practice and aim of capoeira. Literally meaning "wheel," the roda refers both to the circular formation in which capoeira is played and to the unchoreographed movement of two capoeiristas in the middle of the circle set to capoeira music.[38] Though it can take different configurations in different schools, generally two players enter the circle and move around each other; they offer kicks and dodges or simply move together to become accustomed to each other's movement, but usually attempt to stay within arm's reach. The movement is

36. Talmon-Chvaicer, *Hidden History of Capoeira*, 3, 7–48. See also Capoeira, *Little Capoeira Book*, 3–10; Almeida, *Capoeira*, 11–23; Rörhig-Assunção, *Capoeira*, 31–44; Lewis, *Ring of Liberation*, 18–50.

37. Downey, *Learning Capoeira*, 7. Mestre Acordeon, a Brazilian Mestre teaching in Los Angeles, defines capoeira as "a way of living that has given me a better perspective on the game of life." He recalls speaking with the two "fathers" of modern capoeira—Mestre Pastinha and Mestre Bimba—and asking them, "what is capoeira, Mestre?" Pastinha replied, "capoeira is whatever the mouth eats." Mestre Bimba, on the other hand answered, "Capoeira is treachery." Mestre Acordeon interprets their answers as complementary: "For Pastinha, the wise Mestre loved by so many because of his affable personality, it is whatever the mouth eats—all the things that come in life. For Mestre Bimba, the giant with a strong personality . . . Capoeira is treachery, the way of dealing with the dangers of life" (Almeida, *Capoeira*, 3). Whether it is "treachery," "whatever the mouth eats," or "a way of living," capoeira, for those who practice it, moves beyond the boundaries of training and informs the way that they live.

38. Lewis, *Ring of Liberation*, 237. This paper does not focus specifically on the musical element of capoeira, but it is important to note that music and song are integral to capoeira. Lyrics from capoeira songs tell important stories and lessons from the period of slavery and provide the commentary on the capoeira game. See Lewis, *Ring of Liberation*, 133–61 for an in-depth description of capoeira music.

spontaneous and unchoreographed and can incorporate kicks, dodges, acrobatics, and dance movement.[39]

Each capoeira roda, unique and unrepeatable, is created by the improvisation and connection of the players; the movement in the roda can be aggressive or harmonious, awkward or in sync, exciting or boring.[40] By playing close and being ready for any action—kick, playful gesture, silly dance, deadly swing—from one another, capoeiristas cultivate a game that relies on continually responding to new and different movement in an unexpected way. Any player who repeatedly responds to a particular element of the roda in one systematized way will eventually be taught the lesson of improvisation the hard way: a Mestre or another capoeirista will recognize the pattern and take advantage of it, often knocking the player to the ground.[41] Capoeiristas frequently express that in a "good roda" the unexpected happens and because both players move in unanticipated ways the movement of the roda belongs to both capoeiristas.[42] Capoeira unfolds in this shared construction of movement and its ability to teach "a way of being" lies in the sustained participation of the players in the unexpected and unknown action of the roda.

Capoeira as a Pedagogy of Resistance

For centuries, capoeiristas have embodied a resistance to the militarization and domination that Dussel and Panikkar examine in their theories. Capoeira contains specific pedagogical elements that teach a "way of being together" that fosters a consciousness of the human person that resists the alienation and oppression of the militarized context.[43] The qualities

39. Downey, *Learning Capoeira*, 167. See also Lewis, *Ring of Liberation*, xvii–xxiii; Downey, *Learning Capoeira*, 1–6; and Talmon-Chvaicer, *Hidden History of Capoeira*, 140–49. There are rituals, social queues, and nuances whose description will not fit in these pages; I encourage the reader to watch the YouTube videos to get a better sense of what capoeira looks like when played in the roda.

40. Lewis, *Ring of Liberation*, 86–89.

41. Downey, *Learning Capoeira*, 121.

42. Downey, *Learning Capoeira*, 112–13.

43. In defining the pedagogical elements of capoeira, I am in danger of forming capoeira in the image of Panikkar and Dussel's thought and of simplistically comparing hermeneutics, epistemology, and praxis with a complex "way of being" in the world. Although I construct an argument relating *aspects* of capoeira to *aspects* of Dussel and Panikkar's theories, I urge that capoeira is neither completely contained in the elements I explore here nor are all of the characteristics of the game I explore present

of capoeira examined here are analogous to pedagogical aspects of Panik-kar and Dussel's theories although the roda does not conform to their specific academic arguments. Because liberation and dialogical dialogue are a transformation of humanity, Panikkar and Dussel's theories require a pedagogy if they are to effect practical change. Although every roda, studio, and Mestre is different (or even conflicting), I outline basic char-acteristics of capoeira that teach Panikkar and Dussel's philosophies.[44]

Malícia: A Hermeneutics of Suspicion

Malícia is the foundation of the capoeira game and Mestres describe it as capoeira's philosophy.[45] Malícia shares the same Latin root as *malice*, but is better translated as *deception, cunning, trickery,* or *suspicion*.[46] Nestor Capoeira describes malícia:

> a mixture of shrewdness, street smarts, and wariness . . . It may be said that malícia has two basic aspects. The first is knowing the emotions and traits—aggressiveness, fear, pride, vanity, cockiness, etc.- which exist within all human beings. The second is recognizing these traits when they appear in another player, and therefore being able to anticipate the other player's move-ments, whether in the roda or in everyday life. The player who is malicioso is able to dodge under an opponent's kick and prepare for a counter-attack or a takedown before the assailant finishes what he started. In everyday life, he should be able to recognize

---

in every capoeira roda, studio, Mestre, or capoeirista. Capoeira and academic thought belong to different systems of knowledge and experience and trying to see in one a reflection of the other runs the risk of simplifying and constructing meaning that may not be present.

44. I do not claim that capoeira was designed to teach these theories (indeed its practice predates the theories by centuries); nor do I not mean to validate capoeira through Dussel and Panikkar's theories. Rather, I assert that characteristics of capoeira reflect elements of a pedagogy for liberation as outlined by Dussel and Panikkar's theories.

45. Mestre Acordeon describes capoeira as possessing "philosophical insights" and Nestor Capoeira dedicates an entire book to exploring the "capoeira philosophy." Almeida, *Capoeira*, 6; Capoeira, *Street-Smart Song*.

46. Capoeira, *Little Capoeira Book*, 32–33; Downey, *Learning Capoeira*, 123–25; Lewis, *Ring of Liberation*, 32–33; Talmon-Chvaicer, *Hidden History of Capoeira*, 166–69.

the real human being that hides beneath the social mask of someone he has just met.[47]

Malícia is the way of life that an enslaved person learned in order to survive within an abusive, oppressive, and dehumanizing reality.[48]

An examination of the fundamental kick benção demonstrates how malícia was a resistance to the total domination of slavery. Benção is a powerful blow to the solar plexus that often leaves a capoeirista devoid of breath and knocked to the ground but its name translates as "blessing." During the time of slavery, "both children and slaves were supposed to ask for a blessing (benção) on seeing the senhor (master), and he was expected to give it. The slaves were all too aware that the very master who was blessing them today could flog them tomorrow."[49] In a social system where benevolence disguises treachery, the blow of the kick is "compatible with the harshness of the system, both past and present, in which behind every blessing is a potential kick in the gut."[50] Malícia is the ability to see the blessing of the senhor for what it was: a blow to the center of the person. Underlying the practice of capoeira is the ability to unmask the actions of others. Within the system of slavery, the benevolence of the master's blessing was uncovered for the beating it was and in the roda, capoeiristas detect treacherous movement disguised as play or dance.

"Tripping up" or knocking down a capoeirista is a defining characteristic of the capoeira roda and "the ideal seems to be not to use force, but timing and knowledge: to apply gentle pressure at the right time to unbalance the opponent and cause him to fall."[51] Malícia takes the form of "deceiving or faking the opponent into thinking that you are going to execute a certain move when in fact you are going to do something

47. Capoeira, *Little Capoeira Book*, 33.

48. See Essien, *Capoeira Beyond Brazil*, xvii: "Capoeira fueled the souls of those held in the most horrific oppressive conditions. It energized their spirits to carry on, to overcome whatever obstacles they could. Capoeira nourished the existence of countless downtrodden spirits, helping to lift them about their given situation in order to live on . . . One of the fruits of their struggle is the fact that capoeira is still alive."

49. Lewis, *Ring of Liberation*, 31.

50. Lewis, *Ring of Liberation*, 32.

51. Lewis, *Ring of Liberation*, 91. In fact, there are few to no blows to the face using the hands or arms in capoeira and an obvious attack, even if it does bring a capoeirista to the ground, is regarded as inelegant, stupid, or even cowardly. See Downey, *Learning Capoeira*, 123–24.; Lewis, *Ring of Liberation*, 89–96; Capoeira, *Little Capoeira Book*, 30.

completely different and unexpected."[52] A capoeirista with malícia knows both how to execute a fake movement and how to uncover her partner's deceitful action. Malícia is distrust of any overt attack or retreat, aggression or passivity, ability or inability in the capoeira game. Through sustained training, capoeira inscribes "a pervasive wariness and distrust of the world" in the student.[53] Mestre Daniel Noronha describes this distrust as "walking in evil" because malícia develops a suspicious disposition towards a treacherous world.[54] A person with malícia uncovers niceties and blessings of a person and of the world for the danger and treachery they pose.

However, malícia "does not result from merely convincing a person intellectually that the world is a dangerous place. Capoeira as a form of physical education offers detailed practical lessons to a student about how to respond to dangers outside the roda."[55] By repeatedly entering the roda, the capoeirista learns to employ a hermeneutic of suspicion towards the world. In the roda, any movement is a disguise for an attack and capoeiristas learn to suspect each action as a mask, uncovering the possibility of attack that lies beneath. To suspect and react to the reality behind the mask of the kick or the blessing is the foundation of capoeira: "malícia, earned in the roda as in a hard life, is the antidote to naïveté; it is an essential skill for surviving."[56]

Malícia instills the essential ability to question the given that Dussel and Panikkar claim as a propaedeutic to the process of liberation and dialogue. Trusting a social system that oppresses and believing a cultural norm that alienates is dehumanizing for Dussel and Panikkar. For the capoeirista, the "cardinal character flaw . . . is to be too easily duped."[57] By playing capoeira, the person slowly develops (through bodily practice)

---

52. Capoeira, *Little Capoeira Book*, 33. The common practice of "faking" or *finta* can take a range of different forms: pretending to kick from the right side but following with a kick from the left; faking a kick that will cause one's partner to dodge and following it with a "dance" move, laughing at the capoeirista for being afraid of an unthreatening movement; or feigning innocence and inability by performing movements badly in order to lull the other capoeirista into a false sense of security and then taking advantage of their arrogance.

53. Downey, *Learning Capoeira*, 153.

54. Downey, *Learning Capoeira*, 153.

55. Downey, *Learning Capoeira*, 154.

56. Downey, *Learning Capoeira*, 123.

57. Downey, *Learning Capoeira*, 123.

the ability to suspect "the established, fixed, normalized, crystalized"[58] system. Dussel and Panikkar uncover the mask of oppression and alienation that distance human beings from a fuller humanity; and the capoeirista uncovers the mask of a kick or a dodge and reacts to the action beneath it.

Malícia, as "the perspective of the capoeirista, his way of facing life, the world, and other people,"[59] is a disposition of suspicion towards an overt reality, especially an apparently benevolent or natural one. Dussel calls for "the courage to be atheistic vis-à-vis an empire of the center" and outlines specific philosophical requirements to dismantle social systems, asserting that "there is no liberation without economics, without humanized technology, without planning, and without beginning with a *historical social formation*."[60] Panikkar explicitly attempts to cultivate a suspicion of both the Cartesian dualism and the I/non-I ideation, requiring that human communities learn a new and specific way of relating through the I/Thou relationship. Capoeira does not teach Panikkar or Dussel's critique of concrete systems, but its practice imparts a general *dispositionof suspicion* towards the given systems of social domination, including militarization and racialized oppression. Capoeira dismantles learnt understandings of the world by fostering a suspicion of the world that is analogous to a hermeneutics of suspicion.

Improvisation: The Essential Role of Faith

Dussel and Panikkar see faith as the foundation of epistemology; human knowledge of the world develops through an openness to and awareness of the unknown. Panikkar claims that faith is the "existential openness . . . to what one is not" that precedes all human knowing and Dussel asserts that only faith can access "the mystery of the other as other."[61] Both emphasize the vital role of faith for human knowledge and people require a concrete way to learn how to depend on faith as the basis for knowledge. Capoeiristas develop a reliance on faith in the unknown because improvisation is a central component of the roda. A roda never repeats itself and Mestres encourage students to be as unpredictable as possible

58. Dussel, *Philosophy of Liberation*, 59.
59. Downey, *Learning Capoeira*, 124.
60. Dussel, *Philosophy of Liberation*, 8, 63 (emphasis added).
61. Panikkar, *Myth, Faith, and Hermeneutics*, 46.

while playing capoeira.[62] Repeated patterns of movement in the roda are the antithesis of skilled capoeira play because adepts "anticipate an opponent's moves and shift to await an unfolding of vulnerability, already in place to seize any advantage."[63] Predictability increases the risk of being knocked to the ground and therefore students learn to move in increasingly spontaneous and unknown ways.

The capoeira repertoire that a student learns in the classroom is only useful in the roda insofar as the student can improvise and weave movements together in a spontaneous manner.[64] Both players in the roda attempt to be as unpredictable as possible and therefore capoeiristas learn how to respond to the unknown and move with the unexpected movement of the other player. The principle that learnt capoeira movement is "made to be broken" provides students with the consistent challenge of moving in unknown ways and reacting to the unknowable movement of other capoeiristas.[65] Developing knowledge of capoeira originates in the awareness of the unknown and unpredictable movement in the roda.

A capoeirista develops her knowledge of the capoeira game through an existential openness to the unfolding of the unknown movement in the roda. A kick or attack is best delivered when it cannot be anticipated and as capoeiristas attempt to "trip each other up" in the roda, they learn to respond to the unknown movement of the other. Perceiving a kick and "preparing for a counterattack or a takedown before the assailant finishes what he started" teaches the capoeirista that knowing how to move in the roda depends on openness to the unknown movement of the

---

62. Downey, *Learning Capoeira*, 121.

63. Downey, *Learning Capoeira*, 122.

64. Lewis, *Ring of Liberation*, 88–89: In the capoeira classroom, a student "practices a repertoire of named movements and learns how to defend against given attacks, how to attack given defenses. But in the course of actual play, it is up to a player to respond to each situation as he sees fit, even creating a new move on the spur of the moment if necessary. The emphasis on improvisation is related to the ethic of freedom or liberation central to the game." Lewis relates the improvisation of the roda to the principles of freedom and liberation and whether or not every capoeirista understands improvisation in this light, capoeiristas move in improvised, unexpected, and unprecedented ways in the roda.

65. Mestres actively encourage their students to move in unpredictable, unknowable ways because capoeira movement "is made to be broken, in a manner of speaking, either with a sudden surprise attack or with a breach in conventional patterns . . . The more one learns, the more one leaves behind strict dependence upon, and fidelity to, the model." Downey, *Learning Capoeira*, 107–8.

other person.[66] The capoeirista who has malícia sets out from faith in the yet unknown movement of the other and *then* knows how to respond. The roda is a place to which people can return regularly to learn how to create space within their consciousness for the unknown. Improvisation is foundational in the roda and the potential to learn awareness of the unknown is embedded in the practice of capoeira. Whether or not every student learns to depend on faith as a source of knowledge in the roda, the opportunity to learn to walk in the unknown is present when a student takes her place in the roda. A capoeirista's dependence on faith in the unknown movement of the other is analogous to Panikkar and Dussel's epistemology of faith.

Panikkar and Dussel speak specifically about the role of faith in forming knowledge of the world and the improvisational character of the roda suggests that capoeira has the capacity to inscribe faith as the foundation for knowledge as the capoeirista goes out into the world. Capoeira teaches the student not to shrink from a treacherous or unknown world, but instead teaches how to walk in evil, to walk in the unknown. The roda is a space where people can practice depending on faith in the unknown as they interact and dialogue with another person. Through existential openness in the roda, the capoeirista respects the other as capoeirista: source of improvised movement, cunning in his own right, and full of capoeira knowledge.

The Malícia of the Other: A Hermeneutics of Trust

Mestres reproach students for being too trusting and not "malicious" enough, but the antithesis of malícia is "naïveté" rather than trust.[67] On the surface, capoeira impedes the development of Panikkar and Dussel's hermeneutics of trust with respect to the other. A hermeneutics of trust primarily "acknowledges the plausibility and inner coherence" of the other[68] and although capoeira encourages the student to expect attack and distrust the movement of the other, it also teaches the student to acknowledge and be moved by the other. An attack in the roda infrequently elicits a direct opposition to or block of a capoeirista's movement and each player learns to create space within her capoeira game for the game

66. Capoeira, *Little Capoeira Book*, 33.
67. Downey, *Learning Capoeira*, 123.
68. O'Grady and Scherle, "Ecumenics in the 21st Century," 14.

of the other.[69] The ability to react to and move with another player in the roda approaches the notion of a hermeneutics of trust in the Other as understood by Dussel and Panikkar. Because the capoeirista trusts the knowledge and ability of the other player, he is suspicious of his movement; he trusts that the other has malícia and therefore must be wary of him.

If understood as the capacity to allow the other to disclose herself and allow that disclosed Self space within one's own consciousness, the game of capoeira is a physical expression of the I/Thou dialogue in some cases.[70] Moving in the roda employs a hermeneutic of trust with respect to the other insofar as capoeira counterattacks and attacks are mainly about manipulating existing elements of another player's style and movement rather than blocking and forcing the other's movement. A good capoeira player does not fully block an attack or halt the movement of the other player, opting instead for being moved by that player and counterattacking only after escaping an attack in order to preserve the flow of movement in the roda.[71] Because of the emphasis on escaping an attack and then counterattacking, capoeiristas learn to allow the movement of the other to shape their movement. In other words, the capoeira of the other shapes one's own; the capoeira knowledge of the other shapes one's knowledge.

69. Lewis, *Ring of Liberation*, 99–100.

70. Allowing the other space and movement in the roda can differ greatly among capoeira groups and is therefore not as dominant of a characteristic in every roda as malícia and improvisation. Downey, Lewis, Mestre Acordeon, and Nestor Capoeira also acknowledge the space that the other occupies in directing the roda, but emphasize the importance of controlling and even "dominating" the roda through restricting the movement of the other.

71. Lewis, *Ring of Liberation*, 99–100. "Attacks should not be blocked directly, but rather the player should escape from an attack first, then counterattack. This does not mean that there are no blocks in capoeira, but rather that they have reduced importance relative to escapes. A good player will divert the force of a blow with a block in order to protect himself while escaping, or he will block an attack before it is fully formed, to prevent that attack. Such a player will not counter the full force of a blow with a block unless there is no other alternative. This is partly because the emphasis on kicks makes many attacks so powerful that they are difficult or impossible to block effectively, but just as important is the maintenance of the give-and-take, the flow of the game. The emphasis on escape and counterattack reduces body contact and makes possible the dancelike interplay characteristic of beautiful capoeira. This is also the key to establishing the kind of 'turn taking,' typical of normal interchanges, that makes the dialogic, discourse model of the game especially productive. Finally, escape/counter is in tune with the general pattern of indirectness, central to the esthetic of malícia."

Capoeiristas employ a hermeneutic of trust towards the other insofar as they learn to make room within their consciousness for the other. Like Dussel's faith in the "word of the other," the capoeirista and her actions "cannot be comprehended completely or understood perfectly" and the unchoreographed roda allows capoeiristas to "reveal their exteriority, their alterity which reason can never scrutinize from within itself."[72] For Panikkar, humanity cannot "think" alone because "we need dialogue with the *thou* . . . 'I think' acquires its full meaning only in confrontation with what a 'you' . . . thinks."[73] Similarly, one cannot play capoeira alone; the capoeirista needs the "physical dialogue" with another capoeirista because capoeira only attains full meaning in dialogue with another person's way of moving in the roda. Capoeira is only possible when the human person who engages in it moves with the movement of the other as "the other reveals it."[74] Although capoeiristas infrequently express trust towards one another in the roda, the capoeira game teaches adepts to face the other and move "in conformity, harmony with, and/ or reaction to, stimulated by, and in dialogue with, other" capoeiristas.[75] The roda is a space within which people can practice allowing another to reveal herself and dialoguing with others in the fullness of their being.

The Whole Person, Face-to-Face

Dussel and Panikkar advocate for praxis that touches the whole human person and claim that human relationality is "the most essential reality of the person" and the basis of the reality of the Self.[76] Neither Panikkar nor Dussel construct a systematic definition of the human person and instead emphasize the importance of seeing the whole person. The whole person is irreducible to one philosophical characteristic, intrinsically interrelated to others, and part of a social and political system. Both theorists claim social and cultural systems alienate human life, ensuring a piecemeal understanding of the human person as individual unit, discouraging the development of the whole person in relationship. A praxis that shortens the distance between people is the founding act of

72. Dussel, *Philosophy of Liberation*, 46.

73. Panikkar, *Intrareligious Dialogue*, 36.

74. Dussel, *Philosophy of Liberation*, 46.

75. Panikkar, *Intrareligious Dialogue*, 36.

76. Dussel, *Philosophy of Liberation*, 21; Panikkar, *Intrareligious Dialogue*, 25.

liberation and dialogue; capoeira brings practitioners face-to-face with one another, whole person to whole person in the roda.

Dussel and Panikkar understand relationality as the fundamental reality of the human person and the roda provides an opportunity to practice approaching and remaining with the other in the fullness of their being. The roda is a "festival, banquet, liturgy, and *diakonia* of the community in jubilation, [an] originative and final reference" for capoeiristas.[77] It is a place where the I dialogues with the Thou and where neighbors find each other again and anew in flesh and blood. Because practitioners play capoeira face-to-face in close physical proximity, they experience the interdependence of their bodily movement. The capoeira game does not exist independent of the players and yet is not coextensive with them. By emphasizing that capoeiristas take the lessons of the roda out into the world, capoeira can teach people that "they are knots in the continuous weaving of the net of reality."[78]

Although not every capoeirista will see others holistically, it is a practice that touches the whole person, incorporating bodily movement, the mastery of malícia, faith in the unexpected movement, and respect for the other's capoeira game. Capoeira offers the student the opportunity to learn a hermeneutics of suspicion, develop faith in the unknown, and trust in the knowledge of the other through a physical dialogue. Face to face in the roda, capoeiristas have the opportunity to move beyond seeing the other as "just a producer of ideas with which we agree . . . or just a bearer of affinities that make possible a number of transactions."[79] When they move together into the roda, they are capoeiristas, whole, face-to-face. From this sustained experience of proximity, capoeiristas have greater opportunity to accept responsibility for the other and "desire for them the proximity of equals."[80]

Conclusion

Capoeira is a pedagogy of dialogue and liberation; its practice instills specific human capacities that Dussel and Panikkar detail in their theories: a disposition of distrust towards the given, faith in the unknown, trust in

---

77. Dussel, *Philosophy of Liberation*, 20; Capoeira, *Little Capoeira Book*, 32.

78. Panikkar, *Intrareligious Dialogue*, 39.

79. Panikkar, *Intrareligious Dialogue*, xvi.

80. Dussel, *Philosophy of Liberation*, 20.

the knowledge of the other, and regarding the Thou face to face with the Self. However, Dussel and Panikkar understand that dialogue and liberation are only possible when human people and communities are able to name what oppresses and alienates them. As capoeira has moved out of Afro-Brazilian communities, it was often commercialized and marketed as a fitness regime or a martial art for purchase by upper and middle class families.[81] Capoeira was often reshaped to fit the consciousness of new consumers of the practice, ignoring the fact that oppressive conditions within which capoeira was formed—slavery and colonization—continued to mark the current social reality in the form of social dominance, militarization, and racialized oppression.[82]

Conscientization of a community about a specific issue depends both on praxis and reflection according to Dussel and Freire; and for Panikkar, reason and dialectics regarding doctrinal and empirical aspects of culture are essential to dialogue. Reflection on specific social ills and dialectical engagement with doctrinal aspects of lived culture occur when engaged in direct conversation about social and political issues. Many Mestres and capoeiristas view capoeira as a tool for teaching students how to walk in evil and how to be in the world. They often refer to the roda as a metaphor for the wider world and its practice carries specific pedagogical elements necessary for liberation. As capoeira was commercialized and whitened, its social context was stripped from it

81. Talmon-Chvaicer, *Hidden History of Capoeira*, 177. See also Hedegard, "Blackness"; Capoeira, *Little Capoeira Book*, 17–18. Many capoeiristas, such as Mestre Pastinha, actively resisted the whitening of capoeira, seeking to retain its African roots but as capoeira was commercialized, it was whitened as it was marketed to middle and upper class white communities. See Talmon-Chvaicer, *Hidden History of Capoeira*, 176–79.

82. Capoeira was demonized and outlawed in Brazil prior to 1937 because State authorities actively criminalized cultures and peoples of African descent. When a capoeirista from Bahia, Brazil, named Manoel dos Reis Machado or Mestre Bimba founded an academy named Center of Physical Culture and Regional Capoeira in 1927, capoeira moved from the streets and covert practice to training in official studios, marking "the beginning of the institutionalization of capoeira as a sport" (Lewis, *Ring of Liberation*, 59–60). When Brazilian government officially adopted capoeira as the national sport in 1937, they saw it necessary for public authorities to actively remove capoeira's African heritage and transform it and show it as a national sport (Talmon-Chvaicer, *Hidden History of Capoeira*, 177). Capoeira was reshaped in the national consciousness to be a folkloric relic of Brazil's African slaves, ignoring the oppressive conditions within which capoeira was formed and the continued oppression of Brazil's Black communities, repressing the significance of capoeira as resistance to domination.

and liberation necessitates a rigorous and explicit critique of systems of social domination. Armed with the pedagogical elements, capoeiristas can go out into the world and name the current social dominance enshrined in institutions such as police forces, economic systems, private property ownership, criminal "justice" systems and others. However, there is a hermeneutical space between the roda and the wider world that capoeiristas can fill by naming and working to disarm current systems of social domination—militarization, capitalism, police states, etc.—that are an outgrowth of the original system of social domination—slavery and colonization—under which capoeira developed.

I began this research out of a desire to establish a theory of inter-religious liberation and therefore worked with abstract theories of liberation and interreligious dialogue (Dussel and Panikkar). However, as I reworked my research for publication while in the United States during the protests following yet another wave of police murders of Black lives—George Floyd, Sean Reeves, Breonna Taylor, Tony McDade—the next step is to research something more concrete. In future research, I look to examine the ways in which capoeira confronts racial violence in the United States and fails to do so because of the process of whitening and commercialization.

The system under which capoeira was formed—slavery and colonization—continues to be the bedrock of the United States today in the form of our police state, our neoliberal foreign policy, our militaristic intervention, and our violent capitalist economy. Our shared economic, civic, and social life is founded upon these systems. Capoeira was and is resistance to the dehumanization of Black lives that occurred through slavery and continues to occur today through systematic racism that pervades our culture and social institutions. Capoeira can teach that Black lives matter and that our collective liberation depends on humanizing Black and Brown lives in social and political institutions. It can teach us to question and distrust the white social domination present in social and political structures and in the false consciousness of our current definitions of the human person. It can teach us to rely on cunning, creativity, and faith in the unknown of a world without military or police. Capoeira is a way of liberation if we show up willing to learn, question, and change ourselves and our world.

Chapter 10

Facing the Challenge of Zionism

Theological, Hermeneutic, and Interfaith Issues for the Church Today[1]

Mark Braverman

This is the moment of grace and opportunity, when God issues a challenge for decisive action.
—Kairos South Africa, "Challenge to the Church," 1985

Theology itself is not the fighting part here; it stands wholly at the service of the living, confessing, and struggling church.
—Dietrich Bonhoeffer

By leaving out the steps from confession to resistance, one ends up tolerating crimes, turning confession into an alibi, and, in view of the injustice committed, an indictment of the confessors.
—Eberhard Bethge

Any declaration of a status confessionis stems from the conviction that the integrity of the gospel is in danger. It demands of the church a clear, unequivocal decision for the truth of the gospel.
—World Alliance of Reformed Churches, 22nd General Council, Seoul, 1989

---

1. A version of this chapter was presented at the Third Conference of "Radicalizing Reformation," January, 2017, Wittenberg, Germany.

Introduction

In 1935 Dietrich Bonhoeffer lived, taught and prayed at Finkenwalde, an alternative community for study and devotion was established in defiance of the Third Reich's suppression of the Confessing Church. Driven underground by the state, and theologically marginalized by the "German Christians" who had embraced the Nazi regime, at Finkenwalde Bonhoeffer produced some of his most important work on the nature and mission of the Confessing Church and the meaning of the ecumenical movement. "Truth bears within itself the power to divide or it is itself surrendered," he wrote, acknowledging the theological imperative that had prompted the founding of the Confessing Church, its responsibility to challenge the prevailing ecclesial order, and the sacrifice required of those obedient to its call. In a passionate appeal, not only on behalf of the soul of his country but for the integrity and faithfulness of church he loved, Bonhoeffer made it clear that the "Confessing Church does not confess *in abstracto* . . . but *in concretissimo*," referring to the crisis brought on by the actions of "the government of the National Church in Berlin." For Bonhoeffer, it was specific and it was urgent—"a confession in which it is really a matter of life and death."[2] Although the arena of his original struggle was his native Germany, Bonhoeffer perceived early on that the implications were global, not only on the political stage but for sake of the church itself. Bonhoeffer began to see that the implications were global—as long as the church was yoked to ethnic identity and nationalistic strivings, it would betray its mission, with catastrophic results.

As we enter the third decade of the twenty first century, we face challenges even more daunting than those faced by Bonhoeffer and his contemporaries. An increasingly globalized economy has led to a steady rise in inequality and to a process of climate change with calamitous implications. These factors have produced civil wars, insurgencies, and violent repression that have devastated infrastructure and have led to increasing poverty, conflict, internal dislocation and mass migrations on an unprecedented scale. Upsurges in hyper-nationalism and xenophobia accompany these developments. Serving global corporate interests, the predatory systems comprising the neoliberal order are intimately linked to the increase in human suffering and to the fate of the earth. International law and covenants forged by the global community in the aftermath of

---

2. Bonhoeffer, "Confessing Church and the Ecumenical Movement," 409.

the horrors of the twentieth century count for little as governments and global institutions fail to take action against the policies and systems that have brought us to the brink of political and environmental disaster.

Care for Creation, compassion for the poor and oppressed, and an unswerving commitment to equality are at the core of the church's mission. Lamentably, throughout modern history, the church, in collusion or in frank alliance with governments, has lent active or tacit support to the despoiling of Creation and to inequality, racism, colonialism, and slavery itself in its various forms. Fortunately, the previous century has bequeathed to us a legacy of prophetic action—movements, programs and truth-to-power declarations undertaken by denominational and ecumenical church bodies in solidarity with national liberation movements. Originated by Christian theologians, clergy, and lay activists at the grassroots, and then taken up by leaders of national, denominational and ecumenical bodies, these have had a direct impact on human affairs on a global level.

The proud record began with the 1934 Barmen Declaration authored by German church leaders speaking out against a church that had entered into willing partnership with the racism and hyper-nationalism of the Nazi regime. In midcentury, African American pastors and laypersons changed the political and social landscape of America in the struggle to end legal racism. The ecumenical church mobilized in 1968 in Uppsala, Sweden, when the World Council of Churches established the Programme to Combat Racism, affirming in word and deed that combatting racism was the primary mission of the world body at that moment in history. In 1977 in Dar Es Salaam, the Lutheran World Federation declared a *status confessionis*[3] in regard to apartheid, followed in 1982 with the World Alliance of Reformed Churches' declaration of apartheid as heresy at its General Assembly in Ottawa. In 1985, an ecumenical group of South African pastors and theologians took an unequivocal stand against apartheid, declaring that the regime was illegitimate and that it was a Christian duty "to refuse to cooperate with tyranny and to do whatever we

---

3. "Although it came out of specific Lutheran doctrinal debates in the sixteenth century, the term carries a broader connotation. It means that a particular doctrine is essential to who we are as a church. If something is *status confessionis* it means this is a make or break issue. It means that this is not an indifferent matter or one on which we can agree to disagree. It means that if we are to be faithful in confessing the gospel we must confess this." DeYoung, "Status Confessionis Issue."

can to remove it."[4] Arising from and speaking with increasing insistence through these actions was the idea of one church in conciliar unity, transcending denominational and national divisions—in South African theologian John de Gruchy's words, "the church as the community within which God manifests in history."[5]

The Palestinian Call

Even as these momentous developments in the global church were unfolding, the church, in the thrall of theologies that have upheld Jewish privilege over the rights of the indigenous people of Palestine, and at the effect of geopolitical forces supported by neoliberal economic and political theories, slumbered through the relentless taking of Palestinian land and Israel's violent suppression of two Palestinian uprisings. Then, in 2009, the church was awakened by a new kairos call, authored by an ecumenical group of Palestinian clergy, theologians and civil society activists. The Palestine Kairos document, entitled "A Moment of Truth: A Word of Faith, Hope and Love from the Heart of Palestinian Suffering" has called the global church to its mission, summoning the power of the church to move governments and societies. Kairos Palestine sets out a theology that calls for non-violent resistance to the evil of occupation: "resistance with love as its logic." Naming the Israeli occupation a sin, it calls out to the international community, reserving its final appeal for the church itself: "What is the international community doing? What are the political leaders in Palestine, in Israel and in the Arab world doing? *What is the Church doing?*"[6]

The church is called to lead today, as it has been in kairos moments past, embodying the social justice imperative of the first kairos, an indigenous struggle against a tyrannous occupation. Answering this call is not without cost. Today, as in previous struggles, prophetic action produces conflict within the body of the church, surfacing the tension between its core of compassion for the oppressed and the vulnerable, and the caution so often exhibited by the institutional church, often in complicity or overt alliance with temporal power.

4. Kairos South Africa, "Challenge to the Church."

5. De Gruchy, *Theological Odyssey*, 175.

6. Kairos Palestine, "Moment of Truth." Emphasis added.

Toppling the Pillars of Support

In their 2016 *This is an Uprising,* activists and organizers Mark and Paul Engler argue that authoritarian and unjust regimes maintain power not only through the political systems that maintain tyranny and inequality, but through the preservation of seemingly immutable beliefs and assumptions. Political scientist Gene Sharp called these "pillars of support." Racist and authoritarian regimes in particular operate in this way. Colonial powers, for example, rely on the belief in the inferiority of the colonized and enslaved, tyrannous governments on the divine or natural right to wield supreme power over subject, "inferior" groups. Movements for change succeed by challenging and ultimately removing these supports. "Movements succeed," write the Englers, "when they win over ever-greater levels of public support for their cause and undermine the pillars of support."[7] Following Frederick Douglass, Martin Luther King Jr. and other leaders of liberation movements, the Englers further maintain that the creation of division within and disruption of established institutions and systems is not an unintended consequence but a necessary ingredient for achieving sought-after social and political change.

Toppling the ideological, theological and political pillars that supported the apartheid regime was precisely the aim of the authors of the South Africa Kairos document. "The first task of a prophetic theology for our times," reads the document, "would be an attempt at social analysis or what Jesus would call "reading the signs of the times" (Matt 16:3) or "interpreting this Kairos" (Luke 12:56). The South African theologians, church leaders and human rights activists who authored the document laid out a "social analysis that would enable it to understand the mechanics of injustice and oppression."[8] They described what they termed the "church theology" that through the distortion of concepts such as justice, nonviolence and reconciliation served to justify and uphold the political system of racially-based political exclusion, dispossession and extreme economic inequality. They held that the system of apartheid *could not be reformed*, because as long as these pillars of support remained in place, so too did the fundamental ideological and political structures of tyranny. Kairos South Africa called for an end to rule based on a supremacist political ideology supported by the pillars of ethnic nationalism, belief in

7. Engler and Engler, *This is an Uprising,* 193.
8. Kairos South Africa, "Challenge to the Church."

the historic right to supreme power, and a theology that granted divine authority to this political program.

Israel's settler colonial project rests on two pillars.

Pillar 1: Political

Israeli historian Ilan Pappé has argued that what is commonly known as the "Israel-Palestine conflict" is best understood not as a struggle between two powers, indeed not as a "conflict" at all, but as a settler colonial enterprise—the project to ethnically cleanse the indigenous population of historic Palestine in order to establish a Jewish state.[9] The offenses against the Palestinians have been cast as a narrative of national liberation, with Israel as the victim in need of protection from an implacable enemy. For over half a century, this mythology has played out in the political theater of negotiations between equal parties for the division of the territory into two sovereign states. Despite what has been officially put forward by diplomats and politicians, this outcome of "two states, living side by side in peace and security" was never intended, neither by Israel nor its backer, the USA. Nor has the process resembled anything close to a negotiation between two equal parties. Rather, the "peace process" has masked what has been clear for all to see—the inexorable taking of the land of the stateless, unarmed Palestinians by Israel, backed diplomatically and financially by the USA. The land theft has been accompanied by the building of an economic and physical infrastructure of separation and inequality.[10] In fact, the endgame has already been achieved in the reality of a single apartheid state, in which a Jewish minority rules over a subject population of Palestinians.[11] Despite the growing recognition that the "two state solution" is dead, and that the pursuit of such an outcome been a cynically maintained illusion from the beginning, governments

9. Pappé, *Ethnic Cleansing of Palestine*.

10. Khalidi, *Brokers of Deceit*; Khalidi, *Hundred Years War on Palestine*.

11. The 1993 Oslo Accords, which established the Palestinian Authority, was the source of great optimism, especially on the part of Palestinians. But by 2000 it was clear that the Oslo Accords, like the "Peace Process" negotiations, was formulated in bad faith by Israel and the United States, the chief broker of the agreement. Israel used the military and civil control ceded in the agreement to increase its outright annexation of Palestinian lands and to build the infrastructure of political and economic control over the remaining territory west of the Jordan River. The occupation was not ending—rather, it was deepening, with the cooperation of the Palestinian Authority, operating effectively as a client government of Israel.

and supporters of Israel from both liberal and conservative camps continue to call for it. The churches have been complicit in this tragic and criminal process. By and large, recognition of the reality of apartheid in our time has been absent from the statements of denominational, national and ecumenical bodies, who, even as they decry the abridgement of Palestinian rights, continue to strengthen this pillar of support for the Zionist program by repeating the "two states for two people" mantra.

Pillar 2: Theological

Alongside the political stands the pillar of a theologically-informed ideology that is deeply embedded in Western culture, its origins dating back to the English Reformation. This theology finds expression in several forms of Zionism, which, although conceived as a political ideology, has been interpenetrated by theology for Christians as well as for Jews. Since the founding of the state in 1948, Zionism has merged with mainstream Judaism, affirmed across the Jewish theological and cultural spectrum as essential to Jewish identity and belief. Similarly, Zionism has been woven into the fabric of Christian theology because of Christians' sense of responsibility for Jewish suffering at the hands of the church. Following World War II, Christian self-perception became profoundly colored by shame, contrition, and a drive to reconcile with the Jewish people. Christian Zionism, as it is called, now exerts a powerful influence on Christian thought and belief, from progressive to conservative. In mainline Christianity, it effectively grants the Jewish people a right to the land on the basis of their past suffering and confers innocence to the Jewish people for any sins committed in claiming that privilege. Informed by what has come to be called post-Holocaust theology, liberal Christians have come to accept unquestioningly the equation of criticism of Israel with anti-Semitism. Unwritten rules dictate that although Jews and non-Jews alike may pay lip service to the cause for Palestinian rights and to the concept of a Palestinian state, they dare not bring forward any arguments or efforts that challenge core Zionist assumptions. In Christian fundamentalist thought, the primary Jewish claim to land is grounded in a literal interpretation of biblical promises. Belief in the eschatology of a Jewish return to Jerusalem foretelling the imminent return of Jesus was strengthened by Israel's conquest of all of Jerusalem in 1967. While not adhering to the End Times component, most mainline Christians regard the divine promise of land in the Old Testament as literal and in force. This also conveniently serves as a guilt offering: should not the Jews be granted their haven of safety and independence after so much suffering, wandering, and slaughter? Christian Zionism in both these forms is heretical and unbiblical because it negates the core of gospel teachings against territoriality and ethnic triumphalism.[12] Nevertheless, until recently it has remained unchallenged across the ecumenical spectrum and has powerfully influenced political support for Israeli expansionism at the expense of Palestinians.[13]

Liberal Zionism

What has become known as "liberal Zionism" can be considered a third pillar. The aim of liberal Zionism is to salvage the Zionist project through (1) efforts to ameliorate discrimination within "Israel," (i.e. the state established within the 1949 cease-fire lines that served as a *de factor* border until June 1967) against Arab citizens of Israel and people of color (including Jews), and (2) collusion with the fiction that Israel and its Western allies are working toward the establishment of a sovereign Palestinian state in the West Bank and Gaza. As a moderate, reformist response, liberal Zionism exhibits the key features of "church theology" as described in the 1985 South African "Challenge to the Church." It is a theology, in the words of that document, that is in "a limited, guarded and cautious way critical of the oppressive system but that in its superficiality and lack of an adequate analysis of the situation, serves to shore up rather than to challenge the injustice."[14] Indeed, the two-state solution championed by Israel and the Western powers bears disturbing similarity to the black homelands proposed by the South Africa apartheid government in the 1980s. With the accompanying proposals to "share power" with blacks in the federal legislature, the government attempted to hold on to power

12. It is also heretical for Jews because Zionism in its modern incarnation justifies domination, exploitation and dispossession on the basis of race or religion. This negates the transformation of Judaism from a territorial, cult-based national religion into its modern form born in the diaspora, a faith expressing the social justice principles of its monotheistic core.

13. For challenges to Christian Zionism, see Burge, *Jesus and the Land*; Davis and Wagner, *Zionism and the Quest for Justice in the Holy Land*; Prior, *Zionism and the State of Israel*.

14. Kairos South Africa, "Challenge to the Church."

through offers of "reform" in the face of mounting pressure from within as well as from outside the country. Like the South African proposal, the Israeli solution of fragmented Palestinian enclaves surrounded by and under the control of Israel constitutes apartheid under a thin veneer of legitimacy. The liberal Zionist response to criticism of Israel, relying heavily on the two-state fiction, is promoted by institutional Jewish interests and supported by many Christians reluctant or unwilling to create a rift with Jews on personal, professional, and institutional levels. It represents a major challenge for the church and is an important component of both the political and theological pillars of support.

Standing firmly on their pedestals, these pillars have served to uphold Israel's illegal and immoral actions. Like Samson standing between the columns upon which rested the house of his oppressors, both must be toppled in order to bring about the required change in the lives of both Israelis and Palestinians. Dietrich Bonhoeffer declared that "[i]n times which are out of joint . . . the gospel will make itself known."[15] Baldwin Sjollema, the first Director of the World Council of Churches' Programme to Combat Racism, echoes this principle in his 2015 memoir *Never Bow to Racism*: "[T]he struggle against racism" he writes, "is not only a struggle against injustice, it is also a struggle for the integrity of the gospel and the church of Jesus Christ. At that moment, racism becomes an ecclesiological issue because the integrity of Christian faith and praxis is at stake."[16] This is the "necessary bondage" of the church of which Karl Barth spoke. It was the challenge to the church in Germany posed by the Confessing Church, not only to the German pastors who chose to remain "neutral," but to the nascent ecumenical movement itself. John de Gruchy has suggested that "liberal indifference" or passive compliance of church leaders represented the "false church" even more than the outright racist and collaborationist *Deutsche Kristen* [17]

The lessons of the past speak clearly to the present kairos. How can the church learn from and remain faithful to that legacy in meeting the challenge of Palestine? Can a new and renewed ecumenical movement, responsive to the ecclesiological and political conditions of our times, provide the setting and the platform for this work?

---

15. De Gruchy, *Bonhoeffer and South Africa*, 60.

16. Sjollema, *Never Bow to Racism*, 184.

17. De Gruchy, *Bonhoeffer and South Africa*, 60.

Living, Confessing, and Struggling Church

"The question has been posed," wrote Bonhoeffer in the critical year of 1935 in "The Confessing Church and the Ecumenical Movement," asking whether the ecumenical movement would "pronounce judgment on war, racial hatred and social exploitation." "This is not an ideal," asserted the young pastor, summoning his European and American colleagues to fulfil the mission of the nascent international church movement, "but a commandment and a promise."[18] The implications for us today are as broad and as urgent, if not more so, than they were for Bonhoeffer. The question has been posed: words or action? Obedience or equivocation? The emergence of the Palestinian struggle as a cause that unites the church recalls Bonhoeffer's struggle to articulate the meaning of the *oikumene*. Early on, Bonhoeffer addressed the conflict between two very different notions of the nature and purpose of the ecumenical movement. In the first, the ecumenical movement serves as a deliberative body, committed to bringing disparate churches together for mutual understanding and "non-binding" dialogue. The second, in line with Bonhoeffer's vision, was of the ecumenical movement as "a community of faith placing itself under the word of God and therewith coming to an authoritative *decision* on where its obedience to Christ lies" (emphasis in original).[19]

Bonhoeffer arrived at the conclusion that the ecumenical movement did not exist to *serve the churches*, but was a *form of the church*, indeed *the form* of the true church. The Confessing Church, he wrote, stakes its identity and existence on its confession. "There is only a Yes or a No to this confession," he wrote, referring to the proclamations that had emerged from Barmen and Dahlem in response to the heresies of the German church under the Third Reich: "Is it a place for coming to an authoritative decision on where its obedience to Christ lies? Or is there to be endless discussion of possibilities, forever evading a division of the spirits?"[20] "Theology itself is not the fighting part here;" continued Bonhoeffer. "It stands wholly at the service of the living, confessing, and struggling church."[21] In Bonhoeffer's case the confession was in reaction to the heresy of the Reich Church, but the imperative remains through changing contexts. What became known in the Germany of Bonhoeffer's

18. Clements, *Dietrich Bonhoeffer's Ecumenical Quest*, 172.
19. Clements, *Dietrich Bonhoeffer's Ecumenical Quest*, 169.
20. Duchrow, *Conflict Over the Ecumenical Movement*, 320.
21. Clements, *Dietrich Bonhoeffer's Ecumenical Quest*, 62.

time as the *church struggle* has manifested in other times and places: the black liberation movement in the USA, the South African church struggle against apartheid, and now Palestine. In every instance, the cry of those calling for resistance to injustice is met by forces within the church that seek to muffle or neutralize those voices. The form this takes is often not outright suppression, but "softer," through appeals to reason, arguments for caution, and proposals of compromise.

Costly Unity

The question of the identity and mission of the church is one that has followed—one can say productively vexed—the ecumenical movement throughout its history. It was the subject of World Council of Churches General Secretary Willem Visser 'T Hooft's address to the Fourth Assembly of the WCC in Uppsala, Sweden in June 1968. As one who interacted with Bonhoeffer during the years of the young German's struggle with the ecumenical movement, it is more than likely that Visser 'T Hooft had Bonhoeffer's struggle in mind as he spoke these words to the assembled a generation later, as the world body prepared to focus its attention on the anti-racism and anti-colonial movements that were gaining momentum in the decade of the 60s.[22] "So many conceive of unity in terms of uniformity and centralization," Visser 'T Hooft said to the Assembly—but for the church "the great tension [is] between the vertical interpretation of the Gospel as essentially concerned with God's saving action in the life of individuals, and the horizontal interpretation of it as mainly concerned with human relationships in the world." Visser 'T Hooft, however, rejected this division as a false dichotomy—a failure to understand the true nature of God's incarnation in Jesus Christ. Rather than being separate from or in conflict with it, the "vertical" dimension of "God's saving grace in the life of individuals" was inseparable from the "horizontal" imperative for action in the world. "True unity" for the church, Visser 'T Hooft maintained, is found rather in "faithfulness to God's proclamation of the unity of humankind and His incarnation in the life, ministry and sacrifice of Jesus Christ and through the church as a fellowship of faith acting directly in human affairs."[23]

22. Martin Luther King Jr. had been the scheduled keynote speaker. He was assassinated April, and in his stead the WCC invited James Baldwin.

23. Visser 'T Hooft, "Mandate of the Ecumenical Movement," in Kinnamon and

The need for the ecumenical power of the church is as great or greater now than it was in the previous century. But what will serve as the heir to the ecumenical movement in its proudest moments? Sjollema, writing in 2015, acknowledged the World Council of Church's diminished ability to achieve the consensus necessary to mount prophetic actions such as the Programme to Combat Racism, initiated in 1970 following the Uppsala assembly. It had, he maintained, retreated into the comfortable function of supporting the stability and coexistence of church institutions across denominational and national divisions, the very thing against which both Bonhoeffer and Visser 'T Hooft had argued. "After 65 years of existence," lamented Sjollema, "the WCC has lost its pioneering role; its original mandate has changed. It has become a bureaucracy. It no longer takes initiatives on its own; it now depends on its member churches for that."[24] Although the WCC has sponsored programs to benefit Palestinians over the past two decades, its ability to speak and act prophetically on the issue has been constrained by the concern of heads of churches to preserve relationships with the Jewish community, to avoid conflict among its members, and to remain faithful to the post-Holocaust penitential agenda. With respect to contentious issues, the world body is committed to bringing the national churches and global denominations together in consensus—"to act together or not at all" as expressed at a recent World Council of Churches symposium on Palestine. The question must be raised therefore, whether the institutional ecumenical "body" of the WCC today *is* a body in the incarnational sense. This is why we must now revisit Uppsala, Ottawa, Cottesloe, and the letter from Birmingham Jail.[25] Bonhoeffer writes that it is in the *Gemeinde*—the community—in which the true spirit of the church is to be found, that the church can fulfill its mission of obedience to the word of God through its direct involvement in human affairs. This is as true today as it was in Bonhoeffer's time. And it is indeed a costly process, one accompanied by struggle. In Bonhoeffer's formulation the church achieves true unity of purpose *through* disunity:

> Neither unanimity, uniformity, nor congeniality makes it possible, nor is it to be confused with unity of mood. Rather, it is a reality precisely where the seemingly sharpest outward

---

Cope, *Ecumenical Movement*, 38–43.

24. Sjollema, *Never Bow to Racism*, 199.

25. Cottesloe,"Cottesloe Declaration."

> antitheses prevail . . . there unity is established through God's
> will . . . the more powerfully the dissimilarity manifests itself in
> the struggle, the stronger the objective unity.[26]

Never have the issues that divide and the "antitheses" been more acute and more deserving of a direct, unswerving gaze. Writing in the 1980s, German theologian Ulrich Duchrow observed that the emergence of the ecumenical movement in the twentieth century required a "new language" for the church, which had been dominated by the "political and legal principle of territorialism . . . [its] unity conceived of in terms of imperial law, on the Centre-peripheral principle."[27] This fear-based conservatism on the part of church bodies supports the very conditions that threaten human survival and environmental sustainability. Duchrow describes a church limited to viewing "the present and the future as a linear extension of the past" and as such instrumental in bringing "the whole human family . . . [to] the edge of destroying itself and its natural basis by the aimless growth of fragmenting systems of science and technology."[28] We have again arrived at a pass in which we must ask, as did Charles Villa-Vicencio in 1988, "Can religion truly break the iron cage of history? Can religion produce a qualitatively different kind of society? Is the Kingdom of God a real possibility?"[29]

Challenging Empire

The Kairos Palestine Document has engendered a global response to the Palestinian cause. It has spawned documents from kairos organizations worldwide, each responding to the Palestinian call from its own historical and cultural context and experience of struggle.[30] In a 2012 paper, "Bonhoeffer's Legacy and Kairos Palestine," John de Gruchy draws a straight line from Germany, to South Africa, to Palestine. "Bonhoeffer's influence," he states, "is clearly evident in the Kairos Palestine Document just as it was in the original South African Kairos Document in 1986. His personal example of resistance to oppression, his insistence that there can never be security without justice, and his ecumenical commitment to

26. Clements, *Dietrich Bonhoeffer's Ecumenical Quest*, 62.

27. Duchrow, *Conflict Over the Ecumenical Movement*, 298–99.

28. Clements, *Dietrich Bonhoeffer's Ecumenical Quest*, 305.

29. Villa-Vicencio, *Trapped in Apartheid*, 209.

30. Braverman, "Moment of Grace and Opportunity," 42–83.

peace, immediately suggest that what he had to say on such issues during the 1930's is of critical importance today."[31] Steve de Gruchy observed that the abiding influence of South Africa comes increasingly into focus as we become more aware of the global scope of the current struggle. Reflecting on the South African experience, de Gruchy noted that "[t]he global focus on apartheid facilitated much of [the] international networking" that led to the downfall of the regime.[32] Raising the issue of globalization, he argued that ecumenism is key to the emerging role of the church as a force for social justice, citing again the struggle against apartheid, in which "historic confessional differences were shelved in favor of united witness."[33] The importance of Palestine is evidenced in the recognition of the inseparability of each local struggle from every other and from the environmental, social justice, economic and political issues that bear directly on the fate of the earth. This has emerged in the powerful connections made between Palestinian liberation the Black Lives Matter movement in the USA[34] and with the popular struggles for human rights in South America, Asia, and Europe, where the Palestinian story has taken on powerful symbolic value with respect to colonialism, economic oppression, and state-sanctioned racism.[35]

Issues for an Ecumenical Response to this Kairos

Church Struggle

Change originates at the grassroots. Churches, like all institutions, are by nature conservative. Those from within the church who are demanding change are likely to be met with pushback regarding any actions that might cause disharmony within the ranks, challenge traditional beliefs and doctrine, or threaten to disrupt relationships considered vital to church stability and survival. Responding to the Palestinian call requires Christians—clergy, theologians, scholars, and laypersons, to challenge long-held understandings of the Bible with respect to land promise, covenant,

31. De Gruchy, "Bonhoeffer's legacy and Kairos-Palestine," 67–80.

32. De Gruchy, *Church Struggle in South Africa*, 194.

33. De Gruchy, *Church Struggle in South Africa*, 257.

34. Dabashi, "Black Lives Matter and Palestine."

35. "Welcome to Palestine!" read a banner displayed at the entrance to a poor people's tent city in a Brazilian *favela*. A sign reading "Free Palestine" was observed at a demonstration for workers' rights in Norway.

and the status of the Jewish people. Hidden from view but underlying the controversy within churches over the issue of the Jewish claim to Palestine is the implicit challenge to the very notion of land as divinely granted and the exceptionalism thus conferred on the grantees.[36] Very much visible is the heated and often agonized controversy within churches about disrupting hard-won relationships with the Jewish community. For those in positions of responsibility there is the concern that appearing to side with Palestinians "against" Israel will threaten the support of large donors and other powerful interests, including the state itself. For some it raises the risk of loss of members and even the threat of schism. These all exert pressure on administrators, clergy and laypersons at multiple levels of the churches that is not to be minimized. Rather than excusing inaction or temporizing, ineffectual responses, however, the surfacing of these conflictual, vexing issues is a sign that there are very important decisions to be made. Bonhoeffer understood that when its very nature and integrity are at stake, division arising within the church is key to its vitality and relevance—even, he wrote, as it "shudders before the gravity of a cleavage in the church."[37] "Separation is at hand," Bonhoeffer wrote to a friend in September 1933 after the Nazis barred pastors of Jewish descent from serving churches.[38] Over a decade later, writing from prison, he appears to have realized that this statement had represented a wish rather than reality. The church, he observed, will "fight for its own preservation, as if this were an end in itself."[39]

Church struggle results when the conservatism and caution of the church collides with the moral imperative to respond to the cry of the oppressed. Rather than threatening its survival, however, struggle is at the heart of the church's mission. The emergence of the new in response to the signs of the times is the seed of the always changing, always renewing church—at the very times when, in Bonhoeffer's words, "the seemingly sharpest outward antitheses prevail." It is then that division, rather than being feared, is to be welcomed. Perhaps at no time since the global fight against nuclear arms has the church mobilized at the grassroots as it has for Palestine. This is happening at congregational and community levels, within denominations, and in networks of nationally-based ecumenical

36. Brueggemann, *Chosen? Reading the Bible Amid the Israeli-Palestinian Conflict.*

37. Bonhoeffer, "Confessing Church and the Ecumenical Movement," 144.

38. Duchrow, *Conflict Over the Ecumenical Movement*, 321.

39. Bonhoeffer, "Thoughts on the Day of Baptism of Dietrich Wilhelm Rüdiger Bethge," 787.

groups in Britain, Ireland, the USA, Southern Africa, Germany, Sweden, Denmark, Norway, and India. We see costly discipleship manifesting at national and global levels in the mobilization of campaigns against companies profiting from the colonization of Palestine[40] and in the growing response to the 2005 Palestinian call for Boycott, Divestment and Sanctions.[41]

Israel today resembles South Africa in the 1980s: a political system devoted to the economic oppression and cultural erasure of the subaltern population. In the case of South Africa, the world powers, bowing to pressure from around the world, rejected the racist ideology and the political system built upon it. Given the powerful biblical and historical narratives operating in the Israel-Palestine situation, however, the threshold for change is higher. In the South African case, theological support flowed exclusively from the English-speaking, Dutch Reformed and other Afrikaans-speaking churches of South Africa, rooted in the cultural and historical narrative particular to the South African settler population. Simply put, only the Afrikaners believed themselves to be the chosen people. Once the world awoke to the reality of that regime, the governments of the world, spurred by the churches, isolated the white minority government of South Africa and eventually brought about its downfall through economic, political and cultural sanctions. In contrast, there is near-universal support for Jewish "liberation" through settlement of the Holy Land, justified by divine mandate. Nevertheless, the moral and political challenge confronting the world community today with respect to Israel is equally compelling, requiring the same unequivocal, united, and steadfast opposition on the part of national and international bodies.

The Neoliberal Challenge

As pressure on Israel grows over its human rights abuses, and churches and governments are increasingly being challenged to address the injustice, advocacy groups, legislative lobbies and the leadership of Jewish denominations have stepped up their efforts to shield Israel from criticism. They present themselves as committed to the greater good, and as working for a just and peaceful settlement. In effect, however, they are working

40. Who Profits, "Who Profits: the Israeli Occupation Industry."
41. BDS, "Boycott, Divestment and Sanctions."

to preserve the neoliberal order—the status quo of enriching the few at the expense of the many. As in previous struggles, the power imbalance between those standing for justice and the forces arrayed against them appears almost incalculable. Furthermore, the church movement for Palestinian liberation faces a steeper gradient than that faced by previous justice movements. By the time the world became aware of its genocidal programs, few outside the Third Reich had any question about the evil of the authoritarian and racist regime. Likewise, as awareness grew of the brutality and racism of apartheid South Africa, the condemnation of the world at large coalesced into the sanctions that led to the downfall of that regime. Even those secular and church leaders in South Africa who refrained from active resistance acknowledged the political and theological unacceptability of apartheid and were not misled or confounded by the "reforms' proffered by the regime. In the case of the State of Israel, however, the world, on popular as well as official levels has by and large accepted the fiction of Israel as a society committed to human rights and equality for all its citizens, and the down-is-up narrative of Israel as the victim in need of protection.

"Liberal Zionism," discussed above, has emerged as one form of the neoliberal response to efforts to bring an end to Israel's colonial project. Supporters of Jewish hegemony in historic Palestine employ classic reformist strategies, including support for minor, incremental improvements in the human rights situation inside Israel, lip service to the idea of a sovereign Palestinian state, and an attempt to co-opt the Palestinian call for Boycott, Divestment and Sanctions through a parsing and gutting of its three demands—for example limiting boycott to products produced in West Bank Settlements.[42]

Post-Holocaust to Post-Nakba[43]

For almost two millennia, the church defined itself through negation of the Other—the barbarians, unbelievers, and rejecters of the true faith,

42. The three demands of BDS are: (1) Ending its occupation and colonization of all Arab lands occupied in June 1967 and dismantling the Wall; (2) Recognizing the fundamental rights of the Arab-Palestinian citizens of Israel to full equality; (3) Respecting, protecting, and promoting the rights of Palestinian refugees to return to their homes and properties as stipulated in UN Resolution 194.

43. *Nakba,* Arabic for "catastrophe" is the term used by Palestinians for the dispossession and ethnic cleansing of 1947–1949.

vilified in a "binary logic of Us vs. Them."[44] Brigitte Kahl has described
how "nominal Christianity" has authorized "imperial globalization"
through the "aggressive justification of the Western Self and the mental-
ity of conquest."[45] This worldview found particularly toxic expression in
the Reformation, with Luther's demonization of the Jew, the "Turk," and
the "Papists," with far-reaching and disastrous effects on church doctrine
and action through the centuries. Then, in the mid-twentieth century,
a remarkable turnabout occurred. In a paroxysm of horror, shame and
guilt following the Nazi genocide, Christianity, beginning in Germany
and spreading West, undertook a project of penitence through a stunning
reversal of how it regarded the Jewish people. Instead of being despised
for rejecting the foretold Messiah, the Jews were restored as the most
beloved of God—the original, exclusivist covenant now reinstated and
with it the conditional but irrevocable promise of the land.[46] This "post-
Holocaust" formulation stood replacement theology on its head. In the
place of seeing itself as the successor to the Jewish people and inheri-
tor of the covenant, mainline Protestant Christianity now defined itself
negatively in its confession of the sin of anti-Judaism.[47] But Christians
are not left out in the cold in this new order—as "guests in the house of
Israel" they take their place as fellow inheritors of the divine covenant.[48]
This penitential project has not led to obedience to the Lordship of Jesus,
however. Instead, in their preoccupation with correcting historic church
anti-Judaism, Christians have compounded the sin by enabling the Jews'
project of conquest and domination. Thus, the opportunity afforded by
the confrontation with the horror of the Nazi genocide to come face to

44. Kahl, *Galatians Re-imagined*, 10.

45. Kahl, *Galatians Re-imagined*, 6.

46. Braverman, *Fatal Embrace*.

47. German theologian Bertold Klappert describes how the focus of German
Protestant theology in the postwar era shifted from the faithfulness of the church to
its theological core as opposed to the demands of the state, to a penitential focus on
Christianity's culpability for the Nazi genocide. Klappert quotes his teacher and member of the original Confessing Church, Hans Joachim Iwand, who, in a 1959 letter
discussing the Church's "academic and theological guilt" for Auschwitz, asks: "Who
is going to take this guilt away from us and our theological fathers—because there
it started? . . . How can the German people that has initiated the fruitless rebellion
against Israel and his God become pure?" Pollefeyt, *Jews and Christians*, 43.

48. The Roman Catholic church officially repudiated its anti-Jewish doctrine in
the mid-twentieth century. Although partially—and grudgingly—backing off from
the charge of killing Jesus, the Catholic church did not go as far as relinquishing its
exceptionalist and exclusivist claims.

face with the consequences of Christian exceptionalism was squandered. Christian triumphalism has been replaced by *Judeo-Christian triumphalism*, and its language is Zionism.

Today, facing the reality of the ethnic cleansing of Palestine, a seven decades-old crime justified by the Bible and sanctioned by the churches, Christians are now confronted with the need for yet another theological shift, more wrenching and profound than the postwar renunciation of anti-Judaism. We have left the "post-Holocaust" era and entered the "post-Nakba." This shift requires turning the focus from responsibility for past Jewish suffering and toward the obligation to respond to the call of *today's* victims.[49] This does not mean that anti-Semitism, past or present, is to be denied. Anti-Semitism is real, and like all forms of racism, it must be opposed. But vigilance against anti-Semitism is being used to muzzle principled opposition to Israel's oppression of the Palestinians.

This tactic is directed at both Jews and Christians who dare to question Israel's actions. Throwing down the charge that criticism of Israel and challenging its "right to exist" as a Jewish homeland is a form of anti-Semitism is particularly effective as a way to intimidate Christians. It will be difficult, therefore, to accomplish the shift from post-Holocaust to post-Nakba within the current framework of Jewish-Christian relations, because of the rules of the "ecumenical deal." First described by American theologians Rosemary Radford Ruether and Marc Ellis, the terms of this unwritten agreement are that Jews agree to work toward reconciling with Christians for Jewish suffering at the hands of the church as long as any challenge to Israel's policies or to Zionism itself are left out of the conversation.[50] The consequences of breaking this implicit agreement can be severe, from the disruption or severing of hard-won interfaith relations to even worse: the charge of anti-Semitism. *It is a cross to pick up,* but this is to be expected with any prophetic endeavor. It places this effort firmly in the tradition of the church struggles referenced above.

---

49. Jews are also facing a shift, just as demanding, but of a different nature. See Braverman, *Wall in Jerusalem*.

50. Ellis, *Toward a Jewish Theology of Liberation*; Ruether and Ellis, *Beyond Occupation*.

Costly Witness

"Whenever a community of peace endangers or suffocates truth and justice, the community of peace must be broken and the battle must be declared." These were Bonhoeffer's words to an ecumenical conference in 1932, addressing directly the elevation of "peace" as a good in and of itself. "Should the situation arise," he continued, "*the struggle* can protect the openness for the revelation of Christ better than the *external peace* in that it breaks the hardened, self-enclosed order" (emphasis added).[51] These issues are as acute today as they were for Bonhoeffer. Clements writes about the "journey the ecumenical community still has to make in earnest, that is, the discovery and teaching of spirituality which undergird and sustain effective social and political engagement as distinct from cheap statements and easy posturing."[52]

We have witnessed persistent, growing activity at multiple levels of the church in support of equal rights for Palestinians and in opposition to Israel's policies. This has been unfolding on a global level. A vibrant grassroots church movement has arisen in Germany, where the Kairos Palestine Solidarity Network has called the Evangelical Church in Germany (the Lutheran and Reformed Churches) to account for its cautious and temporizing response to the 2009 Kairos Palestine document, adhering to the *Staatsräson* of the German government that places the "security" and stated interests of the State of Israel before principles of human rights. In the USA, denominational mission networks organize pilgrimages in solidarity with nonviolent resistance in Palestine, sponsor resolutions for the study of the Palestine Kairos document, and call for a reassessment of U.S. policy. Protestant denominations have acted to divest from companies profiting from and aiding the dispossession and oppression of Palestinians, instituted educational programs to raise awareness of the human rights situation in Palestine, and promoted study of the theological and hermeneutic issues related to Zionism. Globally, through Kairos networks, student organizations, and Jewish activist groups, the Palestinian call for Boycott, Divestment and Sanctions has received significant support.

But the global church has not yet acted. The "step from confession to resistance," as Bethge warned, has not been taken.

---

51. Clements, *Dietrich Bonhoeffer's Ecumenical Quest*, 77.
52. Clements, *Dietrich Bonhoeffer's Ecumenical Quest*, 293.

"There is still no theology of the ecumenical movement," Bonhoeffer wrote in 1932. He did not mean that there was *no* theology, but that the ecumenical movement was at risk of being at the effect of *false* theology, theology that limited the actions of the movement to "cheap statements and easy posturing." "They abolish Christ by preaching him,' Luther said of those who failed to follow up their faith with action."[53] In Bonhoeffer's embrace of the centrality of church struggle, and through the legacy of those in the struggles that have followed, the stage is set for the work of theology and church renewal in our time. The stakes could not be higher. The Palestinian struggle has enormous power to summon the church to its mission. It surfaces the systems and ideologies that support white supremacy and colonialism on a global scale, as expressed in the 2015 "Dangerous Memory" statement, adopted in Johannesburg on the thirtieth anniversary of the Kairos South Africa document: "Palestine is . . . a microcosm of global empire, a critical site of reflection that can bring experiences in other locales into sharper focus. Palestine does not eclipse other situations around the globe but instead intensifies the need for greater interconnection and mutual engagement."[54] The Palestinian call has awakened church movements at the grassroots around the world, each nationally-based movement responding from the context of its own human rights struggle, such as in the Philippines and Brazil, and in some cases, notably the U.S. and the U.K., from its own confession of complicity.[55]

The historic and ongoing ethnic cleansing and colonization of Palestine represents the most longstanding systematic violation of human rights in the world today. Our outrage increases when we consider the diplomatic and financial support of the Western powers to the continuing colonization of Palestinian land and the abrogation of Palestinians' rights, with the backing of churches at national, denominational and ecumenical levels. In the words of Rev. Edwin Arrison, General Secretary of Kairos Southern Africa: "There is much injustice in the world today, but there is only one that is justified by a misuse of the Bible."[56] The battle is joined today between the neoliberal agenda, in which Zionism is brought into the service of the "contemporary globalized capitalism of modernity

53. Duchrow, *Conflict Over the Ecumenical Movement*, 131.

54. Kairos South Africa, "Kairos 30th Anniversary Statement, Dangerous Memory and Hope for the Future."

55. Palestine Portal, "Mapping the Movement."

56. *Sunday Tribune*, November 15, 2016.

. . . manifest in exploitation, colonization, and genocide in Africa, Asia, and the Americas," and the quest for equality, human dignity, and the survival of the natural environment.[57] When we take on the crime of the dispossession and the political and economic colonization of Palestine we expose the larger, global system of which it is a part.

Conclusion

We are led to responsibility and obedience through the call of the oppressed. The concrete manifestations of this call in our world are as physical as Christ's wounds revealed to the apostles in the final chapter of Luke's Gospel: "Look at my hands and feet!" Jesus entreats his disciples— "and have you anything here to eat?" Jesus was calling on them to understand that his ministry had always been about his humanness—that he suffered, as his people suffered, from being beaten, persecuted, and starved. The wounds and hunger of the poor and dispossessed are as visible today as on that day in Jerusalem. Our responsibility is made visible in the desecration of the landscape of the West Bank by illegal colonies and separation walls, in the misery of the checkpoints, the rubble and starvation of Gaza, the pain and despair in the eyes of the oppressed, and the desperation and fear in those of the oppressors. The confessional process pushes aside the stumbling blocks of compromise, reform, and the resort to endless "dialogue." It calls the question, forcing the church to declare itself as the true church of Jesus Christ, requiring of Christians a decision for obedience—to ask, as did Bonhoeffer, "Who is Jesus Christ for us today?"

57. Radicalizing Reformation, "Radicalizing Reformation: Provoked by the Bible and Today's Crises."

Solidarity as Liberation

Chapter 11

Crucified Bodies and Hope of Liberation

Re-viewing the Cross in the Context
of Black and Dalit Suffering

JOSHUA SAMUEL

On February 23, 2020, Ahmaud Arbery, a 25-year-old unarmed Black man, was killed by two white men when he was jogging through a neigh-borhood in Brunswick, Georgia, USA. Arbery was followed by a father-son duo, Gregory and Travis McMichael, who thought he looked suspicious, with a gun in a truck. When they overtook him, after a brief argument, Arbery was shot and killed.[1]

On May 25, 2020, George Floyd, a 46-year-old Black man was arrested by the Minneapolis police, after receiving information that he had used a counterfeit $20 bill at a local Deli shop. The officer, Derek Chauvin, with three other officers standing by, pinned Floyd to the ground, holding him down by kneeling on his neck for eight minutes and forty six seconds, even as Floyd kept crying out that he couldn't breathe. Chauvin did not remove his knee even after Floyd fell unconscious and the paramedics had arrived on the scene.[2]

---

1. CBS News, "Shooting of Ahmaud Arbery."
2. New York Times, "8 Minutes and 46 Seconds."

On May 23, 2020, the body of Angira Pasi, a 12 year old Dalit girl was found hanging in a village in Rupandehi district, Nepal, after she was raped by a man from an upper/dominant caste community. On the same day, also in Nepal, five Dalit men were killed in the neighboring Rukum West district to protest the marriage of a young Dalit to a girl from a dominant caste.[3]

On June 1, 2020, Vikas Kumar Jatav, a young Hindu Dalit, was shot dead in Uttar Pradesh, North India, during his sleep in his home for trying to enter a Hindu temple. While his father, Omprakash Jatav, alleged that this was a case of caste-based violence, the police claimed that money dispute was the cause of murder.[4]

Introduction

Christian faith is founded and firmly rooted in the cross of Jesus Christ. Even though Jesus' life and message had a powerful influence on his followers—both during and after his time—there can be no doubt that his death on the cross made a significant difference. As Roger Haight rightly observes, Jesus' life would not have had the same effect if he had not been crucified.[5] In other words, there is something significant and critical about Jesus' death on the cross that it has had a profound presence and impact in history. Thus, the cross has not remained as a mere event in history but has become *an experience*, an intimate, life-transforming experience, for many people.

My primary objective in this paper is to reflect on the meaning and relevance of the cross today. However, while I think of a contextual theology of the cross, I am reminded that reflecting on the crucified one from two thousand years ago entails bringing to mind the "crucified peoples"[6] of the world today (to which I will return shortly). Specifically, as a Dalit theologian from India who is now living in the United States of America,[7] this means that I cannot overlook the events that are mentioned above involving the death of women and men from Black

---

3. Human Rights Watch, "Nepal: Ensure Justice for Caste-based Killings."

4. Harveer, "'Barred From Entering Temple.'"

5. Haight, *Future of Christology*, 81, 88–89.

6. Song, *Jesus, The Crucified People*, 215–16. The phrase was also used by the Latin American liberation theologian, Ignacio Ellacuría. See Ellacuría, "Crucified People," 580–603.

7. Hereafter referred to as USA.

and Dalit[8] communities. The names mentioned above are but a few of the many Blacks and Dalits[9] who have been killed by white and caste supremacy in the recent past. In the USA, I remember the racist murders of Black people, including that of Michael Brown, Freddie Gray, Eric Garner, Deborah Danner, Sandra Bland, and Breonna Taylor. In India, I remember Ilavarasan, Muthukumar, Gokulraj, Sankar, and Rajalakshmi who were killed, and the many Dalit women who were raped and murdered to uphold and assert caste supremacy.

Keeping this in mind, as a Christian theologian, I want to ask: what could the cross of Jesus mean to the Black and Dalit communities today? How can the cross be interpreted in such a way that it could become a source of liberation for them?[10] As an attempt to answer these questions, I want to offer some theological reflections on the relevance of the cross within the context of Blacks in the USA and Dalits in India and South Asia. I begin my essay by looking at the cross of Jesus in its socio-political context. Following this, I will explore in brief Black and Dalit theologians' interpretations of the cross. Building on these insights, in the final section, I want to offer some theological reflections on the meaning of the cross in oppressive contexts.

But, before I proceed further, I believe I need to make some important observations and clarifications. To begin with, I confess that the incidents mentioned here are clearly not similar, nor are the Black and Dalit experiences alike. I understand that Black and Dalit contexts or their suffering cannot be compared simplistically. I am all too aware that attempting to conflate and equate race and caste, and their dynamics of dehumanization is certainly problematic. However, while acknowledging that there have been comparisons between the Dalit and the Black

8. Dalits, formerly called as untouchables (among other names), are communities who are discriminated and marginalized as outcastes by the caste system. For more on Dalits, see Webster, "Who is a Dalit?" 76–88.

9. A logistical note is in place here. I want to point out that I intentionally use the terms "Black" and "Dalit" with capital B and D as a sign of assertion of the dignity of these communities which continues to be denied. The only exception to this rule would be quotations from other authors.

10. Let me clarify that though some of the names mentioned here may not be Christians, I still choose to use a Christian symbol, viz. the cross, to interpret their experience, since I believe that, as a symbol of death and life, its meaning and liberative potential transcends religious boundaries. As we shall see, this is especially true in the case of Dalits.

experience in the past,[11] my intention here is not to draw up parallels or argue for similarities (or dissimilarities) but to see how their sufferings can be paradoxically turned into a source of hope and liberation.

But, nonetheless, I see that there are at least two major similarities between Black and Dalit suffering which will be key for this essay. First, the above mentioned Blacks and Dalits were robbed of their lives primarily because of who they were—Black and Dalit. In other words, their socially constructed identities were the fundamental reason and cause for the violence they experienced. Also, it is important to recognize that both the Black and Dalit reality is situated within the larger context of the nation state viz. USA and India respectively. In many cases, the violence against Blacks and Dalits is endorsed, if not encouraged by the state machinery such as the police. In the case of the USA in particular, police shootings of Black women and men is a regular, if not frequent, occurrence. Thus, the state plays a key role in (at least sustaining) the ongoing violence against both Black and Dalit bodies.

The Cross and the Empire

In this section, I seek to situate the cross and the death of Jesus within its context of first century Roman Empire. Firstly, we need to remember that the cross of Jesus was one among many crosses in the Greco-Roman world. New Testament scholar, Brigitte Kahl notes that the cross and the "[C]rucifixion represented an inter-national event, ubiquitous among the vanquished nations under Roman rule, …and was as universal as the Roman Empire itself."[12] Placing the cross along with the arena where gladiator games were held, and the Roman altar(s) where the imperial cult was performed, Kahl argues that together these religio-political symbols created and sustained a hierarchical way of life based on the Aristotelian binaries.[13] This religio-political system was crucial to maintain the law and order for the proper functioning of the empire. Anyone who challenged it or even threatened to destabilize it were accused of rebelling against the

11. For some recent comparative work, see Kapoor, *Dalits and African-Americans* and Barua, "God of the Oppressed," 1–20.

12. Kahl, *Galatians Re-imagined*, 159.

13. These binary notions of the cosmos created an ethos that set the self against/ over the other. Here, "self" denotes male/divine/soul/master and the "other" refers to female/evil/body/slave categories of the Greco-Roman society. Kahl, *Galatians Re-imagined*, 18–19, 156–64.

law of the gods of the empire, and therefore deserved to be crucified or thrown to the wild animals. Thus, the cross was for the 'bad' people—the godless outcastes, rebels, and revolutionaries of the Roman empire.

However, Kahl warns us that the cross was also more than a punishment! She writes,

> the core visual program of a crucifixion is quite stable. What needs to be shown is not just the execution of a criminal but the *elimination of a rebellious, transgressive other and the restoration of the proper order of the world*....it is not human cruelty played out but the sacred violence of divine retribution. A fundamental threat to the divine and human order of the world is eliminated, for everyone's benefit.[14]

In other words, the cross was a *statement*. It was a statement of warning to either follow the "good" hierarchical imperial order and live, or question/ transgress the order and face the consequence of brutal death. Further, the cross was also a statement of failure, the failure of the rebel who had tried to disrupt the *Pax Romana*, the Roman peace, a peace created by violent bloodshed in the first place.[15]

Relating the above observations to Jesus, one can infer that his cross was a statement of warning to anyone who dared to envision an alternative egalitarian society—which according to him was the kingdom of God, a(nother) God who was opposed to the exploitative and oppressive god(s) of the empire—and had the audacity to act upon this vision to make it a reality. Jesus' cross was also surely a failure, failure of a colonized man who had tried to challenge the divisive epistemic and sociopolitical structures of the colonizer.

Yet, the story of Jesus' cross did not end with his death. As the gospels and the epistles spell it out, the cross was followed by the incredible story of resurrection. In fact, without the accounts of resurrection, the cross of Jesus would have lost its significance in the myriad of Roman crosses. As Roger Haight suggests, resurrection stands as a proof that God will not allow an innocent person like Jesus to die or allow his life to go in vain.[16] But, (re-)focusing on the cross, Adam Winn, in his empire critical reading of the Mark's gospel, suggests that Jesus' death itself could be seen as a "thoroughgoing response to Roman imperial power." He writes,

14. Kahl, *Galatians Re-imagined*, 158. Emphasis mine.

15. Longenecker, "Peace, Prosperity, and Propaganda," 33–38.

16. Haight, *Jesus Symbol of God*, 147, 149–150.

On the surface, this narrative presents Roman imperial power as the agent that takes Jesus' life; that is Jesus dies on a Roman cross. But with the use of dramatic irony, Mark mocks those who execute this power. While the Roman actors believe they are defeating Jesus through a shameful execution, Mark presents them as unwittingly giving Jesus a triumph in the process. Thus even in death, the Markan Jesus subverts Roman power and outdoes the Roman emperor. As the passion narrative comes to a close, one Markan character, a Roman centurion, recognizes the irony and declares Jesus 'Son of God.'[17]

This subversive power of the cross is even aptly (re-)presented by the Black liberation theologian, James Cone, in his study of the cross and the lynching tree in the USA. Cone asserts, "[T]he cross is a paradoxical religious symbol because it inverts the world's value system with the news that hope comes by way of defeat, that suffering and death do not have the last word, that the last shall be first and the first shall be last."[18]Thus, we can claim that the cross stands as a living testimony to the fact that, for God, the unjust suffering and death of an innocent person is so precious that She would transform that death into a life-giving and life-affirming story.

Crucified Bodies Today

Having seen the cross within the socio-political context of the Roman Empire, I return to the twenty-first century to reflect on what the cross means today in relation to Black and Dalit suffering. Firstly, as noted earlier, the violence against Black and Dalit people cannot be seen as isolated events. Their murders were conducted within the (constructed) social structures of race and caste under the watchful eyes of the respective nation states. These people were victims of white and caste supremacy which assumed that their bodies were too transgressive or threatening to be allowed to live. For instance, when the police broke into the apartment of Deborah Danner, a Black woman with mental health issues in New York, a pair of scissors in her hand was enough of a 'threat' to shoot and kill her.[19] In March 2016, Sankar, a young educated and well-to-do Dalit

17. Winn, "Gospel of Mark," 104.

18. Cone, *Cross and the Lynching Tree*, 2.

19. New York Times, "In Quick Response, de Blasio Calls Fatal Shooting of Mentally Ill Woman ' Unacceptable.'"

who married someone outside his caste, was enough of a problem for the caste-governed society that he was hacked to death. His good education and secure job did not convince the upper-caste girl's family to accept him as a "respectable" human being.[20] In their eyes, he had transgressed his boundaries and defied the sacred caste rules laid down by the gods and the tradition.[21]

Considering these murders of Blacks and Dalits, I see the social constructs of caste and race as life-regulating (and life-negating) *nomoi* (laws) of our times, particularly visible in their respective (national) contexts.[22] These social constructs have birthed false notions of superiority in the oppressors allowing them to exert dominion over Black and Dalit bodies. The fact that these social "systems"—as internalized by individuals and communities, and supported, perpetuated, and strengthened by the nation-state(s)—control attitudes and actions should remind us that we cannot under-estimate their power.

It is in this sense I believe the violence against Black and Dalit bodies to be similar to the Roman crucifixions during the time of Jesus. That is, their deaths (like that of Jesus) are statements of threat and intimidation made by invisible but ever-active socio-political systems to re-instate hierarchy and hegemony. Therefore, in Christian theological language, we can say that Blacks and Dalits who were killed by white and caste supremacists were indeed "crucified" by the racist and casteist

20. Kumar, "Dalit Youth Killed for Marrying Caste Girl." This murder was even captured on video by CCTV cameras. Similarly, in September 2018, Pranay Kumar was hacked to death for marrying Amrutha Varshini, an upper-caste girl, by his father-in-law. See Times Now Digital, "Telangana Honor Killing."

21. While there are many theories on the origins of untouchability, there is a strong link to the Hindu scriptures and their interpretations. According to the *Purusha Sukta* poem in the *Rig Veda* (ca. fifteenth century BCE), the society is classified into Brahmins (priests), Kshatriyas (warriors), Vaishyas (traders), and Sudras (servants). Using this classification, the Manu Dharmasastra (third century CE) prohibited the mixing of the first three classes—which were considered as the "twice born" classes—with the Sudras. The offspring of those who transgress this sacred norm were the untouchable outcastes, who also (naturally) were forbidden from mixing with the four classes. While the text itself may not have a "legal" hold on all South Asians, mixing of different caste communities, particularly involving Dalits, is still not encouraged. Olson, *Hindu Primary Sources,* 24; Oliville, *Law Code of Manu,* 179–80. Also see Shrirama, "Untouchability and Stratification in Indian Civilisation," 45–75.

22. I am aware that race or caste cannot be limited to any one geographical location any longer. While the universal presence of race is quite obvious, recent researches have pointed out that caste too has gone global. See Zwick-Maitreyi et al., *Caste in the United States.*

power structures. However, this relationship between the crucified Jesus and the crucified people today, in this case belonging to Black and Dalit communities, is not simply accidental. Rather, as womanist theologian, Kelly Brown Douglas argues,

> Jesus' identification with the lynched/crucified class is... intentional. It did not begin with his death on the cross. In fact, that Jesus was crucified signals his prior bond with the 'crucified class' of his day.[23]

Speaking of the crucified people, I believe it is also important to lay special emphasis on the body. This is especially necessary given that the Christian tradition has for long marginalized the body in history. But, as the French philosopher, Michel Foucault, reminds us, "the body itself is invested by power relations" and "directly involved in a political field."[24] Therefore, in the words of, social anthropologist and gender theorist, Athena Athanasiou,

> Our bodies are beyond themselves. Through our bodies, we are implicated in thick and intense social processes of relatedness and interdependence; we are exposed, dismembered, given over to others, and undone by the norms that regulate desire, sexual alliance, kinship relations, and conditions of humanness. We are dispossessed by others, moved toward others and by others, affected by others and able to affect others.[25]

Noting this significance of the body, especially in relation to the power dynamics between the oppressors and the oppressed, Dalit political theologian, John Boopalan, observes that all of us are governed by "grammar of the body" which are "socially conditioned rules by which bodies are habituated to 'speak,'" which "when uncritically followed, condition dominant subjects' actions and reactions to violence" against disenfranchised people.[26] Therefore, given the critical significance of the body in the context of discriminatory epistemic and socio-political systems, it becomes necessary to pay attention to the body, especially of those that are marginalized and violated. This is indeed particularly pivotal for a faith whose foundations lie in "a very earthly, fleshy, physical

23. Douglas, *Stand Your Ground*, 71.

24. Foucault, *Discipline and Punish*, 24 and 25.

25. Butler and Athanasiou, *Dispossession*, 55.

26. Boopalan, *Memory*, 89.

way to connect with one's God,"[27] and is rooted in the story of a person whose body was broken on a Roman cross. Hence, the need to re-turn to the bodies of the broken people today, and uphold the suffering and the hope that is embodied within them. But, before we move on to reflecting on the Black and Dalit crucified bodies, let us consider, in brief, the theology of the cross articulated by Black and Dalit theologians.

Black and Dalit Interpretations of the Cross

Drawing parallels between the violence meted out to Blacks and Dalits, and the crucifixion of Jesus is certainly not new for Black and Dalit theologians. In fact, identifying Black and Dalit suffering with the suffering of Jesus goes (back) to the heart of Black and Dalit liberation theology of which we will have a glimpse here.

As James Cone explains, Blacks, in contrast to white Christians and theologians,[28] were able to readily grasp the deeper meaning of the cross through the sufferings that they endured in enslavement, lynching, and segregation. He writes,

> blacks who first heard the gospel message seized on the power of the cross. Christ crucified manifested God's loving and liberating presence *in* the contradictions of black life—that transcendent presence in the lives of black Christians that empowered them to believe that *ultimately,* in God's eschatological future, they would not be defeated by the "troubles of this world," no matter how great and painful their suffering.[29]

In other words, Blacks were able to comprehend the paradoxical meaning(s) of the cross and believe that in spite of their sufferings, they will not be defeated. Through the cross they believed that evil cannot and will not have the last word. Rather, it is the God of justice and life who is in solidarity with them who will triumph ultimately. Shawn Copeland points out that "[T]he cross was treasured" by the Blacks "because it enthroned the One who went all the way with them and for them..." and

---

27. Isherwood and Stuart, *Introducing Body Theology,* 16.

28. Elsewhere, Cone contrasts the participant approach of the Blacks with the "spectator approach of the Western theological tradition" in interpreting the cross. Cone, *God of the Oppressed,* 169.

29. Cone, *Cross and the Lynching Tree,* 2. Emphasis in the original text.

in it "they saw the triumph over the principalities and powers of death, triumph over evil in this world."[30]

But, Copeland warns us that the cross does not offer "cheap or simplistic solution to the problem of evil."[31] In her book, *Enfleshing Freedom*, Copeland argues that "[T]o place maimed lynched bodies beside the maimed body of Jesus of Nazareth is the condition for a theological anthropology that reinforces the sacramentality of the body, and honors the body as the self-manifestation and self-expression of the free human subject."[32] Relating this to the Eucharist, she notes that this opens new ways of imagining and practicing solidarity in the work of justice.

> Solidarity begins in an *anamnesis*, which intentionally remembers and invokes the black victims of history, martyrs for freedom. Theologically considered, their suffering, like the suffering of Jesus, seeds a new life for the future of all humanity. Their suffering, like the suffering of Jesus, anticipates an enfleshment of freedom and life to which Eucharist is linked ineluctably. Eucharist, then, is countersign to the devaluation and violence directed toward the black body.[33]

This close link between the suffering of Jesus and Black suffering is perfectly captured by Douglas when she says, "[B]ecause of Jesus' death on the cross, there is no doubt that Jesus would have a 'deep and personal' identification with the black pain, heartache, suffering, and death... Just as black people identify with the cross of Jesus, the cross of Jesus means he identifies with them."[34]

In the Dalit context too, the cross has been used to describe the "Dalitness" of Jesus. For them, through his death on the cross Jesus revealed himself as a Dalit in every sense of the word. Correlating the Dalit experience and the cross, pioneering Dalit theologian, Arvind P. Nirmal, writes,

> dalitness is best symbolized by the cross. On the cross, he was the broken the crushed, the split the torn, the driven asunder man—the dalit in the fullest possible meaning of that term... "My God, my god, why hast thou forsaken me?" he cried aloud

---

30. Cited by Cone, *Cross and the Lynching Tree*, 151.

31. Copeland, *Enfleshing Freedom*, 124.

32. Copeland, *Enfleshing Freedom*, 124.

33. Copeland, *Enfleshing Freedom*, 124.

34. Douglas, *Stand Your Ground*, 178.

from the cross. The Son of God felt he is God-forsaken. That feeling of being God forsaken is at the heart of our dalit experience and Dalit consciousness in India. It is the dalitness of divinity and humanity that the cross of Jesus symbolises.[35]

Thus, Nirmal, noticing the parallels between the experiences of Jesus and the Dalits, believes in God's solidarity with them in their suffering. But, as we know, the gospel stories of the cross do not *end* with Jesus' suffering and death. Taking this positive aspect seriously, M. E. Prabhakar believes that just like Jesus' dalitness on the cross culminated in his victorious resurrection, so will the sufferings of the Dalits be turned into liberation. He asserts, "In the Dalitness of Jesus they will be strengthened and upheld for victory against the forces that dehumanize them."[36] Thus, not unlike the Black theologians, Dalits too believe that the cross, not only aptly portrays their suffering, but also gives them hope and strength to resist the powers that cause that suffering. Recognizing this theological proximity between the body of Jesus and the Dalit bodies, we can say that Dalit (along with other crucified) bodies fully (though not exclusively) mediate the immanent Christic presence of God, thus, giving them a sacramental essence. Therefore, in the context of caste oppression, we can say that the Dalit body is the "untouchable sacrament of God."[37]

Deepening and enriching these theological musings, Joseph Prabhakar Dayam identifies that this close connection between the cross and Dalit suffering goes beyond Christianity. In his attempt to re-imagine an Indian theology of the cross using Dalit cultural resources, he notes that many Dalit goddesses have also experienced "rejection and suffering" making them "important categories of the Dalit religious tradition."[38] Thus, based on his research of the Gonthamma tradition among Mala Dalit communities in South India, Dayam locates his theology of the cross within a broader (multi-)religious framework. He writes,

> Perhaps the historical suffering of the Dalits prompted them to see suffering as one of the essential natures of God which is symbolized in the suffering of Kunthi whom they venerate as Goddess Gonthi. Suffering is therefore understood to be the nature of the divine. Their openness to Christ as the suffering

35. Nirmal, "Toward a Christian Dalit Theology," 69.

36. Prabhakar, "Christology in Dalit Perspective," 414.

37. See the section "Sacramentality of the Dalit Body," in Samuel, *Untouchable Bodies*, 70–72.

38. Dayam, "Re-Imagining an Indian Theology of the Cross," 184.

deity must have arose out of their own suffering and their understanding of the divine as the suffering one…. The rejected of the community see their own experience of rejection in the rejection of their deities. Christ as the rejected one as manifested in the cross, naturally became a God of the Dalits. Their experience of suffering and rejection become epistemological keys in knowing the divine. Therefore the cross is the key in knowing the essential nature of God which is the Dalitness of God.[39]

Thus, Dalit engagement with the cross is based on their ability to historically interpret their suffering in relation to the divine well before they met Christianity. In other words, one can say that the Dalit theology of the cross transcends the Christian tradition and has a universal significance beyond any one particular religion.

Recapitulating on the previous sections and the brief study of Black and Dalit theological interpretations of the cross, we can make some summative statements that can serve as signposts for the constructive work in the final section. First, since the cross occupies a central place for Black and Dalit theologies, there is an inevitable comparison of the sufferings in these communities with that of Jesus. Therefore, we are challenged to assert that Blacks and Dalits, in virtue of their unjust sufferings, are the "crucified peoples" of our time. Secondly, however, as (repeatedly) observed, cross as a paradoxical symbol of suffering and liberation also affirms that their sufferings will not and cannot be in vain. In other words, just like the God of Jesus did not allow the Roman capital punishment to have the final word on his beloved child and let him rot in the grave, so will She not allow the sufferings of the oppressed to continue but intervene by *suffering with them* and *fighting for* them. Finally, we need to recognize that any current God-talk that claims to be faithful to the crucified Jesus cannot be blind to the "Jesuses" today. In other words, I believe that any theology of the cross that does not speak about or relate itself to the "crucifixions" of the Black and Dalit bodies in their respective contexts cannot be an authentic Christian theology.

39. Dayam, "Re-Imagining an Indian Theology of the Cross," 184–85.

Crucified and Risen Bodies:
Some Reflections from the Margins

Having noted the significance of the crucified Black and Dalit bodies in relation to the crucified Jesus, in this final section, let me try to offer some theological reflections on the cross within the context of Black and Dalit suffering.

Cross as the Place of Divinization:
Where Demons become Deities

According to Kahl, in the Roman empire, the cross was, among other things, the stage for re-enacting the victory of the (imperial) gods over the (barbaric) demons (of the empire).[40] Thus, those who were crucified were not just enemies of the emperor and the empire but also the gods of the empire. In that sense, the crucified enemies were not just rebellious humans but demons who had defied the sacred laws of the gods. Relating this to Jesus, one may say that in the Roman imperial system he was a demon who was defeated by the divine emperor and the gods of the empire. No wonder then that the cross signified utter hopelessness without any sense of the presence of God. For a God fearing Jew in particular, or any person of faith for that matter, this was an experience of abject misery. One can now understand the intensity of the cry of Jesus, "My God, my God, why have you forsaken me?" (Matthew 27:46; Mark 15:34), which aptly captures the excruciating pain and the sense of abandonment that he experienced on the cross. It was perhaps the moment when Jesus' emotional and physical strength gave away and reached rock bottom.

However, the German political theologian, Jürgen Moltmann believes that it is (with)in this experience of abandonment that Jesus was able to "include" the suffering of all those who suffer unjustly in history.[41] The Latin American liberation theologian, Gustavo Gutiérrez, also commenting on this cry of Jesus, agrees with Moltmann by stating that, through his feeling of abandonment, Jesus is "the *cantus firmus*, the leading voice to which all the voices of those who suffer unjustly are joined."[42] In other words, the suffering of Jesus becomes the meeting

---

40. Kahl, *Galatians Re-imagined*, 159–63.

41. Moltmann, *Way of Jesus Christ*, 151–57.

42. Gutiérrez, *On Job*, 101.

point of all the sufferings of the world. However, as Moltmann is quick to point out, the cross does not symbolize just suffering but paradoxically embodies (within itself) the hope of resurrection as well.[43] But this is not an abstract theoretical hope. Rather, it is a hope that was *experienced* by the communities that believed in Jesus. These communities, by their faith in Jesus and empowered by the Spirit of God, believed experientially that despite his brutal death, Jesus was exalted by God as God's son and was alive *in* God (Acts 2:33). In other words, the communities that believed in Jesus, through their faith and with the help of God, made the resurrection of Jesus possible and real.

In 2014, Michael Brown, an unarmed teenager, was shot dead by a white police officer, Darren Wilson. During his interrogation, Wilson, who is six foot tall, described himself as a "five-year old" who felt intimidated by Brown's appearance. He said that Brown appeared like "Hulk Hogan" and a "demon" with a menacing (Black) body, and therefore, he had to kill him.[44] Now, if Jesus, the demon of the empire, was raised by God, isn't it possible that Brown, and the other crucified people like him, would also be exalted by God as Her children and live on (with)in their communities? If God revealed in Jesus is in solidarity with them, are they not, by virtue of their innocent suffering, also resurrected by God into *theosis* like Jesus? In that sense, I believe we can indeed assert that God who is one with the oppressed, in his gratuitous love,[45] receives the life of innocent sufferers into himself and makes them divine. The cross is therefore, not just a place of God's solidarity with his people but is a place of subversion where "the wretched of the earth,"[46] who are often humiliated as "demons" by imperial/white/caste supremacy, are exalted as the holy women and men of God.

---

43. For Moltmann, resurrection is not about life in a separate realm or time. Rather, "[I]t is the power which enables *this* life to be reborn." Moltmann, *Way of Jesus Christ,* 242. Emphasis mine.

44. New York Times. "Michael Brown's Shooting."

45. As Gustavo Gutiérrez says, "God has a preferential option for the poor not because they are necessarily better than others, but simply because they are poor and living in an inhuman situation that is contrary to God's will." Gutiérrez, *On Job*, 94.

46. Phrase adapted from the title of Frantz Fanon's book. Fanon, *Wretched of the Earth.*

Cross as the Place of Victory: Where Losers Become Victors

Paul, in his letter to the Colossian church, writes that, on his cross, Jesus "disarmed the rulers and authorities and made a public example of them, triumphing over them in it."[47] Who are these rulers and authorities? In the previous verse, Paul says that they are the powers who *controlled* the lives of people through legal demands, which, if we recall the context of the cross, are powers of the Roman empire. It is these powers that had sent Jesus and many others to their crosses, a symbol of defeat. But in the case of Jesus, Paul believes this scheme backfired. According to him, Jesus took the cross—a tool of imperial capital punishment—and nailed the powers of the empire on that same cross, and publically shamed them. René Girard elucidates this climax as follows:

> By nailing Christ to the Cross, the powers believed they were doing what they ordinarily did in unleashing the single victim mechanism. They thought they were avoiding the danger of disclosure. They did not suspect that in the end they would be doing just the opposite: they would be contributing to their own annihilation, nailing themselves to the Cross, so to speak. They did not and could not suspect the revelatory power of the Cross.[48]

In other words, Jesus used, and quite successfully one may add, the "master's tools to dismantle the master's house."[49] As mentioned earlier, God in solidarity with the crucified Jesus used the cross to mock the empire. However, it is important to note again that Jesus, the supposed-to-be loser, became the victor over the powers of divisive imperialism, only in terms of his resurrection *within* his community. To put it differently, the community of followers/believers of Jesus, empowered by the Spirit of God, *ensured* that the purposes of the imperial powers would be thwarted and Jesus would be victorious.

Now, as the crucified people, I believe that the bodies of Blacks and Dalits who experience violence also carry this message of victory. Their sufferings and death were intended by the powers of white and caste

---

47. Col 2:15. All references in this paper are from the New Revised Standard Version Bible.

48. Girard, *I See Satan Fall Like Lightning*, 142.

49. Of course, as Audre Lorde notes, this notion is deeply problematic, and surely cannot be universalized. See "Master's Tools will never Dismantle the Master's House," in Lorde, *Sister Outsider*, 110–13.

supremacy to make them symbols of failure and to mock their worth and dignity. But, these defeats have been turned into symbols of victory and life by various communities of solidarity through their resistance marked by protests and rallies. Obscure Black and Dalit bodies have become the seeds of powerful movements that challenge and shake the powers of white and caste supremacy. For instance, Dalit Mahila Swabhiman Yatra led by Dalit women activists has been working since 2012 to create awareness of sexual violence against Dalit (and Tribal) women in India and challenge caste and patriarchy.[50] Of course, the victory is not yet fully achieved. Nevertheless, the fact that the powers of white and caste supremacy are being publicly paraded and humiliated is a victory in itself. White supremacy tried to nail George Floyd and others like him on the cross (of racism) by demonizing and killing them. But unexpectedly, these crucified ones, in their death (and through their life in their communities) have nailed white supremacy on the cross! And the same may be said of Dalits. The Dalit bodies that were lynched by caste supremacy continue to speak back and mock the powers of casteism. It is in this sense that I believe we can claim the cross to be the place where losers, through the life-giving power of God and the solidarity of their communities, turn the tables around and become victors.

Cross as the Place of Reconciliation: Where Enemies become Family

Finally, I see that the cross can be seen as a place of reconciliation. Once again, turning to Paul, we see that God reconciles divided people together "through the cross, thus putting to death... hostility."[51] Thus, a new humanity of peace is realized *through* the cross. In other words, for Paul, no reconciliation between human communities is possible without the cross. No reconciliatory effort for Christians can bypass the cross. Isn't this yet another paradox about the cross? The Roman imperial cross which was the symbol of hierarchical divisions was subverted by Jesus and made into a symbol of reconciliation.[52]

50. Dalit Mahila Swabhiman Yatra, "Women Activism against Caste and Sexual Violence."

51. Eph 2:16.

52. However, I am aware how the cross has been misused to divide people and as a symbol for violence, for instance, during the crusades. I see this as a gross misinterpretation and misrepresentation of the cross.

In a sense, this is precisely what we see in the protests for the crucified people of our time which have brought divided communities together for the sake of justice. I don't believe we can see the voices for Floyd or Arbery or the lynched Dalit women and men as protests about *individuals*. Rather, it is about bringing justice to their communities that have been unjustly oppressed for many centuries. But at an even deeper level, I see them as protests for the well-being of all humanity and the earth. I see them as dreams for a reconciled (new) world that would not be divided on the basis of race or caste or gender or other such oppressive social constructs. It would be a community where the oppressor and the oppressed will dwell together in justice and peace. Isn't this what Jesus dreamed and spoke of as the reign of God/heaven? However, this also reminds us that the reign of God would have to begin at the cross, the cross of the crucified people. Unless we begin with the unjust sufferings of the Blacks we cannot talk about the reign of God in the USA's context. Similarly, unless we acknowledge and respond to the suffering of the Dalits, we cannot talk about God's reign in the Indian context. A truly reconciled community of God begins at the cross, the place where Black and Dalit bodies have been crucified.

However, speaking of reconciliation, we need to be careful that the cause of the oppressed is not sacrificed in order to bring peace, or to be more precise, for the sake of compromise. Here, I find Mark Taylor's concept of reconciliatory emancipation helpful to keep our priorities right. Taylor reminds us that "[T]he reconciliatory element, the drive for unity amid differences, Christianity's well-known valuation of a koinonia, community of love, is a necessary posture of Christian practice that pervades, qualifies, but never takes precedence over... emancipation."[53] Therefore, it is important to stress that the movement(s) inspired by the crucified bodies, while moving towards reconciliation and the unity of all people, cannot ignore the primacy and urgency of emancipation of the oppressed.

Looking Ahead: Toward a Solidarity of Crucified Bodies

In this essay, I have attempted to reflect on the theology of the cross in light of the sufferings and killings of Blacks in the USA and Dalits in South Asia. Let me conclude with some suggestions for future exploration in

53. Taylor, *Remembering Esperanza*, 176.

Black-Dalit studies even while pointing out historical precedents. First, I hope that a joint study of Black and Dalit suffering creates more interest in learning about the reality and interconnectedness of oppressive systems across the globe. It is heartening to note that this was already attempted by leaders such as W. E. B. Du Bois and B. R. Ambedkar who had an awareness of each other's contexts.[54] Second, I would like this essay to encourage cross-cultural and trans-global learning and mutual inspiration between the marginalized communities of the world. Again we have a precedence, when in the 1970s, Dalit Panthers, a political movement inspired by the Black Panthers in the USA, was formed in Western India and became a major political-cultural force.[55] Finally, I also hope that this chapter engenders solidarity building among the oppressed in the work of justice. Again, we have exemplars to show us the way. We see this effort for global solidarity in the work of Malcolm X in the last few years of his life when he wanted to internationalize the Black rights movement in the USA and build a trans-global justice network, especially among those of African descent.[56] Today we see this in the solidarity among Black and Dalit activists who come together to protest against the killings of Black people.[57] I sincerely wish that this paper would arouse interest in creating networks of learning and activism among the "crucified peoples," since in such solidarity lies the hope and possibility of realizing justice and true peace in the world.

> Dear Prof. Dubois, . . . I belong to the Untouchables of India and perhaps you might have heard my name. I have been a student of the Negro problem and have read your writings throughout. There is so much similarity between the position

54. Dr. W. E. B. Du Bois and Dr. B. R. Ambedkar were aware of the struggles of each other's communities which is evident in the correspondence between them. See UMassAmherst, "Letter from B. R. Ambedkar to Dr. W. E. B. Du Bois, ca. July 1946." and "Letter from W. E. B. Du Bois to B. R. Ambedkar, July 31, 1946." Also see Martin Luther King Jr.'s description of the untouchables in Washington, *Testament of Hope*, 27–28.

55. Though Dalit Panthers was disbanded soon, some of the literature they produced is considered immensely important for Dalit liberation even today. For the history and influence of Dalit Panthers, see Pawar, *Dalit Panthers*, loc. 3565–632. Pawar was one of the co-founders of Dalit Panthers.

56. See the inaugural speech of Malcolm X at the founding rally of the Organization of Afro-American Unity (OAAU). Malcolm X, *By Any Means Necessary*, 57–96.

57. A good case in point is the involvement of Dalit women activists in the Black Lives Matter movement. Equality Labs, "Dalit Women Activists in the Black Lives Matter Movement."

of the Untouchables in India and of the position of the Negroes in America that the study of the latter is not only natural but necessary. —B. R. Ambedkar[58]

My dear Mr. Ambedkar, I have often heard of your name and work and of course have every sympathy with the Untouchables of India. I shall be glad to be of any service I can render if possible in the future.—W. E. B. Du Bois[59]

---

58. UMassAmherst, "Letter from B. R. Ambedkar to Dr. W. E. B. Du Bois."
59. UMassAmherst, "Letter from W. E. B. Du Bois to B. R. Ambedkar."

Chapter 12

Countering counter-insurgency in Grenada, Belize, Bahrain, and Sri Lanka

Investigative Journalism
as Resistance to Imperial Militarization

PHIL MILLER

"Who is responsible? I think of it a little like the Agatha Christie mystery 'The Murder on the Orient Express.' It turned out that all the suspects were involved in the murder. All the people he was exposing had a motive to see him dead—all those who benefited from exploitation, all those who sowed division among the people, those who promoted racism, external powers who wanted control over parts of the island for their strategic interests etc etc. Although which of these forces collaborated to organise the assassination of Sivaram is not definitively known—the fact that they all benefited from his death is clear."
— VIRAJ MENDIS[1]

Introduction

Many people would believe that the UK has had little or no direct involvement with the internal affairs of Sri Lanka, Bahrain, Grenada and

1. Mendis, "Dharmeratnam Sivaram: Murder of a Brilliant Journalist."

Belize since these relatively small territories became independent from British rule in 1948, 1971, 1974, and 1981 respectively. The reality is that the UK has made strategic militarized interventions in each country to ensure that their post-colonial political trajectory aligns with Anglo-American capitalist demands, does not threaten Western hegemony nor present autonomous alternatives to this world order. The recurrence of these counter-insurgency inventions over a broad historical period (70 years) and geographical span (from 88 degrees West to 81 degrees East), and in societies as diverse as indigenous Mayan, African-Caribbean, Gulf Arab, and South Asian demonstrate that the policies were not an aberration from an otherwise benign liberal democratic metropole, but in fact they were fundamental to the maintenance of an imperial system.

Aside from defending the global status quo, the consequences of UK counter-insurgency range from the deprivation of social and economic progress in the fields of healthcare, education and housing, to the denial of civil and political rights including freedom of assembly, expression (such as religious belief) and protection from torture. In two cases discussed here, Sri Lanka and Belize/Guatemala, UK action has ultimately contributed towards genocide. In the face of this counter-insurgency, there has been relentless resistance from communities and people who live in these locations to *counter* counter-insurgency, as well as unlikely acts of solidarity or repentance from sections of the British public or local enforcers of Western hegemony. In this article, I analyze the doctrine of countering counter-insurgency (CCI) as articulated and lived by the Tamil revolutionary Dharmeratnam Sivaram. His doctrine has informed my own work as an investigative journalist based primarily in London, and I provide two in-depth case studies of British counter-insurgency practices in the Americas (Grenada and Belize) that I have unearthed by following Sivaram's method. To conclude, I reflect on my encounters with people of faith from Bahrain and Sri Lanka to draw out how their spirituality serves as a resource for sustaining CCI.

Who is Sivaram?

Sivaram hailed from the East of Ceylon/Sri Lanka and was born in the city of Batticaloa in 1959, just over a decade after the island became independent from British rule. By the time he was old enough to attend university, the country's Tamil minority had developed a national liberation movement that demanded a separate state from the oppressive Sinhalese majority. Sivaram initially engaged in non-violent activism before joining a left-wing Tamil armed revolutionary group and then becoming a journalist in the late 1980s. His intense transformation from campus to sword to pen all took place in a six year period. As such Sivaram's youth encompassed the full spectrum of the doctrine he would later develop: from the insurgency phase against a weak but brutal state; to suffering the counter-insurgency onslaught of a more militarized state (and experiencing the inevitable splits and factions within the insurgent movement); and finally articulating strategies and tactics that might safeguard the insurgent movement against defeat.

Therefore, Sivaram's CCI doctrine is based on the lived experience of an oppressed person who was immersed in the full fury of a national liberation struggle against an enemy —an enemy that would ultimately assassinate him because of the power of his writing. His biographer, Mark Whitaker, said that before his death "Sivaram began to feel that if he could just leave behind in his writings a clear and meticulously accurate picture of exactly how a counter-insurgency campaign is conducted, won, and (most importantly) sometimes defeated, this in itself would constitute a telling blow against repression."[2] Put more simply, "Sivaram was trying to leave behind a set of instructions or a cookbook for defeating counter-insurgency."[3] Whitaker broke Sivaram's approach down into five components:

1. Defining military jargon

2. Presenting geopolitical context

3. Profiling political actors

4. Comparing military history and theory

5. Compiling ethnographic/socio-metric depictions of communities

On every level of his doctrine, Sivaram strove to write in a manner that was clear and accessible. In adopting this approach, he followed (wittingly or otherwise) in the tradition articulated by another prominent Tamil revolutionary writer of the twentieth century, Ambalavaner Sivanandan. As a refugee in London, working in the library of the conservative Institute of Race Relations in the early 1970s, Sivanandan staged a

2. Whitaker, *Learning Politics from Sivaram*, 118.
3. Whitaker, *Learning Politics from Sivaram*, 118.

coup to take over the Institute and transform it from a colonial think tank into an anti-racist think and do tank. The house publication was overhauled from an introspective academic exercise into a "Journal for Black and Third World Liberation." In its founding editorial, Sivanandan took aim at the old guard, condemning their "articles which strike a pose in order to intimidate the uninitiated, articles that are a mere display of academic virtuosity— academics relating to academics over the dead bodies of their subjects."[4] He warned that "the result is scholarship that engenders a colonialism of the mind, brings credibility to power, and helps further to enslave the oppressed and the exploited." In one of his great aphorism, he thundered, "the function of knowledge, however, is to liberate." Sivaram's own desire to spread knowledge among the oppressed saw him pioneer the use of new technologies such as smart phones and websites as tools and platforms for quickly uploading his writing from the field and disseminating it among islanders and the global Tamil refugee diaspora.

My adaptation of the Sivaram's approach has largely consisted of regular research trips to the UK National Archives at Kew in south-west London. From this location, I have viewed declassified British State's records on around a dozen former colonies. Under the Public Records Act, the files are typically made available 30 years after they were written. With reference to Sivaram's five step CCI doctrine, the Kew files offer an insight into (1) British military bureaucracy, (2) geopolitical context as it was then, (3) which political actors were involved in key decisions behind the scenes, (4) military history, and (5) how British authorities analyzed communities in their former colonies. I believe that visiting the Kew archive is consistent with a broader CCI tradition—for instance the Maoist leader in Malaysia, Chin Peng, later went to Kew to read records on how the British had fought his insurgency.[5]

The Kew archive contains records of British policy towards almost every country on earth, and as such provides an opportunity to study all kinds of insurgency and counter-insurgency scenarios from which to inform CCI doctrine. Whilst Peng has comprehensively analysed his own insurgency, other struggles recorded in the Kew archive lie largely untouched. Grenada, a small island in the eastern Caribbean, was among one of the last British colonies to gain independence, and its liberation

4. Sivanandan, "Editorial."
5. Peng, *My Side of History*.

struggle offers a concise case study of a successful insurgency. Similarly, the struggle against military dictatorship in Guatemala has rarely been approached from the study of Britain's support for that regime.

Mining Truths: The Kew Archives

Grenada: Repression of Black Power

Grenada gained international attention in 1979 when the New Jewel Movement (NJM), a revolutionary Black Power movement, overthrew the dictator Eric Gairy. The Grenadian revolution would last until 1983, when US Marines infamously invaded the island. However, the Kew archive reveals how the UK had an almost identical plan to land a battalion of troops on Grenada a decade earlier. The Ministry of Defence had gone as far as preparing a secret invasion plan to restore colonial rule if Gairy lost control. The NJM threatened to nationalize British economic interests in the Caribbean, which were seen as comparable with the UK's investments in India. The Kew archive is most helpful in understanding the geopolitical context and the military mechanisms used by the former colonial power to subvert a struggle against poverty and oppression. This offers lessons for other island nations about the means of repression that might be ranged against them should they challenge the international order.

In summary, a fortnight before Grenada's independence in February 1974, the UK's Chief of the Defence Staff wrote to the Defence Secretary with a secret plan for evacuating 200 British subjects from the island using warships, helicopters and Royal Marine Commandos.[6] Anti-government protests and strikes had gripped Grenada in the months leading up to independence, demanding the resignation of the island's ruthless leader Eric Gairy. The NJM had produced a manifesto which read:

> On February 7th, 1974, we are supposed to become independent. If we do, this will be independence in name only. Gairy believes that independence means pulling down one flag and putting up another, composing a new anthem, creating a new motto, calling the Governor 'Governor General' and the Premier, 'Prime Minister'; playing steelband, jumping up and feteing; cleaning up and beautifying the streets. But after all the

6. National Archives UK (NAUK): FCO 63/1251, "Situation in Grenada," January 24, 1974.

celebrations and bacchanal are over and we wake up next day (or next week) with a hangover, the price of food, clothes and everything else will still keep going up, wages will still be the same (or less), the condition of the schools, hospitals and roads (except for maybe two more roundabouts) will continue to get worse, and the people's housing will still be the same or worse.[7]

The NJM manifesto went on to demand $100 million reparations from Britain "to make up for some of the money stolen from us and the exploitation, human misery, suffering and degradation we have endured at their hands over the last 400 years." Other NJM policies— "Jewel" stood for Joint endeavour for welfare, education and liberation—included primary healthcare, secondary education, low-cost housing, land redistribution, people's assemblies and a non-aligned foreign policy.[8] It was a rousing rallying cry from a former slave plantation whose survivors had the bravery and vision to demand a future comparable to the Cuban revolution.

The Kew archive allows for a detailed analysis of how Britain responded to this kind of political movement. Whitehall did not rule out British forces intervening to "restore law and order after a breakdown of the Gairy Government," deeming that "this is a decision which can be taken only in the light of the circumstances at the time."[9] In the end, the invasion plan was not used, as Gairy clung to power. Other files show that British spies in the security service MI5 were monitoring trade unions in Grenada and running informants inside the revolutionary NJM.

Just days before independence, British intelligence reports described the NJM as: "an extremist organization whose main aim is the overthrow of Gairy and his government (by force if other means fail) and the setting up in its place of a people's revolutionary regime. The NJM is in touch with other similar organizations in the Caribbean, particularly Trinidad."[10] This reminds us of the importance of progressive groups having international contact with similar organizations abroad. The spies speculated that the NJM could try to assassinate Gairy on Independence Day, "when his public presence amongst crowds, noise and fireworks

7. The Grenada Revolution Online, "Manifesto of the New Jewel Movement."

8. Searle, *Grenada*, 18.

9. NAUK: DEFE 25/367, January 25, 1974, and PREM 15/2018, "Grenada: policy on intervention by HM Forces – DOP (74)12," January 29, 1974, secret letter from Deputy Secretary of Cabinet Office, Howard Smith, to the Prime Minister.

10. NAUK: FCO 63/1251, February 3, 1974. Secret telex between MI5 and FCO.

might present a favourable opportunity."[11] The MI5 men noted that "[o]n the other hand, the West Indian temperament does not seem to lend itself to determined and fanatical action except sporadically."[12] It seems that British spies were prone to forming their own ethnographic assessments of peoples, with a view to understanding what forms their resistance might entail. The intelligence officers acknowledged that Gairy's security forces included "ruthless" police aides, "an un-uniformed and undisciplined body ... many of them have criminal records," who were under the Premier's personal control.[13] Known as the "Mongoose Gang" among islanders, this police militia had killed Rupert Bishop, father of the NJM leader, shortly before in January 1974.

The files reveal that MI5 had been watching Grenada's labour movement in the months building up to independence. A planned strike in December 1973 generated a flurry of intelligence reports based on secret sources in the trade unions and other leftwing groups. One memo claims: "Source stated that there would undoubtedly be a general strike on 27 December . . . Source also stated that NJM considered they were not yet ready for final confrontation and had no intention [of] using violence at present . . . Source is in a good position to know and has good entree into NJM."[14] Another intelligence report from December 1973 also examined the likelihood of NJM violence and police capabilities, noting,

> In the past the NJM has tended to exercise restraint in resorting to violence, although we believe that they have the capacity to stir up disorders to the point where the weak and inefficient police force would lose control. Much will depend on whether the NJM judge that their interest will be served by violence. A frigate of the West Indies Squadron will be in Barbados, about 23 hours steaming away, from mid December and early January.[15]

This combination of spies recruiting informants inside labour movements, and naval powers stationing ships on standby off the coast, again help us to understand how counter-insurgency is organized from

11. FCO 63/1251, February 3, 1974.

12. FCO 63/1251, February 3, 1974.

13. FCO 63/1251, February 3, 1974.

14. NAUK: FCO 63/1138, December 16, 1973. Secret telex from MI5 officer in Trinidad.

15. NAUK: FCO 63/1138, "Grenada—security situation," December 17, 1973. Confidential paper for Joint Intelligence Committee Latin America Current Intelligence Group meeting.

a military/intelligence perspective. The MI5 intelligence reports on the trade unions and leftwing groups continued into late February 1974, after independence. More significantly, the secret intelligence reports on Grenada were compiled by the MI5 station in Trinidad, which had orchestrated the overthrow of Guyana's democratically elected government in 1953, where Winston Churchill feared that the country's leader, Cheddi Jagan, was too leftwing.[16] Again, the Kew archive is beneficial because it allows for a comparison of military history and builds our understanding of how Empire uses a network of bases from which to exert control.

In the case of Grenada, the British planners were concerned about the overthrow of Gairy by radical leftwing rebels in the NJM after independence. On January 25, 1974, Foreign Minister Lord Balniel warned his colleagues:

> The internal situation in Grenada has deteriorated seriously in the last few weeks. There have been strikes, interruptions of public services, and demonstrations which have led to violence including shooting, with resultant casualties including three deaths. Nevertheless Mr Gairy's Government is still in control. There is a fair chance that, with the security forces at his disposal (the police and the newly recalled 'police aides') he will succeed in containing the situation at least until independence on 7 February 1974.[17]

However, drastic measures were being contemplated: "In the worst case it is possible that the government may not succeed in retaining control so that it becomes impracticable to transfer sovereignty on 7 February to a cohesive and effective authority." This would put the UK in a difficult position, the minister explained:

> The choice will then have to be made, in the light of the circumstance at the time, between: a) refraining from any intervention, except possibly an operation to rescue 'UK Belongers', and accepting the consequential public criticism of abandonment of responsibility in chaotic circumstances; b) intervening in a state which is legally independent (or on the point of becoming so) to restore law and order and constitutional government. This would involve a reversion to

16. The Guardian, "MI5 files reveal details of 1953 coup that overthrew British Guiana's leaders."

17. NAUK: DEFE 25/367, January 25, 1974.

colonial rule, and place us in a position from which it would be difficult to extricate ourselves. And we could expect strong criticism internationally from certain quarters at least.[18]

This kind of scenario planning is a recurrent feature of British counter-insurgency practice and would also seem to be an important skill for CCI practitioners. Former Labour Party MP Chris Mullin wrote a fictional novel in 1982 about how the British security establishment would respond to the election of a socialist prime minister in the UK, entitled *A Very British Coup*. Fans of the book continue to implement its lessons, and most recently pro-Jeremy Corbyn activists are said to have role played the scenarios from the book. The Kew archive is a unique resource for understanding how UK military chiefs analyze situations at moments of perceived crisis and threats.

For example, Britain's Defence Secretary convened a Defence and Oversea Policy Committee meeting on January 30, 1974 with the military top brass to discuss a secret briefing paper titled "Grenada: Policy on Intervention by HM Forces." The document covered a range of scenarios, which included an invasion plan. On the possibility of "Intervention to restore law and order after a breakdown of the Gairy Government," the briefing noted,

> the Ministry of Defence has examined in general terms how such an operation might be mounted and what forces would have to be used ... The broad proposal is that a Royal Marine Commando or the Spearhead Battalion should be flown from the UK by RAF VC.10 to Trinidad or Barbados, via Bermuda ... At the destination island they would embark in HMS Bulwark, which is within two days' steaming of the area, and be taken by her to Grenada. Bulwark carries a squadron of Wessex helicopters and sufficient logistic support for 28 days' operation.[19]

The invasion plan bears striking resemblance to the 1983 US Operation Urgent Fury, which also relied on troop carriers, helicopters and marines. The UK military chiefs were also asked to consider, "What would be the legal position of British forces sent into the Island? If a Marine, in the course of his duty, should kill a local inhabitant, would he be liable for trial

18. DEFE 25/367, January 25, 1974.

19. NAUK: DEFE 25/367, "Grenada: policy on intervention by HM Forces—DOP (74)12," January 29, 1974. Secret brief for the Defence Secretary and the Defence and Overseas Policy Committee.

by court-martial for the civil offence of, for example, manslaughter?"[20] MOD lawyers decided that the relevant authority would be the UK Forces (Jurisdiction of Colonial Courts) Order 1965. The papers also show how the British planners were concerned about sending paratroopers to Grenada in 1974, because, although the regiment was on stand-by, it was tarred by its involvement in the Bloody Sunday massacre of protesters in Northern Ireland/Six Counties two years previously. The secret briefing noted,

> The Royal Marine Commando is currently on seven days' notice, and if very urgent intervention became necessary, the alternative might have to be adopted, of sending the Spearhead Battalion. We might wish to avoid this, since the battalion is at present the 2nd Battalion the Parachute Regiment, whose associations with Londonderry we might wish to avoid in the Grenada situation.[21]

In November 1973, Gairy's police militia had badly beaten demonstrators in an episode known as Grenada's Bloody Sunday. By this point, Britain had already calculated that it was preferable to grant independence quickly to the island while Gairy was still in charge and let him carry out a crackdown on radical elements without Britain being seen to be involved, before they grew to dominate the opposition. The Foreign Secretary had sent a secret memo to the Prime Minister in May 1973, following a Defence Overseas Planning meeting on Grenada. According to this:

> The Foreign and Commonwealth Secretary takes the view, which is surely right, that our own interest is that Grenada should proceed to independence. He adds that there are signs that the role of the official Opposition in Grenada may before long be taken over by a newly formed Black Power organisation; and he suggests that it might be better that Mr. Gairy should have *a free hand* to keep such developments under control in an independent Grenada than that we ourselves should run the risk of becoming involved in the task. He therefore seeks agreement that he should at once inform the Grenada Government and Opposition that we are willing to terminate association by means of

20. DEFE 25/367, January 29, 1974.
21. DEFE 25/367, January 29, 1974.

an Order in Council; to grant independence; and to amend the existing constitution as necessary.[22] (Emphasis added)

The paper also cited a lack of intelligence on the realities on the ground, which could explain the involvement of MI5 officers in Trinidad to monitor the situation in Grenada. The fact is that we know very little about the local situation. There are certainly Black Power elements at work; and there are some of them in the Joint Endeavour for Welfare, Education and Liberation (JEWEL) which has sprung very rapidly into prominence. It is probably true to say that we simply do not know to what extent Black Power is influential in the movement.[23] The growth of "Black Power" across the Caribbean appears as a consistent concern in Whitehall files from this era. A secret memo titled "The Caribbean: attitude of the United States," from January 1972, stated,

> The Americans are understandably anxious that a collection of mini-states, perhaps orientated towards Black Power or Communism, should not come into existence in the Caribbean as a result of British withdrawal, with consequent political instability in the area which could be exploited by Cuba and other opponents of the United States ... We can therefore go some way towards allaying the Americans' fear of a possibly [sic] proliferation of 'Black Republics' in the Caribbean proper, but probably not in Grenada or the Bahamas.[24]

The files also reveal that Britain's interest in the Caribbean was comparable to investments in India and oil reserves in the Middle East. A document prepared for the Prime Minister in November 1970, called 'Policy in the Commonwealth Caribbean', noted,

> we have a capital investment in the Caribbean, which may be at risk from nationalisation, of at least £250 million. This figure is comparable with our present estimate of British capital investment in India (about £300 million) and would probably be larger if it were possible to include figures for banking, insurance and the oil industry, all of which are, of course, particularly vulnerable to the risk of internal disaffection. And

22. NAUK: PREM 15/2018, "Grenada (DOP (73) 40)," May 23, 1973. Secret document prepared for the Prime Minister.

23. PREM 15/2018, May 23, 1973.

24. NAUK: PREM 15/2018, "The Caribbean: attitude of the United States," January 31, 1972. Secret memo from FCO to Lord Bridges, Private Secretary (Overseas Affairs) to the Prime Minister.

> Trinidad is a source of oil which might be very important to us
> if Middle Eastern supplies were interrupted ... Our economic
> interests in the area (if we want to keep them) require stability.
> So do our (and the Americans') very considerable political and
> strategic interests.[25]

But Britain's reliance on Gairy to safeguard such interests would subsequently become a private joke within the Foreign Office. By 1977, the British High Commissioner to Grenada, Christopher Diggines, who had been involved in the island's independence three years earlier, had become so exasperated by Gairy's increasingly dictatorial behaviour that he wrote a "school report" on him, from the paternalistic position of a headmaster. It is also a crude attempt at political profiling of a key figure. The diplomat told the FCO in London that, "I have just sent off my Annual Review for Grenada. But as Grenada means Gairy, it seems to me that it would be much better and more succinctly covered by something on the lines of a school report on him." The enclosed report for "Gairyland Academy," which a colleague in the FCO thought "rather good," contained the High Commissioner's appraisal of Gairy's ability across a range of school subjects. For scripture, the report said of Gairy, who was now fond of comparing himself to God, that "Having the advantage of direct communications with the Deity, his performance in the subject is outstanding, if unconventional." His health was reported to be "Physically robust—unfortunately." The report alluded to the political intimidation by his Mongoose Gang in the run up to the 1976 elections:

> I have also repeatedly had to warn him about using his pet
> mongoose to frighten the other boys, several of whom it has
> bitten quite painfully. This has had a deleterious effect on their
> exam results. It has made him so unpopular that it has been
> necessary to install special guards in the bushes surrounding the
> House, at considerable expense, to protect him against possible
> attempts at retribution.[26]

The Headmaster's final comment was that Gairy was a "Trying" pupil. But if London was losing patience, the people of Grenada had none left

---

25. NAUK: PREM 15/2018, "Policy in the Commonwealth Caribbean (DOP (70) 35)," November 27, 1970. Confidential document prepared for the Prime Minister.

26. NAUK: FCO 63/1466, January 1977. Personal and confidential letter from Christopher Diggines, High Commissioner to Trinidad and Tobago and Grenada, to Robin Edmonds CMG MBE at the FCO.

at all. Britain's decision to prevent Grenada's revolution in 1974 just made it inevitable by 1979.

Guatemala: The Repression of Mayans, Left-wing Guerrillas and and Liberation Theologians

Although the role of British imperialism in North America and the Caribbean is clearly apparent from the Anglophone legacy, the rest of Central and South America is more often associated with Spanish or Portuguese colonialism, and ongoing US neo-colonialism. However, even in this part of the world, Britain built colonies and continues to wield influence. Apart from the Falkland Islands/Las Malvinas dispute with Argentina, the Belize dispute with Guatemala is probably the other most important (and overlooked) case study in the region. Belize only became independent from Britain in 1981, making it one of the British Empire's last formal colonies. Belize sits on central America's eastern seaboard, facing the Caribbean. It is bordered to the west and south by the larger territory of Guatemala, which considers Belize part of its own land. In the 1980s, Guatemala's government wanted to annex Belize with military force if necessary, and as such Britain left a stay-behind garrison of 1,500 soldiers stationed along the Guatemalan border—explicitly to deter an invasion attempt.

The geopolitics of this flashpoint are complex and seemingly contradictory, although they can be reconciled with a focus on imperialism and anti-communism. Throughout the Cold War and beyond, the US has sought to dominate the politics of Latin America and deny their people any left-leaning leadership. Guatemala was at the forefront of this struggle. The CIA overthrew its progressive president Juan Jose Arbenz in 1954, who had nationalized land belonging to an American-owned banana corporation.[27] In his place, they installed a military leader, resulting in a civil war between the government and a coalition of left-wing revolutionaries, indigenous Mayans and progressive theologians. The US repeatedly backed the Guatemalan Junta with counter-insurgency assistance, on the pretext that it was ridding the region from communism. As one progressive American journalist noted,

> After thirty years of relying essentially upon the CIA and other
> conspiratorial agencies, black warfare subdivisions of the US

27. Schlesinger and Kinzer, *Bitter Fruit*, 8.

Army, "police training" programs to instruct Latin American bullies in the use of US electronic and other technology for coercing prisoners, it is difficult to see what gains we have achieved.

Perhaps, as some in Washington have argued, Communism has been kept out, but if so it is at the price of turning the area over to fascist and neofascist thugs. There is little difference to the man to whose testicles the electrodes are applied whether his torturer is 'totalitarian' or 'authoritarian.'[28]

He wrote these words in 1983, when the repression in Guatemala was reaching a gruesome climax. Guatemala's latest military leader, General Rios Montt, had unleashed a counter-insurgency offensive on indigenous Maya people in the Petén region, near the Belize border. The assault resulted in the murder of 1,771 Maya people from 1982 to 1983, for which Montt was later convicted of genocide.[29]

Geopolitically, this period is instructive because on the surface it seems as though there was a US-backed military regime in Guatemala, committing genocide and poised to invade its neighbour—Belize, a UK-backed liberal democracy. The Guatemalan revolutionaries were under such severe repression in 1982/3 that some sought shelter and solidarity across the border in Belize. The Kew archive shows that at this crucial moment, the UK response was to secretly collude with the Guatemalan military and help them crush the revolutionaries. The files show that British commanders feared the presence of Guatemalan rebels in Belize would give the Guatemalan military an excuse to invade Belize. To prevent this, top British army officers decided to share intelligence on rebels with Guatemalan commanders, even though they were linked to human rights abuses. Royal Air Force pilots made reconnaissance flights over the Belizean jungle looking for guerrilla camps and British troops carried out secret foot patrols. UK soldiers even used a Guatemalan rebel informant for one patrol, before sending him back to Guatemala where he was arrested and later murdered by government gunmen. However, on top of this concern about provoking an invasion, British planners also realized that it was in their interest to support Montt's stance against

28. Salisbury, "Introduction," 4.

29. BBC, "Guatemala's Rios Montt Found Guilty of Genocide," May 11, 2013, his conviction was later overturned in controversial circumstances.

communism in Central America. This was the wider geopolitical context that explains the behaviour of the British authorities.

The unlikely alliance began in early 1983 when the Guatemalan military somehow cultivated an informant inside one of the rebel groups, "FAR" (Rebel Armed Forces). The informant, 27-year-old Pedro Barrera, allegedly claimed that his former comrades had guerrilla bases in Belize. This intelligence was passed to Belizean authorities and British forces, which remarkably agreed to help the Guatemalan regime clamp down on its own opponents. The British High Commissioner sent a UK-Belizean patrol into the jungle, guided by Pedro Barrera, who by this point was effectively acting as a British army agent. When Barrera failed to find the guerrilla camp, the British High Commissioner dismissed his intelligence as "worthless."[30] The patrol was called back after ministers in London panicked about mission creep, with British soldiers now hunting guerrillas instead of just guarding the border.

A former Belizean special branch officer claims he was the interpreter for that patrol with Barrera. The man said: "Pedro Barrera wanted support—that we grant him refugee status in Belize to protect him and stay here, so he started to cooperate with us and he promised that he was going to show us a guerrilla camp." The patrol was inserted into the jungle by a British Gazelle helicopter. When the patrol failed to find any guerrilla activity, the ex-spy claims Barrera started crying, begged for refugee status and offered to "share everything he knew about the Guatemalan army." British officers allegedly recorded as Barrera detailed Guatemalan army massacres of indigenous Maya people. When Barrera was handed into Guatemalan custody, the officer alleges that "the British played the recorded tape . . . [and] upon hearing Barrera's accusations the faces of the Guatemalan officers contorted with anger."[31] The Kew archive supports his claim that the British government had no concern for Barrera's welfare, although they do not refer to the tape recording incident. "Special Branch conducted further interrogation of the guide before returning him to Guatemala," is how the Foreign Office described the handover. Barrera was promptly re-arrested in Guatemala but fled to a Belizean border village of Arenal six weeks later, pursued by three Guatemalan gunmen in civilian clothes. "Barrera tried to run away and was shot first in the leg and then in the head," a telegram on his murder explains.

---

30. NAUK, FCO 99/1693, folio 46.

31. Miller, "We Sent a Man to His Death."

"The victim had been in Guatemalan custody a few hours before he was killed." His assassins then swaggered back across the border where they were greeted by Guatemalan special forces soldiers from the notorious Kaibiles commando unit. "The murderers were themselves undoubtedly official agents," the British High Commissioner in Belize told London.[32] The retired spy was more explicit about the affair. "We sent a man to his death," he later lamented. The spy did not entirely regret working in intelligence, however. "I enjoyed it. Sad to say, but I find it intriguing . . . the James Bond type of thing," he said. However, he reflected that, "At the time, you feel you're doing something good; you don't see the bigger picture. You don't see the consequences; for example, the thousands of peasants that were massacred in Guatemala . . . in time it bothers your conscience."[33] Daniel Carey, a human rights lawyer in London who won an award for his work in Guatemala argues that the conduct of the British personnel involved in that patrol was potentially unlawful. "The British government owes a legal duty of care to agents that it uses to protect them against foreseeable risks. The more exploitative that relationship, the more onerous the duty," commented Carey. "It also has a human rights obligation not to hand prisoners in its custody to regimes where they face a risk of torture or death. On the basis of this account, it appears that both of these duties were breached."

After Pedro Barrera's tip-off, RAF pilots flew reconnaissance missions to photograph the Belize jungle for any sign of Guatemalan guerrillas. The photos were analyzed by defence intelligence staff in Britain and led Prime Minister Margaret Thatcher to authorise further reconnaissance. Two patrols containing British soldiers searched the jungle in vain for guerrilla camps before they were extracted by helicopter. Information from American intelligence later that year led to another search. However, details about these patrols have been censored in the military files, because the information was "supplied by, or relates" to the intelligence agencies or special forces. The SAS regularly operated in Belize. George Hill, an ex-soldier who served in Belize in 1982 with the royal artillery, saw Britain's elite Special Air Service (SAS) twice during his tour. "They were definitely doing covert patrolling," he said. The possible involvement of elite troops on these controversial anti-guerrilla missions is a common view among veteran. "Without a shadow of a doubt it would have been

---

32. NAUK, FCO 99/1694, June 6, 1983, folio 87.
33. Miller, "We Sent a Man to His Death."

special forces," said Chris Slater, who served in the parachute regiment. The regiment's second battalion, "2 para," was in Belize in 1983 and had a specially trained reconnaissance unit, "working exactly the same as (SAS units from] Hereford do', Slater explained. Gus Hales, a "2 para" veteran who served in Belize in 1983, now suspects his jungle patrols were unwittingly aimed at guerrillas. "We were told to look out for drug smugglers who may well be wearing uniforms. But the guys we came across in jungle camps were ordered and tried to conceal their tracks," Hales recalled. "They were Mayan Indians who knew how to live in that terrain, which made it kind of strange. Now it would make sense that they were guerrillas." Hales added: "We were a bit trigger-happy, pumped up and looking for something to come up," Hales said of his time in Belize. His regiment was battle hardened, fresh from winning the Falklands/Malvinas war.

Even though rank and file soldiers possibly did not realize their patrols targeted guerrillas, senior British officers were well aware that was the purpose. The commander of British Forces in Belize, Brigadier Pollard, had secret meetings with Guatemalan military officers linked to serious human rights abuses, where intelligence on guerrilla activity was exchanged. He had several meetings with Colonel Tobar Martínez, who was in charge of Guatemala's northern Petén region. Months before their first rendezvous, Guatemalan soldiers under Colonel Martínez's command massacred 251 villagers in the Las Dos Erres settlement, in one of the worst atrocities during Guatemala's civil war, according to the Inter-American Commission on Human Rights.[34] This did not deter the Brigadier from sharing sensitive intelligence with him about Britain's unsuccessful search for guerrillas, which alluded to Pedro Barrera's failure. Weeks before Barrera's murder, Brigadier Pollard told Colonel Martínez that British troops had carried out a "full search . . . with negative results." Still, Guatemala's president, Rios Montt, was "impressed" when he heard about the intelligence-sharing arrangement with British troops. "President Rios Montt had been impressed by news of this 'interchange' and wished to encourage more informal meetings between the armed forces," one telegram reads.[35] The Kew archive shocked Kate Doyle, an award-winning US archivist on the civil war who has gathered evidence for genocide charges against the former military regime. "Why was anyone in authority talking to Guatemalan forces months after one of worst

34. Inter-American Court of Human Rights, "Case of the 'Las Dos Erres' Massacre v. Guatemala."

35. NAUK, FCO 99/1709, June 9, 1983.

massacres, which was in the Petén?" Doyle said. "The US backed Guatemala with covert aid but openly criticised their human rights record. The British communications are entirely stripped of any human rights dimension, it just does not come up."

The files show that some Foreign Office staff were surprised at the extent of Brigadier Pollard's collaboration, but regarded it as positive. "I don't think we had fully realised the extent to which he keeps in touch with senior Guatemalan military personnel," a British diplomat in Washington remarked approvingly. Pollard was so charming that Martínez wanted to "meet again immediately prior to Christmas on a more social basis to include a meal and perhaps a game of volleyball." Margaret Thatcher's foreign secretary Geoffrey Howe then personally agreed to a volleyball match going ahead. A more explicit document reveals that Brigadier Pollard "was most concerned to reassure GAF (Guatemalan Armed Forces) that if they acquired any hard intelligence on either Guatemalan guerrillas harbouring in Belize or on arms being transported to Guatemalan guerrillas through Belize, and provided GAF passed it to us, we would take action on that intelligence, as we had done in the recent alleged guerrilla camp."[36] Another telegram, seen by MI6, shows that Pollard and his intelligence chief met with the former commandant of Guatemala's Kaibiles commando training school, even though the British army knew Kaibiles were linked to Pedro Barrera's murder months earlier. The British brigadier proudly told the Kaibiles veteran that "my OPs (observation posts) and patrols, by being in the border area, deterred movement of weapons and guerrillas." Human rights organisations regard the Kaibiles as the most barbaric of Guatemala's units, with its own members calling it a "killing machine." However, a British army intelligence report took a different view, describing the Kaibiles acadmey as "probably the best Special Forces school in Central America."

British units in Belize kept detailed intelligence records of Guatemalan troop movements in case of any attempts to invade. These records show that British forces knew Guatemala's military was engaged in a brutal internal crackdown but continued to cooperate with them nonetheless. An intelligence bulletin noted that up to 1,000 guerrillas had been surrounded and that the Guatemalan military "intend to keep them surrounded so as to starve them out." Other bulletins warn of escalating repression against the indigenous Maya population: "There is increasing

36. NAUK, FCO 99/1709, May 26, 1983.

evidence to suggest that the GAF is straying away from its 'bullets and beans' policy, and is taking a tougher line with Indian peasants." In case there was any doubt about the situation in Guatemala, one intelligence report noted: "It is a fact that there has been a certain amount of official involvement in murder and political violence. 'Death Squads' have been part of the Guatemalan way of life for many years." Even on the rare occasions that human rights concerns arose, they were quickly dismissed. A joint UK-Belize intelligence summary said: "A new report by the World Council of Churches claims that President Rios Montt's government was responsible for the deaths of more than 9,000 people between March and August, 1982." However the intelligence officer commented, "Although the report claims to have evidence to support the figure mentioned, there is no collateral in support of the statement."[37]

The Kew archive is also instructive for CCI because it shows how British personnel in Belize also helped police to spy on rebel sympathizers in urban areas. UK aid money funded a British policeman, Alan Jenkins, to "effectively run" the Belize special branch.[38] He put suspected guerrilla activists under surveillance in what the files call "Operation Octopus." The operation found "pretty conclusive evidence of the existence in Belize of cells organised directly by the Fuerzas Armadas Rebeldes (Rebel Armed Forces or FAR), one of the principal Guatemalan guerrilla organisations." The evidence was so alarming that the joint intelligence committee in Whitehall carried out a "threat assessment" and MI5 studied the report. "The FAR leadership in Belize is to begin the selection of FAR members in Belize for guerrilla warfare training in the Petén district of Guatemala," special branch warned. British soldiers responded by giving Belize police more covert surveillance training. The motive for British action against Guatemalan rebels was that guerrilla hideouts in Belize would provoke Guatemala to invade. However, the files also contain evidence that could have led UK military chiefs to make a different decision. The invasion threat was classed as low in 1983 precisely because Guatemala was so busy fighting rebel groups. Arguably then, giving the rebels safe haven in Belize could have precipitated the fall of the military regime in Guatemala. And yet when it came to defeating left-wing rebels, Britain and Guatemala were effectively on the same side. Harris Whitbeck, an unofficial adviser to Guatemala's President Montt, reminded the British

37. NAUK, FCO 99/1694, June 4, 1983.

38. NAUK, FCO 99/1694, December 15, 1983, folio 133.

commander at one meeting that: "[o]f course, seen in the bigger picture, the aim of all of us is to defeat communism in Central America."[39]

At the time, British diplomats appeared to relish the covert nature of this counter-insurgency policy, scribbling in the corner of one telegram that the patrols were "real Sherlock Holmes stuff." The ex-spy has elaborated further on the espionage. He was invited into Guatemala to dine with the military regime, including the officers from the notorious Kaibiles special-forces unit, which is believed to have murdered Pedro Barrera and carried out genocidal massacres. These diners were "characterized by excesses of Guatemalan Gallo beers, game meat and marimba music," he said. "During the night, the Guatemalan soldiers would chauffeur them into the seductive Flores night life," a riverine town almost 100km inside Guatemala. A file found at the UK National Archives supports this allegation, and shows that a Belizean major visited the Kaibiles' notorious training academy, even drawing a crude map of the camp. (Belize's tiny army was then under the command of a British officer.) Despite the Kaibiles appalling human rights record, the document shows that the visitors "had a very good lunch with most of the instructors . . . barbecue chicken, beef, corn tortillas, bread, soup made from carrots and pumpkin, cheese chips, watermelon, pepsi-cola in cans and beers."

According to the file, one Kaibiles officer "was anxious to find out if Belizean security forces were patrolling the (border) area, as he believed that whenever his patrols came near to the guerrillas they would cross into Belize and evade capture." The major replied that British and Belizean soldiers constantly patrolled the border, which made the Guatemalan officer "visibly relieved." The ex-spy also claims he carried out surveillance of left-wing groups in Belize who were supporting the Guatemalan rebels, by providing them with "food, medicine and possibly arms," which they buried in secret dumps along the border. "All of the players in those support groups were interviewed, photographed and monitored by the Special Branch," he said.[40] This detailed account serves to demonstrate the lengths that UK forces in Central America have gone to in their efforts to support US imperialism, and the hallmarks of what such a counter-insurgency strategy involved.

39. NAUK, FCO 99/1694, August 9, 1983, folio 109.
40. Miller, "We Sent a Man to His Death."

Testimonies of Faith from Bahrain and Sri Lanka

Through my investigative journalism at the Kew archive, I have uncovered similar stories of British neo-colonialism in other parts of the world, often during some of the most repressive points in that country's recent history. Although my work on Grenada and Guatemala has largely been confined to the archives, on other stories I have met key activists from the conflicts that I am researching. This is particularly true in the case of Bahrain and Sri Lanka, where UK involvement has been as pernicious, if not more so, than in Grenada and Guatemala. Rather than go into more detail about the abuses that have occurred, I would like to conclude by reflecting on how some of the most inspiring and resilient activists from Bahrain and Sri Lanka are spiritual people, strongly grounded in their respective faiths.

On my field work trips to the Tamil regions of Sri Lanka, I have met priests in almost every town. For security reasons, I will not divulge their names, but it is striking how much they are motivated by liberation theology, a liberative approach to faith most commonly associated with Latin America. One Tamil Jesuit who worked near Batticaloa (Sivaram's home town) told me that:

> Since my student days I was always given to working with injustice. So much so as a Priest also when I lend voice, they gasp and said you are a politician, a priest politician. But then Vatican II came and said 'In the Noble Art of Politics'—early priests had decried politics as a base thing that no one should get involved in. Now Vatican document said 'the noble art of politics'. Then I always quote this document in public when doing my social work or lending voice to the voiceless. The document is the Church in the Modern World ... Every form of injustice, whether against race, culture, religion, language, must be fought against, eradicated and overcome. In the Latin it sounds much more forceful. So I quote this document and I say on whatever political platform that I'm standing, I'm standing to tell the truth because the platform that stands against injustice, and the Church says any form of injustice whether its against race, culture, language, religion, must be fought against eradicated and overcome. How can you do this just saying mass and staying in the church? You must go out and tell the people, and gather the people and say come, we must fight against injustice. So that's what I'm doing now. I'm very happy doing it.

Another Tamil Catholic priest, whose Sunday morning mass was attended by about a thousand worshippers, preferred to be more subtle in his approach. He told me how he uses the sermon as a parable to speak about the occupation of their lands by the Sinhalese military. Without referring specifically to what was happening around them, he could draw on teachings in the Gospel to talk euphemistically about the situation facing his flock, and inspire them. In both cases, the priests had direct experience of the conflict and the churches where I met them had been damaged by the military.

The Tamil church in Sri Lanka presents a form of counter-power to the military-political establishment, with priests, nuns and places of worship all forming a vital network for shelter and respite from life under military occupation—a liberative space where oppressed peoples can find solace and hope for building a better future. Equally, the priests were active in going out into the community, accompanying people through military checkpoints, documenting human rights abuses and even organizing events for remembering people killed in the conflict, even if this came at great personal risk. I travelled with several priests to a remote beach where they planned to host a remembrance day, and saw how plain-clothed intelligence officers monitored their movements.[41]

Through my work, I have also seen how faith has helped challenge UK counter-insurgency in Bahrain, a repressive Gulf monarchy which houses British and American naval bases. Although I have not been able to visit Bahrain myself, I have interviewed several exiles who live and campaign in London.[42] In August 2018, one of them, Ali Mushaima, staged a hunger strike outside the Bahraini Embassy. He aimed to raise awareness about his father, Hassan, who is an opposition leader in Bahrain and was jailed for life after the Arab Spring uprising. The Mushaima's are from the country's Shia majority, which is marginalised by the Sunni monarchy. Hassan Mushaima is notable in Bahraini politics for forming a party, the Haq Movement, that sought to overcome sectarian divisions and brought together Sunni, Shia and Secular figures.

Ali's fast outside the Embassy lasted for 44 days, in which time the solidarity with his struggle gradually built. Every Thursday evening, which marked the start of Jumah or the Muslim holy day, his supporters from London's Shia community would gather outside the Embassy for a *Dua*

41. Miller, "In the Shadow of Military."
42. Miller, "Could a Corbyn Government Change UK Foreign Policy in Bahrain?"

Kumail, a popular supplication.[43] The religious gathering offered a chance to broaden his hunger strike to other nationalities living in London, and saw Shias from Iraq and East Africa also attend. On a logistical level, it was too dangerous for Ali to sleep on his own outside the Embassy at night and he would often be joined by supporters. Sometimes, this would include a Shia Maulana. On other nights, Christian activists from the Quaker community organized sleep outs in support of Ali. The Quakers were particularly active during the hunger strike, as they are already involved in campaigning to stop British arms sales to the Gulf.[44] As such, Ali's hunger strike generated considerable inter-faith activism, and his own faith undoubtedly helped to sustain him throughout those weeks without food, in which he lost 16 kilos.

Conclusion

Returning then to Sivaram's CCI doctrine the phenomenon of spirituality as an aspect of, and agent for, resistance to Empire seems to fit with Sivaram's fifth factor —that of understanding the communities engaged in the struggle. Whether it be in Sri Lanka, Bahrain, Grenada or Guatemala, it would be a grave error to overlook the religious beliefs and practices of the local people, and recognize that this is often a source of immense strength in their efforts at CCI. Whether it can be in drawing lessons from the Gospel or events like Ashura, faith is clearly a factor in resisting Empire. This is something that Grenada's New Jewel Movement, with its focus on doctrinaire Marxist-Leninism and simplistic dismissal of religion as an "opium of the people" appears to have struggled to grasp, much to the delight of the CIA.[45] The US spy agency circulated a paper on "The New Jewel Movement and Religion" and claimed that revolutionary cadres "lamented that there was no 'left' religion in Grenada," and complained that the existing church structures were "reactionary."[46] Whilst this scenario may not resonate to many liberation theologians around the world, it is clearly a factor that needs to be reconciled for a successful CCI strategy.

43. AIM Islam, "Dua Kumail in Solidarity with Bahrain Hunger Strike."

44. Hardy, "Friends Rally Behind Hunger Striker."

45. The full Marx quote was in fact more respectful of faith: "Religion is the sigh of the oppressed creature, the heart of a heartless world, and the soul of soulless conditions. It is the opium of the people."

46. CIA, "New Jewel Movement and Religion."

Contributors

Michael Lujan Bevacqua is assistant professor in Chamorro Studies at the University of Guam and a long-time blogger, artist, writer, and poet. His research is primarily on the effects of colonization on Chamorro people and their islands, and theorizing the possibilities for their decolonization. His work has been published in journals like *American Quarterly, Micronesian Educator,* and *Marvels and Tales.* He is a member of Guam's Commission on Decolonization, the co-chair for the Independence for Guam Task Force and a passionate advocate for the revitalization of the Chamorro language and culture.

Mark Braverman is research fellow in systematic theology and ecclesiology at Stellenbosch University and executive director of Kairos USA, founded in response to the Kairos call of the Palestinian Christians. His work has focused on Christian Zionism, ecumenism, and the role of Christian-Jewish relations in the discourse on Israel-Palestine. He has worked with the Presbyterian, Episcopal, Lutheran, Congregational, Methodist, Baptist, Catholic, Mennonite, and Unitarian Universalist churches on their policies and actions with respect to Israel and Palestine, and has lectured and trained internationally, most recently in the UK, Ireland, Germany, Taiwan, and South Africa. He has served on the Steering Committee of the World Council of Church's Palestine Israel Ecumenical Forum.

Jude Lal Fernando is assistant professor and coordinator of the MPhil in intercultural theology and interreligious studies program at the Irish School of Ecumenics, School of Religion, Trinity College Dublin, and director of the Trinity Centre for Post-Conflict Justice. He is the author of *Religion, Conflict and Peace in Sri Lanka: The Politics of Interpretation of Nationhoods* (Berlin: Lit Verlag, 2013) and the editor of *Resistance to Empire and Militarization: Reclaiming the Sacred* (Sheffield: Equinox, 2020). He was the coordinator of the Peoples' Tribunal on Sri Lanka.

Dan Gonzáles-Ortega is the rector of Comunidad Teológica de México (Theological Community of Mexico). He is the executive secretary of the Latin American Ecumenical Theological Education Community and the executive director of the Ecumenical Theological Education Forum of Latin America and the Caribbean (FETELAC). He was excommunicated from the Presbyterian National Church of Mexico for supporting the ordination of women and currently serves as the pastor of the Mexican Communion of Reformed and Presbyterian Churches (CMIRP).

Young-Bock Kim is a minjung theologian of the first generation. He is the chancellor of Asia-Pacific Center for Integral Study of Life in Korea. He is the former president of Hanil University and Theological Seminary in Chonbuk, Korea. He obtained his MD and PhD from Princeton University, USA, and has been a teaching fellow at Princeton Theological Seminary, USA, and the director of the Doctor of Ministries Studies, a joint program with San Francisco Theological Seminary.

Wati Longchar is a pioneer in Asian indigenous theologies. He taught for 15 years at the Eastern Theological College, Jorhat, Assam. He was a consultant for Ecumenical Theological Education for Asia and Pacific—a joint program of the World Council of Churches and Christian Conference of Asia (2001–2007). He served as the dean of Extension and DMin programme of the Senate of Serampore College (2008–2015). He is the former professor and director at the Asia-Pacific Indigenous Research Institute of Yushan Theological College & Seminary, and the dean of Program for Theology and Cultures in Asia (PTCA), Taiwan. He has authored six books, and edited and co-edited 40 books.

Erin Shea Martin earned her MPhil in intercultural theology and interreligious studies at the Irish School of Ecumenics in Trinity College Dublin. She has trained with capoeira groups in the USA, Turkey, Jordan, and Ireland since 2013 and has worked in refugee services in volunteer and professional capacities since 2004. Her academic and capoeira training as well as her professional experiences inform her current study of law at Loyola University Chicago School of Law, USA.

Phil Miller is a UK-based investigative journalist who has written highly detailed articles on different methods of repression by the imperial powers, particularly the UK. He has published on the British involvement in counter-insurgency warfare in Guatemala, Bahrain, Northern Ireland, and Sri Lanka, and works with many civil society groups in the UK and beyond who oppose militarization. He has led a number of successful anti-deportation campaigns in the UK.

Rasika Sharmen Pieris holds a PhD from Nijmegen's Radboud University, the Netherlands and completed her MPhil in intercultural theology and interreligious studies in the Irish School of Ecumenics in Trinity College Dublin. She is a visiting lecturer at the University of Kelaniya, Sri Lanka and the assistant coordinator of Ecclesia of Women in Asia (EWA). She is a religious sister of the Holy Family Congregation of Bordeaux and works with war widows who belong to different communities in Sri Lanka.

Nidia Arrobo Rodas is the director of Fundación Pueblo Indio Del Ecuador (Foundation for Indigenous People of Ecuador) in Quito who has worked closely with the late renowned campaigner for indigenous people, Bishop Leonidas Proaño and the prominent Belgian sociologist of religion François Houtart. She is a writer and an activist who networks between the indigenous groups and other activist groups in Asia. She is a passionate speaker and an indigenous liturgist.

Joshua Samuel is a visiting lecturer for theology, global Christianity, and mission at the Episcopal Divinity School at the Union Theological Seminary, New York. He previously taught in the Department of Philosophy and Religious Studies at the Marymount Manhattan College, New York. He received his PhD in systematic theology from the Union Theological Seminary, New York, in 2017 and is the author of *Untouchable Bodies, Resistance, and Liberation: A Comparative Theology of Divine Possessions* (Leiden: Brill, 2020). He is an ordained minister of the Church of South India and is currently serving in the Episcopal Church, USA.

Lilian Cheelo Siwila is associate professor in Kwazulu-Natal University, South Africa. Amongst the subjects she teaches are theology and gender in the face of empire, and African feminism and ecological/sacred spaces. She is the president of the United Congregational Church of Southern Africa, and program and training manager of the Ecumenical Church Leaders' Forum, South Africa. She is a peacebuilding practitioner.

Bibliography

AAR Board of Directors. "AARStatement on Racism and George Floyd Murder." https:// aarweb.org/AARMBR/About-AAR-/Board-of-Directors-/Board-Statements-/ AAR-Statement-on-Racism-and-George-Floyd-Murder.aspx.

Acosta, Alberto. *La maldición de la abundancia.* Quito: Editorial Abya Yala, 2009.

Adam, Hussein. *Recognising Sacred Natural Sites and Territories in Kenya.* Nairobi: Institute for Culture and Ecology, 2012.

Adayaalam Centre for Policy Research. "COVID-19: Sri Lanka's Militarized Response Poses Grave Threats to Human Rights." http://adayaalam.org/situation-brief-no-3-covid-19-sri-lankas-militarised-response-poses-grave-threats-to-human-rights.

Adu-Gyamfi, Yaw. "Indigenous Beliefs and Practices in Ecosystem Conservation: Response of the Church." *Scriptura* 107 (2011) 145–55.

AFP. "Brazilian Amazon Mayor Pleads for World Help in Fight against COVID-19." https://www.france24.com/en/20200506-brazilian-amazon-mayor-begs-for-world-help-in-fight-against-covid-19.

Aguon, Mindy. "Guam Gets 90 Days to Review EIS." *KUAM News,* 28 October 2009. http://www.kuam.com/global/story.asp?s=11402872.

AIM Islam. "Dua Kumail in Solidarity with Bahrain Hunger Strike." https://www.facebook.com/events/685949345103897/.

Almeida, Bira. *Capoeira: A Brazilian Art Form.* Berkeley: North Atlantic, 1986.

Arizmendi, Luis. "Necropolitical Capitalism, the State of Exception and Accumulation by Dispossession." In *Resistance to Empire and Militarization: Reclaiming the Sacred,* edited by Jude Lal Fernando, 288–305. Sheffield: Equinox, 2020.

Associated Press. "China Watches U.S. Guam Maneuvers." June 21, 2006. http://www.chinadaily.com.cn/china/2006-06/21/content_622251.htm.

Atkins, Peter J. "Geography of Hunger and Famine." https://www.oxfordbibliographies.com/view/document/obo-9780199874002/obo-9780199874002-0189.xml.

Augustine. *Confessions.* Translated by Vernon J. Bourke. Washington, DC: Catholic University of America Press, 1966.

Barua, Ankur. "The God of the Oppressed and the Politics of Resistance: Black and Dalit Theologies of Liberation." *Culture and Religion* 15 (2014) 1–20.

Balasingham, Adele Ann. "Annai Poopathy's Fast for Freedom." https://eelamview. wordpress.com/2015/04/19/annai-poopathy/.

BBC News. "Coptic Christian Attack: Funerals in Egypt for Seven Murdered Pilgrims." November 3, 2018. https://www.bbc.com/news/world-middle-east-46082927.

———. "Guatemala's Rios Montt found guilty of genocide." May 11, 2013. https://www.bbc.com/news/world-latin-america-22490408.

BDS. "Boycott, Divestment and Sanctions." https://bdsmovement.net.

Bevacqua, Michael Lujan. "Adios Benit." *The Guam Daily Post*, February 24, 2016. https://www.postguam.com/forum/featured_columnists/adios-benit/article_98239518-d9f3-11e5-95e8-63de82e81cc7.html.

Biswas, Soutik. " Coronavirus: How India's Kerala State 'Flattened the Curve.'" https://www.bbc.com/news/world-asia-india-52283748.

Bonhoeffer, Dietrich. "The Confessing Church and the Ecumenical Movement." In *Witness to Jesus Christ*, edited by John W. de Gruchy and Dietrich Bonhoeffer. Minneapolis: Fortress, 1991.

———. "Thoughts on the Day of Baptism of Dietrich Wilhelm Rüdiger Bethge." In *The Bonhoeffer Reader*, edited by Clifford J. Green and Michael P. DeJonge, 297–98. Minneapolis: Fortress, 2013.

Boopalan, Sunder John. *Memory, Grief, and Agency: A Political Theological Account of Wrongs and Rites*. Cham, Switzerland: Palgrave Macmillan, 2017.

Borck, Rita Nakashima. "Anamnesis as a Source of Love." In *Asian and Asian American Women in Theology and Religion: Embodying Knowledge*, edited by Kwok Pui-lan, 31–46. London: Palgrave Macmillian, 2020.

Borja, John I. "25 Years Later, Andersen Air Force Base still Cleaning up Contamination, EPA Says." *Pacific Daily News*. October 15, 2017. https://www.guampdn.com/story/news/2017/10/15/25-years-later-andersen-air-force-base-still-cleaning-up-contamination-epa-says/764211001.

Braverman, Mark. *Fatal Embrace: Christians, Jews, and the Search for Peace in the Holy Land*. New York: Beaufort, 2010.

———. "The Moment of Grace and Opportunity: The Global Kairos Movement for Justice in the Holy Land." *Theologies and Cultures* 11 (2014) 42–83.

———. "Report from the Presbyterian General Assembly, Part 1." http://markbraverman.org/2010/07/report-from-the-presbyterian-general-assembly-part-1.

———. *A Wall in Jerusalem*. New York: Jericho, 2012.

Bravo, Hervi Lara. "Ethical Crisis: Human Rights Situation in Chile, Today." https://comitesromero.org/actual/es/node/226.

Briggs, Robert John. *Craig Santos Perez: Poetry as Strategy against Military Occupation of Guåhan (Guam)*. MA diss., University of Mississippi, 2015.

Brock, Rita Nakashima. "Ending Innocence and Nurturing Willfulness." In *Violence against Women and Children: A Christian Theological Sourcebook*, edited by Carol J. Adams and Marie Fortune, 71–84. New York: Continuum, 1995.

Brooks, Rodney A. "African Americans Struggle with Disproportionate COVID Death Toll." https://www.nationalgeographic.com/history/2020/04/coronavirus-disproportionately-impacts-african-americans.

Brueggemann, Walter. *Chosen? Reading the Bible Amid the Israeli-Palestinian Conflict*. Louisville: Westminster John Knox, 2015.

Buber, Martin. *I and Thou*. Translated by Ronald Gregor Smith. Edinburgh: T. & T. Clark, 1937.

Bumiller, Elisabeth. "Bush Affirms U.S. Role in New 'Pacific Century.'" *The New York Times,* February 19, 2002. https://www.nytimes.com/2002/02/19/world/bush-affirms-us-role-in-asia-in-new-pacific-century.html.

Burge, Gary M. *Jesus and the Land: The New Testament Challenge to "Holy Land" Theology.* Grand Rapids: Baker Academic, 2010.

Business Week Online. "Digital War: The Rumsfeld Doctrine." April 7, 2003. http://www.businessweek.com/magazine/content/03_14/b3827114_mz029.htm.

Butler, Judith. *Frames of War: When is Life Grievable.* London, New York: Verso, 2016.

Butler, Judith, and Athena Athanasiou. *Dispossession: The Performative in the Political.* Cambridge: Polity, 2015.

Cagurangan, Mar-Vic. "Guam Number 1 for U.S. Military Recruitment." *The Marianas Variety,* October 4, 2007. http://www.pireport.org/articles/2007/10/04/guam-number-1-us-military-recruitment.

Camacho, Leevin. "Resisting the Proposed Military Buildup on Guam." In *Under Occupation: Resistance and Struggle in a Militarised Asia-Pacific,* edited by Daniel Broudy et al., 183–90. Newcastle upon Tyne: Cambridge Scholars, 2013.

Camara, Dom Helder. *Hoping Against All Hope.* Maryknoll, NY: Orbis, 1984.

Capoeira, Nestor. *The Little Capoeira Book.* Translated by Alex Ladd. Berkeley: North Atlantic, 1995.

———. *A Street-Smart Song: Capoeira Philosophy and Inner Life.* Berkeley: Blue Snake Books, 2006.

Catechism of the Catholic Church. Vatican City: Vatican, 1997.

CBS News. "Shooting of Ahmaud Arbery." https://www.cbsnews.com/news/ahmaud-arbery-killing-hate-crime-justice-department-investigation.

Cervenka, Zdenek. "The Effects of Militarization of Africa on Human Rights." Paper submitted to the Conference on Human Rights: The African Context, Port Harcourt, Nigeria, June 9–11, 1987.

Chirongoma, S. "Motherhood and Ecological Conversation of Mother Earth." *Women in God's Image* 10–11 (2005) 1–11.

Christ, Carol P., and Judith Plaskow. *Goddess and God in the World: Conversations in Embodied Theology.* Minneapolis: Fortress, 2016.

Chung, Hyun Kyung. "Ecology, Feminism and African and Asian Spirituality." In *Ecology: Voices from South and North,* edited by D. G. Hallman, 175–203. Geneva: WCC, 1994.

———. *Struggle to Be the Sun Again.* New York: Orbis, 1990.

Clements, Keith. *Dietrich Bonhoeffer's Ecumenical Quest.* Geneva: World Council of Churches, 2015.

Clinton, Hillary. "America's Pacific Century." *Foreign Policy,* October 11, 2011. https://foreignpolicy.com/2011/10/11/americas-pacific-century.

CIA, Grenada. "The New Jewel Movement and Religion." https://www.cia.gov/library/readingroom/document/cia-rdp86t00303r000500680024-9.

CNN Editorial Research. " Korean War Fast Facts." https://edition.cnn.com/2013/06/28/world/asia/korean-war-fast-facts/index.html.

Commander, Joint Region Marianas. "Marianas Island Range Complex." CNIC. https://www.cnic.navy.mil/regions/jrm/om/MIRCOPS.html.

Cone, James. *Black Theology of Liberation.* New York: Orbis, 1970.

———. *The Cross and the Lynching Tree.* Maryknoll, NY: Orbis, 2012.

———. *God of the Oppressed.* Maryknoll, NY: Orbis, 1997.

Conrado, Flavio. "Manual de Capacitación para la Construcción de Redes Interreligiosas Juveniles." https://www.academia.edu/5660993/Manual_de_Capacitacion_para_la_Construcion_de_Redes_Interreligiosas_Juveniles_-_Religiones_por_la_Paz.

Copeland, M. Shawn. *Enfleshing Freedom: Body, Race, and Being.* Minneapolis: Fortress, 2010.

Cottesloe. "The Cottesloe Declaration (1960)." https://kerkargief.co.za/doks/bely/DF_Cottesloe.pdf.

Coulter, Persson, et al. *Young Female Fighters in African Wars Conflict and Its Consequences.* Uppsala: Nordiska Afrikainstitutet, 2008.

Dabashi, Hamid. "Black Lives Matter and Palestine: A Historic Alliance." *Electronic Intifada.* https://www.aljazeera.com/indepth/opinion/2016/09/black-lives-matter-palestine-historic-alliance-160906074912307.html.

———. *Islamic Liberation Theology: Resisting Empire.* New York: Routledge, 2008.

Dalit Mahila Swabhiman Yatra. "Women Activism against Caste and Sexual Violence." https://dalitwomenfight.org/dalit-mahila-swabhiman-yatra.

Davis, Walter T., and Donald E. Wagner. *Zionism and the Quest for Justice in the Holy Land.* Eugene, OR: Pickwick, 2014.

Dayam, Joseph Prabhakar. "Re-Imagining an Indian Theology of the Cross Using Dalit Cultural Resources." PhD diss., Graduate Theological Union, 2009.

De Gruchy, John W. *Bonhoeffer and South Africa: Theology in Dialogue.* Grand Rapids: Eerdmans, 1984.

———. *The Church Struggle in South Africa.* Minneapolis: Fortress, 2004.

———. *Dietrich Bonhoeffer, Witness to Jesus Christ.* Minneapolis: Fortress, 1991.

———. *A Theological Odyssey: My Life in Writing.* Stellenbosch: Sun Media, 2014.

D'Souza, Radha. "Wars Beyond the Armed Forces: Colonialism and Militarization of Ethno-national Conflicts in Contemporary South Asia." In *Resistance to Empire and Militarization: Reclaiming the Sacred,* edited by Jude Lal Fernando, 25–44. Sheffield: Equinox, 2020.

Desjarlais, Orville, Jr. "Andersen AFB: Growing to Meet its Mission." *Air Force Print News,* January 17, 2006. https://www.af.mil/News/Article-Display/Article/132233/andersen-afb-growing-to-meet-its-mission.

DeYoung, Kevin. "A Status Confessionis Issue." https://www.thegospelcoalition.org/blogs/kevin-deyoung/a-status-confessionis-issue.

Douglas, Kelly Brown. *Stand your God: Black Bodies, and the Justice of God.* Maryknoll, NY: Orbis, 2015.

Downey, Greg. *Learning Capoeira: Lessons in Cunning from an Afro-Brazilian Art.* Oxford: Oxford University Press, 2005.

Duchrow, Ulrich. *Conflict Over the Ecumenical Movement.* Geneva: World Council of Churches, 1980.

Dumat-ol Daleno, Gaynor. "20 Years of Growth in 5." *The Pacific Daily News,* 14 September 2008. http://www.perezbrosinc.com/newsDtls.aspx?id=20.

Dupuis, Jacques, and Josef Neuner. *The Christian Faith in the Doctrinal Documents of the Catholic Church.* 6th ed. Bangalore: Theological Publications in India, 1996.

Dussel, Enrique. *Philosophy of Liberation.* Translated by Aquilina Martinez and Christine Morkovsky. Eugene, OR: Orbis, 2003.

DW. "Latin America: The Wealth of its Endangered Biodiversity." https://www.elmostrador.cl/cultura/2018/03/31/america-latina-la-riqueza-de-su-biodiversidad-en-peligro.

Ellacuría, Ignacio. "The Crucified People." In *Mysterium Liberationis: Fundamental Concepts of Liberation Theology*, edited by Ignacio Ellacuría SJ and Jon Sobrino SJ, 580–603. Maryknoll, NY: Orbis, 1993.

Ellis, Marc H. *Toward a Jewish Theology of Liberation: The Challenge of the 21st Century.* Waco: Baylor University Press, 2004.

Engelhardt, Tom. "Can you Say Permanent Bases? The American Press Can't." *Tomdispatch*, February 14, 2006. http://www.tomdispatch.com/post/59774/a_permanent_basis_for_withdrawal_.

Engler, Mark, and Paul Engler. *This is an Uprising: How Nonviolent Revolt is Shaping the Twenty-first Century.* New York: Nation, 2016.

Equality Labs. "Dalit Women Activists in the Black Lives Matter Movement." https://www.equalitylabs.org/the-movement-for-black-lives.

Essien, Aniefre. *Capoeira Beyond Brazil.* Berkley: Blue Snake, 2008.

Evans, Gareth. "Tip of the Spear: The Global Importance of America's Guam Base." *Naval Technology*, November 16, 2017. https://www.naval-technology.com/features/tip-spear-understanding-global-importance-americas-guam-base.

Fabella, Virginia. *Beyond Bonding: A Third World Women's Theological Journey.* Manila: The Ecumenical Association of Third World Theologians and the Institute of Women's Studies, 1993.

Fanon, Frantz. *The Wretched of the Earth.* New York: Grove, 1963.

Fernando, Jude Lal. "Introduction." In *Resistance to Empire and Militarization: Reclaiming the Sacred*, edited by Jude Lal Fernando, 1–24. Sheffield: Equinox, 2020.

———. "People, Land, and Empire in Asia: Geopolitics, Theological Imaginations, and Islands of Peace." In *People and Land: Decolonizing Theologies*, edited by Jione Havea, 125–40. London: Lexington, 2020.

Flores, Cara, and Leevin Camacho. "We Are Guåhan." *Guampedia*, August 22, 2013. https://www.guampedia.com/we-are-guahan.

Foucault, Michel. *Discipline and Punish: The Birth of the Prison.* Translated by Alan Sheridan. New York: Vintage, 1995.

Freire, Paulo. *Pedagogy of the Oppressed.* Translated by Myra Bergman Ramos. London: Penguin, 1993.

Galarza, Napoleon Saltos. " New Imperialisms and Struggle for Peace." In *Resistance to Empire and Militarization: Reclaiming the Sacred*, edited by Jude Lal Fernando, 270–89. Sheffield: Equinox, 2020.

Gholz, Eugene. "The Nixon Doctrine in the 21st Century." *World Politics Review*, July 22, 2009. https://www.worldpoliticsreview.com/articles/4106/the-nixon-doctrine-in-the-21st-century.

Girard, Rene. *I See Satan Fall Like Lightning.* Maryknoll, NY: Orbis, 2001.

Goodreads. "Vandana Shiva Quotes." https://www.goodreads.com/author/quotes/144748.Vandana_Shiva.

The Grenada Revolution Online. "The Manifesto of the New Jewel Movement." https://www.thegrenadarevolutiononline.com/manifesto.html.

Grossman, Karl. "The Democrats and Star Wars." http://www.space4peace.org/articles/democrats.htm.

———. "Weapons in Space." http://www.thirdworldtraveler.com/Militarization_Space/Weapons_Space.html.

Grossman, Karl, and Judith Long. "Waging War in Space." https://www.thenation.com/article/archive/waging-war-space.

The Guardian. "MI5 files reveal details of 1953 coup that overthrew British Guiana's leaders." https://www.theguardian.com/world/2011/aug/26/mi5-files-coup-british-guiana.

Gudmarsdottir, Sigridur. "Rapes of Earth and Grapes of Wrath: Steinbeck, Ecofeminism and the Metaphor of Rape." *Feminist Theology* 18 (2010) 206–22.

Gudynas, Eduardo. "Prologue: El buen vivir más allá del extractivismo." In *La maldición de la abundancia*, 15–20. Quito: Editorial Abya Yala, 2009.

Gutiérrez, Gustavo. *On Job: God-talk and the Suffering of the Innocent.* Maryknoll, NY: Orbis, 1987.

———. "The Task and Content of Liberation Theology." Translated by Judith Condor. In *The Cambridge Companion to Liberation Theology*, edited by Christopher Rowland, 19–38. Cambridge: Cambridge University Press, 1999.

———. *A Theology of Liberation: History, Politics and Salvation.* New York: Orbis, 1988.

Haight, Roger. *Future of Christology.* London: Continuum, 2007.

Halloran, Richard. "Guam Seen as Pivotal U.S. Base." *The Washington Times*, March 11, 2006.

Hanlon, David. *Remaking Micronesia: Discourse Over Development in a Pacific Territory, 1944–1982.* Honolulu: University of Hawaii Press, 1998.

Hara, Kimie. "Micronesia and the Postwar Remaking of the Asia-Pacific: 'An American Lake.'" *The Asia-Pacific Journal* 5 (2007). https://apjjf.org/-Kimie-Hara/2493/article.html.

Harden, Blaine. "On Guam, Planned Marine Base Raises Anger, Infrastructure Concerns." *The Washington Post*, March 22, 2010. http://www.washingtonpost.com/wp-dyn/content/article/2010/03/21/AR2010032101025.html.

Hardy, Rebecca. "Friends Rally Behind Hunger Striker." https://thefriend.org/article/friends-rally-behind-hunger-striker.

Harjo, Suzan Shown. "Just Good Sports." In *For Indigenous Eyes Only: A Decolonization Handbook*, edited by Waziyatawin Angela Wilson and Michael Yellow Bird, 31–52. Santa Fe: School of American Research, 2005.

Harveer, Dabas. "'Barred from Entering Temple': Dalit Youth, 17, Argues with Four Upper Cast Men, Found Shot Dead in Amroha." https://timesofindia.indiatimes.com/city/meerut/up-barred-from-entering-temple-dalit-youth-17-argues-with-4-upper-caste-men-found-shot-dead-in-amroha/articleshow/76267143.cms.

Hattori, Anne Perez. "Righting Civil Wrongs: The Guam Congress Walkout of 1949." *Kinalamten Pulitikat: Sinenten i Chamorro: Issues in Guam's Political Development: The Chamorro Perspective.* Agaña, Guam: Political Status Education Coordinating Committee, 1995.

Hattori, Anne Perez, et al. "Unified Chamorro Response to the DEIS." February 10, 2010. http://www.minagahetzine.com/chamorroresponse.

Haynes, Jeffrey. "Religion, Ethnicity and Civil War in Africa: The Cases of Uganda and Sudan." *The Round Table* 96 (2007) 305–17.

Hedegard, Danielle. "Blackness and Experience in Omnivorous Cultural Consumption: Evidence from the Tourism of Capoeira in Salvador, Brazil." *Poetics* 41 (2013) 1–26.

Higginbottom, Andy. "Colonialism Still Matters: Militarization and Imperial Grand Strategy in the Era of US versus China." In *Resistance to Empire and Militarization:*

Reclaiming the Sacred, edited by Jude Lal Fernando, 251–69. Sheffield: Equinox, 2020.

Hikey, Michael. "The Korean War: An Overview." http://www.bbc.co.uk/history/worldwars/coldwar/korea_hickey_01.shtml.

Hossein-zadeh, Ismael. "The Globalization of Militarism." https://www.huffingtonpost.com/ismael-hosseinzadeh/the-globalization-of-mili_b_798843.html.

Houtart, François. *Deslegitimar el Capitalismo. Reconstruir la esperanza, Cuestiones geopolíticas*. Caracas: Fundación Editorial el Perro y la rana, 2007.

Howard, Keith. *True Stories of the Korean Comfort Women*. London: Continuum, 1995.

Hubert, J. "Sacred Beliefs and Beliefs of Sacredness." In *Sacred Sites*, edited by D. Carmichael et al. London: Routledge, 1994.

Human Rights Watch. "The Miss World Riots: Continued Impunity for Killings in Kaduna." https://www.hrw.org/reports/2003/nigeria0703/2.htm.

———. "Nepal: Ensure Justice for Caste-Based Killings." https://www.hrw.org/news/2020/06/01/nepal-ensure-justice-caste-based-killings.

Humphreys, Macartan, et al., eds. *Escaping the Resource Curse*. New York: Columbia University Press, 2007.

Ifil, Gwen. "Guam, Against the Tide, Wants Air Base Closed." *New York Times*, April 20, 1991. https://www.nytimes.com/1991/04/20/us/guam-against-the-tide-wants-air-base-closed.html.

Inter-American Court of Human Rights, "Case of the "Las Dos Erres" Massacre v. Guatemala." https://www.corteidh.or.cr/docs/casos/articulos/seriec_211_ing.pdf.

Interfaith Peacemakers. "Roman Catholic Theologian and Advocate for Interfaith Cooperation." https://readthespirit.com/interfaith-peacemakers/hans-kung.

Isherwood, Lisa, and Elizabeth Stuart. *Introducing Body Theology*. Sheffield: Sheffield Academic Press, 1998.

Itano, Nicole. "The Sisters-in-Arms in Liberia's War." https://www.csmonitor.com/2003/0826/p07s01-woaf.html.

Jankunas, Jediminas T. *The Dictatorship of Relativism: Pope Benedict XVI's Response*. New York: St. Pauls, 2010.

John Paul II. *Apostolic Letter Salvifici doloris of the Supreme Pontiff John Paul II to the Bishops, to the Priests, to the Religious Families and to the Faithful of the Catholic Church on the Christian Meaning of Human Suffering*. Vatican City: Libreria Editrice Vaticana, 1984. http://www.vatican.va/content/john-paul-ii/en/apost_letters/1984/documents/hf_jp-ii_apl_11021984_salvifici-doloris.html.

Joseph, M. P. "Introduction: Searching Beyond Galilee." In *From Galilee to Tainan: Towards a Theology of Chhutpthau-thin* (ATESEA Occasional Paper No. 15), edited by Huang Poho, 1–13. Tainan: ATESEA, n.d.

Kahl, Brigitte. *Galatians Re-imagined: Reading with the Eyes of the Vanquished*. Minneapolis: Fortress, 2010.

Kairos Britain. "Time for Action, a British Christian response to A Moment of Truth, the Kairos Palestine document." http://www.kairosbritain.org.uk/wp-content/uploads/2015/01/Time-for-Action.pdf.

Kairos Palestine. "A Moment of Truth. A Word of Faith, Hope and Love from the Heart of Palestinian Suffering." http://www.kairospalestine.ps/content/kairos-document.

Kairos South Africa. "Challenge to the Church: A Theological Comment on the Political Crisis in South Africa." https://kairossouthernafrica.wordpress.com/2011/05/08/the-south-africa-kairos-document-1985.

———. "Kairos 30th Anniversary Statement: Dangerous Memory and Hope for the Future." https://kairossouthernafrica.wordpress.com/2015/08/20/kairos-sa-30th-anniversary-conference-statement.

Kaoma, Kapya J. *God's Family, God's Earth: Christian Ecological Ethics of Ubuntu.* Zomba: Kanchere Series, 2013.

Kapoor, S. D. *Dalits and African-Americans: A Study in Comparison.* Kalpaz, 2004.

Khalidi, Rashid. *Brokers of Deceit: How the U.S. Has Undermined Peace in the Middle East.* Boston: Beacon, 2013.

———. *The Hundred Years War on Palestine: A History of Settler Colonialism and Resistance, 1917–2017.* New York: Metropolitan, 2020.

Kim, Dae-jung. *Conscience in Action: Autobiography of Kim Dae-jung,* Singapore: Palgrave Macmillan, 209.

Kim, Nami, and Ann Joh Wonhee. *Feminist Praxis against US Militarism.* London: Lexington, 2020.

Klare, Michael T. "Imperial Reach." *The Nation,* April 25, 2005. https://www.thenation.com/article/imperial-reach.

Koenig, H. G., et al., eds. *Handbook of Religion and Health.* New York: Oxford University Press, 2001.

Kumar, Vimal R. "Dalit Youth Killed for Marrying Caste Girl." http://www.thehindu.com/news/national/tamil-nadu/dalit-youth-killed-for-marrying-caste-hindu-girl/article8350431.ece.

Kumaragamage, Kumari. *Ureippu Sappada, Noasu Kan Walata [For the Ears the Haven't Heard].* Colombo: Neo Graphics, 2010.

Kwok, Pui-lan. *Introducing Asian Feminist Theology.* Sheffield: Sheffield Academic Press, 2000.

Leahy, Stephen. "La protección de la biodiversidad en América Latina." http://www.fao.org/in-action/agronoticias/detail/es/c/512653.

Lewis, J. Lowell. *Ring of Liberation: Deceptive Discourse in Brazilian Capoeira.* Chicago: University of Chicago Press, 1992.

Lizama, Jude. "No Secrets." *Marianas Variety,* May 22, 2009. http://decolonizeguam.blogspot.com/2009/05/jgpo-no-secret-but-admits-to.html.

Longchar, Wati. *Transforming Cultures and Praxis: Engaging Peoples in the Margins.* PTCA Study Series No. 16. Kolkata: PTCA & YTCS, 2017.

Longenecker, Bruce W. "Peace, Prosperity, and Propaganda: Advertisement and Reality in the Early Roman Empire." In *An Introduction to Empire in the New Testament,* edited by Adam Winn, 15–45. Atlanta: SBL, 2016.

Lopez, C. Todd. "DOD Finalizes Purchase Plan for F-35." https://www.defense.gov/Explore/News/Article/Article/2002585/dod-finalizes-purchase-plan-for-f-35-aircraft.

Lorde, Audre. *Sister Outsider: Essays and Speeches.* New York: Random, 2007.

Lumen. "The Korean War." https://courses.lumenlearning.com/boundless-ushistory/chapter/the-korean-war.

MacFarlane, S. N. "Taking Stock: The Third World and the End of the Cold War." In *The Third World Beyond the Cold War: Continuity and Change,* edited by L. Fawcett and Y. Sayigh, 15–33. Oxford: Oxford University Press, 1999.

Malcolm X. *By Any Means Necessary.* New York: Pathfinder, 1992.

Mama, Amina, and Okazawa-Rey, Margo. "Militarism, Conflict and Women's Activism in the Global Era: Challenges and Prospects for Women in Three West African Contexts." *Feminist Review* 101 (2012) 97–123.

Mbiti, J. *An Introduction to African Religion.* 2nd ed. Dar er Salaam: East African Educational, 1991.

McIntyre, Jamie, and Mike Mount. "U.S. Sub Leaked Radioactive Water, Possibly for Months." *CNN*, August 1, 2008. http://edition.cnn.com/2008/US/08/01/navy.sub. leak.

Mendis, Viraj. "Dharmeratnam Sivaram: Murder of a Brilliant Journalist." http://www. jdslanka.org/index.php/analysis-reviews/media-a-culture/1-dharmaratnam-sivaram-silencing-a-brilliant-mind.

Miller, Phil. "Could a Corbyn Government Change UK Foreign Policy in Bahrain?" https://novaramedia.com/2018/09/29/could-a-corbyn-government-change-uk-foreign-policy in-bahrain/Phil-Miller-Editing Now.doc.

———. "In the Shadow of Military: Sri Lanka's 'new democracy' and Tamil people." http://www.jdslanka.org/index.php/news-features/human-rights/530-in-the-shadow-ofmilitary-sri-lankas-new-democracy-and-tamil-people=.

———. "'We Sent a Man to His Death': How the British Army Betrayed Its Own Informant to a Murderous Junta." https://www.vice.com/en_uk/article/xd3vv3/spy-claims britain-sent-man-to-his-death-in-guatemala.

Millette, Alan R. "Korean War: 1950–1953." https://www.britannica.com/event/Korean-War.

Moltmann, Jurgen. *The Way of Jesus Christ: Christology in Messianic Dimensions.* New York: HarperCollins, 1990.

Molyneaux, L.B. *The Sacred Earth: Spirits of the Landscape, Ancient Alignments and Sacred Sites Creation and Fertility.* London: Duncan Braid, 1994.

Muslim Network for Peace. *Jihad against Violence: The Struggle of Muslim Women for Peace.* Text adapted and expanded from the first campaign of the Shura Muslim Council of the International Network, 2009.

Mwagiru, M. "Women and Children in Conflict Situations: The Culture of Rights as a Missing Link in Africa." *Africa Media Review* 11 (1997) 1–24.

Naputi, Tiara. *Charting Contemporary Chamoru Activism: Anti-Militarization and Social Movements in Guåhan.* PhD diss., University of Austin, Texas, 2013.

Naputi, Tiara, and Michael Lujan Bevacqua. "Militarization and Resistance from Guåhan: Protecting and Defending Pågat." *American Quarterly* 67 (2015) 837–58.

Natividad, LisaLinda, and Gwyn Kirk. "Fortress Guam: Resistance to U.S. Military Mega-Buildup." *Asia-Pacific Journal* 8 (2010). https://apjjf.org/-LisaLinda-Natividad/3356/article.html.

Natividad, LisaLinda, and Victoria-Lola Leon Guerrero. "The Explosive Growth of U.S. Military Power on Guam Confronts People Power: Experience of an Island People Under Spanish, Japanese and American Colonial Rule." *Asia-Pacific Journal* 8 (2010). https://apjjf.org/-LisaLinda-Natividad/3454/article.html.

New York Times. "8 Minutes and 46 Seconds: How George Floyd was Killed in Police Custody." https://www.nytimes.com/2020/05/31/us/george-floyd-investigation. html.

———. "In Quick Response, de Blasio Calls Fatal Shooting of Mentally Ill Woman 'Unacceptable.'" https://www.nytimes.com/2016/10/20/nyregion/nypd-sergeant-fatal-shooting-bronx-woman.html.

———. "Michael Brown's Shooting." https://www.nytimes.com/interactive/2014/08/12/us/13police-shooting-of-black-teenager-michael-brown.html.

Nirmal, Arvind P. "Toward a Christian Dalit Theology." In *A Reader in Dalit Theology*, edited by Arvind P. Nirmal, 53–70. Madras: Gurukul, 1990.

O'Grady, John, and Peter Scherle. "Ecumenics in the 21st Century." In *Ecumenics from the Rim: Explorations in Honour of John D'Arcy May*, edited by John O'Grady and Peter Scherle, 3–20. Berlin: Lit Verlag, 2007.

Oliville, Patrick, trans. *The Law Code of Manu*. Oxford: Oxford University Press, 2004.

Olson, Carl, trans. *Hindu Primary Sources: A Sectarian Reader*. New Brunswick: Rutgers University Press, 2007.

Palestine Portal. "Mapping the Movement." https://www.palestineportal.org/mapping-movement/the-global-network.

Palomo, Tony M. *An Island in Agony*. Agaña, Guam: Self-published, 1984.

Panikkar, Raimon. *The Intrareligious Dialogue*. Mahwah: Paulist, 1999.

———. *Myth, Faith, and Hermeneutics*. New York: Paulist, 1979.

Pappé, llan. *The Ethnic Cleansing of Palestine*. London and New York: Oneworld, 2006.

Pawar, J. V. *Dalit Panthers: An Authoritative History*. New Delhi: Forward, 2017, Kindle edition.

Pena, Alex. "Afghan Deployment is a Family Affair for Guam National Guardsmen." *Stars and Stripes*, November 17, 2013. https://www.stripes.com/news/afghan-deployment-is-a-family-affair-for-guam-national-guardsmen-1.253334.

Peng, Chin. *My Side of History*. Singapore: Media Masters, 2003.

Petrovich, Lynn. "2019 Defense Budget." https://popularresistance.org/2019-defense-budget-supports-883-overseas-bases-and-is-lethal-to-humanity.

Phar Kim Beng. "The Pentagon's Paradigm Shift in Asia." *Asia Times Online*, June 10, 2003. http://www.atimes.com/atimes/Korea/EF10Dg01.html.

Phillips, Mike. "Land." In *Kinalamten Pulitikat: Sinenten i Chamorro: Issues in Guam's Political Development: The Chamorro Perspective*. Agaña, Guam: Political Status Education Coordinating Committee, 1996.

Pieris, Aloysius. *Fire and Water: Basic Issues in Asian Buddhism and Christianity*. New York: Orbis, 1996.

Pollefeyt, Didier. *Jews and Christians: Rivals or Partners for the Kingdom of God?* Louvain: Peeters, 1997.

Porter, Robert Odawi. "The Decolonization of Indigenous Governance." In *For Indigenous Eyes Only: A Decolonization Handbook*, edited by Angela Wilson Waziyatawin and Michael Yellow Bird, 87–108. Santa Fe: School of American Research, 2008.

Prabhakar, M. E. "Christology in Dalit Perspective." In *Frontiers of Dalit Theology*, edited by V. Devasahayam, 402–32. Delhi: ISPCK, 1997.

Prior, Michael. *Zionism and the State of Israel, a Moral Inquiry*. New York: Routledge, 1999.

Proaño, Msgr Leonidas. "El intervencionismo norteamericano en América Latina." In *Foro Provincial Anti-intervencionista de Chimborazo*, 35–46. Riobamba, Ecuador: Fundación Pueblo Indio del Ecuador, 1982.

————. "El Profeta del Pueblo." In *Coedition Ciudad*, 35–46. CEDEP. Quito: Fundación Pueblo Indio del Ecuador, 1992.

————. *Fe y Política*. Riobamba. Ecuador: Instituto de Pastoral, ERPE, 1983.

Radicalizing Reformation. "Radicalizing Reformation: Provoked by the Bible and Today's Crises: 94 Theses." http://www.radicalizing-reformation.com/index.php/en.

Raheb, Mitri. *Faith in the Face of Empire: The Bible Through Palestinian Eyes*. Maryknoll, NY: Orbis, 2016.

Rao, Naveen. "Centred on the Margin." *Clark Journal of Theology* 5 (2015) 6–15.

Religions for Peace. *The Kyoto Declaration on Confronting Violence and Advancing Shared Security*. Kyoto: Religions for Peace Eighth World Assembly, 2008.

Rhem, Kathleen T. "Korean War Death Stats Highlight Modern DoD Safety Record." https://archive.defense.gov/news/newsarticle.aspx?id=45275.

Robson, Seth. "Pivot to Asia Will Remain a Priority for U.S. Military, Experts Say." *Stars and Stripes*, June 22, 2017. https://www.stripes.com/news/pivot-to-asia-will-remain-a-priority-for-us-military-experts-say-1.474950.

Rogers, Robert. *Destiny's Landfall: A History of Guam*. Honolulu: University of Hawai'i, 1995.

Rörhig-Assunção, Matthias. *Capoeira: The History of an Afro-Brazilian Martial Art*. New York: Routledge, 2005.

Ruether, Rosemary Radford. "Ecofeminism: The Challenge to Theology." https://www.unive.it/media/allegato/dep/n20-2012/Ricerche/Riflessione/4_Ruether_Ecofeminism.pdf.

Ruether, Rosemary R., and Ellis, Marc H., eds. *Beyond Occupation: American, Jewish, Christian and Palestinian Voices for Peace*. Boston: Beacon, 1990.

Ryan, Samuel. "Outside the Gate, Sharing the Insult." In *Leave the Temple: Indian Paths to Human Liberation*, edited by Felix Wilfred, 125–45. Eugene, OR: Wipf & Stock, 2009.

Samuel, Joshua. *Untouchable Bodies, Resistance, and Liberation: A Comparative Theology of Divine Possessions*. Leiden: Brill, 2020.

Santos, Nicole Adapon. *The Paradox of Guam: Brief Essays on Culture, the Military, and a U.S. Pacific Territory*. MA thesis, University of California at Santa Cruz, 2007.

Schlesinger, Stephen, and Stephen Kinzer. *Bitter Fruit: The Untold Story of the American Coup in Guatemala*. New York: Anchor, 1983.

Schüssler Fiorenza, Elisabeth. *Sharing Her Word: Feminist Biblical Interpretation in Context*. Edinburgh: T. & T. Clark, 1998.

————. *Wisdom Ways: Introducing Feminist Biblical Interpretation*. New York: Orbis, 2001.

Searle, C. *Grenada: The Struggle against Destabilisation*. London: Writers and Readers, 1983.

Sen, Amartya. *Identity and Violence: The Illusion of Destiny*. London: Penguin, 2006.

Shrirama. "Untouchability and Stratification in Indian Civilisation." In *Dalits in Modern India: Vision and Values*, edited by S. M. Michael, 45–75. New Delhi: Sage, 2007.

Sideris, Tina. "War, Gender and Culture: Mozambican Women Refugees." *Social Science and Medicine* 56 (2003) 713–24.

Sivanandan, A. "Editorial." *Race and Class* 15 (1974). https://journals.sagepub.com/doi/pdf/10.1177/030639687401500401Phil-Miller-EditingNow.doc.

Siwila, L. "Tracing the Ecological Footprints of our Foremothers: Towards an African Feminist Approach to Women's Connectedness with Nature." *Studia Historiae Eclesiasticae* 40 (2014) 131–47.

Sjollema, Baldwin. *Never Bow to Racism: A Personal Account of the Ecumenical Struggle.* Geneva: WCC, 2015.

Sobrino, Jon. *Jesus the Liberator: A Historical-Theological View.* New York: Orbis, 1994.

———. *Witnesses to the Kingdom: The Martyrs of El Salvador and the Crucified Peoples.* Maryknoll, NY: Orbis, 2003.

Solano, Boris Tobar. "La Teología de la Liberación del Ecuador: Lideres, Principios y Estilo de Iglesias." *Revista PUCE* 102 (2016) 385–404.

Song, C. S. *Jesus, The Crucified People.* New York: Crossroad, 1990.

———. *Theology from the Womb of Asia.* New York: Orbis, 1986.

Stade, Ronald. *Pacific Passages, World Culture and Local Politics in Guam.* Stockholm: Stockholm Studies in Social Anthropology, 1998.

Stencel, S., et al., eds. *Tolerance and Tension: Islam and Christianity in Sub-Saharan Africa.* Pew Research Center, 2010. http://www.pewforum.org/2010/04/15/executive-summary-islam-and-christianity-in-sub-saharan-africa.

Talmon-Chvaicer, Maya. *The Hidden History of Capoeira: A Collision of Cultures in the Brazilian Battle Dance.* Austin: University of Texas Press, 2008.

Tamayo, Juan José. *Para comprender la Teología de la Liberación.* Navarra, Spain: Editorial Verbo Divino, 1982.

Tauran, Jean-Louis. "Vaticano: Formar jóvenes cristianos e hindúes para ser artífices de paz." http://www.aciprensa.com/noticias/vaticano-formar-jovenes-cristianos-e-hindues-para-ser-artifices-de-paz-84497/#.Ui9EQdJFVcg.

Taylor, Mark Kline. *Remembering Esperanza: A Cultural-Political Theology for North American Praxis.* Maryknoll, NY: Orbis, 1990.

Terlaje, Therese (Office of the Senator). "MITT SEIS, Informational Presentation for the Community." Office of Senator Therese Terlaje, 2017. http://senatorterlaje.com/wp-content/uploads/2017/08/MITT-Presentation-2.pdf.

Times Now Digital. "Telangana Honor Killing." https://www.timesnownews.com/india/article/telangana-honour-killing-nalgonda-honour-killing-pranay-kumar-caste-crime-amrutha-varshini-father-t-maruthi-rao-drushyam-movie-alibi-contract-killers/287137.

Tomaselli, Alexandra. "A Journey Towards Mother Earth: Listening to Indigenous Voices in the COVID-19 Pandemic." https://blogs.eurac.edu/covid-19/indigenous-voices-in-the-covid-19-pandemic.

Turshen, Meredeth. "Women, War and Peace in Africa: A Reflection on the Past 20 Years." http://www.unrisd.org/beijing+20-turshen.

UMassAmherst. " Letter from B. R. Ambedkar to Dr. W. E. B. Du Bois, ca. July 1946." https://credo.library.umass.edu/view/full/mums312-b109-i132.

———. " Letter from W. E. B. Du Bois to B. R. Ambedkar, July 31, 1946." https://credo.library.umass.edu/view/full/mums312-b109-i133.

Underwood, Robert. "Afterword." In *Campaign for Political Rights on the Island of Guam*, by Penelope Bordallo Hofschneider. Saipan: CNMI Division of Historic Preservation, 2001.

———. "Teaching Guam's History in Guam High Schools." In *Guam History Perspectives*, edited by Lee Carter, Rosa Carter and William Wuerch, 56–69. Mangilao, Guam: University of Guam Press, 1997.

United Nations Secretariat. "Working Papers on Non-Self-Governing Territories." www.un.org/en/decolonization/nonselfgovterritories.shtml.

United Pacific Command. "USPACOM Facts." http://www.pacom.mil/web/Site_Pages/USPACOM/Facts.shtml.

Utas, Mats. "West-African Warscapes: Victimcy, Girlfriending, Soldiering: Tactic Agency in a Young Woman's Social Navigation of the Liberian War Zone." *Anthropological Quarterly* 78 (2005) 403–30.

Villa-Vicencio, Charles. *Trapped in Apartheid*. Maryknoll, NY: Orbis, 1988.

Visser 'T Hooft, Willem. "The Mandate of the Ecumenical Movement." Fourth Assembly of the World Council of Churches, Uppsala, 1968." In *The Ecumenical Movement: An Anthology of Key Texts and Voices*, edited by Michael Kinnamon and Brian E. Cope, 38–43. Grand Rapids: Eerdmans, 1997.

Wagner, Donald E. *Zionism and the Quest for Justice in the Holy Land*. Eugene, OR: Pickwick, 2014.

Warheit, Vanessa, dir. *The Insular Empire: America in the Mariana Islands*. Horse Opera Productions, 2010.

Warren, K., ed. *Ecofeminism: Women, Culture, and Nature*. Bloomington: Indiana University Press, 1997.

———. *Ecofeminist Philosophy: A Western Perspective on What it is and Why it Matters*. Lanham, MD: Rowman & Littlefield, 2000.

Washington, James M., ed. *A Testament of Hope: The Essential Writings and Speeches of Martin Luther King Jr*. New York: Harper One, 1986.

Waziyatawin, Angela Wilson. "Relieving Our Suffering: Indigenous Decolonization and the United States Truth Commission." In *For Indigenous Eyes Only: A Decolonization Handbook*, edited by Angela Wilson Waziyatawin and Michael Yellow Bird, 189–205. Santa Fe: School of American Research, 2005.

Waziyatawin, Angela Wilson, and Michael Yellow Bird. "Beginning Decolonization." In *For Indigenous Eyes Only: A Decolonization Handbook*, edited by Angela Wilson Waziyatawin and Michael Yellow Bird, 1–2. Santa Fe: School of American Research, 2008.

We Are Guåhan Coalition. "Buildup Basics." http://www.weareguahan.com/about-the-eis/build-up-basics.

Webb, James. *Micronesia and U.S. Pacific Strategy*. New York: Praeger, 1974.

Webster, John C. B. "Who is a Dalit?" In *Dalits in Modern India: Vision and Values*, edited by S. M. Michael, 76–88. New Delhi: Sage, 2007.

West, Cornel. "Cornel West Moves Anderson Cooper to Tears with His Call for Racial Justice." https://www.youtube.com/watch?v=ZGETF3MO3pQ.

Whitaker, Mark P. *Learning Politics from Sivaram*. London: Pluto, 2007.

Who Profits. "Who Profits: the Israeli Occupation Industry." https://whoprofits.org.

Widome, Daniel. "The List: The Six Most Important U.S. Military Bases." *Foreign Policy*, May 2006. http://www.foreignpolicy.com/story/cms.php?story_id=3460.

Williams, Dana M. "15,000 Troops on Guam, Northern Marianas for Valiant Shield Exercise." *Pacific Daily News*, 16 September 2018. https://www.guampdn.com/story/news/2018/09/16/15-000-troops-here-valiant-shield-exercise/1324243002.

Williams, Delores S. *Sisters in the Wilderness: The Challenges of Womanist God-Talk*. New York: Orbis, 1993.

Winn, Adam. "The Gospel of Mark: A Response to Imperial Propaganda." In *An Introduction to Empire in the New Testament*, edited by Adam Winn, 91–106. Atlanta: SBL, 2016.

World Council of Churches. "Just and Inclusive Community." In *Mission from the Margins*, edited by World Council for Churches, 153–69. Amsterdam, Netherlands: World Council of Churches, 2012.

Zwick-Maitreyi, M., et al. *Caste in the United States: A Survey of Caste among South Asian Americans*. N.d.: Equality Labs, 2018.

Index

Note: page numbers containing n
    refer to footnotes.

Abya-Yala 65–68, 80
    see also Latin America
Acosta, Alberto 68
Acosta, Marino Samayor 76
Adam Hussein, Adam 122
Adu-Gyamfi, Yaw 122–23
Afghanistan 39, 172
Africa 15, 17, 52, 112–28, 219
    Christianity/Islam in 124, 128
    demilitarization in 128
    and ecofeminism *see*
        ecofeminism
    independence movements in
        114–15
    interreligious violence in 125
    neocolonial violence in 113–16
    rape in 113, 119–21
    sacred sites in 113, 116, 117,
        118, 119, 121–23
    see also specific countries
African Americans *see* Black people
Ainu people 50
Akan people 122–23
alienation 54, 68, 177, 183, 190
Amazon 68, 83–84
Ambedkar, B. R. 21, 240–41
American Academy of Religions 4–5
Americas, School of (SOA) 76,
    79–81, 82, 84
Anabaptists 168
ancestors 119, 122, 123
androcentrism 46–47

Angola 175
Annai Poopathy 89, 89n1, 90
anthropocentrism 46
anti-human gods 2, 3, 11, 16
anti-Semitism 204, 216
apartheid 200–201, 202–3, 205–6,
    208, 211, 213, 214
    and Israel-Palestine 21, 203, 204,
        206, 213
Aquinas, Thomas 93, 179
Arbenz, Juan Jose 254
Arbery, Ahmaud 223, 239
ARENA (nationalist Republican
        Alliance, El Salvador) 76
Argentina 49, 79, 83, 161, 254
Aristotle 178, 179
arms race 85, 140–41, 143
Arrison, Edwin 218
Asia 15, 17, 52, 53–55, 103–4, 111,
    219
    and USA 7, 29, 32, 35
    see also East Asia; South Asia;
        West Asia; *and see specific*
        countries
Athanasiou, Athena 230
Atkins, Peter J. 127
atonement doctrine 13
Augustine 93
Australia 49, 50

Bahrain 22–23, 242–43, 263–64
Balasingham, Adele Ann 89
Balniel, Lord 249
Banzar, Hugo 79
Barmen Declaration (1934) 200, 207

Barrera, Pedro 256–57, 259, 261
Barth, Karl 206
Basic Human Communities 14,
    21, 23
BDS (Boycott, Divestment and
    Sanctions) 213, 214, 214n42,
    217
Belize 22–23, 243, 254, 255, 256,
    257–58, 259, 260, 261
Bethge, Eberhard 198, 217
Bezmer Air Base (Bulgaria) 39
Bible 45–46, 71, 86, 152–54
    indigenous translations of
        51–52, 80
    see also Gospels
binaries, Aristotelian 226–27,
    226n13
biodiversity 17, 67
biological weapons 84
Birds against Shotguns collective 84
Bishop, Rupert 248
Black Lives Matter movement
    176n2, 211, 240n57
Black people 3–4, 20, 171, 200,
    223–41
    and crucified Christ 4, 21, 224,
        225, 231–32, 231n28, 234,
        236, 237–39
    as crucified people 224, 228–31,
        239
    and Dalit people, compared
        225–26
    liberation struggles of 21
    and racial violence 3, 4–5, 8, 21,
        22, 176, 197, 223, 225, 226,
        228, 239
    see also African Americans
black theology 103
Blazer, Plan 78
Bloody Sunday massacre (1972) 251
body, the 230–31
Boko Haram 125
Bolivia 78, 79
Bonhoeffer, Dietrich 198, 199, 206,
    207–8, 209–11, 212, 217,
    218
Booplan, John 230
borders 82, 115, 126

solidarity across 21, 23, 24, 168
Boycott, Divestment and Sanctions
    see BDS
Bravo, Hervi Lara 66
Brazil 5, 8, 143, 164, 170, 171, 218
    and capoeira see capoeira
Britain (UK) 6, 134, 145, 213, 218
    and Caribbean 252–53
    Foreign Office 253, 256, 259
    MI5 247–48, 249, 252, 260
    Ministry of Defence (MOD)
        246, 251
    RAF 255, 257
    Royal Marines 246, 250–51
Britain and counter-insurgency 7,
    22–23, 242–64
    and Grenada see Grenada
    and Guatemala see Guatemala,
        counter-insurgency in
    and Institute of Race Relations
        244–45
    and Kew Archives see Kew
        Archives
British Empire 50, 139, 246, 249,
    254
Brock, Rita Nakashima 13, 103
Brown, Michael 11, 225, 236
Buddhism 19, 133, 135, 178
    and nonviolence 159, 162
Buddhist war widows 104–6, 109–10
Buddhist–Christian dialogue
    159–65
    and peace/justice 159–60
    and prayer/meditation 162–65
    and self-criticism 160–61, 162
    and silence 162
Bush, George W. 38
Butler, Judith 10–11

Camara, Dom Helder 1–2, 77, 164
Cambodia 54
capitalism 3, 6, 56, 66, 69–70, 74–75,
    86, 115, 141, 197
capoeira 4, 19, 20, 175, 184–97
    and benção 188
    blocks in 192, 193, 193n71
    commercialization of 196–97
    and dialogue 192, 193, 194, 195

and epistemology of faith 190,
192
and hermeneutics of trust
192–94, 195
and improvisation 190–92,
191nn64, 65
and *malícia* 187–90, 192–94,
195
origins of 184–85
pedagogical elements of 186–95,
186–87n43, 187n44, 196
and resistance 177, 184, 185,
186, 196n82
and *roda* 185–86, 186n39, 188,
190–91, 193n70
as treachery 185n37, 188, 189
as whatever the mouth eats
185n37
and whole person 194–95
Capoeira, Nestor 187–88, 187n45
Caribbean 52, 79, 80, 243, 252–53
see also Grenada
Carriles, Luis Posada 79
Cartesian dualism 181, 182, 190
caste system 22, 47, 224, 225n8,
229–30, 229nn2122, 237–38
Castro, Fidel 83
Catholic Church/Catholicism 19,
77, 78, 135, 157, 215n48
Catechism of (CCC) 92–93, 94–95
and ecumenism 157
and Vatican II 157, 160, 262
CCI (countering counter-
insurgency) 243, 250, 260
and Sivaram 243–246, 264
Central America 67, 75, 77, 254,
256, 261
Cervenka, Zdenek 114, 116, 128
Chamorro people 7, 15–16, 27,
33–34
land stolen from 35, 36, 40, 41
powerlessness of 43–44
resistance of 29, 34, 41–43, 44
sacred sites of 41
in US Armed Forces 29, 34
Chauvin, Derek 223
children 17, 19, 55, 57

and social/cultural colonization
49, 50
and war 112–13, 115, 117, 118,
119–20, 125, 171
Chile 79
Chin Peng 245
China 6, 16, 132–33, 137, 137n3
and Korean War 138–39
and Sino-Japanese Wars 134,
135, 136
and US 142
Chŏndogyo 135–36
Chosun Dynasty 134, 136
Christ, Carol P. 99–100, 107
Christianity
in Africa 124, 125, 178
and Buddhism 159–62
conservative 149
and Empire 16, 51–53
in India 56
lack of unity in 165–66
minjung 19
and resistance 150
and suffering/sacrifice 18
and Zionism 12, 21
Chung, Hyun Kyung 107, 118
Churchill, Winston 249
CIA (Central Intelligence Agency)
75, 79, 144, 254, 264
citizenship 36, 50, 144, 145
Ciudad Juarez (Mexico) 156, 171
civil–military relations 144
Clements, Keith 217
climate change 70, 199
Clinton , Hillary 38
Cold War 79, 80, 137, 140, 141, 145,
149, 254
ending of 37, 147
collective struggle 9, 16, 17, 19, 20,
23, 46, 60, 83, 108
Colombia 79, 80
colonialism 15–16, 28, 32, 42, 44,
113–14, 115, 140, 200, 202,
254
colonization process 48–53
and Christianity 51–53

colonization process (*continued*)
  cultural/social colonization
      48–50, 51, 52
  and denial of right to life 50–51
  land confiscation 48
commercialization 47, 58, 196–97
communism 37, 137, 145, 149, 254,
      255, 256, 261
Cone, James 59–60, 228, 231,
      231n28
Confessing Church 199, 206, 207,
      215n47
Confucianism 19, 131, 135, 136
Congo, Democratic Republic of
      (DRC) 114
Conrado, Flavio 158
Contreras, Manuel 79
Copeland, Shawn 231–32
coral reefs 31, 40
Corbyn, Jeremy 250
corruption 57
cosmos 3, 9, 55, 143, 152–54,
      226n13
  sacredness of 10, 12
Costa Rica 67
Coulter, Persson 126
Council for World Mission (CWM)
      52
counter-insurgency 7, 22–23, 79, 80,
      242–64
  and Britain *see* Britain and
      counterinsurgency
  countering *see* CCI
  and faith 262–64
courage 7, 63, 90
COVID-19 pandemic 2, 3–7, 8, 24,
      112
  in India 6
  and indigenous people 5
  and militarization 10
  and racism 4–5
  in Sri Lanka 6–7
creativity 13, 14, 20, 24, 151, 177,
      197
critical consciousness/reflection 21,
      58, 64, 71, 77, 111, 173
cross, theology of 4, 8, 11, 22, 76, 94,
      95, 96, 98, 100, 224, 230, 231

and abandonment 235
Black/Dalit 231–34
and hope 228, 231, 233, 236
and reconciliation 238–39
and Roman Empire 226–28,
      235, 237, 238
and solidarity 231, 232, 233,
      236, 237, 238, 240
and victory 237–38
crucified peoples 76–78, 96, 224,
      228–31, 236, 239, 240
  and body 230–31
Cuba 75, 83, 252
cultural/social colonization 17,
      48–49, 51, 52
CWM (Council for World Mission)
      52

Dalit Panthers 240, 240n55
Dalit people 8, 21, 47, 60, 171,
      223–41
  and Black people, compared
      225–26
  and crucified Christ 4, 11, 22,
      224, 225, 231, 232–34, 236,
      237–38
  as crucified people 224, 228–31,
      239
  dehumanization of 21–22
  killing/suffering of 224–26,
      228–29, 239
  and scriptural basis of
      untouchability 229n21
  women 224, 225, 238
Danner, Deborah 225, 228
d'Aubuisson, Roberto 76, 79
Dayam, Joseph Prabhakar 233–34
de Gruchy, John 201, 206
de Gruchy, Steve 211
Deepawali 170–71
dehumanization 8, 176, 185, 188,
      189, 197
  and caste/race 21, 225
  of indigenous people 15, 47
  of women 18
DEIS (Draft Environmental Impact
      Statement, USDOD) 40
democracy 28, 68, 150

dependency theory 71
development 114, 123, 141
    and indigenous people 16, 48,
        53–56, 58
dialogue 180–82, 187, 189, 196, 197
    and capoeira 192, 193, 194, 195
Diggines, Christopher 253
diversity, cultural 54, 58, 67, 68
Dominican Republic 75
Donghak Peasant Revolutionary
        Movement 134, 135, 136
Douglas, Kelly Brown 230
Douglass, Frederick 202
Doyle, Kate 258–59
DRC (Democratic Republic of
        Congo) 114
drug abuse 55
Du Bois, W. E. B. 21, 240–41
Duchrow, Ulrich 210
Dussel, Enrique 20, 177–80, 183
    and alienation 183, 190, 196
    and capoeira 186, 187, 187n44,
        189, 190, 195–96, 197
    and epistemology of faith 190,
        192
    and false consciousness 179,
        180, 180n14
    and hermeneutics of trust 192,
        193
    and relationality/humanity
        178–80, 179–80n14, 183,
        183–84n31

East Asia 20, 32, 36, 38, 132, 134,
        135, 137n3, 142, 151
Ebola 112
ecofeminism 113, 116–18, 122, 127,
        128
    and militarization 120–21
economic growth 2, 53, 57, 141
    see also development
Ecuador 17, 68–69, 80, 81–84
    see also Proaño, Msgr. Leonidas
ecumenical movement 20, 152, 157,
        200, 206, 207–10, 217, 218
    and conservatism 210, 211, 212
    and lack of Christian unity
        165–66, 209–10

    and Palestine 207, 208, 209,
        211–13
    and Protestant churches 168–69
    and social networks 167–68
    and victims of violence 169
    see also Buddhist–Christian
        dialogue
education 145, 148, 176, 217, 243,
        247
    and capoeira 186–95, 186–
        87n43, 187n44, 196
    and indigenous peoples 49, 51,
        51n6, 54, 57
Egypt 125, 127–128
Eisenhower, Dwight 145
El Salvador 75, 76–77, 79, 83
Elisha 61–62
Ellacuría, Ignacio 76
Ellis, Marc 216
Empire 2, 7, 8, 28, 46–48
    and colonization see
        colonization process
    divide and rule policies of 6, 51,
        56, 58
    global 132, 150, 218
    and spirituality 132
    value systems 46, 48, 50, 52
    and whiteness 52
Engler, Mark/Engler, Paul 202
environmental destruction 2, 16, 18,
        19, 31–32, 40, 55, 68, 70, 84
    as rape 119
    and war 117, 118, 119, 126–27
epistemology 190, 192, 234
ethnic conflicts 55, 113, 114
Eucharist 232
exclusion 46, 66, 71, 180, 202
    see also marginalized people
Exodus 72
experience, categories of 99–100
Ezekiel 45–46, 153–54

Fabella, Virginia 108
faith
    and counter-insurgency 262–64
    epistemology of 190, 192
    and fearlessness 20, 156, 160, 163
    and hope/liberation 2, 9, 11–12

faith groups 23
Falk, Richard 149
Falkland Islands/Las Malvinas 254, 258
Fallon, William 32
false consciousness 179, 180, 180n14, 181–82, 183, 184, 197
FAR (Rebel Armed Forces, Guatemala) 256, 260
far right 3, 4
femicide 155–56
feminism/feminist theology 15, 17–19, 18, 92, 96, 97–100
  and categories of experience 99–100
  eco- see ecofeminism
  and militarization 120–21
  and patriarchy 97, 98, 103–4, 113
  and suffering 97–99, 103–4, 106, 107, 111
Fiji 52
Finkenwalde community (Germany) 199
firing ranges 30–31, 40, 41, 42–43
First Sino-Japanese War (1894–95) 134, 135, 136
Floyd, George 4, 22, 24, 197, 223, 239
food insecurity 56, 58, 117, 118
Foucault, Michel 230
Foundation for Indigenous Peoples 17
Francis, Pope 76, 156
Franklin, Benjamin 28
Free trade Agreements (FTAs) 81
Free Trade Area of the Americas (FTAA) 80–81
freedom 91, 114
  and far right 3, 5
Freire, Paolo 183, 196
Friedman, George 147

Gairy, Eric 246, 247, 248, 249, 250, 251–52, 253
Garner, Eric 22, 225
gender stereotypes 126

Genesis 93, 153, 155
genocide 65–66, 68, 70, 80, 85, 149, 219, 243, 255
  see also Holocaust
Germany 134, 213, 217
  Nazi 139, 144, 145, 199, 200, 207–8, 212, 214, 215
Ghana 114
Girard, René 237
global militarization 9, 139–49
  and civil–military relations 144–45
  and class 144, 145–46
  and gender relations 146
  and militarization of space 8, 141, 142, 147–49
  and police 146
  and race relations 145
  and technological revolution 140–41, 142
  and US planetary empire 147–49
globalization 38, 139, 141–42, 143, 199, 211
God 12, 22, 58–62
  crucified see cross, theology of
  and Empire 46, 57, 72
  encounter/union with 19–20
  healing power of 60–62
  of justice 11, 13, 85, 231
  and liberation 9, 17, 23, 58, 71–72, 74–76, 127, 128
  of life 8, 9, 11, 149
  of the oppressed 2, 8, 11, 14, 16, 58
  of the powerless 58–60
  and suffering 92–93, 95
  universality of 23–24, 136
  will of 72, 95, 100, 103, 106
godlessness 11, 22, 23
gods of death 8, 9
Gojong, King 134
Gokulraj, V. 22, 225
Gospels 71, 72, 73, 155, 156, 208, 263
  see also John; Luke; Mark; Matthew

Grenada 22–23, 242–43, 245–54,
        262, 264
    and British intelligence 247–48,
        252
    and British invasion plan
        250–51
    and British Navy 246, 248, 250
    and British scenario planning
        249–51
    and British support for Gairy
        251–52, 253
    and NJM/Black Power 246–47,
        248, 249, 251, 252, 264
    and police violence 248, 251,
        253
    and trade unions 247, 248, 249
Guam 7, 15–16, 27–44
    Congress of 35–36
    contamination/environmental
        destruction in 31–32
    indigenous people of see
        Chamorro people
    land-taking in 35, 36, 40, 41
    Litekyan 42–43
    militarization of 28–31, 35–36,
        40–41, 42
    military buildup in 40–41, 42
    and Nixon Doctrine 36–37
    Pågat 40, 41, 42
    political status of 28, 29, 32–33,
        44
    resistance in 29, 34, 41–43
    and Rumsfeld Doctrine 37–39,
        40
    sacred sites in 16, 41, 42
    strategic importance of 28, 32,
        33, 35, 36
    in World War II 28, 29, 33–34,
        43
Guantanamo Bay 39, 75, 85
Guatemala 75, 79
Guatemala, counter-insurgency in
        23, 75, 79, 243, 246, 254–61,
        262, 264
    and Belize see Belize
    and British military action
        255–56

    and intelligence 255, 256–57,
        258, 259, 260, 261
    and Kaibiles commando unit
        257, 259, 261
    and killing of Maya people 243,
        254, 255, 256, 258, 259–60,
        261
    Petén region 255, 258, 259, 260
    and Rebel Armed Forces (FAR)
        256, 260
    and SAS 257–58
    and US 254–55, 259, 261
Gudmarsdottir, Sigridur 121
Gudynas, Eduardo 68–69
Gutiérrez, Gustavo 10, 14, 71, 95–
        96, 235–36, 236n45
Guyana 249

Haig, Alexander 75
Haight, Roger 224, 227
Hales, Gus 258
Hanlon, David 37
healing 60–62
healthcare 243, 247
heterosexism 47
hierarchies 2, 3, 22, 59, 98, 226, 227,
        229, 238
    religious 6–7, 103–4
Hinduism 170–71, 178, 229n21
    and divine suffering 233–34
Hindutva ideology 13, 57
HIV/AIDS 112
Holocaust 138n3, 144, 145, 204,
        215–16
Honduras 75, 79, 85
hope 9, 11–12, 58, 77n22, 90, 98,
        109–10
    and interreligious dialogue 164,
        165, 166, 167, 169
Hossein-zadeh, Ismael 30
Houtrart, François 73, 86
Howe, Geoffrey 259
Hubert, J. 123
Humala, Ollanta 79
human dignity 15, 23, 52, 54, 73, 78,
        79, 169, 173, 219
human rights 22, 54, 58, 68, 71, 76,
        79, 81, 115, 258, 259

human rights (*continued*)
  liberal/imperial 11, 23
  and Palestine 211, 213, 214, 217,
    218
human trafficking 55
humanity/human person 23, 91, 94,
    103, 106, 111, 176, 177, 194
  as in-relation 178
  and individualism/plurality
    180–81
  and people of centre/periphery
    178–80, 179–80n14, 183,
    183–84n31
  philosophy of 178–80, 182n25,
    183
Humboldt, Alexander Von 68

I/Thou relationship 181–82, 183,
    190, 193, 195
identity 124, 125, 146, 199, 204, 226
  of the church 207, 208
  indigenous 48, 49–50, 54
idolatry, militarization as 8, 9, 11
Ilavarasan, E. 22, 225
IMF (International Monetary Fund)
    75, 81
imperialism 2, 7, 10, 17, 34–35, 80,
    86, 114, 141
  and counter-insurgency 243,
    254
  and Korean peninsula 134–36,
    140
  power structures of 46–48
independence movements 56, 71,
    72, 114–15
  and counter-insurgency *see*
    counter-insurgency
  neo-colonial 82–83, 115
India 4, 170, 213
  and COVID-19 pandemic 5
  Dalits in *see* Dalit people
  indigenous people in 46, 51, 53
  Muslims in 5, 8
  North East nEI) 6, 16, 46, 51,
    56–57, 59, 64
indigenous people 5–6, 8, 15–17, 46,
    47, 69

colonization of *see* colonization
    process
  conflict amongst 55, 56, 57
  and COVID-19 pandemic 5
  and development 53–56
  genocide of 17, 65–66, 68, 70
  and legal systems 47, 48, 49
  and liberation theology 70,
    72–73, 82–84
  and natural resources 68, 69–70
  and sacred sites *see* sacred sites
  and sacredness of cosmos 12
  *see also specific indigenous
    peoples*
individualism 180–81
Indonesia 50, 143
inequality 69, 199, 200, 202, 203
Institute of Race Relations 244–45
intelligence 247–48, 252, 255, 256–
    57, 258, 259, 260, 261, 263
international community 29, 199–
    200, 211
International Criminal Court 83
International Monetary Fund (IMF)
    75, 81
interreligious dialogue 14, 19–21,
    110, 155–74, 175–76, 197
  and peace 156–58, 159–60, 167,
    168–69, 171–74
  and shared security 158, 170,
    173
  and social networks 167–68
  and victims of violence 169
  and women 172–73
  see also Buddhist–Christian
    dialogue; ecumenical
    movement
Iraq 36, 38, 264
Ireland 12
Isaiah 86
Islam 172, 263
  see also Muslims
Islamic State 13
Israel 144
  see also Palestine
Itano, Nicole 127

Japan 33, 34, 42, 43, 50, 142, 161,
    162
    and Korea 131, 133, 133n2, 134,
        135, 136, 137, 150
    nuclear attacks on 137, 149
    and Sino-Japanese Wars 134,
        135, 136
Jatav, Vikas Kumar 224
Jenkins, Alan 260
Jesus Christ 8–9, 72, 202, 207, 208,
    219
    atheism of 11
    birth of 59
    crucified see cross, theology of
    and Empire 48, 85
    and fearlessness 156, 160, 163
    as light 163
    and the powerless 62–63
    Resurrection of 63, 172, 227,
        233, 236, 236n43, 237
    and suffering 92, 94–95, 96, 98
    and transformation 63–64
John 155, 156, 163
John Paul II 93–94
John XXIII 157
Judaism 172, 204
    see also Israel; Zionism
justice 5, 11, 12, 14, 48, 54, 56, 74,
    78, 86, 167, 202
    and crucified Christ 231–32,
        239, 240
    eco- 127
    and God 16, 59, 62, 85
    and human rights 81
    restorative 159–60
    social/ecological 55n8
    and suffering 77n22, 98

Kaduna nigeria) 125
Kahl, Brigitte 215, 226, 227, 235
Kaibiles commando unit
        (Guatemala) 257, 259, 261
Kaoma, Kapya J. 120
karma 7, 11, 100, 103
Kashmir 12, 85, 171
Kepappilavu (Sri Lanka) 89–91
Kerala (India) 6

Kew Archives (UK) 246, 247, 249,
        255, 256, 260, 262
    insights of 245, 250
Kichwa people 83
Kim, Dae-jung 131
King, Martin Luther Jr. 103, 149,
        202
Kings, II 60–62
knowledge
    commodification of 15
    and liberation 245
Korean peninsula 8, 19–20, 131–54
    Buddhism in 133
    and China 132–33, 134, 135,
        136, 137, 140
    and Chŏndogyo 135–36
    Chosun Dynasty 134, 136
    Confucianism in 19, 131, 135,
        136
    and conservative Christianity
        149
    division of 137–39, 140
    and Donghak Peasant
        Revolutionary Movement
        134, 135, 136
    and global militarization 139–44
    indigenous spirituality in 135
    and Japan 131, 133, 133n2, 134,
        135, 136, 140, 150
    March First Independence
        Movement 136, 137, 151
    Mongol invasions of 133–34
    and name-changing 131
    nationalism/militarism in 133
    resistance in 136–37, 150–52
    and USA 134, 137n3, 138, 140
    and zoegraphy/thanatography
        132–34, 149–50
Korean War 34, 137–38, 142
Kumaragamage, Kumari 102
Küng, Hans 156–57
Kurds/Kurdistan 12, 36, 85
Kwok, Pui-Lan 103–4, 111

land-grabbing 16, 35, 40, 41, 48, 54,
        58, 90, 103
    and Palestine 201, 203
    and restitution 74

language 7, 8, 14, 67
    and colonization 16, 27, 27–
        28n1, 49–50, 51–52
    faith- 10
    and name-changing 131
Laos 50
Lasprilla, Jaime 79
Latin America 6, 7, 15, 17, 65–86,
        254–55
    biodiversity of 67
    capitalism in 75
    Catholic Church in 77–78
    cultural/linguistic diversity of 67
    genocide in 65–66, 68, 70
    indigenous peoples of 65, 67–68,
        69, 82–83, 85
    liberative praxis in 81–85
    and School of the Americas 76,
        79–81
    and Summer Institute of
        Linguistics (SIL) 80
    torture/murder of Christians in
        76–77, 78, 82
    see also specific countries
Latin American Conference of
        Bishops 77
Lazarus 60
Leahy, Stephen 67
legal systems 47, 48, 49
leprosy 60–62
LGBTIQ peoples 47
liberation 9–15, 16–17, 24, 64, 78
    Dussel's/Panikker's philosophy
        of 20, 177, 178, 180
    God of 17, 23, 58
    interreligious 20, 176, 197
    and knowledge 245
    and material spirituality 10–15
    and solidarity 21–23
    and women 18, 90, 91, 98, 106,
        107
liberation movements see
        independence movements
liberation theologians, massacre of
        (1989) 76–77
liberation theology 10, 14, 15, 17,
        19, 65–86
    and Bible 71–72, 73

and counter-insurgency 262–63
Ecuadorian see Proaño, Msgr.
    Leonidas
four conditions for development
    of 71
and liberative praxis 81–85
principles of 73
and suffering 92, 95–97
targeted by US 78
life, fiesta of 133, 152–54
Life, Story of see zoegraphy
light, festival of (Deepawali) 170–71
light metaphor 163, 164, 165, 168,
    170
Litekyan (Guam) 42–43
López, Amando 76
López Obrador, Andrés Manuel 174
López y López, Joaquín 76
love 13
    and resistance 8–9, 77n22
    and suffering 94
LTTE (Liberation Tigers of Tamil
    Eelam) 101, 102, 105, 109
Luke 60, 63, 72, 73, 202, 219
Luther, Martin 215, 218
Lutheran Church 168n9, 200,
    200n3, 217

Mahuad, Jamil 81
Malcolm X 240
malícia 187–90
Mama, Amina 115, 116, 120
Manas Air Base (Kyrgistan) 39
March First Independence
    Movement 136, 137, 151
marginalized people 55, 56, 77, 91,
    97
    God of 58–60
    women as 103–4, 109
Marianas Island Range Complex/
    Training and Testing area
    (MIRC/MITT) 30–31
Marianas Islands 28, 30, 32
    see also Guam
Mark 62, 63, 227–28, 235
Marshall Islands 31
Martin-Baró, Ignacio 76
Martínez, Tobar 258, 259

martyrdom 77, 77n22, 96, 168
masculinity 146
material spirituality 10–15, 16, 21
materialism 2, 15, 24, 53
Matthew 63, 163, 202, 235
Maya people 65, 243, 254, 255, 256,
    258, 259–60
Mbiti, John 124
media 43, 84, 113, 166
    see also social media
meditation 163–64
Mendis, Viraj 242
Mennonites 168
Meredeth, Turshen 115
Mexico 16, 20, 80, 82, 163, 170, 174
    femicide in 155–56, 171
    Protestant tradition in 167
MI5 247–48, 249, 252, 260
Middle East 7, 39, 252, 253
migrants 6, 8, 81, 82, 85, 199
militarism 139–40
militarization 2, 10, 15, 47, 57
    characterized as common good
        7
    and civil–military relations 144
    and false consciousness 184
    global *see* global militarization
    and liberative praxis 81–85
    resistance to *see* resistance
    see also war
military service 145–46
military training 30–31
minjung theology 19
MIRC/MITT (Marianas Island
    Range Complex/Training
    and Testing area) 30–31
misogyny 103–4
missionaries 51, 51n6, 114, 128
Moltmann, Jürgen 235
Molyneaux, L. B. 120
Monroe Doctrine 75
Montes, Segundo 76
Montesinos, Vladimiro 79
Montt, Efraín Ríos 79, 255–56, 258,
    260
Moreno, Juan Ramón 76
mother earth 12, 54, 69, 70, 81, 85,
    112, 113

rape of 119, 121
mothers 17, 90, 96, 126
Mother's Front 89
Mott, John R. 157
Movement for Peace with Justice
    and Dignity 20, 170
Mozambique 119–20
Mullin, Chris 250
multinational corporations 53, 54,
    77, 78, 80, 83–84, 115, 199
Mushaima, Ali 263–64
Muslim war widows 91, 102–3, 104,
    108
Muslims 23, 91, 102–3, 124, 125,
    171, 172
Myanmar/Burma 50, 162

Naaman 60–62
Nagaland (India) *see* NEI
national security 1, 8, 11, 78, 143
nationalism 6, 13, 23, 133, 158, 199,
    200, 202
Native Americans 149, 152
natural resources 67
    denial of access to 48, 55, 117
    destruction of 17, 18, 19, 113–
        14, 115, 116
    and development 68–69
    exploitation of 46, 48, 66, 69, 83
nature 9, 67, 128
    and anthropocentrism 46
    conquest of 53
    and eco-human
        interdependence 5–6
    and women 19, 113, 116, 117,
        121
Nazis 139, 144, 145, 199, 200, 207–
    8, 212, 214, 215
NEI north East India) 6, 16, 46, 51,
    56–57, 59, 64
neo fascists 4
neo-colonialism 23, 69, 82–83, 128,
    254
    and violence 52, 75, 77, 85, 112,
        113–16
neoliberalism 21, 115, 197, 199, 201,
    213–14
Nepal 50, 224

New Jewel Movement nJM,
Grenada) 246–47, 248, 249,
251, 252, 264
New Tribes Mission 80
Nicaragua 75
Nigeria 114, 125, 127, 143
9/11 attacks (2001) 38
Nirmal, Arvind P. 232–33
Nixon, Richard 37
Noriega, Manuel 79
North Korea 16, 43, 138, 149
Northern Ireland 251
nuclear weapons 38, 43, 85, 137,
140, 142, 147, 149
and resistance 150
in space 148
Nyerere, Julius 114

Obama, Barack 140, 149
oil industry 83–84, 114, 252, 253
Okazawa-Rey, Margo 115, 116, 120
Okinawa (Japan) 29, 40
ontology 178–80, 183
oppression/oppressed people 2, 3, 8,
16–17, 90, 91, 176
criminalization of 8
dual consciousness of 183
hopelessness/despair of 45–46
and liberation 9–10, 18, 21
and material spirituality 10–15,
16, 21
solidarity with see solidarity
and suffering 96, 97
ordinariness 90, 92
original sin 92, 93

pachamama 12, 69
Pacific Region 7, 16, 34, 36–39, 44,
137
and Guam/Nixon Doctrine
36–37
and Rumsfeld Doctrine 37–39
see also Guam
pacifism 168
PACOM (US Pacific Command)
29–30, 32
Pågat (Guam) 40, 41, 42

Palestine 8, 12, 20–21, 85, 137n3,
156, 201–6
apartheid in 21, 203, 204, 206,
213, 214
and BDS movement 213, 214,
214n42, 217
and Black Lives Matter/human
rights struggles 211
and church mission 207, 208,
209, 211–13, 214, 216,
217–19
and criticism of Israel as anti-
Semitism 204, 216
as ethnic cleansing 203, 216, 218
and Kairos Document (2009)
138n3, 201, 210, 217
and Nakba 214n43, 216
and neoliberal order 213–14
and Oslo Accords (1983)
203n11
and two-state solution 203–4,
205
and Zionism see Zionism
Panama 79
pandemics 112
see also COVID-19 pandemic
Panikkar, Raimon 2, 177–78,
180–83
and alienation 183, 190, 196
and capoeira 186, 187, 187n44,
189, 190, 195–96, 197
and epistemology of faith 190,
192
and hermeneutics of trust 192,
193
and humanity 177, 178, 194
and Self/Other relationship
181–82, 183, 194
Pappé, Ilan 203
Pasi, Angira 224
patriarchy 13, 17–18, 97, 98, 103–4,
108, 113
Paul 237, 238
peace 11, 12, 18, 59, 82, 86, 127,
150–54, 217
and crucified Christ 238, 239,
240
and fiesta of life 152–54

and interfaith dialogue 156–58,
    159–60, 167, 168–69, 171
paradigm of 8
and prayer 163, 165
Peace Corps 75
Pentagon 32, 80
Pentecost 63, 161, 162
Perez, Craig Santos 27
Peru 84
Petén region (Guatemala) 255, 258,
    259, 260
Philippines 53–54, 218
philosophy 178–80, 182n25, 183
Pieris, Aloysius 10, 13, 14, 17, 18
Plaskow, Judith 99–100, 107
plurality 177, 180–81
police forces 146, 176, 197
police violence 4, 5, 6, 223, 226, 227,
    236, 248, 251, 255
political analysis 2–3, 14–15, 60
Pollard, Brigadier 258, 259
Poopathy, Kanpathipillai (Annai
    Poopathi/Poopathi *amma*)
    18, 89, 89n1
Porter, Robert Odawi 49
poverty 2, 3, 6, 48, 55, 56, 58, 113,
    199
    and pastoral work 70–71, 76, 77
    and suffering 92, 95–96, 110,
    111
power structures 11, 18, 19, 46–48,
    60, 61, 91, 103, 109, 147
    and transformation 63–64
    and war 113
    see also caste system
powerlessness 43–44, 46, 58–60,
    62–64
Prabhakar, M. E. 233
praxis 184, 186n43, 194–95, 196
    critically reflective 3, 16, 24, 173
    feminist 14n24
    historical 24, 64, 71, 73, 77, 111
    liberative 72, 81–85
    and peace 163, 168
    and suffering/poverty 95–96
prayer 16, 123, 125, 135–36, 162–65
precariousness of life 11
privatization 12, 38, 114

Proaño, Msgr. Leonidas 17, 65,
    70–78, 81, 85
    arrest/persecution of 78
    and Bible 71–72, 73
    and God of liberation 74–76
    on imperialism/capitalism
    74–75
    and indigenous peoples 70,
    72–73
    pastoral work of 70–74
    and restitution of land 74
    and School of the Americas
    79–80
    and Solidarity Front of
    Chimborazo 83
    on USA 75–76
prophetic tradition 21, 152, 166,
    169, 200, 202, 209, 216
Protestantism 157, 167, 168–69, 170
    and Israel-Palestine 215,
    215n47, 217
punishment 92, 94
PwD (Persons with Disabilities)
    47, 60

Quakers 264
quality of life 48, 53

racism 6, 15, 33, 47, 57, 69, 145,
    171, 200
    and COVID-19 pandemic 4–5
    as ecclesiological issue 206
    and liberals 4
    resistance to 2, 4, 24
    and World Council of Churches
    200, 206, 209
radioactive waste 32
RAF (Royal Air Force) 255, 257
Raheb, Mitri 12
Ramos, Celina 82
Ramos, Elba 76
Rand Corporation 77, 78
rape 9, 11, 19, 23, 56, 106, 113,
    119–21
    of mother earth 119
Reagan, Ronald 75, 78, 148
reconciliation 238–39
Reformation 215

refugees 36, 85, 126, 175, 214n42
Reign of God 60, 63, 71
religion, imperial manipulation of
46, 47, 50, 51, 52, 53
religious fundamentalism 13, 23, 78,
128, 150, 158, 162, 204–5
religious pluralism 20
resilience 20, 23, 90, 177, 262
resistance 2, 29, 54, 77n22, 91, 98,
176
and capoeira 177, 184, 185, 186
and Christ 8–9, 22
and indigenous people 6, 16, 17
and religious pluralism 20
and sacred sites 121–23
of women 13–14, 18
Resurrection 63, 172, 219, 227, 233,
236, 236n43, 237
Revelations 152–53
Ricoeur, Paul 161
right to life, denial of 47, 50–51
rights, civil/political 243
see also human rights
Rohingya people 171
Roldós Aguilera, Jaime 83
Roman Empire 63, 64, 139, 173,
226–28, 229, 235
Romero, Msgr. Óscar Arnulfo 76, 84
Royal Air Force (RAF) 255, 257
Royal Marines 246, 250–51
Ruether, Rosemary Radford 116,
118, 216
Rumsfeld Doctrine 37–39, 40
Russia 134, 135, 137n3, 138n3, 142
see also Soviet Union
Russo-Japanese War (1904–05) 135,
136
Ryan, Samuel 2, 11, 16

sacred sites 16, 19, 41, 58, 112, 113,
117, 118
and development 123
gendering 123–27
and rape 119, 120–21
and resistance 121–23
sacredness 12–13, 16
of cosmos 10, 12
salvation 71, 73

and suffering 13, 18, 95, 96, 98
Sankar, Udumalai 228–29
Schüssler Fiorenza, Elisabeth 99,
111
Second Sino-Japanese War (1937–
45) 136
self-criticism 160–61, 162, 167, 172
self-determination 82, 85, 136
Self/Other 181–82, 183, 226n13
Sen, Amartya 172
sex industry 47, 53
sexual abuse/violence 13, 17, 115,
117
Shamanism 19
Sharp, Gene 202
Shia Islam 263, 264
Shiva, Vandana 112
SICSAL (Christian Secretariat
of Solidarity with Latin
America) 84–85
Sideris, Tina 119–20
SIL (Summer Institute of
Linguistics) 80, 83
silence 108, 162, 163
Silla Kingdom 132, 133
sin
original 92, 93
punishment for 92, 94
and resistance 48
social/structural 18, 64, 73, 77,
96, 98, 100–103
Sinhala Buddhist state 6, 13, 90,
101–3
Sinhala war widows 91, 101
Buddhist 104–6, 109–10
Christian 104
Sivanandan, Ambalavaner 7, 244–45
Sivaram, Dharmeratnam 7, 243–46,
262
and CCI doctrine 244, 245, 264
Siwila, L. 117
Sjollema, Baldwin 206, 209
Slater, Chris 258
slavery 20, 52, 54, 113, 114, 127–28,
177
and capoeira 177, 184–85, 188,
188n48, 196, 197
and humanity 179

SOA (School of The Americas) 76,
    79–81, 82, 84
Sobrino, John 95–96
social class 7, 47, 69, 70, 84, 145–46
    and global militarization 144,
        145–46
    and women 96, 97, 98, 99, 107,
        117
social economy 86
social justice 201, 205n12, 211
social media 41, 42, 43
social systems/orders 48, 177, 179,
        180, 189, 190, 194, 229
Solano, Boris Tobar 70
solidarity 4, 15, 24, 58, 86
    and crucified Christ 231, 232,
        233, 236, 237, 238, 240
    and interreligious dialogue 14,
        167, 168
    as liberation 21–23
Solidarity Front of Chimborazo 83
Somalia 127
Song, C. S. 104
soteriology see salvation
South Africa 19, 114, 160
    apartheid in 200–201, 202–3,
        205–6, 208, 211, 213, 214,
        218
    Kairos Document (1985) 21,
        198, 200–201, 202–3, 205,
        210, 218
South Asia 50, 225, 239, 243
South Korea 32, 43, 138, 139, 142,
        143
South Sudan 127
Southern Command 80–81, 80n26
sovereignty 80, 81
Soviet Union 137, 141, 142
    collapse of 37, 147
space, militarization of 8, 141, 142,
        147–49
Spanish American War 28, 33
Spanish Empire 65–66, 68, 254
Special Air Service (SAS) 257–58
spirituality 66, 132, 150–52
    across borders 24
    and CCI 64, 243

of contemplation/struggle 164,
        165
    indigenous, denial of 50, 51,
        53, 55
    of solidarity 21
    this-world see material
        spirituality
    and war 117, 118
    water metaphor for 160–61
Sri Lanka 6–7, 18, 22–23, 51, 89–92,
        162
    counter-insurgency in 242–43,
        262–63, 264
    suffering of war widows in see
        war widows, suffering of
Stade, Roland 32–33
status confessionis 200, 200n3
Stencel, S. 124
stewardship 118
Stiglitz, Joseph 68
story-telling 107
suffering 18, 60, 91–110
    and CCC 92–93, 94–95
    as evil 93
    and feminist theology 96–99
    glorification of 92–95
    and hope 109–10
    and Jesus 92, 94–95, 96, 98, 219
    and liberation theology 92,
        95–97
    overcoming 107–9
    and salvation/redemption 13,
        18, 95, 103
    of Sri Lankan war widows see
        war widows, suffering of
    as structural 95–97
    theology of 91–99
    as will of God 95, 100, 103
    of women 77n22, 90, 91
Summer Institute of Linguistics
        (SIL) 80, 83
Syria 170, 171

'T Hooft, Willem Visser 208, 209
Taiwan 49, 50, 51, 52–53
Tamayo, Juan José 71
Tamil Eelam 8, 12, 85, 101–2

Tamil Eelam (*continued*)
    Liberation Tigers of (LTTE) 101,
        102, 105, 109
    see also Sivaram, Dharmeratnam
Tamil war widows 6–7, 89–92
    Christian 100–101, 102, 105,
        106, 107, 108, 109
    Hindu 101, 103, 105, 108, 109
Tanzania 114
Taoism 19
Tauran, Jean-Louis 171
Taylor, Mark 239
technology 140–41, 142
terrorism 33, 37, 38, 140
Tertullian 93
Texaco 83–84
Thailand 50, 53
thanatography 8, 132–34, 136,
    138n3, 149–50
Thatcher, Margaret 257, 259
torture 23, 56, 77, 243
tourism 55, 184
trade 69, 80–81, 134, 139
transformation 10, 18, 20, 46, 60, 62,
    91, 151
    and Jesus 63–64
    societal 97
Trinidad 247, 249, 250, 253
Truman, Harry S. 145
Trump, Donald 43
trust, hermeneutics of 192–94,
    195–96
Turkey 175

Union of Peoples 83–84
United Nations 36, 138, 148
United States (USA) 15, 175
    anti-racism protests in 2, 4
    border control 82
    and Caribbean 246, 252, 253
    CIA 75, 79, 144, 254, 264
    COVID-19 pandemic in 3–5
    defense budget 142–43, 147
    Evangelical movement in 13
    as global empire 147–49
    and Guam *see* Guam
    and Guatemala 254, 259, 261

    and Israel-Palestine 203,
        203n11, 217, 218
    killing of George Floyd in 4–5
    and Korean peninsula 16, 43,
        134, 137n3, 138, 140, 142
    and Latin America 6, 74n17,
        75–76, 77–81, 85, 254–55
    militarization of space by 8, 141,
        142, 147–49
    militarization of world by 20,
        140
    military service in 145
    and Monroe Doctrine 75
    motto of 9, 85
    National Security Act (1947)
        144
    National Security Doctrine 78,
        79, 80
    Pacific Command (PACOM)
        29–30, 32
    Pentagon 32, 80, 147
    and postwar rebuilding 34–35
    racial violence in 3, 4–5, 8, 21,
        22, 176, 197, 223, 225, 226,
        228, 239
    and School of the Americas 76,
        79–81, 84
    Southern Command 80–81,
        80n26
    US Air Force 32, 34, 36, 142–43,
        147
US Army 34, 79, 142–43, 254–55
US Congress 28, 35, 148
US Marines 29, 40, 75, 84, 246
US military 29–31, 34
    and Rumsfeld doctrine 38–39
    and School of the Americas 76,
        79–81
    and training/firing ranges
        30–31, 40, 41
US military bases 35, 38, 39, 40, 80,
    142
US Navy 29, 31–32, 33, 34, 35–36,
    142–43
USDOD (US Department of
    Defense) 29, 30–31, 37, 40,
    42–43, 144
    Report (2019) 142–43

Vásquez, Romeo 79
Vatican II 157, 160, 262
Venezuela 79, 80, 170
Videla, Rafael 79
Vietnam 54
Vietnam War 34, 36, 37, 144, 146
Villa-Vicencio, Charles 210
Viola, Roberto Eduardo 79
violence 20

war 2, 11, 17, 69, 140
    new 115
    paradigm of 7–9
    and women 17–18, 19, 112–13,
        115, 116–21, 125–26, 127
    see also counter-insurgency
War on Terror 140
war widows, suffering of 6–7, 90, 91,
    92, 99–111
    and challenging power
        structures 91, 103, 109
    and experience 99–100
    and feminist theology 97–99,
        103–4, 106, 107, 111
    and hope 109–10
    and justification for suffering,
        rejection of 103–6
    Muslim 91, 102–3, 104, 108
    and new image of God 106
    overcoming 107–9
    and patriarchy 97, 98, 103–4,
        108
    Sinhala see Sinhala war widows
    and story-telling 107
    and structural sin 100–103
    Tamil see Tamil war widows
WARP (World Assembly of
    Religions for Peace) 158,
    159–60
Warren, Karen J. 118
water metaphor 160–61
water resource 67
Waziyatawin, Angela Wilson 51–52
WCC (World Council of Churches)
    157, 200, 206, 208, 209, 260
West Asia 132, 137–38n3
West, Cornel 8–9
Whitaker, Mark 244

Whitbeck, Harris 260–61
white supremacy 3, 4, 5, 21, 22, 176,
    218
whiteness 52
widows 18
Williams, Dolores 103
Winn, Adam 227–28
women 6–7, 46–47, 60, 146
    Dalit 224, 225, 238
    and evil 93
    Korean, mass suicide of 132–33
    in military 126
    and nature 19, 113, 116
    and peace 172–73
    powerlessness of 63
    rape of see rape
    and religion 124
    resistance of 13–14
    and sex industry 47, 53
    suffering of 77n22, 93, 96–99
    and war 17–18, 19, 112–13, 115,
        116–21, 125–26, 127, 171
    see also war widows, suffering of
Word, the 62, 71, 72, 169
World Alliance of Reformed
    Churches 198, 200
World Assembly of Religions for
    Peace (WARP) 158, 159–60
World Bank 81
World Council of Churches (WCC)
    157, 200, 206, 208, 209, 260
World Mission Conference
    (Edinburgh, 1910) 157
World War I 140, 146, 157
World War II 28, 29, 33–34, 43, 133,
    136, 137, 140, 144
    technological advances in
        140–41

Yatra, Dalit Mahila Swabhiman 238
Yemen 170, 171

Zaccagnini, María Elena 67
Zambia 114
Zelaya, Manuel 79
Zimbabwe 114
Zionism 12, 13, 21, 204–6, 211–12,
    213, 217–18

Zionism (*continued*)
    Christian 204–5
    liberal 205–6, 214
    and post-Holocaust theology
        204, 215–16
zoegraphy 8, 19–20, 132–34, 138n3,
        149–50, 154

CPSIA information can be obtained
at www.ICGtesting.com
Printed in the USA
BVHW041756200421
605297BV00002BA/162